# LAND SETTLEMENT POLICIES AND POPULATION REDISTRIBUTION IN DEVELOPING COUNTRIES

# LAND SETTLEMENT POLICIES AND POPULATION REDISTRIBUTION IN DEVELOPING COUNTRIES

## Achievements, Problems & Prospects

EDITED BY

## A.S. OBERAI

A study prepared for the International
Labour Office within the framework of the
World Employment Programme, with the
financial support of the United Nations
Fund for Population Activities

New York
Westport, Connecticut
London

The designation employed in ILO publications, which are in conformity with United Nations practice, and the presentation of material therein do not imply the expression of any opinion whatsoever on the part of the International Labour Office concerning the legal status of any country, area or territory or of its authorities, or concerning the delimitation of its frontiers.

The responsibility for opinions expressed in studies and other contributions rests solely with their authors, and publication does not constitute an endorsement by the International Labour Office of the opinions expressed in them.

Reference to names of firms and commercial products and processes does not imply their endorsement by the International Labour Office, and any failure to mention a particular firm, commercial product or process is not a sign of disapproval.

**Library of Congress Cataloging-in-Publication Data**

Land settlement policies and population redistribution in
  developing countries.

  "Study prepared for the International Labour Office."
  Includes bibliographies and index.
  1. Land settlement—Government policy—Developing
countries—Case studies.   I. Oberai, A. S.
II.  International Labour Office.
HD1131.L364      1988        333.3′1′1724        87-15837
ISBN 0-275-92799-7 (alk. paper)

Library of Congress Catalog Card Number: 87-15837
ISBN 0-275-92799-7

First published in 1988

Praeger Publishers, One Madison Avenue, New York, NY 10010
A division of Greenwood Press, Inc.

Printed in the United States of America

The paper used in this book complies with the
Permanent Paper Standard issued by the National
Information Standards Organization (Z39.48-1984).

10  9  8  7  6  5  4  3  2  1

# Contents

*List of Tables*                                                        vii

*Preface*                                                               xiii

1.  Introduction                                                          1
    *A. S. Oberai*

2.  An Overview of Settlement Policies and                                7
    Programs
    *A. S. Oberai*

3.  Transmigration in Indonesia                                          48
    *H. W. Arndt*

4.  Land Settlement in Malaysia: A Case Study of                         89
    the Federal Land Development Authority
    Projects
    *Tunku Shamsul Bahrin*

5.  Land Settlements in the Philippines                                  129
    *Cayetano Paderanga, Jr.*

6.  Land Settlement in Ethiopia: A Review of                             161
    Developments
    *Eishetu Chole and Teshome Mulat*

7.    A Case Study of the Resettlement of Nomads in          202
      Somalia
      *Tod A. Ragsdale and Abdullahi Scek Ali*

8.    Land Settlements and Population Redistribution          237
      in the United Republic of Tanzania
      *P. S. Maro*

9.    Colonist Constraints, Strategies, and Mobility:         271
      Recent Trends in Latin American Frontier Zones
      *Sally E. Findley*

10.   The Colonization Experience in Brazil                   317
      *María Helena F. T. Henriques*

11.   Settlement Policies in the Forest Highlands of          355
      Peru
      *Jorge Carpio*

Index                                                         387

# List of Tables

3.1    Number of migrants in Lampung settlement, 1905–41    79

3.2    Number of migrants in colonization settlements, all Indonesia, end of 1940    79

3.3    Population growth in Java and Indonesia, 1900–76    80

3.4    Transmigrants by area of settlement, 1950–68    81

3.5    Number of migrants by area of origin, 1969–74    82

3.6    Transmigration projects in Lampung, 1952–March 1973    83

3.7    Number of transmigrants, 1950–82    84

3.8    Number of persons settled under transmigration program during 1969–70 to December 31, 1982, by place of settlement    85

3.9    Transmigrants and spontaneous migrants from Java, 1950–72 and 1975–80    86

3.10   Growth rates of area, production, and yield of wet rice (*sawah*), Sumatra, 1951–60 to 1976–80    86

3.11   Transmigration: Central government development budget allocation and number of families settled, 1969–70 to 1983–84    87

3.12    Outflow of transmigrants and spontaneous migrants
         from Java to Sumatra by province of settlement, 1950–
         72, 1975–80                                                      88

4.1     Settler selection points system, 1961                           120

4.2     Pattern of development of a pre-1966 FELDA scheme               120

4.3     FELDA staff, 1982                                               121

4.4     Malaysia: Progress in land development, 1971–80, and
         target area, 1981–85                                           121

4.5     Area developed and number of families settled by the
         FELDA up to 1982                                               122

4.6     Projected and actual intake of settlers in FELDA
         schemes                                                        122

4.7     Distribution of infrastructural facilities in FELDA
         schemes, 1981                                                  123

4.8     Settlers' occupation prior to entry into FELDA schemes          123

4.9     Settlers' average monthly income (1976) by age and
         duration of stay in FELDA scheme                               124

4.10    Settlers' average monthly net income                            125

4.11    FELDA: Cost of resettling one family, 1976                      125

4.12    Intrastate and interstate migration to FELDA schemes,
         1957–83                                                        126

4.13    Settlers' migration by distance, 1957–76                        127

4.14    Age-sex distribution of settlers' children by residence,
         1977–78                                                        127

4.15    Labor force of dependents in FELDA schemes, 1957–90             128

5.1     Percentage distribution of output, industrial
         employment, and population by broad regional
         grouping, 1903 and 1975                                        152

5.2     Population and density by region, 1903                          153

5.3     Some indicators of agricultural growth, 1950–70                 153

5.4     Origins of migrants to Digos-Padada valley                      153

5.5     Educational attainment: Persons 20 years or older,
         1964–65 migrant survey                                         154

5.6     Total number of hectares farmed per farm family in
         Digos-Padada settlement                                        154

5.7     Average area owned by setters, Palawan Resettlement
         Project, 1978                                                  155

5.8     Estimated costs of establishing a 5-hectare rice farm
         through government-assisted and self-financed
         settlement                                                     155

5.9     Estimated net migration by region, 1903–75                      156

5.10   Population density by region, 1903–75                                    157

5.11   Percentage distribution of employment and number of
       industrial establishments by region, 1903, 1948, 1971–
       72                                                                        158

5.12   Percentage distribution of agricultural output by region,
       1939, 1960, and 1971                                                      159

5.13   Percentage of farm area and cultivated area operated by
       tenants, 1939                                                             159

5.14   Estimates of relative costs of land settlement and
       irrigation                                                               160

6.1    Land use in Ethiopia                                                     186

6.2    Types of settlement under the Relief and Rehabilitation
       Commission, 1983                                                         187

6.3    Percentage distribution of household heads by age in 24
       settlements, 1983                                                        188

6.4    Age distribution of total settlement population, 1983                    189

6.5    Sex distribution of household heads and total settlement
       population, 1983                                                         189

6.6    Unmarried settlers in 56 settlements, 1983                               190

6.7    Total number of participants in literacy programs                        191

6.8    Percentage distribution of settlers (household heads) by
       occupation prior to settlement, 1984                                     192

6.9    Land productivity in settlement schemes, 1983                            193

6.10   Settlement productivity by settlement types, 1983                        194

6.11   Regression results: The determination of settlement
       productivity                                                             195

6.12   Planned settlement growth, 1978–82                                       196

6.13   Various facilities provided at settlement sites, 1983                    197

6.14   Some settlement cost estimates, 1978–82                                  198

6.15   Frequency of settlements without access to items of
       social and economic infrastructure, 1983                                199

6.16   Some settlement problems                                                 200

6.17   Regression results: Determination of settlement
       "abandonment" rates                                                      201

7.1    Percentage distribution of settlers by place of origin,
       1981                                                                     230

7.2    Percentage distribution of resettlement, urban, rural,
       and nomadic populations, by age and sex, 1980–81                         231

7.3    Percentage distribution of settlers by age and sex, 1980                 231

7.4    Distribution of settlers who received training at
       agricultural resettlement schemes during 1977–80, by
       major occupational categories                                           232

7.5    Crude work activity rates for Somalia, 1975, and for
        fishing and agricultural settlements, 1980–81                    232

7.6    Percentage distribution of working male and female
        population at CDP/SDA settlements, by occupational
        groups, 1980–81                                                    233

7.7    SDA settlements: Target and actual number of schools,
        teachers, and classrooms, 1980–81                                  233

7.8    SDA proposed budget, 1975–80                                        234

7.9    Percentage of heads of households at SDA settlements
        reporting specified diseases, 1981                                 234

7.10   Total number of settlers at the three SDA agricultural
        and three CDP fishing settlments, 1976–80                          235

7.11   Expenditures on selected projects in the agricultural and
        fisheries sectors in the Five-Year Development Plan,
        1974–78, and the Three-Year Development Plan, 1979–
        81                                                                 235

7.12   SDA agricultural settlements: Targets and
        achievements, 1979–81                                             236

7.13   Proposed resettlement program for Somalia's
        agricultural sector, 1980–2000                                     236

8.1    Number of *ujamaa* villages and population by region,
        1970–74                                                           267

8.2    Summary of the process of villagization, 1967–79                   268

8.3    Percentage distribution of settlers by distance moved              268

8.4    Production of major agricultural commodities, 1970–80              269

8.5    Share of agricultural production in GDP, 1965–81                   269

8.6    Rural household income distribution trends, 1969 and
        1976–77                                                           270

8.7    Percentage distribution of households by level of
        income, 1969 and 1976–77                                          270

9.1    Proportions of colonists previously landless                       312

9.2    Percentage of colonists coming from within frontier
        zones                                                             313

9.3    Percentage of colonists remaining in settlement                    314

9.4    Colonist households with off-farm incomes                          315

9.5    Colonist evaluation of improvements                                316

10.1   Annual rates of growth for the urban and rural
        populations by states, 1940–80                                    341

10.2   Rondônia, 1979: Directed colonization projects                     343

10.3   Percentage of households with access to basic services
        and ownership of domestic appliances: Rondônia,
        1960, 1970, and 1980                                              344

10.4    Age-specific fertility rates and total fertility rate for
        urban and rural women: Rondônia, 1970 and 1980          344

10.5    Life expectancy at birth, 1970 and 1980                 345

10.6    Mean size of plots by size of holding: Rondônia, 1960,
        1970, 1975, and 1980                                    345

10.7    Percentage distribution of the number and area of
        holdings by landholding status: Rondônia, 1970,
        1975, and 1980                                          346

10.8    Distribution of income, by area and sex: Rondônia, 1980 346

10.9    Percentage distribution of settlers and *agregados*, by type
        of house, type of water provision, and type of sewage
        disposal facilities, Rondônia, 1980                     347

10.10   Percentage distribution of settlers and *agregados*, by the
        extent to which illness led to an interruption of
        normal activity and by type of care received,
        Rondônia , 1980                                         348

10.11   Percentage distribution of settlers by project, state of
        birth, and state of previous residence, Rondônia, 1980  349

10.12   Percentage distribution of settlers, by project and year
        of arrival in Rondônia                                  350

10.13   Percentage distribution of settlers by land titles,
        Rondônia, 1980                                          350

10.14   Percentage distribution of settlers in Rondônia,
        according to whether they had ever used rural credit    351

10.15   Percentage distribution of settlers, according to whether
        they had received technical assistance                  351

10.16   Percentage distribution of settlers by type of crops,
        cultivated area, and volume of production, Rondônia,
        1979–80                                                 352

10.17   Percentage distribution of settlers and *agregados* in the
        Gy-Paraná project, by the duration of wage work in a
        year, Rondônia, 1980                                    353

10.18   Percentage distribution of settlers and *agregados*, by
        comparison of their present and previous situations,
        Rondônia, 1980                                          353

10.19   Percentage distribution of settlers and *agregados*, by their
        preference whether to stay in or move out of
        Rondônia, 1980                                          354

11.1    Size and growth of population by natural regions,
        1940–81                                                 381

11.2    Land tenure in the forest region                       382

11.3    Clearing of forest areas for shifting cultivation, 1925–99   382

11.4    Rank classification of the basins of the forest highlands
        according to some indicators of development                383

11.5    Family labor input and incomes in agricultural
        households                                                 384

11.6    Direct production costs and gross profits of rice
        cultivation in Alto Mayo                                   385

11.7    Distribution of cultivated land by crop, 1979             385

11.8    Land owned by indigenous communities, 1974                386

# Preface

The availability of public land has prompted many developing countries to adopt schemes bearing such labels as resettlement, transmigration, land colonization, or land development. These have often been presented as potentially tidy solutions to a number of problems, including the need to increase agricultural production, correct spatial imbalances in the distribution of population, exploit frontier lands for reasons of national security, and defuse potentially serious political problems resulting from the existing agrarian structure, poverty, rising landlessness, and unemployment.

Despite the substantial amounts that are being invested in planned settlement schemes, however, their performance has not been very encouraging. If not complete failures, they have given settlement officials and policymakers serious cause for concern in almost all parts of the world. They are costly relative to the number of persons settled, and frequently suffer from low productivity and high rates of desertion.

And yet, strangely, little is known about the actual causes of success or failure of resettlement schemes. It is not even clear whether land settlements or colonization schemes are in fact an effective way of settling large numbers of people on virgin or reclaimed land. To fill this information gap the International Labour Organisation (ILO) initiated a number of case studies on land settlement schemes. The major focus of these studies was the identification of the factors that had contributed to the success or failure of resettlement schemes from the point of view of the populations concerned, in relation to the original objectives of the policymakers, and with respect to development objectives other than population redistribution.

The present volume reports the findings of the case studies conducted in Indonesia, Malaysia, the Philippines, Somalia, Ethiopia, the United Republic of Tanzania, Brazil, and Peru. In addition, the land settlement experiences of several other countries such as India, Nepal, Sri Lanka, Kenya, Bolivia, Colombia, Ecuador, and Costa Rica are also discussed. The volume thus provides a comparative analysis of land settlement policies and programs in developing countries under various socio-economic conditions.

Many people in addition to the authors of the chapters have contributed to this volume. It is difficult to single out individuals, but a large number of government officials in settlement agencies have provided useful information on matters of policy and practice and on their experience in the formulation and implementation of land settlement programs. I am indebted to all of them.

I am also grateful to Richard Anker, Jacques Gaude, Ajit Ghose, Eddy Lee, Peter Peek, Guy Standing, and René Wéry for their valuable comments on the earlier drafts of the chapters.

The work of typing the manuscript was handled by Mrs. C. Farley and Mrs. F. Piccoli. I gratefully acknowledge their assistance.

Finally, I wish to express my thanks to the United Nations Fund for Population Activities (UNFPA) for its support of this work.

Needless to say, the views and opinions expressed in this volume reflect those of the individual authors, and not necessarily those of the ILO or the UNFPA.

# LAND SETTLEMENT POLICIES AND POPULATION REDISTRIBUTION IN DEVELOPING COUNTRIES

A. S. Oberai                                                    1

---

# Introduction

---

Success in settlement schemes is, after all, nothing but the process of reducing or minimizing the number of failures.[1]

A. J. Schwelm

## BACKGROUND

Land settlement or colonization schemes have been adopted in many countries, often at enormous cost. Although they have the common aim of raising the incomes and living standards of the rural landless, land settlements nevertheless appear to differ in their approaches and aims. Issues of population redistribution and efficient utilization of waste land are predominant in Indonesia and Sri Lanka; in Malaysia, the United Republic of Tanzania, and Brazil, settlements of various kinds have been regarded as a prerequisite to the overall development strategy of the country. There have also been instances where extensive land settlement programs have been adopted in place of more radical agrarian reform measures.

In social and economic terms, however, the record of past schemes has been discouraging (see, for example, Jones and Richter 1982). All too often settlement projects have stagnated, while attempts to stimulate regional development by implementing policies of settlement have served merely to accentuate the dichotomy between urban and rural areas (see, for example, Standing 1984). Settlement schemes have been extremely expensive in relation to the number of persons settled. In some cases they also appear to have created social tensions in the areas concerned.

It is easy to advance reasons for the failure of a particular program, but these are not always convincing. A lack of training and extension services has sometimes been advanced as one cause of failure, as in Indonesia, but in other cases considerably better services have not led to greater success. Thorough and detailed analysis is therefore necessary to assess the efficiency of different types of settlement programs, the conditions tending to produce success or failure, and the social costs and benefits of such programs.

It is in this practical context that the ILO initiated a number of case studies in several countries in Asia, Africa, and Latin America. The purpose of these national case studies was to examine the historical antecedents of resettlement schemes, the objectives of these schemes, their planning and implementation, and the extent to which they have achieved their stated objectives. Within this framework a number of policy-related questions were examined. For example:

1. Have settlement schemes achieved their stated objectives?
2. How do income and productivity in settlements compare with other rural areas?
3. To what extent have planned settlement schemes succeeded in improving settlers' socioeconomic well-being?
4. Have "drop-outs" from settlement schemes been significant?
5. What types of settlement schemes are most successful in attracting and retaining migrant settlers?
6. What are the principal factors that contribute to the success or failure of settlement schemes?
7. Have planned settlements demonstrated greater socioeconomic benefits and ecological stability than spontaneous settlements?
8. Is spontaneous migration more cost-effective? If so, what policies are needed to encourage it?
9. Is resettlement a feasible way of preventing urban overcrowding?
10. What lessons can be learned and applied to future settlement schemes?

This volume contains eleven chapters. After a brief introduction, the rest of this chapter is devoted to a discussion of the criteria for assessing the success or failure of settlement programs. Chapter 2 attempts to synthesize the main conclusions of the national case studies presented in subsequent chapters and to bring out the implications for policy design. Chapter 3 outlines the history of Indonesia's transmigration program, assesses its successes and failures, and analyzes the extent to which the program is an appropriate policy response to population distribution problems in Indonesia. Chapter 4 provides a detailed description and analysis of the planning and implementation of the Federal Land Development Authority (FELDA) projects in Malaysia. It also assesses the impact of resettlement policy on internal migration and examines the question of whether this policy is a feasible way of reducing rural–urban migration. Chapter 5 deals with the process of resettlement in the Philippines and examines the ways in which national economic and social policies influence settlement patterns. Chapter 6 provides a critical examination of Ethiopia's settlement experience and identifies factors that facilitate the success of resettlement schemes. Chapter 7 analyzes Somalia's resettlement program and assesses the demographic and socioeconomic implications of settling Somalia's nomadic population. Chapter 8 evaluates the United Republic of Tanzania's "villagization" strategy and attempts to identify the achievements made and the major problems encountered in implementing this strategy, especially at the grass-roots level. Chapter 9, based on settlement experiences in several Latin American countries, describes different phases of the colonization process, outlines the problems and constraints encountered in each phase, and discusses possible state interventions that could facilitate transition from one phase to another. It also illustrates how the pattern of relocation and settlement, with and without subsequent circular mobility, has contributed to the success of settlement projects in retaining settlers. Chapter 10 reviews Brazilian colonization policies from the perspective of their ability to attract and retain migrants. It focuses specifically on the Rondônia region, which has experienced one of the most massive influxes of rural population ever witnessed in Brazil, and whose colonization projects have received considerable government support during the past few years. Finally, Chapter 11 places the evolution of colonization policies in Peru in a historical perspective and examines the economic and social consequences of the process of colonization in the forest highlands. It also highlights the ecological implications of large-scale deforestation and suggests appropriate measures for maintaining ecological balance.

For the purposes of this volume, a relatively simple definition of land settlement is used—the planned or spontaneous movement of people to areas of underutilized agricultural potential. As such, the volume does not deal with urban resettlement.

## EVALUATION OF PLANNED SETTLEMENT SCHEMES

The criteria by which to judge the "success" or "failure" of planned settlement projects are themselves a subject of debate. A variety of approaches have been used in the evaluation of settlement projects. Many schemes are scrutinized solely in terms of profitability. This type of evaluation is attempted to see if the scheme repays its investment. In some cases "economic" analysis of scheme performance amounts to little more than a statement of the annual earnings from the major cash crops. Schemes are justified solely in terms of their aggregate production of the crop. This practice is especially common where new crops are introduced through settlement schemes. The realization of crop targets is then taken as evidence of success, even where individual settler households cannot rely on the scheme for a living.

Some evaluations use farm income per settlement unit as an indicator of success. It is often looked at in conjunction with preplanned farm budgets, to see if the settler attains a set target. Many of the early East African schemes had as their goal a specified cash income level per family. This measure is insensitive to variations in family size, however, and so frequently gives misleading indications of family welfare.

Many schemes have as their goal the redistribution of the nation's resources, especially increased access to agricultural opportunities. The success of such schemes is measured in terms of the total number of households accommodated. In many cases, the long-term viability of farm communities is the most important criterion of successful settlement.

The assessment of schemes from the viewpoint of the national economy is conducted by means of benefit-cost analysis. The present discounted value of the scheme must be positive; that is, the benefit-cost ratio must be greater than one. If this is not the case, the scheme is considered to be of doubtful economic benefit to the country.

Two purposes are served by benefit-cost analysis. First, it is useful for assessing the viability of individual schemes. Second, it provides a standard by which different schemes may be compared with each other and with alternative development projects.

This exercise does, however, involve the usual theoretical problems of benefit-cost calculations. What discount rate is appropriate? What importance should be attached to externalities? What multiplier effect should be assumed?[2] There is also the problem of distinguishing between costs that are attributable to a scheme and those that are not. Sometimes this distinction is not very clear, and the decision to include or exclude a particular cost item is often arbitrary.

If the objectives of the project are unquantifiable, however, they cannot be subject to manipulation through benefit-cost analysis. If they are conflicting, a system of weighting has to be introduced. The benefit-cost ratio is usually supported, therefore, by extensive qualifying remarks extolling the externalities and noneconomic benefits to be derived from the project. In some cases the ratio may be accompanied by a financial analysis and cost-effectiveness estimates, that is, public expenditures per unit of the factors to be maximized, such as new employment generation, total number of beneficiaries, and net foreign exchange saving (Nelson 1973).

One major problem in evaluating settlements stems from the time scale involved. Land settlement is by its nature a long-term process in which results often show slowly. In most cases, it will be at least ten years before real benefits are fully apparent. Evaluation is therefore a difficult process in which excessive preoccupation with benefit-cost ratios in the early years can give a very distorted picture (Higgs 1978).

It must also be recognized that the choice between different projects is not always based simply on economic criteria. In the United Republic of Tanzania, for example, the government regards settlement schemes as a means of achieving a social revolution in the rural areas, transforming a subsistence tribal economy into a modern cash economy of small farmers gathered into producer cooperatives. In the United Republic of Tanzania, therefore, investment in settlement schemes is not merely a means of increasing material wealth, but also a way of modernizing rural society.

The evaluation of the success of a settlement project thus largely depends on the objectives of the project. In countries where the objectives of land settlement policy are to increase agricultural production, generate new employment, and reduce income disparities, the performance of settlement projects can be assessed in terms of their achievement of these objectives. This is the approach followed by most of the country case studies included in this volume.

With regard to the success of individual settlers, they can be considered basically successful if the majority of their household cash or subsistence needs are met by working within the settlement area. Other indicators of success might include the settlers' own estimation that life is better since settlement, a net settler income that exceeds that attainable at the place of origin, and partial or full commercialization of production (see Chapter 9). Settlements can be considered successful if they have a high rate of retention of settlers or if the number of households remains fairly stable over time, despite some turnover.

## NOTES

1. A. J. Schwelm, "Some Thoughts on Colonisation," cited in Maos (1974: 24).

2. The implementation of a settlement scheme will not only result in immediate incomes for the settlers. It will also generate new or secondary incomes through the expenditure incurred in the operation of the scheme, and through settlers spending their income (the multiplier effect).

## BIBLIOGRAPHY

Higgs, J. 1978. "Land Settlement in Africa and the Near East: Some Recent Experiences." In *Land Reform, Land Settlement and Cooperatives*. Rome: FAO.

Jones, G. W., and H. V. Richter, eds. 1982. "Population Resettlement Programmes in Southeast Asia." Canberra: Australian National University. Development Studies Centre. Monograph no. 30.

Maos, J. O. 1974. "The Spatial Organization of New Land Settlement in Latin America." Ph.D. diss., Johns Hopkins University.

Nelson, M. 1973. *"Development of Tropical Lands."* Baltimore, Md.: Johns Hopkins University Press.

Standing, G. 1984. "Population Mobility and Productive Relations: Demographic Links and Policy Evolution." Geneva: ILO. Mimeo.

A. S. Oberai

# 2

# An Overview of Settlement Policies and Programs

The purpose of this chapter is to provide an overview of the performance of national resettlement programs. Some of the programs are discussed in greater detail in subsequent chapters. The major focus of the discussion here is on the similarities and differences in the policies and implementation of different resettlement projects. An attempt is also made to identify the problems facing settlement programs and to indicate what *should* or *could* be done to improve settlement performance.

There are five sections in this chapter. The first provides a discussion of the performance of settlement projects, concentrating on the extent to which they have achieved their objectives. The second section discusses major economic and social problems confronting settlement programs. The third section analyzes the factors affecting success or failure of settlement projects. The fourth section considers whether resettlement is an appropriate policy response to the problems of population redistribution, unemployment, and poverty. Finally, the last section brings together the overall findings and highlights their major policy implications.

## ACHIEVEMENT OF SETTLEMENT OBJECTIVES

### Population redistribution

Population redistribution—the movement of excess population from one part of the country to other, more sparsely populated parts—is often one of the principal objectives of land settlement policy.

In Sri Lanka the policy of colonization and irrigation is considered to have had a major impact on population distribution. The concept of large-scale colonization had been conceived by the policymakers in the pre-independence era. Because land suitable for cultivation in the wet zone was scarce and what remained was comparatively inaccessible, the existing demand for land could not be fully met without using the resources of the dry zone. Several colonization schemes were therefore initiated. With independence the process of colonization was accelerated.

Several studies point to the success of land settlement and irrigation schemes, which have resulted in increased food production and considerable relief of population pressures in the wet zone (Indraratna et al. 1983). About 75,000 families were resettled between 1946 and 1971. Taking into account the estimated average size of the resettled households, this means that nearly 4 percent of the island's population was resettled within a period of 25 years (Indraratna et al. 1983).

In Indonesia, too, the idea of population transfer is far from new. The Dutch tried it in 1905, but for economic reasons rather than to relieve population pressures, when they moved Javanese to southern Sumatra, where additional labor was needed. Between 1905 and 1950 the government moved about 220,000 people to the outer islands.

Since independence, however, the pace has increased dramatically. Between 1950 and 1977, the program resettled about 771,100 people, while at least as many moved independently without being officially recorded (see Chapter 3). Throughout most of the period, however, there have been wide gaps between the targets set for the program and the actual numbers moved, due both to overenthusiasm in setting the targets and to political and administrative problems (Oey and Astika 1978). Recently, the program has been much more successful in meeting its targets. The target for the Five-Year Plan (1979–84) was to move about 2 million people. It was a daunting goal, but the government appears to have achieved it. Encouraged by this success, the authorities want to move twice as many in the next five years.

In the case of the most often quoted objective, however—relieving population pressure—the program has had only a minimal impact in Java. While the official transmigration program moved at most 991,100 people in the 1905–77 period, the population of Java increased by more than 35 million during the same period.

With Java's population increasing by about 2 million a year, government officials no longer claim that the transmigration program could correct the population imbalance between Java and the outer islands. Arndt's analysis presented in Chapter 3 shows that even if it were possible to sustain transmigration at the Third Five-Year Plan (1978–79 to 1983–84) target rate, this would remove from Java only one-fifth of the annual increase in Java's population. A recent study has also noted that the number of people who move from the outer provinces to Java is about two and a half times greater than that of people migrating from Java to the outer islands (Bahrin 1979: 300).

This is not to say that, in terms of numbers, the effort has been pointless. The removal of between 300,000 and 400,000 people a year during the period 1979–84 must have done something to relieve the population pressure and consequent social problems in some of the poorest areas of Java. Moreover, as Arndt argues, if the outflow of spontaneous migrants was to some extent induced by the transmigration program, the program can be credited with a greater total effect on the population balance than the official transmigration statistics would suggest. The influx of transmigrants also represents a significant addition to the human resource base of the outer islands, where low population density and a shortage of labor undoubtedly constitute obstacles to economic development. But it would clearly be difficult to justify the program simply in terms of its effects on the population imbalance.

In Malaysia, while population redistribution as such was never an objective of land development programs, FELDA was seen as having a role in regulating and stabilizing population movement within the rural areas. Except in Pahang, which depends on migrants from other states, the FELDA settlers are predominantly from their own states. This is largely because most states have a quota requiring a minimum of 50 percent of the settlers to be from their own states (Chan 1983).

In this way the FELDA schemes succeed in retaining migrants from rural villages within the rural areas. Rural–rural migration is therefore encouraged, and this minimizes rural–urban movement. It will be noticed that, except where states have a land availability problem, most of the FELDA schemes are located in states that suffer from out-migration. This deliberate location of land development projects in such states provides FELDA with a stabilizing role, and partly explains Malaysia's relatively slow rate of urbanization, compared with other developing countries. Ying has shown that between 1957 and 1970 the urban population grew at the same rate as the rural population (2.6 percent a year). Since the natural population growth was somewhat lower in urban areas, some rural–urban migration obviously took place over the period, but the rate appears to have been low (Ying 1977: 87).

## Colonization and development of new areas

There are many reasons why a government might wish to colonize and develop a sparsely populated, underdeveloped area: increased agricultural output, considerations of national security, the provision of land for landless or displaced people, the relief of population pressures in overcrowded areas. The colonization of new areas is not, then, so much an end in itself as a means of achieving certain other goals.

In the Philippines the earliest settlement projects had the colonization of the frontier as their major objective. It was considered that the unexplored areas of Mindanao, Palawan, and Cagayan Valley had resources that were being underutilized. It was also thought that an influx of Christian settlers into these regions would lead to the assimilation of cultural minorities, or at least reduce the threat of raids or warfare against other regions. This was an important aim in the early settlement of the Mindanao regions. The initial projects therefore sought to achieve a major shift of population, with the aim of changing the economic and political character of the frontier area. From this point of view, the settlement program was very successful. From almost one-seventh of the average population density of the country's traditional agricultural areas at the beginning of the century, Mindanao's density had risen to almost one-half by 1975.

The pacification of cultural minorities appeared at first to have been achieved, but now looks to be one of the more palpable failures of the program. As the frontier areas rapidly filled up, conflicts began to arise between the original tribal inhabitants and the settlers. Early frictions returned, due both to cultural differences and to conflicts over land. Land disputes contributed to the problems, which culminated in the violent uprising led by Muslim separatists in the early 1970s.

Paderanga's study (see Chapter 5) does suggest, however, that an increase in agricultural output has been a major benefit of frontier migration. Quoting the ILO mission report, he points to the expansion of the cultivated areas as a major factor in the growth of national agricultural output (ILO 1974). The same report also suggested that land colonization could play an even greater role in increasing agricultural output, since a substantial amount of unutilized land still remained to be exploited.

Paderanga argues, however, that land settlement cannot be seen as the only option here. Other instruments for increasing agricultural output such as intensified cultivation, which would entail investment in rural infrastructure (irrigation, rural roads, etc.), must be considered.

His analysis suggests that benefit-cost ratios for irrigation of rice land are higher than those for land resettlement.

The cultivation of hitherto unutilized land is also a major issue in parts of Africa; in Somalia, for example, where nearly 70 percent of the 5.7 million population consists of nomads, only 1.5 million of the 8 million hectares of land potentially available for cultivation is actually cultivated.

Three agricultural and three fisheries settlements were established to settle war refugees and the 1974 drought-stricken population, but the achievements of these settlements have been much below target. The original target laid down by the Settlement Development Agency (SDA) for developing irrigated and nonirrigated agricultural land during the Five-Year Development Plan (FYDP) of 1974–1978 was 56,000 hectares for its three settlements. This target was subsequently scaled down to 30,000 hectares. By the end of 1978, only 2438 hectares of rain-fed land had been reclaimed and improved (see Chapter 7).

During the next development plan (the Three-Year Development Plan of 1979–81), the SDA's objective was to develop 22,000 hectares of land, half of it irrigated. However, since 10,000 hectares of this was to be at Dujuma, the overall target was reduced to 12,000 hectares when Dujuma was abandoned at the end of 1980, because the land was found to be unsuitable for irrigated agriculture and only marginally suitable for rain-fed agriculture. Soon after, even this modest goal was further scaled down to a mere 3050 hectares.

The analysis in Chapter 7 suggests that Somalia's fisheries settlements are doing slightly better than the agricultural settlements, although neither appears to have been sufficiently successful in economic terms to make it worth emulating in future resettlement programs.

In Ethiopia, a recent land use survey has shown that only 15 percent of arable land is now under cultivation. There is, therefore, a great potential for developing land and moving people from high-density to low-density areas.

The settlement program in Ethiopia started after the 1974 drought. The target was to settle a population of 520,000 over a period of ten years. By the end of 1983, however, only 103,500 persons (31,506 households) had been settled in 83 settlements (see Chapter 6).

In Peru it was hoped that the colonization of the Amazon, and in particular the forest highlands, would absorb a significant proportion of the country's population increment. Until the 1940s, the principal means used by the state to colonize the region was to establish and promote large estates. However, ecological problems, the decline in international prices for cash crops, and the relative shortage of manpower proved detrimental to the consolidation of these estates. From the 1940s onwards, the emphasis was on the development of small family farms. In addition, the government encouraged the cultivation of crops that were required to satisfy urban consumption needs.

Carpio's study suggests that although the population of the forest highlands has increased in recent decades, the region has absorbed less than 10 percent of the population growth of the country as a whole (see Chapter 11). Similarly, less than 20 percent of the Andean migrants have chosen the valleys of this region as their destination in the last 40 years. It thus appears that the forest highlands have not constituted a major alternative for human settlements.

## Provision of land for the landless

In certain cases (although resettlement programs must necessarily involve the settlement and cultivation of hitherto little populated areas) the main emphasis of the program has been on the provision of land for landless people.

When FELDA was established in Malaysia in 1956, its principal objective was to develop land for the landless and unemployed. In 1966 the government created an additional organization, the Federal Land Consolidation and Rehabilitation Authority (FELCRA), in order to assist other poor rural groups such as those with small and fragmented holdings.

By the end of 1982, FELDA had developed 331 schemes with a total of 559,906 hectares of agricultural land, involving about 76,786 families (see Chapter 4). Assuming that the household size is six (five dependents and the settler), FELDA would appear to have moved more than 460,716 people. This does not include additional labor needed during the initial period of establishing the land schemes (viz. the use of migrant casual labor in land clearing, road construction, etc.). Although during the fourth plan period (1981–85), FELDA hoped to settle 6000 families annually, it had been able to exceed this figure by 500 and 219 for 1981 and 1982, respectively.

In India, on the other hand, rural resettlement projects have mainly been much less successful. In an evaluation of the Dandakaranya project, for example, Bose observes that the project has totally failed to achieve its objectives (Bose 1983). When it was set up in 1958, its aim was to resettle 20,000 displaced families by 1959. It was thought that it could eventually absorb as many as 2 million displaced persons. Bose's study indicates that by August 1979 only 31,007 families had been settled, and of these 11,364 (36.6 percent) had already deserted. The number of deserters has been increasing in recent years; during 1978–79, 844 new families were settled, while 2504 deserted.

In an assessment of the Rondônia project in Brazil, Wood and Schmink suggest that the colonization program's most pertinent failure relates to the very size of the population, which has effectively benefited from the program. The goals have turned out to be far higher than the actual achievements. By mid–1974 only around 7000 families had been settled in the three major pilot projects, instead of the 100,000 families estimated initially (Wood and Schmink 1979).

The failure to meet targets has led to large numbers of people arriving in the settlement areas and failing to find land within the settlement projects. By mid–1977, the number of agricultural families who had not managed to obtain a plot by legal or illegal means, and had thus joined the marginal population of newly created urban areas, was estimated at 30,000 (*O Globo* 1977).

Recognizing the impossibility of absorbing the rural population that was migrating to Rondônia in growing numbers, the government was forced to adopt measures aimed at discouraging these flows at their origin. At the end of 1977, disincentive pamphlets were distributed in several municipalities in the states from which the majority of migrants to Rondônia had come.

Since then, however, the migration flows have continued. Henriques' analysis in Chapter 10 shows that northeasterners and other spontaneous migrants have been attracted in much greater numbers than could effectively be absorbed by official programs. For each family settled by the official programs, four others have established themselves spontaneously on vacant land. The authorities now say that they can no longer cope with the torrents of migrants that are being attracted by the 1 million free land titles being distributed by the government. New arrivals now have to wait up to four years for a title to 100 hectares of virgin forest (South 1985).

The authorities in Rondônia are now faced with growing problems. There are violent conflicts over land, and uncontrolled urban growth and its attendant problems. Some of the settlers have become disillusioned by the lack of easy wealth. They are ready to sell their holdings and move back to their places of origin or to even remoter jungle areas. Nevertheless, Rondônia's population continues to swell by 13 percent a year (six times the national average), and crime, disease, and competition for available land are mounting (South 1985).

The same sort of thing has tended to happen in Nepal. Planned resettlement started with the establishment of the Nepal Settlement Company in 1964, with the dual objectives of coping with the pressure of population in the hills and settling landless peasants, as well as peasants with inadequate lands in the Terai and Inner Terai areas. The provision of land at a nominal price, and the availability of social and economic infrastructure (such as schools, drinking water, roads, agricultural extension services and credit facilities within the project area), were important attractions for the hill people. They began to migrate to the resettlement project in large numbers, and the project could not keep pace with the demand for land through forest clearing. Those who had come in the hope of acquiring land encroached on forests in and around the project area, and the project had in turn to involve itself in resettling these encroachers.

At the beginning of 1969, the government established the Resettlement Department, with the objective of organizing land settlement on a massive scale. The program implemented by the Department has been largely ineffective, however, in meeting the objectives of resettling landless peasants and controlling forest encroachment (Kansakar 1983).

## Promotion of regional development

Land development programs have sometimes been seen, at least partly, as a means of promoting regional development. In Indonesia, for example, this was certainly one objective of the transmigration program.

If by regional development is meant the promotion of industry and trade, the exploitation and processing of minerals, forestry and other natural resources, and the improvement of transport and communications necessary to integrate the region more effectively into the national economy, then the contribution of the transmigration program has so far been quite marginal.

Arndt argues that the whole notion of promoting regional development by means of land settlement is unrealistic (see Chapter 3). Land settlement is perhaps useful for the people who are given the opportunity of growing some crops in somewhat better conditions than at home in Java. It is a form of social relief for poor people, but it cannot contribute significantly to the industrial and commercial development of the outer islands. For this it would be necessary to provide wage employment opportunities, which in turn would attract a large flow of spontaneous migrants from Java. But where would the jobs come from? Arndt and Sundrum have suggested that in the first instance they have to come from public employment, on public works, to create the infrastructure, in transport and other areas, without which regional development of the outer islands is in any case impossible (Arndt and Sundrum 1977).

Some observers argue, however, that the approach suggested by Arndt and Sundrum would require diversion of a huge percentage of the national budget to the construction of infrastructure in the islands outside Java. While it is undeniable that infrastructure of all kinds needs to be expanded, there is obviously a point beyond which no central government can go when it comes to allocating funds to the development of relatively unpopulated areas (Perez-Sáinz 1983).

While it is almost certainly totally unrealistic to regard a land development program in itself as a viable means of promoting regional development, such a program could well be a valuable part of a broader regional development strategy.

In Malaysia, land development and settlement constitutes one of the most important instruments of the regional development program. The available evidence suggests that land settlement schemes in Malaysia, combined with broader rural development programs, have been rather successful in increasing rural production, raising rural incomes and reducing rural–urban migration. The reduction in rural–urban differentials in income and employment opportunities, and the provision of social and economic infrastructure in rural areas, have discouraged potential migrants from leaving the rural areas.

In fact, it was also thought that the FELDA model of land development would include urbanization (or at least semi-urbanization) in the rural areas, something that is vitally necessary if the second and subsequent generations are to be retained in the rural areas. This would have tailored neatly with the goals of the New Economic Policy: to urbanize and modernize the Malays. Somehow this has not occurred. A physical aggregation of settlers engaged in agricultural activities does not constitute an urban center. While it is true that the Malays have migrated from the rural villages, they have in fact transplanted themselves to another rural and agricultural environment that is only physically more "modernized." If the FELDA type of land development is to function effectively as an urbanizing agent, it must offer a socioeconomic environment that is different from that of the *kampong* (village). The social, economic, and commercial structure must be different, and it must offer opportunities for the sort of competitive endeavors that are usually found in urban centers. Thus, while FELDA has physically influenced the demographic landscape, it has not really succeeded in establishing urban growth centers.

Partly in response to this problem, FELDA has initiated a larger-scale integrated regional development. A number of projects have been designed and some of them have been implemented. Prominent among these are the Jengha Triangle and the Pahang Tengyara Region in Pahang and the Johore Tengyara Region in Johore. Unfortunately, whereas the land development and settlement part of some of these projects has developed according to schedule, thus bringing in the settlers, the growth of urban centers and the spontaneous movement of business and services are still lagging behind.

## Agricultural Development

Agricultural development is often included among the objectives of settlement programs. Here again, performance has more often than not been disappointing.

In Nepal, for example, productivity has been lower in new settlements than in surrounding cultivated areas. This is due to several reasons. First, as most of the settlement projects are located on ground higher than the surrounding older cultivation areas, irrigation through canals from the rivers is not feasible. The intensity of cultivation in the resettlement projects is therefore very low compared with the surrounding areas. Second, the quality of land in the resettlement projects is not good compared with the surrounding lowlands. Third, the settlers do not get adequate loans and credit in time. In such a situation, they have to take the recourse of borrowing from moneylenders at exorbitantly high rates of interest. And, finally, the inaccessibility of projects, coupled with the absence of marketing facilities, has acted as a major constraint on the settlers' securing reasonable prices for their farm produce. Usually they have to sell their produce at low prices to moneylenders or local grain traders. Low farm incomes adversely affect their ability to improve the land and consequently result in low productivity.

In Indonesia, too, several studies indicate that in the northern Sumatran provinces, which have received relatively fewer transmigrants, the rate of growth of productivity has been higher than that in southern Sumatra. Overall, the evidence suggests that productivity is abysmally low, except in the 10 percent of settlements that have tree crops or irrigated rice fields. None of the other settlements have returns anything like what the World Bank regards as the minimum feasible if the program is to be economically justifiable. There has been a small net increase in food production, but it can hardly justify the huge investment (Carelfield 1984).

Settlement programs have not always been so unsuccessful in achieving their agricultural objectives, however. As we have already seen, frontier migration in the Philippines has been a major factor in increasing national agricultural output.

Bahrin's analysis, presented in Chapter 4, suggests that in Malaysia, too, FELDA's land settlement schemes have made a significant contribution to the development and diversification of agriculture. The area developed and maintained by FELDA constitutes approximately 12 percent of peninsular Malaysia's cultivated land. Although it has helped to create a community of modern and relatively prosperous rubber smallholders, it is actually with respect to the expansion in the cultivation of oil palm that its contribution has been the greatest. By 1982, FELDA schemes were responsible for producing 4,734,605 tons of palm oil, representing nearly 30 percent of Malaysia's total production. The newly established smallholders thus appear to be playing a significant role in making Malaysia the biggest producer of palm oil in the world.

In some cases specific increases in output have occurred despite generally low levels of productivity. In Sri Lanka, for example, average yields have normally (though not always) proved to be considerably lower than the national average, and projects have suffered from serious problems of social cohesion and even, on certain occasions, of social distress. On the other hand, one major benefit of the land settlement program has been the increase in food production. It is estimated that more than one-third of Sri Lanka's paddy output is produced on major irrigation schemes in the colonization areas (Indraratna et al. 1983).

In Somalia, too, the total output from settlements has generally been quite modest, while the costs of developing and running the schemes have been high. From the standpoint of the SDA settlements' contribution to the import substitution, however, it is noteworthy that, among food commodities alone, sugar imports actually decreased from 90,818 tons in 1978 to none by 1981 (see Chapter 7). Dujuma's newly transferred former nomads, contributing their labor to the new Juba Sugar Estate, were in large part responsible for this success.

## Improved welfare of migrants

Reducing poverty and providing improved standards of living for the poorest in society (the landless, those with inadequate holdings of land, refugees, drought victims, and so on) is advanced as one of the objectives of most land settlement programs. It is thought both that the settlements will provide migrants with better incomes and that the concentration of people into settlements will make it easier to provide social services such as housing, health, and education.

### Settlers' incomes

As far as settlers' incomes are concerned, settlement performance has been mixed. In Peru, for example, the evidence suggests that the farmers of the forest highlands enjoy a higher standard of living than in their regions of origin. In a survey carried out in Alto Huallaga in 1973, for example, two-thirds of the respondents indicated that their situation had improved since moving or simply that they were satisfied. Even in the case of Tambopata, which has been described as one of the most depressed settlement areas in terms of development and availability of basic services, only 47 percent of migrant families had real incomes below the legally established minimum rural wage, as compared with 56.3 percent in the areas of origin (see Chapter 11).

In Malaysia, it seems that a poor rural farmer of any age who decided to join a FELDA scheme enjoyed, after a few years of settlement, a steady increase in the level of real income between 50 and 74 percent, compared with farmers of the same age who did not join the FELDA schemes, but who might have been benefiting from other rural development programs during the same period (see Chapter 4). While the average income of rural workers in Malaysia increased from M$200 per month in 1970 to M$355 in 1980, the corresponding figures for the average income of urban workers were M$428 and M$675. Although the average income of the FELDA settlers in rubber schemes is still well below urban levels, the income of the oil palm settlers is definitely comparable.

In Indonesia, too, migrants do seem to experience some improvements in their incomes, although the available evidence suggests that benefits are still extremely variable and on average relatively small. The average income of transmigrants is only a little above that in rural Java. Even in settlements assisted by the World Bank, farmers with an average of just over 1 hectare under cultivation are found after three to four years on the site to reach an annual family income of only about U.S. $600 (at 1982 prices). This may be compared with an estimated average per capita consumption expenditure of about U.S. $120 in rural Java (see Chapter 3). It must be remembered, however, that most of the transmigrants are not average Javanese. The majority are recruited from among the landless and poorest. To them, even an average migrant standard of living, including a piece of land of their own, represents a big improvement.

Unfortunately, in many countries land settlement programs have not had even this limited degree of success. Evaluations of colonists' returns in coastal northeastern Brazil and Costa Rica show that most colonists earn less than the minimum wage. In the Satipo region of Peru and the Eje Norte of Paraguay, the average colonist spends more than he earns.

In Somalia, the SDA had estimated that the gross family income for 1976 would be around 12,921 shillings, of which about 47 percent was to be returned in kind or cash to the SDA for operational costs, leaving each family with about 6848 shillings net average income. This was to be compared with an estimated national family income of only 3504 shillings in 1976.

Obviously the settlers had high expectations that their income would rise substantially once the program was implemented. Despite enthusiasm and hard work on the part of the settlers, however, most settler households received less than 2400 shillings, an income considerably below the projected net income of 6848 shillings (see Chapter 7).

Low farm incomes force many colonists to seek off-farm work to supplement their farm earnings. Here again, a lack of off-farm employment opportunities is a problem in almost all settlements, so settlers often cannot solve their problems by seeking work away from their farms. Low incomes often cause settlers to abandon the settlements.

In Latin America, for example, while earnings from off-farm work may enable the family to meet subsistence needs, most frontier jobs pay poorly, and only rarely do they provide enough to invest in commercialization. For many settlers, off-farm earnings simply cannot fill the gap between net farm income and consumption expenses, with the result that they have to obtain credit from local merchants to tide their families over until the next harvest. When they cannot clear their debt, they have to sell their land. The debtors either start anew, become tenants or sharecroppers on a large landowner's farm, or become casual workers in the frontier zone. The net result is that, despite the fact that colonists start off with similar holdings, land is increasingly held by a smaller and more select group of rich individuals, while the poorer colonists find themselves on successively smaller plots after each forced sale.

*Provision of social services*

Here once again, settlement performance is very mixed. In the United Republic of Tanzania, the provision of social services such as improved access to clean water, primary education, and health services to a vast majority of the rural population has been among the most notable achievements of the "villagization" strategy. The availability of these services has led to a reduction in mortality and an increase in life expectancy, a reduction in the incidence of some diseases, and an ability on the part of a more literate society to comprehend and implement technical and scientific innovations. As social and economic development indicators show, since independence, and particularly in the post–1967 period, the enrolment rate in primary schools has almost tripled, with over 70 percent of school-age children (7–13 years) attending school; health services are within easy access at 5 kilometers for over 50 percent of the population; around 40 percent of the population now has access to safe water, as compared with only 13 percent in 1970; and the average life expectancy has increased from 37 years in 1967 to 50 years in 1981 (see Chapter 8).

One important social consequence of villagization has been the improved position of women in society. Women are now entitled to village membership in their own right and play an active role in communal agriculture. In most villages women are represented on the village councils. The provision of clean water in many villages has relieved women of the arduous task of fetching water from great distances from the village (Shayo 1984).

In Somalia, though income and production targets have not been met, the settlements have been quite successful in creating a social infrastructure that has improved hygiene, nutrition, and educational opportunities for some 15,000 families.

The provision of education and health care at the settlements appears to be well above the national norm. In 1981, the elementary school program at the settlements ranked behind only 5 of the 16 administrative regions in terms of the rate of enrollment. At the intermediate (grades

5–8) and secondary levels, the settlement enrolment was less than only two and three regions, respectively (see Chapter 7).

Health facilities at the settlements also appear to be above average. Each of the settlements at Kurtunwary and Sablaale has a central hospital with about 130 and 140 beds, respectively. Each settlement has a lower ratio of persons per dispensary than the national average (and much lower than the home regions of the settlers).

While health facilities are generally at a higher level than the national norm, however, the former nomads face unprecedented health hazards in bilharzia and in the year-round incidence of malaria.

Housing has also presented problems, and the housing pilot projects at the agricultural settlements remain a point of controversy. By 1981, the targeted 400 houses at Sablaale and Kurtunwary were still far from completion. At Sablaale, only 58 houses had been completed. The situation at Kurtunwary was not much better. The housing was expected to be low cost, but turned out to be expensive, with a large component of imported materials.

In many other countries, however, the provision of social infrastructure has been totally inadequate and has often constituted a major reason for settlement abandonment. A 1979 report on the Dandakaranya project in India found, for example, that only eight of the 381 villages had been electrified; that the supply of drinking water was far from adequate; that of 296 primary schools, as many as 169 were housed in temporary structures; that there was a shortage of medicines in the hospitals and dispensaries; and that several vacancies for technical staff had not been filled.

Nor does the implementation of a colonization policy in Brazil's Rondônia appear to have significantly enhanced people's well-being. The analysis of data from a recent survey shows that in 1980, 93 percent of the settlers' houses were made of unfinished wood (see Chapter 10). A similar percentage of houses had no source of water other than a nearby river or an untreated well. Sewage facilities were also lacking; 73 percent of the settlers had none at all and 22 percent only a rudimentary cesspool.

Health standards were also found to be low among both settlers and *agregados* (agricultural laborers). Disease was part of their lives. Sixty percent of the settlers reported that they had felt sick during the month prior to the survey, and most of them had had to interrupt their normal activities as a result.

The available evidence on the Bura project in Kenya suggests that here, too, the settlers run serious health risks. Malaria and malnutrition are widespread, and infant mortality is high compared with other rural areas of Kenya. The provision of social infrastructure has also not kept pace with that of the settlement. This is largely because of the National

Irrigation Board's (NIB) comparatively weak resources for coordination and planning in sectors where they rely on action by other ministries.

## Broader social objectives

Land settlement programs have sometimes had extremely far-reaching social objectives. In the United Republic of Tanzania, the objective could be described as a complete transformation of rural society. The villagization program was an attempt by the nation's leadership to evolve a coherent rural development strategy with the aim of fostering communal production on the *ujamaa* (socialist) model, thus achieving growth with equity. After the Arusha Declaration (1967), which ushered in the philosophy of socialism and self-reliance, the United Republic of Tanzania embarked on the collectivization of the entire rural population into nucleated settlements (ujamaa villages) as a precondition for rural development. Although ujamaa villages were conceived as a voluntary association of people living and working together, some force had to be used to move people into them.

Maro's study (see Chapter 8) indicates that today, practically the whole of the rural population of the United Republic of Tanzania is living in more than 8000 villages. The total cost of moving around 5 million people has been estimated at 800 million Tanzanian shillings, which is a very large sum of money, since it was not initially planned or budgeted for. The opportunity cost of spending this sum of money on moving people to villages must have been great, but has never been assessed.

The objectives of the nucleated settlements were to mobilize land and labor for communal production and to achieve equitable income distribution. Although the growth of rural incomes has been slow compared with that of urban incomes, there has been a lessening of inequality in the rural areas, as shown by the decline in the Gini coefficient from 0.57 in 1969 to 0.49 in 1976–77 (see Chapter 8, Table 8.6). One of the factors that accounts for this trend is the redistribution of land and introduction of income-generating communal activities through the villagization program.

In spite of the villagization program, however, levels of agricultural production and productivity have continued to be low, and as a result rural incomes have remained far from adequate. In fact, there are some indications that agricultural productivity and output have actually declined. There are several reasons for this. First, the communal farms have not been successful. At the same time, private farms have not been allowed to borrow money. Only the communal farms have had privileged access to credit and technical assistance. Second, there has been greater emphasis on the transformation of the institutional structure for rural development than on measures such as the adoption of new technology and the increased use of fertilizers, which would improve agricultural productivity directly. Third, young adults have been moving to the urban centers, leaving behind the children and older people. This has adversely affected land and labor productivity in the rural areas.

## PROBLEMS CONFRONTING SETTLEMENT PROGRAMS

### Settlers' abandonment of settlement schemes

The problem of settler retention is one that confronts most settlement schemes to some degree. Where settlement performance and achievement of objectives are poor, and the settlers are disappointed in their often unrealistically high expectations, the natural tendency is for settlers to abandon the settlement and seek better opportunities elsewhere.

In one completed project in Nawalpur, in Nepal, where the land titles have been conferred, nearly 50 percent of the original settlers have already disposed of their plots and left. Of the remaining 50 percent, very few families have holdings of 4 bighas (1 bigha = 0.7 hectares), most of them already having sold a portion of their land (Kansakar 1983: 243).

Here, low productivity seems to be at the root of the problem. Despite facilities such as agricultural etension services, agricultural development in settlement projects, as discussed earlier, has not been remarkable compared with the surrounding older areas of cultivation. In a recent review of planned resettlement in Nepal, Kansakar (1983: 244) concludes:

the programme has not been able either to emerge as an example of agricultural development or to raise the standard of living of the resettlers. The apathy on the part of the resettlers in agricultural development and the discouraging environmental conditions of the settlement projects indicate that the resettlers are just waiting to acquire land ownership certificates in order to sell the allotted land and go elsewhere.

Settler retention is also a major problem for most settlements in Ethiopia. Several factors account for the high but variable rate of settler abandonment of the settlements. Initially settlers were not allowed to bring in their families. This resulted in a shortage of labor and low productivity. As a consequence, many of the settlers left the settlements. The multivariate analysis in Chapter 6 suggests that the more distant a settlement is from the origin of the settlers, the smaller is the degree of settlement abandonment.

In Somalia, because achievement of production targets has been unsatisfactory, income in settlement areas is considerably below the target levels and is not adequate. As a result, many of the settlers, particularly the adult males, have been abandoning the settlements in search of work elsewhere, leaving behind the children and the older members. By 1981, only 75,000 of the original 120,000 former nomads remained in the settlement schemes (see Chapter 7). This has adversely affected agricultural productivity and incomes in settlement areas. The family members are left behind so that they can take advantage of the free education and the health and housing facilities available in the settlements.

In Indonesia, lack of infrastructural facilities, such as housing, drinking water, roads (essential for marketing), and irrigation; lack of farming experience; and scarcity of nonagricultural employment are among the important factors that have induced people to abandon the land settlement projects. The available evidence suggests that in most settlement projects between 6 and 10 percent of settled families have already abandoned the settlement sites.

## Lack of non-farm employment opportunities—second generation problems

The provision of non-farm employment is an area where most settlement schemes seem to have failed totally.

Even in Malaysia, where the land settlement program is conceived as part of an integrated regional development program, the problem has not been solved. Initially one plot of land (4–5 hectares) is perhaps adequate to provide a minimum income for the family, utilize the family labor, and satisfy the emotive need for land ownership. This is workable during the early years while the settler's family is small. As it grows, however, the triple functions of land fail. One of the rigid principles of FELDA is that the settler's land cannot be subdivided, for fragmentation creates uneconomic holdings. This means that the settler's dependents will have to leave the land settlement scheme to seek employment opportunities elsewhere. A new cycle of out-migration is thus generated. Already, though the problem is not acute yet, this new wave of out-migration is occurring, particularly among those who have received a higher level of education and who have developed some inclination toward urban living (Chan 1983).

Under such circumstances, what is needed is the establishment of urban-based industries and activities in the schemes. As we have seen, this has so far not been achieved. Thus, although land settlement programs have given potential rural–urban migrants the alternative of remaining in the rural areas, they can play only a temporary role in combating rural–urban migration.

Nepal provides another typical case. As agriculture is characterized by slack seasons, the resettlement program should provide alternative employment opportunities outside agriculture during the slack seasons to generate additional income for the settlers. As it has not been able to do this, the settlers are unemployed or underemployed for a large part of the year. Moreover, with the gradual increase in the size of settlers' families, the allotted holdings in the resettlement projects have not been large enough for families to maintain a livelihood. Fragmentation of land in the resettlement projects has therefore led to the emergence of landless families or families with inadequate land within the settlement areas. The program thus completely lacks a plan of action to deal with second-generation problems.

In the Dandakaranya project in India, the failure to provide non-farm employment seems to have had particularly distressing consequences. The available evidence suggests that due to lack of employment opportunities in the schemes, there are large numbers of young men and women who have grown up in the Dandakaranya area who are totally frustrated. Some of the young men have turned to crime, and there are reports of young women taking to prostitution, especially in the nearby Bhilai industrial region (Bose 1983). The human suffering generated by the failure of the Dandakaranya project has yet to be assessed.

## Land concentration

A serious problem for land resettlement programs in Latin America is that of land concentration, which defeats many of the aims of the programs, such as providing land for the landless and promoting greater equality in land and income distribution.

The process of land concentration is well documented by Martine (1982) in his study of the colonization in Brazil's Rondônia. Concentration often results from the sale of land by failed colonists. By 1976, the small farmer colonists (those with less than 50 hectares) made up 31 percent of the farms but owned only 1 percent of the land. Almost 60 percent of the land was controlled by a minority of 1.2 percent of the landowners, each with 5,000 hectares or more (see Chapter 9).

The analysis in Chapter 10 also suggests that significant changes are taking place in Rondônia's land tenure system. The mean size of larger holdings has almost doubled during the last five years, a clear sign of a land concentration process. Several other reports also indicate that up to one-third of colonists sell shortly after receiving their land titles. Eighty percent sell their land within five years (South 1985). By the time the roads and infrastructure arrive in the settlement areas, the original colonists are often exhausted. Since prices have usually doubled in the meantime, they accept any cash offer and move on. The pioneer region thus becomes like a stock exchange; many people think that they can make more money by selling land than by planting it. Many of those who sell their land end up as day laborers.

Some who sell their land, however, are not compelled to do so by debts or lack of capital. With the rise in land values, colonists sometimes find it more profitable to sell their land after only two or three years of occupation. They obtain a plot of land, clear it, work it for a few years and then sell the improvements. In Colombia's Llanos Abrierto and Departmento de Meta, for example, professional colonists can earn up to U.S. $30,000 per hectare of improved land sold (see Chapter 9). Some of them hope to amass enough capital eventually to establish their own cattle ranches, but for many clearing and selling becomes a way of life.

The result of this process is the emergence of the *minifundia–latifundia* pattern so evident throughout settled, traditional areas of Latin America. In Bolivia's Santa Cruz zone, for example, the majority of the settlers no longer possess their original 20 hectares. Despite relatively equal plot sizes at the start of colonization, after 10–15 years over one-third of the land is possessed by one-sixth of the colonists (Maxwell 1980). This process of concentration has been observed in virtually all Latin America's frontier zones.

Shifts in crop patterns and labor force demand accompany the land concentration process. Like large landholders in traditional settled zones, the large landholders in frontier zones concentrate on raising livestock or commercial crops that do not require large or year-round labor inputs. This can only have an adverse impact on the population retention potential of the colonization zones, where many colonists depend on off-farm agricultural wage labor.

## Social tensions between settlers and indigenous populations

Tensions are likely to arise between settlers and indigenous populations if the settlers are perceived to have larger landholdings and better provision of social services or to be encroaching on land traditionally farmed by the local community.

As the Andean settlements in Peru's forest highlands have grown, land areas that had always previously been held by indigenous forest communities have been taken over. The competition for both land and labor has led to serious ethnic conflicts (see Chapter 11).

The lack of adequate communication with the indigenous tribal population regarding the resettlement scheme was an important factor contributing to the failure of the Dandakaranya project in India. This led to misgivings on the part of the tribal communities and tension between them and the migrants. As we have seen, there have also been serious conflicts between separatists and Christian settlers in the Philippines.

It is a crucial part of the resettlement agency's job to ensure that there is adequate communication between settlers and the indigenous population. It should also anticipate that feelings of jealousy are likely to arise among the native population if superior services and housing are provided to the settlers. If possible, education, water, health, and other services should be made available to both groups, and a suitable social climate generated for their integration.

In fact, spontaneous migration is less likely to create the social problems that occur in many governmental resettlement schemes between migrants and local residents. This is because spontaneous migrants are more likely to have had some contact with the local residents before migrating, or once they have arrived might work out acceptable relationships with the local population in order to succeed in the new areas.

## Ecological problems

In many Latin American countries, the practice of shifting cultivation by settlers has resulted in the excessive deforestation and serious ecological deterioration that is at present occurring in the different basins of the forest highlands. In Peru, for example, during the period 1925–84, approximately 7 million hectares of forest are estimated to have been destroyed (see Chapter 11, Table 11.3). The cultivation of crops unsuitable for the forest highlands has also contributed to the environmental problems (Hyman 1984).

Because of this practice of shifting cultivation, a significant proportion of the agricultural land is now uncultivated. Although this has been done largely to maintain soil fertility, measures should be taken to use land more intensively and to adopt more appropriate technologies.

## High settlement costs

The prohibitively high costs of planned settlements constitute one of the major reasons advanced in favor of spontaneous settlement, particularly where large numbers of people need to be resettled.

Arndt's analysis presented in Chapter 3 shows how the proportion of the development budget allocated to Indonesia's transmigration program has risen from 0.7 percent in 1969–70 to 6.1 percent in 1982–83, though it was slightly less (5.8 percent) in 1983–84. Expenditure per family settled reached nearly U.S. $12,000 in 1982–83. Taking the target size of 800,000 families most commonly mentioned for the Five-Year Plan 1985–89, the direct cost to the government would add up to U.S. $10 billion, or U.S. $2 billion a year.

In the Bura irrigation and settlement scheme in eastern Kenya, the estimated cost of settling one landless family on a small (1.25 hectare) plot is now U.S. $40,000 (Gunnel 1983). The rapidly escalating costs of this project have proved a serious drain on government resources at a time when it can little afford it. The World Bank, backing the Bura scheme with a loan of U.S. $34 million, estimated total project costs at U.S. $91.7 million in 1977, of which 52 percent was to be financed by external loans and grants. The latest estimate is now about U.S. $200 million, and the Kenyan government has to pay the increase, as well as repayment of capital and interest on loans.

On the economic viability of the scheme, Gunnel (1983) writes:

The World Bank had predicted a 13 percent rate of return on the project based on assumptions that now seem ridiculously optimistic: high cotton yields (they are poor to average); stable export price of cotton; and strict adherence to the construction schedule. The Bank's predicted rate of return would drop 1.5 percent points for every 10 percent increase in costs or one year delay in construction schedule. On these estimates the project has already hit zero.

Looked at in purely economic terms, few land settlement schemes are likely to be "viable," although this is not necessarily a useful way of looking at them. Certainly most schemes have not been profitable in terms of the returns on capital invested. The benefit-cost ratio of the Nagadeepa project in Sri Lanka, for example, is estimated to range from 0.42 to 0.82, according to the discount rates adopted, which vary between 6 and 15 percent (Kunasingham 1972). Similarly, commenting on the economics of the Gal Oya project, which had produced a benefit-cost ratio of only one-half, the Farmer Committee concluded in 1970 that "this finding makes it necessary that policymakers take a long, hard look at the advisability of diverting resources to what is essentially a social welfare function in an economy where the greatest need is to maximize production" (Dunham 1982).

This conclusion was reiterated by the ILO mission to Sri Lanka the following year. The economic viability of major colonization programs was questioned, and serious doubts were expressed about the wisdom of continuing to pursue a policy of large-scale capital-intensive land development. Before the report of the ILO mission was formally published, however, the bill creating the Mahaweli Development Board had passed through parliament, and a project committing the country to massive investment for a full 30-year period had been endorsed by the government (Dunham 1982).

The picture is not universally gloomy, however. The data presented in Chapter 4 show that FELDA spent approximately M$26,600 in 1976 to resettle one family. This seems a large sum compared with the cost of settling an Indonesian farmer in a transmigration project. But Bahrin's analysis suggests that economic returns more than compensate for the investment. Moreover, the settlers are obliged to repay the costs of clearing the jungle, preparing the land, planting the main crop, developing house sites, and constructing houses, and the cost of maintenance, including materials and subsistence allowance, before crop production.

Despite declining commodity prices, the collection of loan repayments can be considered satisfactory. The first batch of settlers had fully repaid their loans and were awarded their land titles in 1977, exactly 21 years after the establishment of FELDA. By the end of 1982, a total of 2724 settlers, comprising 1822 rubber settlers and 902 oil palm settlers, had fully repaid their loans. By 1982, the collection rate was 91.2 percent from palm oil settlers and 67.6 percent from rubber settlers (see Chapter 4).

## FACTORS AFFECTING SUCCESS OR FAILURE OF LAND SETTLEMENT PROGRAMS

### Planning

A lack of detailed and comprehensive planning has been a major factor behind the poor performance (and even total failure) of settlement projects.

Reporting to the Indian parliament in April 1979 on the many failures of the Dandakaranya project, the Estimates Committee mentioned the fact that no master plan for the region had yet been prepared, in spite of repeated recommendations to prepare such a plan by successive Estimates Committees, and that no serious attention had been paid to the essential input and infrastructure for the development of small-scale industries, with the result that attempts to develop these industries had ended in failure.

The achievements of the land settlement program in Peru seem to have fallen short of expectations, largely because land development in the forest highlands has been characterized by a piecemeal approach. In no case were the settlement projects preceded by serious, comprehensive, in-depth economic and social feasibility studies. Even the objectives to be pursued were often stated after the technical and credit assistance programs were already under way. In most cases, no detailed soil studies were undertaken, which could have served as a guide in recommending the most suitable crops. As a result, there has been low productivity per hectare. No serious consideration has been given to improving agricultural technology or solving the problems of large-scale deforestation. Moreover, there has been a neglect of complementary investments in forestry, industries, and services in colonization areas, which would have generated alternative employment and improved the living standards of the settlers.

Settlements in both Ethiopia and Somalia have also suffered from a lack of planning. Because they were mostly conceived during a period of national emergency, settlements tended to be created long before any social or economic planning could be carried out. Things were done quickly, and ambitious and unrealistic goals were set to be achieved in far too short a time. The resettlement scheme at Dujuma in Somalia had to be abandoned five years after it was established because of the salinity of the soil. Obviously no soil studies had been carried out.

In the United Republic of Tanzania, too, people were moved in a hurry without any proper planning, with the result that some of the villages are now overcrowded, some with a population of more than 10,000. This has implications for the availability of sufficient land for communal and individual plots within a reasonable walking distance. In order to reduce the pressures on land, the government is already thinking of moving people again, by creating satellite settlements (a revillagization program). These settlements are likely to increase both effective working time, by reducing travel time to the fields, and the average size of farm holdings.

## Selection of site

One of the most crucial aspects of planning is the selection of suitable sites. We have already seen how the Dujuma project in Somalia had to be abandoned after five years because the salinity of the soil made it unsuitable for cultivation, and how in Nepal the fact that the settlers were on higher ground than existing cultivated areas made it impossible to provide irrigation through canals from the rivers, and so led to low productivity.

As far as the selection of a site is concerned, the physical aspects must be appropriate; the soil must be fertile, the rainfall adequate, the draining and environmental conditions acceptable. The settlement must be conveniently located to afford it accessibility to essential infrastructural services as well as to markets for the settlers' produce at a later stage. Settlement schemes in many countries have failed where these considerations have not been properly understood.

In Indonesia, for example, a major shortcoming of the transmigration program has been the choice of sites that are unsuitable with respect to location, accessibility, and soil conditions; this has led to slow development of the projects, and sometimes to their abandonment and perhaps costly resurrection at a later stage.

Poor choice of sites has also been a problem in Ethiopia. In some cases settlement sites were selected without prior studies of the suitability of land and moisture conditions for permanent crops. Other settlements are located far out of easy reach, near the border regions or in disturbed areas, and face serious security problems.

## Size of plot

The size of the holding allocated to settlers is an important factor in attracting them. Two principles frequently used in determining farm size are (a) farms must be large enough to provide settlers with a standard of living higher than what they had in their areas of origin (if colonists are to be attracted to confront pioneer conditions) but not very much higher (lest tensions develop between existing farmers and favored settlers), and (b) farms must not be larger than the settler can cultivate (Farmer 1974; Amerasinghe 1974). Farm size must vary, however, with the type of crop, market conditions, soil characteristics, management capacities, and technological changes.

It is futile to settle people on holdings that do not provide them with enough elasticity to allow for changes in the number of dependents or variations in the pattern of rainfall, and which do not fulfil food crop requirements. The size of holdings should therefore be worked out in order to anticipate full use of family labor. Very small holdings will not provide the necessary income, while holdings that are too large will favor the employment and most probably the exploitation of permanent non-family labor.

The Gezira Scheme in the Sudan is an example of a project where many of the beneficiaries have become absentee landlords, because the land initially allocated to them exceeded the labor requirements of their families (Sabry 1970).

If productive and economic efficiency are to be achieved, it is also important that new land development should not be viewed within a static framework. As a region evolves, the system must be flexible enough for those with ability and savings to put these assets to productive use in the form of expanded agricultural operations. During the past two decades, for example, FELDA in Malaysia has modified several times the size of agricultural holdings allotted to its settlers. A 2.5-hectare holding planted with rubber was considered adequate initially; but over the years, due to changes in prices and other factors, increases in the size of holdings to 5 hectares for rubber and 6 hectares for oil palm were deemed necessary in order to meet the objective of providing a "fair income" to the resettled families (Bahrin and Perera 1977).

Although such changes were sensible, the size of holdings cannot be increased indefinitely, however. There are two main reasons for this. First, the changes in holding size have already created land inequalities among FELDA's own settlers. Second, with an increasing demand for land, an "optimum" size has to be worked out whereby the limited resources can be made to benefit the maximum number of people without depressing family incomes to the "poverty" level (Chan 1983).

When land is scarce, and the number of potential settlers large, some underemployment may be inevitable. In these circumstances, the welfare of society is likely to be better served by accommodating larger numbers of landless people on smaller holdings than by giving fewer settlers holdings large enough to make full use of family labor, while unsuccessful candidates go without meaningful employment altogether.

Unfortunately, most settlement programs do not make explicit the degree of income improvement sought, nor do they indicate priorities in case of conflict between income distribution and productivity objectives.

## Selection of settlers

Issues of settler selection are quite complex. The selection criteria largely depend on the national objectives and the target group to which the program is directed. It is therefore difficult to provide a general mode of selection.

One thing that is certainly important is that a clear explanation be given to applicants at the time of selection of what will be expected of them and what they can expect in return, so that people do not come in with a misunderstanding of what the project is all about. An opportunity to participate in a settlement scheme often unrealistically raises people's expectations, even in successful settlements. This may contribute to settlement failure. Settlement usually requires a major commitment from the settlers, but few families are prepared to wait ten or more years for results that they feel should come immediately.

Gunnel's report on the unsuccessful Bura project in Kenya points out that the newly arrived settlers at Bura who were interviewed in 1982 had a number of misconceptions about the scheme. Many thought that they would be able to build houses on their own land. Some thought they would become rich. None had any clear idea about the repayments for housing and services that they would be required to make. Tenurial rights to land and houses were not clearly understood. As far as some of these aspects of the scheme are concerned, the authorities themselves have yet to decide on the financial and legal position of the settlers.

In most countries, the selection criteria are biased in favor of young persons. This means that villages in rural areas are losing energetic and young labor. This dimension of the migration effects of land development schemes on the sending areas has yet to be studied.

The priority given to agriculturists with experience obviously has merit. The principle need not be rigidly applied in all schemes, however. Where resettlement need not emphasize agricultural development (for example, where the chief objective of a scheme is to resettle refugees or enhance national security), insistence on agricultural experience would be misplaced.

The selection procedure is open to abuse, however. In Indonesia, a reduced emphasis on farming experience has tended to serve as an excuse for including in transmigrant groups all sorts of unskilled and unwanted people. With the expansion of the transmigrant program in the 1970s, official policy statements began to stress the need to include among transmigrants an admixture of people with other skills apart from agriculture, for building and construction and for services of many kinds. Social welfare departments and village officials were then tempted to solve their own problems by sending out of Java the landless, homeless, and jobless, who did not necessarily have the skills and pioneering spirit needed. A recent report based on the field visits to several settlement sites in Sumatra indicates that a significant number of transmigrants (50 percent) had never owned or managed farmland before, and many (approximately 25 percent) had not engaged in farming at all. The report also concludes that lack of knowledge of appropriate clearing and cultivation techniques has been a major cause of failure for many transmigrants (World Food Program 1985).

There is also some merit in resettling people who speak the same language, belong to the same tribe, or come from the same group of villages, in order to minimize social tensions. Experience has shown that settlement projects with diverse "social groupings" can create intergroup conflicts, as in the Philippines, India, and Peru. In Latin America generally, it has been found that settlements tend to be more successful where settlers are a fairly homogeneous group, drawn predominantly from nearby areas (see Chapter 9). This seems to result in less dislocation and more continuity and cooperation between settlers.

It may not always be possible to resettle distinct social groups, however. If settlers are selected on the basis of their individual qualifications, as in FELDA projects in Malaysia, or if selection is done on a first-come, first-settled basis, then resettlement of social groups can be difficult. In some cases, it may not even be desirable, particularly in a multiracial society where national integration is a major aim of the government resettlement program.

The preference for settlers with capital should also be assessed within the context of the overall objectives of resettlement. If, as in the majority of cases, land settlement projects are designed specifically for the most disadvantaged segment of the population (i.e., the landless and the poor), then giving priority to those with capital conflicts with the overall intention.

As far as the success or failure of individual colonists is concerned, of course, those with capital must have a greater chance of success than those without. Findley argues, however, that initial capital is not the only prerequisite for a settler's success. In his study of Brazilian colonists, for example, Galjart distinguishes innovators, or commercialized farmers, from noninnovators, concluding that a major distinction is that the innovators are committed to staying in the colony and making the frontier their life (Galjart 1968). They therefore treat their farm as a commercial venture, invest their savings in it, and develop a wide network of political and social contacts that may be tapped for help or advice as needed.

Findley's review does suggest, however, that even with such a commitment to the frontier zone, not all who attempt commercialization succeed. Not infrequently, hard work and commitment fail to overcome the initial handicaps, such as too little capital and poor location.

## Land tenure and farming systems

The land tenure system defines rights and obligations with respect to acquisition and use of land in agricultural settlements, and is a critical determinant of the size and distribution of agricultural incomes. The ideal land tenure system is one that provides adequate incentives to produce, to adopt improved technologies, and to invest. It should afford reasonable security to those who till the land. A good tenure system can also be the means for generating adequate employment opportunities and promoting a more equal distribution of income.

Technical efficiency and economic viability are best achieved by a project design that promotes individual landholdings through the issuance of freehold or leasehold titles. Exceptions do exist, however. Existing land settlement projects incorporate a wide array of tenure systems, reflecting both local customs and unique project objectives.

In practice, the degree of freedom with which planners in different countries can create alternative tenure systems is greatly constrained by sociopolitical factors. Within these constraints, however, several general considerations apply. Equity and security are essential under any tenure system. Subdivision into uneconomic units must be strongly discouraged. Settlers must be aware of their rights and obligations, and the settlement authority must have the necessary enforcement authority.

In general, settlers' rights over the land should bear a direct relationship to their contribution to its development. When a government's contribution is large relative to that of the settlers, as in costly irrigation projects, the settlement authority should retain a large element of control over use of the land. In lower-cost settlements, where the settlers' contribution is correspondingly larger, it is both appropriate and necessary for incentive purposes to grant more extensive land rights to settlers.

It is common, however, for governments to impose some restrictions or conditions on the land titles. The usual argument is that without such conditions the settlers would either sell the land and thus become landless or subdivide the land among their heirs and make the holdings uneconomic. Both these situations are considered undesirable, as they contradict the basic objectives of the settlement programs. In some countries, the issuing of titles is tied to the repayment of loans by the settlers (Kansakar 1983). But, whatever the restrictions imposed, it is important that the settlers are guaranteed titles to their land.

The failure to do this has caused serious problems in the Dandakaranya project in India. Even though allotment of land had been completed in many areas as far back as 1963, *patta* (land ownership) rights have not been conferred so far. This has led to unrest, and was one of the major factors behind the mass exodus of displaced persons in 1978 (Bose 1983).

In most circumstances, individually owned and operated farms are likely to be the most conducive to productive efficiency and the development of settlers' initiative and entrepreneurial capabilities (Amerasinghe 1978). The advantages of freehold tenure may decline, however, as distributional and egalitarian objectives are accorded greater priority.

The choice between cooperative and individual family farms appears to have stood out as the most controversial issue in land development and settlement policy in many countries, particularly in Africa. Cooperative farming has often been regarded as a means of combining land development with equity, introducing scientific management, and achieving economies of scale. Cooperative farm ventures do, however, depend heavily for success on the motivation of the members. Lack of incentives and "cooperative" spirit is sufficient to mask whatever economies of scale may be obtainable. Cooperative enterprises also demand a high order of leadership and management. Where these are lacking, whatever advantages cooperative farming may have are lost. Although there are a few exceptions (e.g., Honduras, Israel), cooperative farming in many countries such as India, Sri Lanka, Somalia, and Ethiopia has not been very successful. The yields in cooperative settlements have been lower than those in private settlements (see Chapter 6).

In order to promote communal farming it would be necessary, therefore, to increase its economic advantages as a system of production and to devise appropriate incentives to bring about a shift in labor allocation and other resources in its favor. This means, above all, giving careful attention to methods of work organization, payment systems, and the allocation of proceeds from communal production between distribution and accumulation. So far, the major emphasis has been placed on exhorting people to devote more labor time to communal work. What is really needed, however, is to devise strategies that would generate group feelings and solidarity among the settlers to a greater degree than at present.

Even in the United Republic of Tanzania, there is a low level of commitment to collective undertakings in many villages. Inducing faster growth in communal production, which at present accounts for only a small fraction of total agricultural output, remains a serious problem. This may be due to several reasons: the predominance within the village economy of individual farming, which is still the main source of livelihood; the relatively poor performance of some collective undertakings, due to poor organization of production, lack of work discipline, and lack of financial control; poor management; and lack of incentives for individual participation in communal production. The answer may be some form of inducement to make villages expand the communal farms to a size that would allow the introduction of appropriate technology and large-scale use of modern inputs. The average of 40 hectares suggested in 1980 is too small on a per capita basis, and most villages do not have communal farms even as large as this.

## Management and administration

Good management and administration are important in determining a program's degree of success. Since land development lends itself to an integrated type of development process, it is essential that the agency entrusted with implementation be able to harness the help and assistance of other government departments, especially if the settlement agency itself has not been given the funds and the necessary supporting personnel. The success of FELDA in Malaysia can be attributed in part to its ability to obtain the assistance of other departments. Conversely, projects in Indonesia and elsewhere have been less successful partly because such assistance has not been forthcoming.

To be successful, resettlement operations require a gradual transfer of responsibility from settlement agencies to the settlers themselves. Otherwise, a dangerous relationship of dependency may arise and agency resources may become tied up in a limited number of permanently supervised schemes. Action should be taken from the outset to prepare for the transfer of management responsibilities to the settlers. If settlement agencies overcome the tendency to retain decision-making and managerial functions and encourage the emergence of recognized community leaders, this will stimulate local initiative and greatly facilitate the transfer of responsibilities.

## Settler dependency

It should be remembered that settlers are prone to dependency if paternalistic help policies are applied, as in many land settlement schemes in Asia and Africa. Not only does this have the result of escalating the costs of settlement, but it also discourages self-mobilization and undermines the settlers' commitment to self-reliance and development. Government assistance should therefore be an interim measure. Care must be taken to avoid implanting in the minds of the settlers the idea that they have become permanent wards of the state.

In Somalia it seems that work incentives and family incomes have not been given adequate weight because the settlement agencies have often provided the settlers with all their basic needs. The maintenance of the settlements as "relief camps" has produced a large measure of apathy and dependency among the settlers, and has adversely affected the settlements' economic performance. A shortage of labor for agricultural production continues to be a problem, as a large number of working-age men have left the settlements for presumably more profitable endeavors elsewhere.

Similar problems have occurred in Ethiopia. When the settlement program was initiated, it was thought that settlers would become self-sufficient in two years. But experience shows that this has not been the case. In fact, they become increasingly dependent on the government, which provides free food, transportation, inputs and equipment, training, and technical services. This system is in part responsible for the high settlement costs.

The extent of site preparation to be carried out should be considered in relation to the more general issue of settler dependency. The decision concerning the degree of settlers' participation in site development is a critical one. It is obviously possible to admit settlers to a new area without prior preparation of the site, allowing them to succeed or fail by their own efforts. On the other hand, land preparation can be so comprehensive that the settlers have little to do on arrival. Between these two extremes are many possible degrees of site development, and the amount of preliminary work to be done in each case must be a matter for close deliberation and careful decision, giving due consideration to the resources available.

The extent of site preparation should also be considered in relation to the objectives of the program and the number of people to be resettled. If the settlement is intended to be a development project to improve the living standards of the people and to contain urban drift, then site preparation should be extensive. Settlers' failure to start their agricultural work immediately because of the time required for clearing has forced many settlement agencies in the Philippines, Indonesia, and Ethiopia to extend their subsidy period and thus delay the settlement process.

## Planned or spontaneous settlements?

The issue of settler dependency is closely related to the question of whether settlements should be planned or spontaneous.

Planned movement often entails a high degree of government involvement, including a selection of colonists, provision of services, and financial aid. In planned settlement, the issue is how much should be left to individual settlers and how much should be organized or guided. There is no one answer. The ideal, of course, is to have a combination of both, but a great deal depends on the structure of the project and the types of crops to be cultivated.

If people are settled on individual family units with subsistence as the objective, then the need for guidance and group work is reduced. In this case, settlement becomes an end in itself and not a means to overall economic development. If, on the other hand, the crops are grown for sale, and if the family-size farm is to be economically viable, some central agency must organize all matters that are best done on a large scale (e.g., mechanical operations, irrigation, research and technical advice, processing and marketing of the crops, provision of credit, and purchase of supplies).

Government-sponsored settlements, as currently structured, appear to have major disadvantages, however. The relatively high costs limit the number of participants to such an extent that little may be achieved in terms of relieving population pressure in densely populated areas. Moreover, the excessive rate of defaults on assistance loans often places the settlement agency in an untenable financial position. In his study of colonization in Latin American countries, Nelson found that most governments recoup on average only 10–20 percent of their expenditures on these projects, which thus create subsidized rural elites (Nelson 1973). The agencies themselves have sometimes mismanaged funds, and over-all the settlement programs have proved to be excessively costly in terms of the limited number of beneficiaries. As we have already discussed, erroneous and incomplete preliminary natural resource surveys have been almost universal shortcomings of the directed projects.

Since the record of planned colonization has generally been mixed, planners have sometimes been of the opinion that the process of opening up the frontier areas through migration should be left to the voluntary and spontaneous choice of individuals. Where the number needing to be resettled is large, the eventual savings to the government would be substantial.

A recent study indicates that nearly 75 percent of the current rate of new rural land settlement is due to spontaneous settlement (World Bank 1978). Although spontaneous migration without government assistance is widespread, it does present problems of its own. Since spontaneous settlements are established by individuals, community services and facilities are usually poor and take a long time to become available. Unsupervised farming systems and disregard for proper land management have produced erosion and other environmental problems.

However, in spite of the bad reputation of spontaneous settlement has acquired because of natural resource destruction and shifting subsitence agriculture, it does offer the best chance of success in developing new lands where capital and administrative resources are scarce. The analysis in Chapter 9 suggests that the more complex and costly government-assisted settlement projects are in fact no more likely to succeed than largely spontaneous settlements. A similar conclusion was reported by Nelson in his study of 24 settlement projects ranging from spontaneous to highly planned and directed ones. The study examined the effect of settlement projects on employment and their economic viability.

Eight projects were classified as "dynamic," seven as "acceptable," and the remaining nine as "poor." Significantly, no projects with extensive government assistance appear among the "dynamic" group. Inadequate technical and administrative capacity in the implementing agencies was identified as the major factor behind this disappointing performance. Six of the nine projects rated "poor" received extensive government support. On the other hand, three of the eight "dynamic" projects were largely spontaneous settlements, while the other five were either private (domestic or foreign) ventures or received limited government assistance (Nelson 1973).

The various studies also indicate that spontaneous migration is not random and unplanned, but rather that it involves systematic cooperation between early migrants and those who follow. It is for this reason that spontaneous migration usually takes place in areas where development has been initiated by others.

## LAND SETTLEMENT PROGRAMS AND OTHER POLICY OPTIONS

If land settlement programs have not been notably successful in achieving their stated objectives, why is it that they continue to be adopted by so many governments? Some observers have argued that the real goal of colonization programs, particularly in Latin American countries, is to open frontier areas for capital accumulation by creating a labor reserve to be used by capitalist enterprises (Moran 1981: 69–84; Wood and Schmink 1979). The redirection of surplus rural population to frontier areas by means of the settlement schemes provides low-cost labor as the workers get their subsistence out of their own plots. As Pacheco (1977: 106–7) points out: "In the directed colonization projects, based on family units, a trend was observed that within two or three generations the process of small farming starts enabling the formation of a rural reserve army. . . . The plot provides for the workers' subsistence through the periods of seasonal unemployment and at the peak of labor demand they are hired as paid workers by the enterprises."

Perhaps the most important reason for pursuing colonization rather than integrated rural development programs is that the latter usually include land reforms, which for political reasons most governments are usually reluctant to implement. Yet a strong demand for land may exist among the landless and *minifundistas* in the more densely populated areas. In such a situation colonization is offered as a substitute for land reform. Colonization programs are also favored by urban-industrial interests, particularly if such schemes hold out the promise of cheaper food for urban industrial workers, thereby enabling employers to keep down wage rates (Standing 1984).

The evidence suggests, however, that the existing agrarian structure is being reproduced in most new settlement areas, thus giving little scope for solving the problems of unemployment and poverty. Despite initial efforts directed to the rural poor and to small farmers, the eventual outcome is generally the reappearance of the modes of production that prevail in the traditional agricultural areas. In Brazil, for example, government efforts to effect a distribution and use of land consistent with its land settlement policy lasted only for the first five years following the implementation of settlement projects. After that, the process took its own course and land distribution became more skewed, with increases both in very large farms and in squatting (see Chapter 10). The Philippine study also shows that the land settlement program had no perceptible effect in terms of alleviating agrarian problems in overcrowded or high-tenancy areas. In fact, the situation had deteriorated over the years. Even more discouraging was the perceived reversion of the pattern of land ownership in the frontier areas to that prevailing in the regions of origin (see Chapter 5).

How is it that government programs that are intended to assist all colonists end up benefiting only a few? The analysis in Chapter 9 suggests that most government credit and assistance programs are based on the premise that the colonist has title to a piece of land. But the evidence contradicts this premise. In many developing countries such as Indonesia, India, and Nepal, settlers sometimes have to wait between five and ten years before they get a title to their land. In most Latin American countries, at least half of all colonists are spontaneous settlers, of whom only a minority obtain title on arrival. A majority of colonists are thus barred from seeking institutional credit. Those who have access to institutional credit, on the other hand, can meet their requirements for capital relatively easily, which encourages investment in commercial agriculture and capital-intensive technologies. With greater access to new technology, some colonists become richer, while others who find the new technology too expensive and risky are left behind. Because the subsequent increase in productivity and output brings down prices, colonists using traditional forms of production and receiving lower prices experience declining incomes. Many colonists are forced to sell their land to richer colonists and seek wage labor in the area, to work as temporary or seasonal workers in other areas to supplement their farm income, or to permanently migrate away from the area. As we have seen, however, some who sell their land are not in fact compelled to do so by debts or lack of capital; many colonists sell their land with improvements in order to make a profit. The net result is that land is increasingly held by a smaller and a more select group of rich individuals (see Chapter 9).

The ambiguous and limited support received by smallholder colonists in frontier areas has therefore led to the reproduction of the productive relations found in the areas from which the peasants have migrated. The upshot has been a growing rural reserve army; this greatly limits the bargaining power of tenants and farm workers vis-à-vis landlords. Unless these and other more basic conditions are altered, it is doubtful whether land settlement programs will have a lasting impact on agrarian problems. What land colonization programs can do, however, is to give tenants and landless rural workers temporary help until the effects of more basic changes begin to be felt.

What, then, is the alternative? The ideal solution for the absorption of rural surplus population would involve the adoption of a range of strategies to create employment and reduce inequalities in the distribution of land and income. Of particular relevance here would be the implementation of comprehensive land reform. In many countries, bold redistributive programs could release large areas of land, already equipped with basic infrastructure, for settlement at costs lower than those entailed in opening up new land (World Bank 1978). Such programs should involve the transfer of land from the noncultivating owners (landlords) to the actual tillers of the soil (and this usually implies an abolition of both wage labor and tenancy). Governments should also regulate the activities of intermediaries such as traders and money lenders and, to the extent possible, they should provide credit and marketing facilities through cooperative and state-controlled institutions.

An immediate consequence of such measures, however, may be a decline in the volume of the agricultural surplus available to the urban industrial sectors, particularly in view of the prevailing poverty of the direct producers. Such a decline may involve either a shift in crop patterns (from cash crops to food crops) or a decline in the proportion of food output marketed, or both. To overcome these short-term problems, state policies would therefore be needed to promote modern technologies to raise productivity and increase the agricultural surplus. On the demand side, some adjustment may also be necessary in the urban industrial structure and other sectors of the economy, particularly if they depend on the agricultural sector for raw materials or export crops (Ghose 1983).

Nor should new land development be seen as the only option for increasing agricultural production. Other instruments for increasing agricultural output, such as intensification of agriculture, must be considered. Additional resources for an already settled agricultural area, where the basic physical infrastructure is in place, can be expected to generate greater economic returns than resources invested in new areas, where a good portion is needed for essential infrastructure. The Philippine study clearly demonstrates the greater cost-effectiveness of investing in irrigation rather than attempting to achieve an increase in output through an organized settlement program (see Chapter 5). Some studies suggest, however, that production intensification in already settled areas will leave unchanged both the pattern of land ownership and the distribution of rural incomes (Bal 1981). The experience of several countries in Asia shows that the "green revolution" has benefited the rich rather than the poor and has led to an absolute as well as a relative deterioration in the conditions of the already underprivileged tenant farmers and agricultural laborers. On the other hand, several observers have argued that by providing access to land, new land development can have a greater egalitarian impact on income distribution. However, the evidence suggests that although there are a few exceptions (Malaysia and the United Republic of Tanzania, for example), land settlement programs in many countries (Bolivia, Peru, Brazil, Chile) have worsened income distribution, particularly where the beneficiaries have not been among the poorest groups in rural society.

In practice, the method of benefit-cost analysis can be used to compare the relative performance of the two methods of increasing agricultural production. However, benefit-cost analysis as a guide to the choice between colonization and production intensification needs to be disaggregated if it is to be meaningful. It is not reasonable to assume that for a whole country the choice should be either colonization or production intensification. The analysis must relate to specific projects and areas.

## CONCLUSIONS

The above review of land settlement programs suggests that they have so far made no more than a modest contribution to the solution of the problems of population distribution, unemployment, and poverty. Very few programs have achieved their stated objectives. Although an increase in agricultural production and an improvement in settlers' living standards can be observed in some countries, the overall impact on employment and production remains limited, while the cost per settler of successful settlements has been high. Despite government efforts, settlement or resettlement of the rural population has been on a small scale, compared with the potential numbers of people that need some assistance.

Notwithstanding their limited success, land settlement programs are popular in most developing countries, mainly because they are politically more desirable, more expedient, and relatively easier to execute than other agrarian reform measures. However, the evidence suggests that land settlement programs alone cannot be expected to solve agrarian problems. At best, they are palliatives that buy time so that other policies can operate fully.

This review of various colonization programs also shows that both a process of land concentration and an increasing fragmentation of holdings are taking place in most settlement projects as a result of insufficient support to smallholder farmers. In fact, the distribution of land in many colonization projects is as skewed as in other traditional agricultural areas. This has adverse consequences for the absorption of manpower and the capacity of settlement projects to retain settlers.

The emergent differentiation was certainly not intended. Nonetheless, the evidence suggests that in many instances the chances of success have been biased in favor of colonists with more land or capital. As in traditional settled areas, those who are able to take best advantage of government assistance and agricultural credit are the capitalist farmers, not the subsistence farmers for whom the programs were seemingly designated.

As colonization is likely to move in the future to more and more marginal land, at ever increasing real costs, there is an urgent need to review colonization policy in light of the benefits and costs of alternative means of increasing agricultural output and achieving a more equitable distribution of land and incomes—for example, by intensification of cultivation, coupled with comprehensive land reforms. Whatever the outcome of such a review, some colonization may well continue for other reasons, such as to correct spatial imbalances in the distribution of population, to settle war refugees, or to exploit frontier lands for the purposes of national security. But, since government-sponsored projects have been very expensive, semi-directed or spontaneous colonization may be promoted as the best means of maximizing settlement per unit of state investment. In fact, the success of government land resettlement programs can to some extent be measured by the degree to which they stimulate spontaneous movement.

Efforts should be made to improve settlement performance. One major problem is that many governments do not have a consistent, well-thought out, long-term settlement policy that looks ahead to problems of adjustment, of second-generation settlers, and of integrating these settlements into regional plans. In many countries there is a tendency to put a major effort into the initial settlement and to fail to plan for

settlers' long-term requirements. These include not only the consolidation and perhaps expansion of the original settlement, but the means
of ensuring that potential earnings remain realistic, that tenancy systems
do not revert to unjust forms, and that there are alternative employment
outlets available as the settlement area grows. Land settlement should
not be considered either as an end in itself or as a convenient means of
redistributing the population. It should be conceived as a proper strategy
for creating new and viable communities.

To be successful, the planning and implementation of settlement projects require a close scrutiny of the essential needs of the settlers. High
priority should be attached to providing community infrastructure and
social services such as housing, schools, health care, and water supplies.
Government support for housing should be limited to helping with site
selection and planning, provision of building materials on credit, and
technical assistance. This should help make settlers self-reliant and reduce the risk of creating a class of dependent farmers.

As low productivity in settlements results in low incomes for the settler
(which in turn leads to high rates of settlement abandonment), it is vital
for the future of land development that the problem should be overcome.
The introduction of incentives, the provision of inputs and training, and
the guarantee of favorable prices for settlement-produced goods and
services would all contribute to improved productivity.

In many Latin American countries, the practice of shifting cultivation
by settlers and the resultant excessive deforestation are the major reasons
for the serious ecological deterioration that is taking place. The cultivation of crops that are unsuitable for the forest highlands has also
contributed to environmental problems. There is thus an urgent need
to improve agricultural technology and to provide educational programs
for the settlers covering the various aspects of environmental protection.

All government plans to settle nomads must recognize the nomadic
existence as a cultural system that has evolved over several centuries.
From their mobility they derive not only subsistence but the values and
satisfactions of social life. The idea of forcing them to settle in faraway
agricultural areas at a tremendous cost therefore needs to be reconsi-
dered, particularly in light of the finding that more than one-third of
nomad settlers have already abandoned settlement schemes in Somalia.
Help for nomads must first take the form of helping them to make better
use of the resources they have, rather than attempting to settle them.
This should perhaps be done by creating growth centers or poles of
attraction where they are provided with water, training, and health and
other social services. This would reduce the radius of their movement,
and as these poles of attraction grew in size they would automatically
develop into settlements. This type of strategy is likely to be more successful and cost-effective than a settlement program.

Alternatively, a policy of encouraging voluntary spontaneous settlement of nomads in regions where agricultural potential is greatest may be a more efficient alternative to planned settlement programs.

It is not sufficient, however, to look at settlements simply in terms of their agricultural potential, for the concept of a purely agricultural settlement is inadequate for present-day needs. Most settlement planners fail to give explicit consideration in project design to generating non-farm employment, particularly for settlers' children as they mature and enter the labor force. It is frequently assumed that settlers' children will carry on with agricultural work, although the evidence strongly suggests that not all intend to remain in agriculture, in part because of the limited possibilities they perceive to exist there, and in part because of the wider range of employment opportunities and social services believed to await them in urban areas. Land settlements should therefore be planned within an integrated regional framework that includes development of related agro-industrial and services sectors.

Although some countries have already taken measures to provide nonagricultural employment in settlement areas, there seems to be few instances of this being carried out successfully. One of the reasons for this is that the ministries responsible for rural industrial development are rarely closely concerned with settlement planning. One country that has attempted to provide nonagricultural employment is the United Republic of Tanzania (where a National Small-Scale Industries Corporation has recently been established to promote industries in rural areas), but so far the results have not been spectacular.

Malaysia has also adopted the concept of integrating land settlement with regional development. But, as we have already seen, whereas the land development and settlement part of the integrated projects have developed according to schedule, the growth of urban centers and the spontaneous movement of businesses and services have lagged behind. It is probably too early to expect the growth of urban centers. One weakness of the whole approach may be that in the early stages of settlement, the immediate needs of the settlers are those basic to their rural way of life and agricultural economy. The urban centers that could cater to that stage of development would be agriculturally based market towns. Only when the schemes were in an advanced state of development, with commercial and industrial and other sectors pressing for a higher order of demand, would a fully fledged urban center be able to take off on its own. "Phases" or "stages" of urban development strategy may therefore be an answer to this problem.

Overall, this review of settlement schemes suggests that resettlement should not simply be a matter of logistics—moving people physically from one region to another—but rather should embrace more concerted and imaginative planning in the areas of destination, emphasizing the human element. The settlers must be provided with basic infrastructural facilities, and a noticeable improvement in income, if they are to remain within the scheme. To reverse the trend toward increased concentration of land in settlement projects requires significant changes. Instead of explicitly or implicitly aiding concentration and large-scale commercialization of agriculture, programs need to be redirected toward commercialization among the colonists with smaller landholdings. Unless this is done, there will be an increased movement back to the areas of origin.

## BIBLIOGRAPHY

Amerasinghe, N. 1974. "The Determination of the Size of Holdings in Settlement Planning: A New Approach." In *Land Reform, Land Settlement and Cooperatives*. Rome: FAO. No. 1–2.

———. 1978. "Cooperative Settlements: A New Approach to Land Development in Sri Lanka." In *Land Reform, Land Settlement and Cooperatives*. Rome: FAO. No. 1.

Arndt, H. W., and R. M. Sundrum. 1977. "Transmigration: Land Settlement or Regional Development." In *Bulletin of Indonesian Economic Studies* (Canberra) 13(3): 72–90.

Bahrin, T. S. 1979. "Development Planning: Land Settlement Policies and Practices in Southeast Asia." In *Migration and Development in Southeast Asia: A Demographic Perspective*, edited by Robin J. Pryor. Kuala Lumpur: Oxford University Press.

———. 1981. "Review and Evaluation of Attempts to Direct Migrants to Frontier Areas through Land Colonization Schemes." In *Population Distribution Policies in Development Planning*, pp. 131–43. New York: United Nations, Department of International Economic and Social Affairs.

Bahrin, T. S., and P. D. A. Perera. 1977. *21 Years of Land Development*. Kuala Lumpur: Ministry for Land and Regional Development.

Bal, H. S. 1981. "New Farm Technology and Income Distribution of Punjab Farmers." Ph.D. diss., Punjabi University, Patia.

Bose, A. 1983. "Migration in India: Trends and Policies." In *State Policies and Internal Migration: Studies in Planned and Market Economies*, edited by A. S. Oberai, pp. 137–82.

Carelfield, C. 1984. "The Great Migration of the 1980s." *Fiji Times* (Suva), July 2.

Chan, P. 1983. "Population Distribution and Development Strategies in Peninsular Maylasia." In Oberai, *State Policies*, pp. 27–78.

Christodoulou, D. 1970. "Settlement in Agriculture of Nomadic, Semi-Nomadic and Other Pastoral People: Basic Considerations from a World View." In *Land Reform, Land Settlement and Cooperatives*. Rome: FAO. No. 1.

Dunham, D. 1982. "Politics and Land Settlement Schemes: The Case of Sri Lanka." In *Development and Change*, vol. 13, pp. 43–61. London and Beverly Hills, CA: Sage.

Farmer, B. H. 1974. *Agricultural Colonization in India Since Independence*. London: Oxford University Press.

Galjart, B. 1968. Itaguai: Old Habits and New Practices in a Brazilian Land

Settlement. Wageningen, Netherlands: Centre for Agricultural Publishing and Documentation.

Ghose, A. K. 1983. *Agrarian Reform in Contemporary Developing Countries*. London: Croom Helm; New York: St. Martin's Press.

Government of India. Estimates Committee. 1979. *Dandakaranya Project—Exodus of Settlers (1978)*, 30th Report. Presented to Lok Sabha on April 9. New Delhi: Sixth Lok Sabha, Lok Sabha Secretariat.

Gunnel, B. 1983. "Hopes Turn to Dust." *Guardian* (London), May 31.

Hyman, E. L. 1984. "Land-Use Planning to Help Sustain Tropical Forest Resources." In *World Development* (Washington, D.C.) 12 (8): 837–47.

International Labour Organisation. 1971. *Matching Employment Opportunities with Expectations: A Report on a Programme of Action for Sri Lanka*. Geneva.

———. 1974. *Sharing in Development: A Programme of Employment, Equity and Growth for the Philippines*. Geneva.

Indraratna, A. D. V de S., H.M.A. Codipilly, A.W.A.D.G. Abayasekera, and A.T.P.L. AbeyKoon. 1983. "Migration-Related Policies: A Study of the Sri Lanka Experience." In Oberai, *State Policies*, pp. 79–136.

James, W. E. 1983. "Settler Selection and Land Settlement Alternatives: New Evidence from the Philippines." In *Economic Development and Cultural Change*. Chicago, IL: University of Chicago Press.

Kansakar, V. B. S. 1983. "Population Distribution Policies and Planned Resettlement in Nepal." In Oberai, *State Policies*, pp. 229–50.

Kunashingham, A. S. 1972. "Economics of New Land Settlement Projects in Ceylon." Ph.D. diss., University of Hawaii.

MacAndrews, C. 1978. "Transmigration in Indonesia: Prospects and Problems." *Asian Survey* (Berkeley, CA) (May): 458–72.

Martine, G. 1979. "Recent Colonization Experiences in Brazil: Expectations versus Reality." In *Why People Move*, edited by J. Balan. Paris: UNESCO.

———. 1982. "Colonisation in Rondônia: Continuities and Perspectives." In *State Policies and Migration: Studies in Latin America and the Caribbean*, edited by P. Peek and G. Standing. London: Croom Helm.

Maxwell. S. 1980. "La differenciacion en las colonias de Santa Cruz: Causes y efectos." Working Paper no. 13. Santa Cruz, Bolivia: Centro de Investigacion Agricola Tropical (CIAT). May.

Moran, E. F. 1981. *Developing the Amazon*. Bloomington, IN: Indiana University Press.

Nelson, M. 1973. *Development of Tropical Lands*. Baltimore, MD: Johns Hopkins University Press.

Oberai, A. S., ed. 1983. *State Policies and Internal Migration: Studies in Planned and Market Economies*. London: Croom Helm; New York: St. Martin's Press.

Oey, M. 1982. "The Transmigration Programme in Indonesia." In *Population Resettlement Programmes in Southeast Asia*, edited by G. W. Jones and H. V. Richter, pp. 27–52. Canberra: Australian National University, Development Studies Centre.

Oey, M., and K. S. Astika. 1978. "Social and Economic Implications of Transmigration in Indonesia: A Policy-Oriented Review and Synopsis of Existing Research." Jakarta: Fakultas Ekonomi, Universitas Indonesia.

*O Globo*. 1977. (Rio de Janeiro) May 15.

Oucho, J. O. 1983. "The Kenyan Land Settlement Programme: Its Demographic and Socioeconomic Implications." Geneva: ILO. Mimeo.

Pacheco, L. M. T. 1979. "Colonização dirigida: Estrategía de acumulaçao e legitimaco de un estado autoritário." Translated by Maria Helena and F.T. Henriques. M.A. thesis, Department of Social Sciences, University of Brasília (August).

Perez-Sáinz, J. P. 1983. "Transmigration in Accumulation in Indonesia." In *State Policies*, Oberai, pp. 183–228.

Sabry, O. A. 1970. "Starting Settlements in Africa." In *Land Reform, Land Settlement and Cooperatives*. Rome: FAO. No. 1.

Shayo, F. P. 1984. "Living Together and Working Together: Can ujamaa Be Delivered?" In *Development: Seeds of Change*, vol. 2, pp. 40–45. Rome: Society for International Development.

*South*. May, 1985. London.

Standing, G. 1984. "Population Mobility and Productive Relations: Demographic Links and Policy Evolution." Geneva: ILO. Mimeo.

Wood, C. H., and M. Schmink. 1979. "Blaming the Victim: Small Farmer Production in an Amazon Colonization Project." *Studies in Third World Societies* 7: 77–93.

World Bank. 1978. *Agricultural Land Settlement*. Washington, D.C.

World Food Program. 1985. *Project Indonesia 2812: Regional Development through Transmigration in Sumatra*. Rome. Mimeo.

Ying Soon Lee. 1977. "An Analysis of Internal Migration in Peninsular Malaysia: Dimensions, Causes and Some Policy Implications." University of the Philippines, Council for Asian Manpower Studies, Discussion Paper Series 77–06. Quoted in Alan B. Simmons: "Slowing Metropolitan City Growth in Asia: Policies, Programs and Results." *Population and Development Review* (New York) (March) 97.

# H. W. Arndt

3

# Transmigration in Indonesia

## INTRODUCTION

The idea of trying to alleviate population pressure and poverty in Java by organizing and encouraging the movement of people from Java to the outer islands of Indonesia is almost 100 years old. During the 1970s, fueled by the oil boom, Indonesia's transmigration program became one of the largest voluntary land settlement programs in the world. While many of the formidable technical, logistic, and administrative problems of moving and settling 100,000 or more families a year are being energetically tackled, the future of the program is subject to two serious constraints: increasing shortages of land and financial resources.

After a short historical account in section 1, section 2 describes the main features of the program: policies regarding selection of migrants, identification of sites, preparation of land, assistance to transmigrants in the form of transport, food, and other inputs, housing and other social welfare services, relations with the indigenous population, and administrative organization. Section 3 deals with interprovincial movement of spontaneous migrants. Section 4 assesses the effects of the

Emeritus Professor of Economy, Australian National University, Canberra program on population distribution, on the living standards of the transmigrants, on food production, and on regional economic development. Section 5 discusses the two main problems now facing the program, land availability and finance. Section 6 considers the options available for coping with the fundamental problems that the program has been designed to remedy. Section 7 consists of a short conclusion.

## HISTORY

The history of transmigration in Indonesia goes back to the early years of the twentieth century. A census conducted by the Netherlands colonial administration in 1905 had shown that, of the total population of the Netherlands East Indies of 37.5 million, 30 million or 80 percent lived in Java-Mandura, which accounted for little more than 7 percent of the land area. Mounting evidence of declining welfare in rural Java led to the adoption of a "colonization" policy, aimed at relieving population pressure in Java by settling "colonies" of Javanese on the outer islands, initially mainly in southern Sumatra. Migrant families were given free transport, up to 1 hectare of reasonably fertile and watered land, and money (at first grants and later, to save expense, loans) for the purchase of housing materials, tools, and seeds. There was substantial investment in irrigation in Lampung, the province of Sumatra nearest to Java (Hardjono 1977).

Between 1905 and 1922, some 22,000 people were moved to two main settlements in Lampung, and to smaller ones in Bengkulu and South Sumatra. In the 1920s colonization virtually stopped, although there was some spontaneous migration to the Lampung settlements. In 1932, as the depression cut into the export incomes of smallholders, the Netherlands government decided to resume colonization. The needs of established settlers for harvest labor were met by bringing migrants to work for one season as harvest (*bawon*) laborers before becoming settlers themselves in new villages. By 1940, some 200,000 government-sponsored migrants are estimated to have been settled under the Netherlands colonization policy, at an average rate of about 4000 a year, more than two-thirds in Lampung (Tables 3.1 and 3.2). There was also, during the 1930s, a large flow of spontaneous migration of labor to the Sumatran plantations. With the Japanese occupation in 1942, colonization came to an end.

For the next 15 years, the Indonesian economy was wracked by war and political instability, while the population continued to grow and the problems of population pressure and poverty in Java (and neighboring Bali) intensified. By 1966, the population of Java had risen to over 70 million (Table 3.3) and was virtually certain to increase to 150 million by the end of the century. In Java population density was already near

600 persons per square kilometre, 50 percent larger than that of Bangladesh and nearly three times that of the Netherlands. Per capita income had been falling for much of the preceding decade, and two-thirds of the population was estimated to live below the poverty line.[1] From 1966 on, under the Soeharto regime, economic development began to be given priority over political objectives, and during the 1970s the oil boom provided Indonesia with the external resources for exceptionally rapid economic growth.[2]

Even before the Republic of Indonesia was formally born in 1950, the new leadership had begun to make ambitious plans for transmigration. A 1947 plan to move 31 million people over 15 years gave way in 1951 to a plan to move 49 million over 35 years. But political and economic circumstances were not propitious, even for much less grandiose plans than these, and they became still less so under Sukarno's Guided Democracy from 1959. Between 1947 and 1966, ministerial and departmental responsibility for transmigration was changed ten times. In practice, the Netherlands transmigration policy continued, by which families of Javanese subsistence farmers, or of landless people hoping to become subsistence farmers, were moved, mostly to southern Sumatra. The numbers moved in any one year rarely exceeded 25,000 and fell to a trickle in the chaotic years of the mid–1960s (Table 3.4).

As rational economic policymaking again became possible after the 1965–66 change of government, interest in transmigration revived, but with a different perspective. It came to be recognized that transmigration could not solve, or even substantially alleviate, the problem of "population imbalance" between Java-Bali and other islands, if indeed that was a problem. Transmigration was now seen primarily as having a welfare objective, to raise the living standards of the migrants and those of their home villages in Java.[3] It was also hoped that transmigration could serve as a strategy for regional economic development on the outer islands.

The first few years were devoted chiefly to the rehabilitation of existing settlements that had been allowed to run down. Transmigration to new settlements was resumed under the First Five-Year Plan (Repelita-I, 1969–70 to 1974–75), which put the emphasis on increased food production. For some years there were high hopes that this would be achieved through swamp reclamation in coastal regions of southern Kalimantan and eastern Sumatra. When the practical obstacles proved too formidable for quick settlement of significant numbers, attention shifted to settlement on unirrigated (rain-fed) land in other provinces of Sumatra, Kalimantan, and Sulawesi.

The OPEC oil price increases of 1973–74 and 1979–80, which brought hitherto undreamed-of foreign exchange earnings to the country and revenue to the government, raised Indonesian development targets all round, and transmigration became one of the main beneficiaries of the windfall. Both the scale of the transmigration program and its regional development objectives became more ambitious. The income of migrant settlers was to be raised by giving them enough land to grow cash crops as well as food for their own needs, with special emphasis on tree crops, such as rubber and oil palm. The pace of transmigration was to be accelerated to the point where settlements would economically justify the provision of new infrastructure and community facilities, such as schools, clinics, and local government. The land settlements themselves were increasingly to serve as growth centers by attracting spontaneous migrants from Java and by promoting regional development beyond agriculture, in processing and other industries, as well as in trade and services.

The Second Five-Year Plan (Repelita-II, 1974–75 to 1978–79), with its strong emphasis on social welfare and regional development, at first adopted a transmigration target of 250,000 families (50,000 families or over 200,000 persons a year), a figure four times as high as the highest achieved in any previous year. This target was subsequently recognised to be unrealistic, and in 1976 was scaled down to 108,000 families for the plan period. The Third Five-Year Plan set its sights even higher, with a transmigration target of 500,000 families or over 2 million persons for the years 1978–79 to 1983–84, but within a year of its adoption the second oil price increase seemed to make this vast program financially feasible. Development budget allocations for transmigration rose from an annual average of Rp. (rupiah) 2 billion in Repelita-I (about U.S. $5 million) to Rp.40 billion in Repelita-II and Rp. 218 billion (about U.S. $340 million) in Repelita-III. The latter figure represented a more than fourfold increase in real terms and raised the share of transmigration to the development (capital) budget to almost 6 percent. Since the early 1970s, the transmigration program has also received an increasing flow of external assistance, from the World Bank, the Asian and Islamic Development Banks, United Nations specialized agencies, and bilateral donors.

## POLICIES

### Selection of transmigrants

From the beginning, the Indonesian transmigration program has aimed at land settlement. With this objective in view, selection of transmigrants has rested on three principles. Transmigration should involve family units. Participation should be voluntary. And priority should be given to people from "critical" areas. The three principles have not always been easy to reconcile with one another and with the requirements of effective land settlement.

The official criteria for selection of transmigrants in terms of personal characteristics have changed little since the days of the Netherlands colonization policy. The family head should be between 20 and 40 years of age, and married with a family of not more than five members. No member of his household should be over 60 or under six months, and no pregnant women may join the group. Farming skills are desirable but not a condition for selection (Suratman and Guinness 1977). The available evidence suggests that the great majority of transmigrants have indeed been nuclear families, but that in other respects the official criteria have been applied with considerable latitude.

Official statistics for families and persons moved in the past decade show a fairly stable average family size of around 4.2 persons, with a slight tendency for the average to decline (from nearly 4.3 in 1974–75 to just over 4.0 in 1982–83). But there have been wide variations around the average. A 1976 survey indicated that over 30 percent of the respondents had more than four dependants with them. Another survey showed that one-third of transmigrant family heads had been over 40 on departure, and many complained that they lacked the strength to clear the land. More important is the fact, brought out in numerous surveys, that many transmigrants had had little, if any, experience in farming. Since one aim of the policy was to help the landless, it is not surprising that nearly one-third in one survey had never owned or managed farmland before, and 16 percent had not been engaged in farming at all (Suratman and Guinness 1977).

With the expansion of the program in the 1970s, official policy statements began to stress the need to include among transmigrants an admixture of people with other skills in building and construction and in services of many kinds. But there is little evidence that this had influenced selection, although teachers, nurses, agricultural extension workers, and other government employees with requisite skills (or at least nominal qualifications) have been sent to settlement areas. If anything, the reduced emphasis on farming experience has tended to serve as an excuse for including in transmigrant groups unskilled and unwanted people from Jakarta and other cities.

All voluntary migration contains an element of self-selection, since the willingness to tear up one's roots and face the risks and burdens of building a new life in unknown surroundings implies a certain amount of courage and determination. But in the circumstances of Java, the push of poverty has often made desperation the dominant motive. Willingness to move has not always gone hand in hand with suitability for the arduous life of the transmigrant settler. "Too often those who agreed to move were the less enterprising and less resourceful people in the village" (Hardjono 1977: 36), and the official priority given to "critical" areas, with heavy population pressure and/or poor soils and/or affected by natural disasters, has reinforced this tendency. Social Welfare Department and village officials have been tempted to solve their own problems by sending out of Java the landless, homeless, and jobless, who do not necessarily have the skills and pioneering spirit needed. Nor has participation always been entirely voluntary.

Recruitment and selection of transmigrants have been the task of transmigration branch offices set up in the capitals of the provinces of Java and Bali and some of the larger district (*kabupaten*) capitals. One function of these officials has been to spread information among village communities, to interest farmers and landless laborers in moving away from overcrowded areas. Another function has been to make selections from lists of willing transmigrants prepared by village heads. As program targets were raised during Repelita-II and III, quotas were allocated for each province and kabupaten. The need to fill quotas not infrequently led to the use of persuasion, to put it no more strongly. There have also been periods when political factors have influenced the selection of transmigrants. Thus, the very large number of people moved in 1965 has been attributed to pressure by the Indonesian Communist party, which was seeking to strengthen its influence in certain outer island provinces (Hardjono 1977: 37). But this does not seem to have happened more recently.

Another qualification of the principle of voluntary participation has been the practice of moving whole communities affected by natural disasters (such as the eruption of the volcano Gunung Agung on Bali in 1963) or displaced by flooding for hydro projects (as for the Wonogiri dam in 1976, when individual families were given little choice). In the latter case, however, government determination to make the settlement of the Wonogiri community at Sitiung (South Sumatra) a showplace helped to overcome whatever reluctance might have been felt.

By and large, one gets the impression that the principle of voluntary participation has been adhered to. Few transmigrants have returned to their home villages, and most areas of Java normally report an excess of registered applicants over places.

As Table 3.5 shows, during the period of Repelita-I (1969–73), the vast majority (87 percent) of transmigrants came from Java, and most of the rest from Bali. No corresponding figures for the more recent periods are available, but the proportions have not changed much, except that somewhat larger numbers have come from the island of Lombok (on the eastern side of Bali), which has suffered periods of famine.

## Identification of sites

Under the Netherlands colonization policy, selection of sites for transmigration settlements was governed chiefly by two criteria: suitability for irrigation (for wet rice production) and proximity to Java (to keep down transport costs). As the areas in Lampung and South Sumatra available for wet rice farming became increasingly crowded, attention shifted elsewhere. Most of what good agricultural land there was on the outer islands, chiefly in North Sumatra and South Sulawesi, was already under cultivation by 1965. The choice was therefore between the relatively poor soils of the rain-fed uplands (whether under primary forest or under grass with secondary timber growth) and reclaimable swamp.

For a few years after 1966, the latter alternative excited most interest among transmigration planners, partly because food production was a high-priority objective, and reclaimed swampland, with its opportunities for tidal irrigation, seemed suitable for wet rice cultivation. (Tidal irrigation operates on the principle of using the tides for controlled inundation by backed-up fresh water of fields on either side of great rivers, sometimes up to 100 kilometres inland.) Nearly 40 million hectares, or one-quarter of the total land area of Indonesia, consists of swamps, and of this some 2 million hectares is believed to be potentially cultivable.

Swamp reclamation was pioneered in Indonesia by spontaneous migrants. Buginese (from South Sulawesi) in Jambi and Riau (eastern Sumatra) and local Bandarese in southern Kalimantan. Some efforts at swamp reclamation for land settlement were made in South Kalimantan under government auspices before and after World War II, but while canals were dug, mainly for improved communications, few people were settled.

Enthusiasm for swamp reclamation reached a peak in the years 1967–69, when a special unit in the Department of Public Works was created to accelerate the program, but by the end of Repelita-I barely 7000 transmigrant families had been settled on newly reclaimed tidal swampland. With the oil boom, the high capital cost of swamp reclamation no longer seemed a major obstacle, and Repelita-II initially set an ambitious target of 1 million hectares of tidal swamp development. But after the Pertamina crisis of 1975, this was scaled down to 250,000 hectares, and by the end of Repelita-II (March 1979) even this target had not been reached. Of 208,000 hectares of newly "opened" land, 117,000 had received no settlers at all, and of the remaining 91,000 hectares only 60 percent was occupied by transmigrant families. The number of families settled on swampland during Repelita-II was just over 9000. For Repelita-III (1979–1984), the swamp reclamation target was set at 400,000 hectares, but once again performance lagged well behind in the first three years.

The disappointment of early hopes for swamp reclamation as a major source of land for transmigration settlements is partly accounted for by technical constraints. Not all coastal land is suitable for tidal irrigation. "The site chosen must be close enough to the coast for tidal effects to be felt daily but not so close that crops are affected by the salt water that penetrates some miles inland in the dry season. At the same time, the location must be such that annual floods in the wet season are not too extensive.... Obviously, a thorough knowledge of the local river regime is necessary before a site can be chosen for tidal rice fields" (Hardjono 1977: 73). By the end of Repelita-I, it had become apparent that few suitable project sites were left in Riau, Jambi, or West Kalimantan, and that future swamp reclamation would be confined in the main to the Palembang (South Sumatra) and Banjarmasin (South Kalimantan) areas, apart from even more remote Irian Jaya. Canal design and construction also presented greater technical problems than had been expected, the capital costs were considerably higher, and for organizational and other reasons long time lags occurred between the ostensible "opening" of land by the construction of canals and the completion of clearing, housing, and other preparations necessary for settlement.

With little scope for more settlement on irrigated lowland, and swamp reclamation lagging, the transmigration program has had to look for settlement sites primarily in the rain-fed upland areas of the outer islands. None of these can compare in soil fertility with Java or with the relatively fertile areas of North Sumatra or South Sulawesi. Very large parts of Sumatra, Kalimantan, Sulawesi, and Irian Jaya (50 million hectares or more) are said to have some agricultural potential, but they consist mostly of red-yellow podzolic soils, which are highly susceptible to erosion and leaching. Their natural fertility is low, more suited to tree crops than other crops.

Poor site selection was a major source of failure of settlements in the 1950s and 1960s. The job was left to provincial governments, most of which had little enthusiasm for the settlement of poor Javanese in their provinces. Virtually no systematic survey work was carried out to ascertain the nature of the soils and/or the availability of water or to determine appropriate crop patterns. "Transmigration officials simply accepted whatever land was made available" (Hardjono 1977: 39).

Procedures for site identification were improved under Repelita-I and II. Responsibility for selection remained with provincial governments, subject to approval from Jakarta, but the central government laid down specifications, usually a minimum area of 15,000 hectares where five adjacent villages of 500 families each could be established. Soil surveys and enquiries into land rights were made mandatory before a final selection was made. This helped but did not altogether overcome the problems. Some surveys, particularly those conducted by overseas financing bodies or by local university teams in conjunction with the transmigration authorities, have been reasonably thorough, but most presettlement surveys have been confined to cursory inspection over a month or two. Too often the result was that, after a few years of settlement, crops failed, soil fertility declined, and land disputes with local villagers disrupted farming activities (Suratman and Guinness 1977: 90).

In 1978, as part of a major reorganization of the transmigration program, responsibility for selection and evaluation of large sites was assigned to the Directorate of Regional and City Planning (DITADA) within the Department of Public Works. Although without any previous experience of agricultural planning, DITADA, with increasing assistance from the World Bank, soon developed staff resources and appropriate procedures. The standard planning program prior to land clearing covered provisional selection of sites based on regional development criteria, such as proximity to existing or proposed roads and regional growth centers, screening of sites using existing data and aerial photography, topographic mapping, soil surveys and analysis, examination of land claims, tentative indication of roads and villages, and designation of clearing blocks. To cope with the acceleration of settlement required by Repelita-III targets, an emergency PAYP (plan as you proceed) procedure was formulated under which site investigation and land development proceeded simultaneously.

While PAYP has inevitably tended to repeat the mistakes due to perfunctory identification procedures, the standard planning program has been demanding in money and skilled manpower and has come up against ever more serious constraints on availability of suitable land on the scale demanded by plan targets. The requirements for technical specialists of various kinds, under plans currently being worked out with the help of the World Bank, are to be met by domestic and foreign consulting firms, as well as by the training of government officials. World Bank and other financial sources are to meet a major part of the considerable costs involved. The land availability problem is much less manageable. By 1981, for example, of over 2 million hectares identified for transmigration along with the new Trans-Sumatra Highway, almost 95 percent had been rejected as unsuitable for one reason or another. Large areas were excluded because the soil was toxic or swampy, or the land too steep (an 8 percent limit on slope was thought necessary to avoid erosion); or because of possible land claims, forestry regulations, or inadequate access to services and markets; or simply because of poor coordination with local officials. More will be said about this below (see "Key Constraints").

## Land preparation

Under the Netherlands colonization program, transmigrants received 0.7–10 hectare irrigated plots (though irrigation often did not become available until some years after settlement), and the migrants were required to give 75 days' labor to the construction of irrigation facilities

(Hardjono 1977: 18ff). Experience in Lampung demonstrated that so small a plot allowed neither for an income above subsistence nor for expansion for children or newcomers. During the 1950s and 1960s, therefore, it became standard practice to give each migrant family 2 hectares of land, of which one was cleared by the government before the migrants arrived, while the second was to be cleared by the migrants themselves. But clearing of the second hectare often proved beyond the migrants' capacity, and 2 hectares of rain-fed land at best yielded only a subsistence income. In the 1970s, initially on World Bank–assisted projects, plots of 3.5–5.0 hectares were allocated to each transmigrant family, of which the major part, including 1 hectare already cleared and planted, was reserved for tree crops. The government also assumed responsibility for the provision of an increasingly complex infrastructure for settlements.

Experience suggests that adequate preparation of a site, from soil surveys and land acquisition to the clearing of land, construction of roads and bridges, and building of houses for settlers and community buildings for villages, can take up to six years. Until 1973, the transmigration program provided for a category of semi-assisted (*spontan*) transmigrants who received only cash for transport, a plot of land (in some cases uncleared), and housing materials, and were expected to build their own houses. Since the category was abolished, all transmigrants, at least in principle, have housing ready when they arrive.

Until 1978, the Directorate General of Transmigration was itself responsible for village planning, land clearing, and construction of houses and other village infrastructure. In that year, village planning and land clearing were transferred to a new Directorate for Land Planning (PTPT) in the Department of Public Works. Clearing is now performed by private contractors under contracts awarded and supervised by the PTPT. Clearing of the fields does not include removal of the stumps, a task that takes migrants up to five years. There has been a good deal of debate about methods of clearing. The government agencies prefer mechanical clearing to keep up with timetables, while World Bank and other consultants advise manual clearing with chain saws, for employment and soil conservation reasons and because mechanical clearing requires large blocks of land to offset equipment costs.

## Assistance to migrants

The amount and kinds of other assistance given to transmigrants, apart from land and housing, have varied greatly. In the 1950s it was assumed that it was sufficient to settle migrants on the land, and to provide seed and a food allowance for the first few months until the first crop was harvested. This proved unrealistic, either because the land was not cleared when the settlers arrived or because the first crops were disappointing due to poor soil, inadequate water, or pests (Hardjono 1977: 42). From the early 1970s, regular transmigrants received support during the first 12 months (18 months in tidal swamp areas) and therefore had time to invest in clearing and cultivating their fields. The standard support package consisted of a monthly ration of rice, salted fish, salt, kerosene, and cooking oil, in addition to an initial supply of farming tools, fertilizer, pesticides, seeds and seedlings, and in most projects one draught animal. Failure to ensure that these essential variable inputs reach the settlers when they need them has been one of the chronic logistic problems of the program. In 1972, the World Food Program began to provide settler families in five projects with a food ration (wheat, dried milk, fish, pulses) to replace rice and supplement the government ration, and additional amounts were offered as an incentive to perform specified works in subsequent years.

There has been even more variation in the range of services provided to transmigrants. In principle, though by no means always in practice, prospective settlers are assembled in transit centers in Java where they are briefed on what to expect in their new environments, while designated group leaders receive a three-month training in organization and administration of settlement units. For official transmigrants, transport is normally provided by the authorities, first to the transit centers and then, often over long distances, by ship, train, or bus to the project site. In recent years, to reduce delays, a large number of transmigrants have been flown to the settlement province, an expensive operation. At the project site, transmigrants are supposed to receive help from project staff, including courses in agriculture, animal husbandry, health care, and so on. But much of this, even in the more accessible and better organized large settlements, has remained on paper for lack of sufficient skilled staff, particularly agricultural extension officers, health workers, teachers, and social workers.

One of the most effective forms of assistance to transmigrants has been the promotion of tree crop cultivation. For the past ten years, the World Bank has provided large-scale financial and technical assistance in support of tree crop projects, chiefly rubber, based on the nucleus estate principle. The primary object has been to raise the income of migrants by enabling them to grow a cash crop besides food. The essential feature of the nucleus estate scheme is that the layout, technical know-how, and organizational capacity of established estates (mostly government-owned but commercially operated) are drawn on to assist smallholders (initially mainly local but now increasingly transmigrant settlers) by planting the first hectare with immature trees and subsequently providing extension-type help. The estates are permitted to retain 20 percent of the land for their own profitable operation, and they therefore cooperate keenly through special production management units (PMUs). Much of the finance for land development, infrastructure, and planting is raised by borrowing—in some cases rather too freely. The program in the longer run undoubtedly promises a more secure livelihood for transmigrants than the traditional agricultural package for food production, as well as supporting Indonesia's policy of expanding non-oil exports. Its chief disadvantage, apart from its long time horizon and consequent problems in the early years, is its high cost, currently estimated at some U.S. $15,000 in direct costs per family.

## Relations with the indigenous population

Indonesia's outer islands are sparsely inhabited, but they *are* inhabited, by millions of Indonesian people differing in varying degrees from the Javanese and Balinese in language, culture, and way of life, from the relatively backward Dyak people of Kalimantan to the Minangkebau, Bataks, Buginese, and Acehnese, with their highly developed and distinctive traditions. In some cases, as in the eastern provinces of Maluku and Irian Jaya, there are conspicuous differences in ethnic composition, skin color, and physiognomy. It is fair to say that the indigenous people of the outer islands have not generally welcomed the settlement of Javanese transmigrants among them, especially where the Javanese have threatened to become a majority. Indigenous villagers not unnaturally tend to resent the special facilities, such as roads, schools, clinics, and other assistance given to settlers.

The Netherlands policy was, for this very reason, to concentrate Javanese transmigrants in compact "colonies," with the result that they tended to become enclaves. Relations have generally proved easier where land claims have presented no major problem and where local people have benefited from employment or business opportunities opened up by new settlements. But there has been little genuine assimilation based on intermarriage, partly because transmigrants, often recruited from among the poorest in Java, have not enjoyed sufficient social standing in Minangkebau, Buginese, or Batak communities.

The transmigration authorities have tried to deal with this problem in four main ways. One has been planned movement of indigenous people into project settlement areas, with the object of helping them to benefit from project facilities and thus improve their own economic position. In some project areas, up to 20 percent of each settlement site is now reserved for locals who receive the same benefits, and must share the same duties, as the transmigrants. They are selected by the *kabupaten* administration on the basis of criteria similar to those used for transmigrants. Second, some attempt has been made to put arrangements for land acquistion and compensation (one of the sorest points in relations with the indigenous population) on a sounder institutional and financial basis. Third, indigenous people have been encouraged to establish stores and other businesses that cater to the needs of the new settlers. Compensation for village land sometimes provides the necessary capital. Finally, efforts are being made to improve cooperation between the central government's transmigration and other departments involved in the program and the provincial authorities, in the hope that closer involvement of provincial officials and decentralization of decision-making will help smooth relations.

In all these respects, practice still lags a good deal behind formulated policies. In any case, there is no escaping the fact that a sustained large-scale movement of people from Java, whether by government-sponsored transmigration or spontaneous migration, implies increasing "Javanization" of the outer islands. This fact, which is implicit in all notions of correcting or moderating the population imbalance, and the suspicion in the minds of some that this is one of the motives behind the program, may yet give rise to sociopolitical problems.

## Administration and management

As was mentioned earlier, overall control of Indonesia's transmigration program suffered many changes and vicissitudes in the 1950s and 1960s. The expansion of the program to mammoth dimensions during the 1970s placed an enormous strain on the country's limited administrative capacity. Efforts to improve administration and coordination among the numerous agencies involved in the program have been made year by year, with indifferent success.

During Repelita-I, transmigration became the responsibility of a Directorate-General within the Department of Manpower, Transmigration and Cooperatives, assisted by coordinating bodies (BPPDT) set up at central, provincial, and district levels to provide regular contact with the other departments concerned. In March 1978, a major reorganization created a post of Junior Minister for Transmigration, but transferred responsibility for project implementation from the Directorate-General to the seven departments (and by now over 50 directorates-general) involved in the Repelita-III program, coordinated by a board consisting of the relevant ministers. This does not seem to have worked very well, and the March 1983 cabinet reconstruction brought yet another change. The Directorate-General became a department on its own, now including also the important transmigration sections of the Department of Public Works, with the former junior minister as minister.

By 1982 the Directorate-General of Transmigration had grown into a very large apparatus, with nearly 10,000 employees. As numbers of staff have increased to meet the demands of a considerably expanded program, quality has inevitably suffered, especially among on-site staff on project areas. Many of the Project Management Units and Project Co-ordinators appointed by the Directorate-General to look after individual projects are reported to be dedicated and effective in often very difficult and frustrating conditions. But it is not easy to persuade people with the requisite skills and experience to leave Jakarta and other cities to live in remote areas under pioneering conditions on meager Indonesian government salaries. The shortage of settlement staff for extension and all other services and the inadequacy of training facilities have been recurrent themes in reports on transmigration settlements over the last few years.

Another has been the problem of coordination. A 1977 study of the program pointed out the lack of coordination between central, provincial, and district offices of the Transmigration Department as "a major source of failure to reach targets and spend budgets" (Suratman and Guinness 1977: 88). Since then the number of departments with responsibility for different aspects of the program (and the number of directorates-general and subdirectorates in each) have steadily increased. To improve coordination was one of the objectives of combining the functions of the former Directorate-General for Transmigration and the transmigration sections of the Department of Public Works into a single separate department in March 1983. But this covers only part, though a major one, of the unwieldy bureaucracy in charge of the program.

Not the least difficult aspect has been the division of responsibility between central and local authorities. In principle, the central government transmigration authorities retain responsibility for settlements until they become "self-supporting," when they are transferred to the local authorities, ultimately to be integrated into provincial and kabupaten administration. As Table 3.6 shows, in the difficult years before and during Repelita-I, transfer was often long delayed. If, as frequently happened, older projects were transferred irrespective of their level of economic development, the local authorities were saddled with problems for which they were usually not well equipped. There has been some improvement in this respect, but hardly enough to match the rate of expansion of the program.

## SPONTANEOUS MIGRATION

Before returning to the results achieved by Indonesia's official transmigration program, something needs to be said about the flow of spontaneous migrants that has occurred alongside it.[4] There has always been movement of people among the islands and provinces of Indonesia, and at times such movement has assumed considerable proportions.

The first large flow from Java to the outer islands in the twentieth century consisted of labor needed by, and attracted to, the plantations established by the Netherlands and other Western enterprises, especially in North and South Sumatra. In the 1920s some of this labor was recruited and transported by private contractors (*mandor*). The need of the plantations for labor was also a factor in the Netherlands colonization policy, since settlement of farm families near the plantations in South Sumatra was expected to help improve the labor supply, partly through off-season employment of the settlers themselves, but chiefly through the attraction to the settlement of a flow of friends and relations of settler families, as harvest workers or as permanent members of settler households (Hardjono 1977).

The concept of "chain migration" (transmigration or settlements established by government acting as "seed communities" and attracting unsponsored migration through family ties) has been an important element in thinking about transmigration in Indonesia ever since. Indeed, it has sometimes been suggested that "the ultimate goal in transmigration is to set up a flow of spontaneous migrants who move from overcrowded areas of their own accord and without government assistance" (Hardjono 1977: 30).

Such chain migration has undoubtedly occurred on quite a large scale, particularly in the provinces closest to Java, where two-way communications are easy. Sometimes unsponsored migrants would take up land abandoned by disappointed settlers. More often, they would share the work and income of settler families, or move on to seek employment on estates or logging concessions. In favorable circumstances, spontaneous chain migration can reinforce the official transmigration program, achieving its purposes at relatively little cost to the government through a kind of multiplier process, by accelerating the growth of settler communities and providing additional labor for clearing, planting, and other agricultural tasks. But chain migration continuing over many years can also add to overcrowding in settlement areas. This has been a major problem in Lampung and adjoining parts of southern Sumatra.

A third kind of spontaneous outward migration has been that of independent settlers, some from Java but chiefly from Bali. The Parigi settlement in central Sulawesi is the best-known example (Davis 1976). The settlement began in 1950 with 17 Hindu families from Bali who had been exiled to Sulawesi for breaches of *adat* (customary) law. They were joined in 1957 by a group of Christian Balinese. Over the next 25 years, nearly 10,000 people from Bali followed, all in some way connected with the original settlers. Many were personally recruited in Bali by Parigi settlers in need of labor or anxious to help friends and relatives, particularly in the aftermath of the communal and political conflict in Bali that accompanied the change of regime in 1965–66. For a time, provincial and national government assistance was secured, but during the 1970s the flow continued entirely independently, even in the face of government discouragement. The introduction of the new, rapidly maturing varieties of rice, which permitted two to three crops a year, produced higher incomes but also labor shortages. Both these factors attracted spontaneous migrants in increasing numbers, not just as farmers or farm laborers, but also as schoolteachers, shopkeepers, craftsmen, and others who found their services in demand in the thriving communities that spread out from the initial settlement along the coast of the Gulf of Tomini.

There has been much discussion of the reasons for the exceptional success of these Balinese settlements. One undoubtedly was the fact that the area into which the Balinese moved, the *Tana Boa* (empty quarter), had been depopulated at the end of the nineteenth century and was virtually empty. Another was the close cohesion of the Balinese, who brought to the settlement their distinctive culture and tradition of village cooperation. This has frequently been observed among arrivals from Bali, whether government-sponsored or spontaneous migrants.

The Balinese settlers, who have generally been allotted land in a contiguous area, have worked together in clearing the land, and improving irrigation, and have created many of the organisations that characterized their home culture. Each month they meet together to discuss social or agricultural matters, and group work activities are regarded as compulsory for all Balinese, as are contributions to celebrations of any of their group. (Suratman and Guinness 1977: 95ff)

A third factor was the process of self-selection referred to earlier, which means spontaneous migrants tend to be above average in initiative and self-reliance. These qualities have also characterized other spontaneous settlers, such as the Buginese, who pioneered settlement in eastern Sumatra.

Partially offsetting spontaneous outward migration from Java in these various forms, there has always been a reverse flow, from the outer islands to Java. As economic growth accelerated in the 1970s, which was heavily biased toward Java, this reverse flow became very substantial, motivated by perceived employment opportunities and the attractions of city life. It has not directly affected the transmigration program, but it has certainly made the objective of mitigating Indonesia's population imbalance still more difficult to attain.

## RESULTS

### Number of transmigrants

Judged merely by the number of people moved from Java to the outer islands, the transmigration program has achieved remarkable results in the past ten years. As Table 3.7 shows, the number of families (and persons) moved annually doubled during Repelita-I, as compared with the preceding two decades, doubled again during Repelita-II, and at least quadrupled in Repelita-III. (Statistics are so far available only for the first four years. If the Repelita-II target is reached in the current fiscal year, the increase, compared with Repelita-II, will be nearly six-fold.) Table 3.8 indicates that the majority of transmigrants have been settled in Sumatra (around 60 percent in each of the three Five-Year Plan periods). The proportion settled in Kalimantan has also remained fairly stable at around 15–18 percent. But the proportion moved to Sulawesi has declined, from 26 percent in Repelita-I to 12 percent in Repelita-III, in favor of the eastern provinces of Maluku and Irian Jaya, whose share has risen to 7 percent.

The importance of total numbers should not be underestimated. When the Repelita-III target of 500,000 families was announced, it was widely regarded as unrealistic and unattainable. To have managed the movement and settlement of between 60,000 and 100,000 families a year in the often extremely difficult conditions of the Indonesian archipelago is an organizational achievement of no mean order.

Even this tremendous effort, however, has merely underlined what has now become obvious and almost universally admitted—that transmigration cannot hope to correct the population imbalance between Java and the outer islands. The population of Java (including Bali) is now close to 100 million and is growing at about 2 percent a year. This means that, even if it were possible to sustain transmigration at the Repelita-III target rate, this would remove from Java only one-fifth of the annual *increase* in Java's population. The population imbalance in Indonesia is an irremediable fact of life. The real question is whether whatever economic or other disadvantages it may entail can be remedied *within* Java.

This is not to say that, in terms of numbers, the effort has been pointless. The removal of between 300,000 and 400,000 people a year must have done something to relieve the population pressure and consequent social problems in some of the poorest areas of Java; and in so far as low population density and a shortage of labor constitute obstacles to the economic development of the outer islands, the influx of this number of transmigrants represents a significant addition to their natural increase (of about 1.4 million a year).[5] But it would clearly be difficult to justify the transmigration program simply in terms of its direct effects on the relative rates of population growth in Java and the outer islands.

Side by side with government-sponsored transmigration there has been, as we have noted, for many decades a flow of spontaneous migrants in the same direction, and in the past decade also a substantial reverse flow. Table 3.9 presents a rough estimate of the magnitude of these flows, based on a comparison of official transmigration statistics with population census data on interprovincial migration in two periods, 1950–72 and 1975–80 (approximately coincident with Repelita-II). In the earlier period, the net outflow from Java of spontaneous migrants was considerably larger than the outflow under the official transmigration program. In the Repelita-II period, this was no longer the case. As economic development accelerated in Java, a large number of people from the outer islands were attracted to Java, and especially to Jakarta, by the business and employment opportunities that seemed to be opening up. While the gross outflow of spontaneous migrants still exceeded that of government-sponsored transmigrants, the net outflow, after allowing for the reverse movement to Java, was smaller.

In this crude form, these figures do not tell us much. Their relevance to an assessment of the transmigration program depends on whether there was a causal connection between spontaneous and government-sponsored migration. If the outflow of spontaneous migrants was to some extent directly or indirectly induced by the transmigration program, the program can be credited with a larger total effect on the population balance than the official transmigration statistics would suggest. If, on the other hand, spontaneous migration was wholly or largely independent, this might suggest that the effort and resources that have been expended on transmigration would have been better devoted to facilitating and encouraging spontaneous migration. We shall return to this important question below (See "Options"). But even the most favorable (and certainly unrealistic) assumption that the spontaneous outflow from Java was entirely induced by transmigration, and the spontaneous inflow entirely independent of it, the gross outflow of all migrants from Java still fell well short of Java's natural population increase during Repelita-II. No comparable figures for the most recent period of Repelita-III are yet available, but it is unlikely that the conclusion would be different.

If the transmigration program cannot be justified solely by its effects on the population balance, what of its achievements in terms of the two other objectives which have been most commonly held out in the past decade, a better life for the transmigrants and the promotion of regional development in the outer islands? In the absence of any reliable measure or data by which the results can be quantified, there is room for wide differences of opinion. A personal judgment, based entirely on secondary sources, is that in both respects there has been a marked improvement in recent years but that the benefits are still extremely variable and on average relatively small.

## Transmigrant welfare

There is now a fairly general consensus that the Netherlands colonization policy and the transmigration program in the first 25 years after independence, which continued that policy in all its essentials, did little more than reproduce, in Lampung and other settlement areas, the problems of rural Java. As one well-informed commentator put it, "settlements were more or less expected to remain at subsistence level" (Hardjono 1977: 44).

The realization that cash crop cultivation is necessary if settlers are ever to achieve higher standards of living lies behind the shift of emphasis during Repelita-II and Repelita-III in favor of combined food and cash crop production on larger holdings, a shift strongly supported by the World Bank. This, and many other improvements in the program to which reference has already been made, have, it seems, done a great deal to ameliorate conditions and prospects in the average settlement. Life is still hard, especially in the early years, and what little evidence there is suggests that average income is only a little above that in rural Java. Even in the new World Bank assisted settlements, farmers with an average of just over 1 hectare under cultivation are found after three to four years on the site to reach an annual family income of only about U.S. $600 (at 1982 prices). This may be compared with an estimated average per capita consumption expenditure of about U.S. $120 in rural Java.[6] Even optimistic projections put target family income on the most favored World Bank assisted projects at no more than Rp.2 million (1982 prices) at full development in 1990, or about U.S. $450 per capita, little above estimated per capita income for Indonesia as a whole.

Surveys of farmers in the older upland settlements suggest that crop yields and incomes are both low and extremely variable. In one survey, nearly two-thirds of farmers were found to obtain 500 kilograms of paddy (*gabah* or unhulled rice) or less from their holdings in a year. These farmers relied on crops other than rice for subsistence and obtained cash largely from off-farm work. In the dry grassland areas particularly, where soil fertility diminishes quickly, yields decline after a few good harvests and farmers revert to cassava as the subsistence crop (Suratman and Guinness 1977: 94). In tidal swamp areas, higher rice yields (of around 1 ton per hectare) are usually achieved, but even this is much below the average in Java and Bali.

In assessing the significance of these data, however, it must be remembered that most of the transmigrants are not *average* Javanese. The majority are recruited from among the landless and poorest. To them, even an average migrant standard of living, including a piece of land of their own, represents a big improvement. The flow of spontaneous migrants to the settlements supports this conclusion. They must at least *believe* that they will be better off.

All reports agree that there is a wide dispersion around the average income of settlers. On one hand, there are some quite prosperous settlers, such as the Balinese spontaneous migrants at Parigi, and some official transmigrants, among them those at Belitang and Baturaja in South Sumatra. On the other hand, there are the overcrowded areas of Lampung, comparable to some of the poorest in Java, and isolated transmigrant settlements in Central Kalimantan and Irian Jaya, where life is a struggle for survival. Over the years many disappointed settlers have abandoned their holdings to seek a livelihood in logging or other work. One survey of a project in a rather remote grassland area of Lampung, which was settled in the early 1970s with "social welfare" families (mostly urban unemployed with no experience of the hard work of clearing and the constant effort of farm life, and little stomach for it), found that by 1977 only just over half of the original families were still on-site. But subsequently, as conditions on the settlement improved and more opportunities for off-farm employment became available, quite a few returned to their plots. Certainly, on publicly available evidence, very few transmigrants appear to have returned to their home villages in Java.

Opportunities for off-farm employment are clearly a major determinant of settlers' living standards and of income differentials between more and less successful projects. Off-season wage employment may be essential for subsistence, and may be the only source of cash income until marketable crops can be grown. In upland areas, the most important opportunities have been in logging and construction, although misguided regulations have forbidden household heads in some areas to work in construction. In tidal swamp settlements, apart from fishing, settlers have generally had to depend on limited opportunities of wage employment as laborers working on site development.

Another major factor determining a project's success is the accessibility of marketing outlets for cash crops, which in turn depend largely on access to towns or major roads. (In tidal swamp areas, canals provide easy transport, but towns or other larger communities are liable to be far away.) While roads or canals may give adequate access, marketing networks linking settlers to local and regional markets take time to evolve. Even in relatively prosperous settlements, such as that in the Luwu district of Sulawesi, economic improvement has been held back by isolation. Migrants have lacked the incentive to produce more than they could consume, or to cultivate commercial crops, because of the difficulty of selling their products. In some settlement areas, indigenous traders with capital to acquire and market produce in larger quantities render a valuable service to transmigrants.

## Regional development

One's judgment as to the contribution that transmigration has made to regional development in the outer islands depends very much on what one means by regional development. Without doubt, large areas of Sumatra, Kalimantan, and Sulawesi have been developed in the sense that primary forest has given way to cultivation of rice, cassava, and other food crops, that some 2 to 3 million people have been settled in new village communities, and that, associated with the program, there has been considerable investment in infrastructure, especially roads, irrigation, and swamp reclamation.

There is also statistical support for the assumption that transmigration has contributed to one of the major policy objectives of the three Five-Year Plans, increased food production. Table 3.10 presents growth rates of rice (*sawah*) production in the various provinces of Sumatra since the 1950s. Over the period as a whole, the northern Sumatran provinces, which have received relatively fewer transmigrants, have shown somewhat higher rates of yield increase than those of southern Sumatra. But in the southern provinces, harvested area increased at an average annual rate of over 4 percent and production at over 5 percent; and in the last 5 years, even yield per hectare rose fastest in the two chief transmigrant settlement provinces, Lampung and South Sumatra, resulting in an annual rate of growth of output twice as rapid as that of Java. There is no reason to doubt that the inflow of transmigrants and opening up of land to irrigated rice production has been a major factor in this. There remain, of course, the questions as to how much longer such rates of increase in area or yield can be sustained in these provinces, and whether such rates can be matched in the rain-fed upland areas.

If by regional development is meant the promotion of industry and trade, the exploitation and processing of mineral, forestry, and other natural resources, and the improvement of transport and communications necessary to integrate the region more effectively into the national and world economy, the contribution of transmigration to the outer islands has so far been quite marginal. Members of settler families and spontaneous migrants initially attracted to transmigrant settlements have at times eased labor supply problems for timber concessionaires and for smallholder and estate producers of cash crops. The roads built in association with transmigration have incidentally improved market access for timber, cash crops, and processing industries. But the major industrial developments in the outer islands over the past decade, chiefly based on oil and natural gas, mineral processing, and plywood construction, have occurred entirely independently; and manufacturing development has continued to be largely confined to Java, because the outer islands cannot effectively compete with Java's domestic market; labor supply; physical, business, and administrative infrastructure; and lines of communication.

To expect transmigration to have registered a marked impact on regional development in this sense may be unreasonable. Large-scale transmigration has been going on for only a few years. In opening up large tracts of jungle and swamp, it may be said to have laid the foundation for a process that must be thought of in terms of decades, taking us into the period in the next century when the oil sector can no longer be relied on to propel the development of the outer islands.

How much weight can be given to this argument depends in large part on two sets of questions. One relates to the prospects for overcoming the many difficulties that the transmigration program has had to face and still faces. The other concerns the availability of alternatives to transmigration for the broad purposes this program has been designed to promote.

## Program problems

Little needs to be added to what has already been said about some of the major problem areas of the program—migrant selection, assistance to migrants with inputs and services, cropping systems, rations with the indigenous population, and administration.

The central dilemma in migrant selection has been between the criteria of need and suitability. So long as relief of population pressure in the most poverty-ridden areas of Java and the welfare of the transmigrants remain major objectives of the program, the dilemma is inescapable. But it has come to be increasingly recognized that the prospects for successful land settlement, let alone for regional development outside agriculture, depend on a sufficient admixture of people with leadership qualities and a wide range of skills. The answer lies partly in deliberate emphasis on such qualities in selection and partly in the provision of further training facilities in or near the settlements.

Most of the deficiencies in assistance to transmigration can be traced to logistic problems connected with inefficient administration and co-ordination. These, in turn, are endemic in Indonesia as in other developing countries, and have merely been aggravated by the pace at which the whole program was expanded in the atmosphere of euphoria engendered by the oil windfall of the 1970s. There are no easy solutions, and most of what needs to be done is obvious enough.

As regards farming systems on transmigration settlements, transmigration policymakers and consultants now mostly see agricultural diversification as the main answer to the problems encountered by the earlier policy of transferring to the outer islands the Javanese system of wet rice cultivation. Since Repelita-II, as we have already noted, it has been official policy to provide settlers in the rain-fed uplands with larger plots, to enable them to supplement their income by cash crop production. Other measures now proposed to improve settlers' incomes and prospects are better preliminary soil surveys to determine the most appropriate cropping pattern in each area, whether for food crops of different kinds or other cash crops; facilities for timber disposal for the benefit of settlements, whether by contractors or the settlers themselves; encouragement of animal husbandry; and with respect to all of these, more adequate extension and advisory services.

In contrast to these problems, which are in principle manageable, there are two, the full seriousness of which has emerged only in the last year or two. They are shortage of land and shortage of money. Both deserve fuller discussion.

## KEY CONSTRAINTS

### Shortage of land

The idea that there should be a shortage of land for transmigration settlements in the vast areas of Indonesia's outer islands usually meets with incredulity. The statement that one hears quite frequently that Sumatra, Kalimantan, and Sulawesi are "full" is certainly an exaggeration. But even with improved procedures for site identification, for which the World Bank is providing considerable financial and technical assistance, the lack of suitable sites is regarded by many informed observers as the crucial constraint on continuance of the program on anything like its present scale.

We have already noted the great contrast in soil fertility between Java and most of the outer islands. Much of the land area of the latter that is not already cultivated is unusable—it is either mountains or swamp. And much of the rest consists of poor soils and/or steep terrain subject to leaching and erosion. It is difficult to believe that in coming decades new technology will not make much of this land cultivable, by new kinds of fertilizer, new techniques of farming, or cheaper methods of swamp reclamation. But such technological advances cannot be counted on to transform the situation within the next Five-Year Plan period or the one after. Apart from these basic limitations, three other factors limit the amount of land available for transmigration sites.

The first is concern for conservation and rational exploitation of Indonesia's forest resources. It has been forcefully argued that sustained-yield forestry represents a more economic use of primary forest land than agricultural development, unless all timber is fully recovered during clearing and makes a major contribution to agricultural development in the first year (Burbridge et al. 1981). This case is now substantially conceded by the transmigration authorities. Mapping and surveying, moreover, are more difficult in primary forest, and the cost of clearing is ten times as high in forest as in grassland areas. In practice, increasingly effective control of forest land by the government forestry agencies has now led to a situation where primary forest is virtually unavailable for transmigration settlement sites.

The alternative is grassland or land cleared of forest by logging. The problem here is *alang-alang* grass (*Imperata cylindrica*), which has long been recognized as the chief obstacle to agricultural use of upland areas not under virgin forest in much of Sumatra and Kalimantan. Intensive research has been undertaken for many years on the possibilities of mechanical, chemical, or vegetative eradication of *alang-alang*. A few years ago, experiments with vegetative control by means of a leguminous cover crop (*stylosanthus*) seemed very promising (Daroesman 1981). More recent reports cast doubt on the effectiveness of this approach when it is extended from controlled pilot plots to smallholder agriculture.

A third frequent source of difficulty in procuring settlement sites has been the assertion of prior land claims by the indigenous people of the region. One feature of the system of shifting cultivation long customary in much of Sumatra and Kalimantan was the formation of *marga* groups claiming hereditary rights to large, unmapped tracts of land. In the absence of legal records or precise boundaries, disputes have been common, often well after transmigrants have settled on the land in the belief that they hold secure title. The problem has also recently become an issue in Irian Jaya. It is now acknowledged that the development of a legal framework for transfer of the title from local people to transmigrants is an urgent task. But while this should reduce the incidence of disputes, it is likely to increase rather than diminish the shortage of land for transmigration sites.

That this problem is serious, and acknowledged as such by the Indonesian authorities, is shown by the proposal said to be under consideration in Jakarta to shift the emphasis in Repelita-IV (1984–85 to 1988–89) heavily toward Irian Jaya. One can hardly think of a less satisfactory solution. Apart from the obvious logistic problems presented by that distant and in large part very inaccessible province, Irian Jaya exemplifies the problem of ethnic relations in its starkest form. Any attempt to settle in Irian Jaya a million Javanese who would submerge the indigenous population of 750,000 Papuans would risk serious conflict.

## Shortage of money

The financial constraints are hardly less worrying. The transmigration program involves a formidable administrative superstructure, costly efforts to improve conditions for transmigrants—by provision of transport (largely now by air), adequate preparation of sites, clearing and planting of larger holdings, provision of housing, food rations and other inputs, irrigation and roads, education, health, and other facilities—and a heavy reliance on expensive consultant services, and all this has considerably increased the cost per transmigrant family. At the same time, target numbers have been rising and, in the view of some of the planners, should rise further. Until recently, even so lavish a transmigration program appeared to be supportable, side by side with many other imaginative economic and social development projects, by Indonesia's oil earnings. This is no longer the case. The prospect is for much leaner years ahead, as the government has fully recognized and acknowledged. The question is how the transmigration program now stands in competition with other essential or worthwhile uses of much more limited funds.

Table 3.11 relates the central government's annual development budget allocation for transmigration to the number of families settled in each year since the beginning of Repelita-I. For various reasons, this is a very crude measure of the cost of the program. On one hand, disbursements may have fallen short of budget allocations (though this does not seem to have been the case to any significant extent in the first eight years for which figures are available). On the other hand, the figures cover only part of the cost. They include neither the allocation for transmigration in the routine budget (not a large figure, about Rp.10 billion in 1983–84), nor the amounts attributable to the program in the development and routine budget for other central government departments, such as public works, health, education, and home affairs (some of which would, of course, have been incurred for the same people had they remained in Java), nor the expenditures on transmigration by provincial authorities (which absorbed an unknown proportion of very large central government grants to them—Rp.1.423 trillion in the 1983–84 development budget). The figures, however, do give some indication of the growth in expenditures that has occurred with the expansion of the transmigration program in the course of the first three five-year plans.

The proportion of the development budget allocated to the transmigration program has risen from 0.7 percent in 1969–70 to 6.1 percent in 1982–83 and slightly less (5.8 percent) in 1983–84. Expenditure per family settled reached nearly U.S. $12,000 in 1982–83. (If the revised target of 150,000 families is reached this fiscal year, and expenditures are to remain within the budget allocation, the cost per family would have to drop dramatically to U.S. $3,590, which seems improbable.) Most of the recommendations for improvement of the program would, if adopted, raise the cost still further, though there is undoubtedly also scope for economies that would increase the cost-effectiveness of expenditure. But taking the figure of U.S. $12,000 per family as a benchmark, and relating it to the target size of 800,000 families most commonly mentioned for Repelita-IV, the direct cost to the development budget would add up to nearly U.S. $10 billion, or U.S. $2 billion a year.

Some of the cost of the program has been met by external financial assistance, and such assistance can be expected to continue. By far the largest contributor, and indeed one of the most committed and influential supporters of transmigration in the past decade, has been the World Bank. Motivated in part by the increased emphasis on social objectives under the McNamara presidency, the Bank took up the cause of transmigration in the mid–1970s. Its Transmigration I project initiated in 1976 provided a loan of U.S. $30 million for two test schemes, one for rehabilitation of an existing project in Lampung, the other for an experimental project combining tree and food crop cultivation at Baturaja in South Sumatra. The Transmigration II agreement, signed in 1979, provided a U.S. $90 million loan and U.S. $67 million International Development Agency (IDA) support for the Repelita-III transmigration program. A third project, still being negotiated, is to meet U.S $100 million of the foreign exchange cost (chiefly consultants) of site identification, extension of the Baturaja project, and general program support, especially training of transmigration officials. Other multilateral assistance for transmigration has come from United Nations specialized agencies (United Nations Development Program, World Food Program), from the Asian Development Bank (U.S. $34 million), and from the bilateral donors grouped in IGGI (the Inter-Governmental Group for Indonesia). All this assistance has been valuable, especially in supplementing and strengthening the managerial and technical capabilities of Indonesian government departments in charge of the program. But it is clear that it has contributed only a small percentage of the overall financial cost of the program.

The questions that are naturally being asked, and which must be asked, among Indonesian policymakers as much as by foreign donor agencies, are whether Indonesia can afford to continue to spend this much on transmigration in the conditions of the much more severe resource constraints that are likely throughout the rest of the 1980s (Arndt 1981).

## OPTIONS

We have seen that transmigration has in the past decade achieved a momentum that few would have thought possible and that, even when all allowances are made for failures and setbacks, it has almost certainly yielded significant benefits in terms of relief from population pressure in some of the poorest areas of Java, in terms of improvements in income and economic security for the majority of transmigrants, and in terms of development of land in the outer islands. We have seen that the program has run into a host of problems, but that most of them are being energetically tackled and, with reasonably efficient administration and external help, should be remediable. But we have also seen that the program is now running into two constraints that may necessitate serious reconsideration of the more ambitious plans for the future: shortage of land and shortage of money.

Many question the whole concept of transmigration. They argue that the underlying notion of a population "imbalance" in Indonesia is an illusion, based on looking at a map, which makes no more economic sense than similar notions about population imbalance between Egypt and the Sahara or between southeast and central Australia. It is no accident, they say, that fertile Java is so much more densely populated than the inhospitable jungle and swamplands of Kalimantan or the craggy mountains of Irian Jaya; and to attempt to correct this "imbalance" is, beyond a point that has probably already been reached, counterproductive. Grant (and this is now granted by the most fervent enthusiasts of transmigration) that the key to a better life for the people of Java lies in Java, transmigration, so the critics would argue, merely diverts resources and effort from the task of raising farm incomes and increasing nonagricultural opportunities for productive employment in Java, and attention from the need for population control through family planning.

There are others who, without questioning either the desirability of some movement of people from Java to the less densely populated parts of Indonesia or the potential for economic development of large parts of the outer islands, do not believe that the traditional policy of transmigration for land settlement, whether for subsistence or cash crop farming, represents a realistic approach. A recent study has suggested an altogether different one. It argues that mere land settlement can never achieve industrial and commercial development of the outer islands, that regional development in this sense is inhibited by backward transport and other infrastructure, and would soon be held back by a shortage of manpower if it gained any significant momentum; if only for reasons of cost, any really large-scale movement of people from Java must therefore depend primarily on spontaneous rather than government-sponsored migration. The authors of the study therefore propose a scheme for massive public works expenditure in the outer island provinces, which would attract labor from Java by opening up wage employment opportunities (Arndt and Sundrum 1977).

Others have objected that it is the promise of land, above all else, that motivates landless and other poor people to volunteer for transmigration. They maintain that land settlement has proved the most effective catalyst for spontaneous migration, in the form of chain migration (settlers in need of labor to help with clearing, planting, and harvesting encouraging their relatives and friends to join them), and that land settlement constitutes and promotes regional development by opening up upland and swampland for cultivation. In their view, it does so by improving transport and establishing communities as well as improving the labor supply through the attraction of spontaneous migrants (Hardjono 1978).

This debate turns largely on the empirical question touched on earlier, concerning the extent to which the outflow of spontaneous migrants is itself dependent on transmigration, through chain migration and in other ways, or whether it could be induced equally or more effectively by the offer of visible and large wage employment opportunities. The question cannot be conclusively settled either by case studies or by available aggregate statistics. Several studies have pointed to the large spontaneous outflow of labor to the plantations of Sumatra under the Netherlands government and in the first two decades of independence, and to East Kalimantan during the timber boom of the late 1960s (Manning 1971), as well as to the inflow to Java and especially Jakarta in the 1970s, all propelled by opportunities, or at least hopes, of wage employment. The critics of these studies, in turn, point to the substantial evidence in favor of chain migration in Lampung and other settlement provinces.

Table 3.12 presents a further breakdown of the figures given in Table 3.8. It suggests that during the period 1950–72, nearly 20 times as many spontaneous migrants and transmigrants moved to the northern provinces of Sumatra, as compared with less than three times as many to the main provinces of transmigration settlement, Lampung and South Sumatra. In the more recent period, 1975–80, the situation was reversed. Almost the whole of the flow of spontaneous migrants to Sumatra went to the two southern provinces. The figures for Lampung are particularly striking, with 399,000 spontaneous migrants but only 30,000 transmigrants in the latter period, as compared with 667,000 spontaneous migrants and 213,000 transmigrants in the earlier period.

These figures, however, are open to alternative interpretations. They do suggest a very effective, though considerably lagged, chain migration process. But if it is true, as Joan Hardjono and others have reported, that by the mid–1970s Lampung was already severely overcrowded, with fragmentation of holdings and increasing landlessness, it is arguable that transmigration did indeed act as a catalyst for spontaneous migration, "but only by reinforcing the tendency of the official program to recreate in much of neighboring Lampung the Malthusian situation of rural Java" (Arndt and Sundrum 1977: 80). Clearly, this need not be the consequence of chain migration, as the example of Parigi shows. But it greatly weakens the case for treating chain migration as an automatic bonus of the official transmigration program.

## CONCLUSIONS

The Indonesian government is strongly committed to the transmigration program. It would be pointless, even if it were sound, to recommend that it be abandoned.

The last five years have demonstrated that the policymakers and administrators in charge of the program are capable of moving very large numbers of transmigrant families from Java to the outer islands and coping with most of the immense logistic and organizational problems. There is scope for much further improvement, as our brief survey of policies and summary of program problems has shown, and further technical assistance from the World Bank and others is available. Some of the most pressing of these problems are due to deficiencies of administration, and here no rapid improvement can be expected. Others call for the application of technical know-how—new technology to improve and adapt cropping patterns and animal husbandry to varying soil and other conditions; to develop higher-yielding planting materials and more efficient methods of cultivation of tree crops, such as rubber, oil palm, and coconut; and, perhaps most important of all in view of the constraint of land availability, to eradicate *alang-alang* grass and develop less expensive techniques of swamp reclamation.

But it is unduly optimistic to believe that technology can answer all the financial, economic, and sociopolitical questions posed by the transmigration program. Long-standing doubts about the relative advantages of transmigration and alternative ways of achieving the same objectives are now being strongly reinforced by the two key constraints to which the present study has referred. There is a danger that an inflexible attachment to ambitious transmigration targets and the search for new settlement sites may create sociopolitical problems in the outer islands, and that the effort to make ends meet may mean that social and economic development programs in Java are cut back. In the longer run, serious thought needs to be given to the tradeoff between economic and social development in Java, the official transmigration program, and a spontaneous migration approach aimed at creating wage employment opportunities through public works in the outer islands. In the short run, it is obviously desirable to restrain the escalating financial demands of the transmigration program by introducing more economical and cost-effective ways of running it. But it may also be necessary to contemplate a marked reduction in the planned size of the program, at least for Repelita-IV.

## NOTES

1. For an account of economic developments in Indonesia in the Sukarno period, see Glassburner (1971).

2. Cf. Booth and McCawley (1971); also the regular *Survey of Recent Developments* series in *Bulletin of Indonesian Economic Studies* (BIES) published by the Australian National University, Canberra.

3. Transmigrants (and spontaneous migrants) have come from Bali and re-

cently from Lombok, as well as from Java. Unless specifically indicated, "Java" as the source of migrants in this paper includes these two small islands.

4. Nonsponsored migrants are sometimes referred to as "voluntary," but this usage offends against the principle that all recruitment to the transmigration program is, or should be, voluntary. The word "spontaneous" was inconvenient so long as official terminology in Indonesia distinguished a *spontan* or semi-sponsored and a fully sponsored category of transmigrants. Since this distinction was abolished in 1973, we have opted for *spontaneous* as the least confusing term.

5. The population of the outer islands was 54 million in 1980, growing at 2.6 percent a year.

6. U.S. $104 at 1980 prices; from V. V. Bhanojii Rao, "Poverty in Indonesia, 1970–80" (mimeographed), based on SUSENAS (national household expenditure survey) data. This figure is, of course, very much smaller than that for GDP per capita, even for rural Java. The *World Development Report for 1983* puts GDP per capita for Indonesia as a whole in 1981 at U.S. $530.

# BIBLIOGRAPHY

Arndt, H. W. 1981. "*Survey of Recent Development.*" *Bulletin of Indonesian Economic Studies* (Canberra) 18, no. 3 (November): 1–24.

Arndt, H. W., and R. M. Sundrum. 1977. "Transmigration: Land Settlement or Regional Development?" *Bulletin of Indonesian Economic Studies* 13, no. 3 (November): 79–90.

Booth, A., and P. McCawley, eds. 1971. *The Indonesian Economy During the Soeharto Era.* Kuala Lumpur: Oxford University Press.

Burbridge, P., J. A. Dixon, and B. Soewardi. 1981. "Land Allocation for Transmigration." *Bulletin of Indonesian Economic Studies* 17 (March): 108–13.

Daroesman, R. 1981. "Vegetative Elimination of Alang-alang." *Bulletin of Indonesian Economic Studies* 17 (March): 83–107.

Davis, G. 1976. *Parigi: A Social History of the Balinese Movement to Central Sulawesi, 1907–74.* Dissertation, Stanford University.

Fachurrozie, S. A., and C. McAndrews. 1978. "Buying Time: Forty Years of Transmigration in Belitang." *Bulletin of Indonesian Economic Studies* 14 (November): 94–103.

Glassburner, B., ed. 1971. *The Economy of Indonesia: Selected Readings.* Ithaca, NY: Cornell University Press.

Hardjono, J. 1977. *Transmigration in Indonesia.* Kuala Lumpur: Oxford University Press.

———. 1978. "Transmigration, a New Concept?" *Bulletin of Indonesian Economic Studies* 14 (March): 107–12.

Hull, T. G., and Ida Bagus Mantra. 1981. "Indonesia's Changing Population." In *The Indonesian Economy During the Soeharto Era*, edited by A. Booth and P. McCawley. Kuala Lumur: Oxford University Press.

Jones, G. 1979. "Recent Development and the Transmigration Programme." In *Migration and Development in Southeast Asia: A Demographic Perspective*, edited by R. J. Prior. Kuala Lumpur: Oxford University Press.

Manning, C. 1971. "The Timber Boom with Special Reference to East Kalimantan." *Bulletin of Indonesian Economic Studies* 7 November: 30–60.

Suratman, and P. Guinness. 1977. "The Changing Focus of Transmigration."
    *Bulletin of Indonesian Economic Studies* 13 (July): 78–101.
Suratman M. Singarimbun, and P. Guinness. 1977. "The Social and Economic
    Conditions of Transmigrants in South Kalimantan and South Sulawesi."
    Gadjah Mada University, Institute of Population Studies, Yogyakarta,
    Gadjah Mada University, Institute of Population Studies.
Tanjungkarang, Director of Transmigration. 1973. *Report for the Year 1972–73.*
    Lampung Province.

Table 3.1
Number of migrants in Lampung settlement, 1905-41

| Period | Government-sponsored migrants | Total number at end of year* |
|--------|------------------------------|------------------------------|
| 1905-11 | -- | 6,073 |
| 1912-22 | 16,838 | 22,274 |
| 1923-33 | 8,693 | 37,257 |
| 1934 | 1,375 | 37,477 |
| 1935 | 12,524 | 51,605 |
| 1936 | 12,181 | 62,764 |
| 1937 | 14,938 | 73,499 |
| 1938 | 20,014 | 91,595 |
| 1939 | 27,826 | 120,464 |
| 1940 | 31,173 | 144,619 |
| 1941 | 35,251 | 173,959 |

Source: Hardjono (1977).
*Total number of transmigrants resident in the settlements, i.e. cumulative inflow (plus natural increase) less outflow (and deaths).

Table 3.2
Number of migrants in colonization settlements, all Indonesia, end of 1940

| Area | Total population in settlements |
|------|--------------------------------|
| Residency of Lampung | 144,619 |
| Residency of Palembang | 19,876 |
| Residency of Bengkulu | 7,443 |
| Jambi and West Sumatra | 1,920 |
| Kalimantan | 3,107 |
| Sulawesi | 23,600 |
| Total | 200,565 |

Source: Hardjono (1977).

Table 3.3
Population growth in Java and Indonesia, 1900-76

| YEAR | JAVA | | INDONESIA | |
|------|------------------------|--------------------------------------------------|------------------------|--------------------------------------------------|
| | Population (thousands) | Growth rate over previous period (percent per annum) | Population (thousands) | Growth rate over previous period (percent per annum) |
| 1900 | 28,746 | -- | -- | -- |
| 1905 | 30,098 | 0.9 | n.a. | n.a. |
| 1917 | 34,157 | 1.1 | n.a. | n.a. |
| 1920 | 34,984 | 0.8 | n.a. | n.a. |
| 1930[a] | 41,718 | 1.8 | 60,727 | n.a. |
| 1940 | 48,400 | 1.5 | 70,400 | 1.5 |
| 1950 | 50,456 | 0.4 | 77,200 | 1.0 |
| 1961[a] | 62,993 | 2.0 | 97,019[b] | 2.1 |
| 1971[a] | 76,102 | 1.9 | 119,232 | 2.1 |
| 1976 | 82,103 | 1.5 | 126,093[c] | 2.0 |

Source: Hull and Mantra (1981: 273).
n.a., Not available.
[a] Census year, other years are official estimates.
[b] Including an estimate of 700,000 for Irian Jaya.
[c] Excluding rural areas of Irian Jaya, East Nusatenggara, and Maluku. Growth rate adjusted for boundary changes.

Table 3.4
Transmigrants by area of settlement, 1950-68

| Year | Sumatra | Kalimantan | Sulawesi | Elsewhere | Total |
|------|---------|------------|----------|-----------|--------|
| 1950 | 77      | --         | --       | --        | 77     |
| 1951 | 2,453   | --         | 96       | 402       | 2,951  |
| 1952 | 16,585  | --         | 338      | 682       | 17,605 |
| 1953 | 33,212  | 2,619      | 310      | 3,868     | 40,009 |
| 1954 | 26,430  | 1,736      | 1,078    | 494       | 29,738 |
| 1955 | 17,609  | 2,033      | 1,314    | 433       | 21,389 |
| 1956 | 22,135  | 2,119      | 96       | --        | 24,350 |
| 1957 | 17,456  | 4,184      | 1,590    | --        | 23,230 |
| 1958 | 25,700  | 463        | --       | 256       | 26,419 |
| 1959 | 44,124  | 1,412      | 298      | 262       | 46,096 |
| 1960 | 19,128  | 2,947      | --       | --        | 22,075 |
| 1961 | 14,876  | 4,330      | 263      | 140       | 19,609 |
| 1962 | 13,966  | 7,543      | 420      | 200       | 22,129 |
| 1963 | 28,903  | 1,808      | 1,448    | --        | 32,159 |
| 1964 | 11,787  | 2,448      | 987      | --        | 15,222 |
| 1965 | 46,287  | 5,019      | 1,919    | --        | 53,225 |
| 1966 | 771     | 375        | 2,774    | 728       | 4,648  |
| 1967 | 7,149   | 652        | 1,015    | 750       | 9,566  |
| 1968 | 9,664   | 2,010      | 1,922    | 287       | 13,883 |

Source: Hardjono (1977).

Table 3.5
Number of migrants by area of origin, 1969-74

| Area of origin | 1969-70 | 1970-71 | 1971-72 | 1972-73 | 1973-74 | Total |
|---|---|---|---|---|---|---|
| West Java | 2,105 | 3,004 | 2,647 | 7,936 | 8,170[a] | 23,862 |
| Central Java | 4,093 | 5,979 | 4,119 | 15,455 | 27,778 | 57,424 |
| Special area of Yogyakarta | 5,397 | 2,636 | 2,739 | 5,916 | 6,212 | 22,900 |
| East Java | 4,726 | 3,475 | 4,139 | 16,850 | 24,966 | 54,156 |
| Bali | 1,527 | 4,901 | 5,226 | 5,761 | 4,380 | 21,795 |
| Lombok | -- | -- | -- | -- | 1,451 | 1,451 |
| Local[b] | -- | -- | -- | -- | 108 | 108 |
| Totals | 17,848 | 19,995 | 18,870 | 51,918 | 73,065 | 181,696 |

Source: Hardjono (1977).
[a] The 1973-74 figure for West Java includes 1433 people from the Capital Territory of Jakarta.
[b] "Local" refers to indigenous people moving into project areas.

Table 3.6
Transmigration projects in Lampung, 1952-March 1973

| Project | Period of settlement | Project area (ha) | Population (1973) | Year of transfer |
|---|---|---|---|---|
| **South Lampung** | | | | |
| Balau Kedaton | 1961-73 | 12,000 | 7,041 | 1970 |
| Palas | 1958-73 | 14,300 | 15,127 | 1970* |
| Sidomakmur | 1967 | 500 | 977 | |
| Sidomulyo | 1958-73 | 14,500 | 27,053 | 1970* |
| Tanjungan | 1968-73 | 1,000 | 1,867 | |
| | | 42,300 | 52,065 | |
| **Central Lampung** | | | | |
| Banjaratu | 1959-63 | 6,000 | 4,209 | |
| Lb. Maringgai | 1953-56 | 142 | 3,023 | 1956 |
| Lempuyang | 1959 | 12,000 | 732 | |
| Pekalongan | 1953-57 | 1,000 | 8,711 | 1963 |
| Punggur | 1953-57 | 10,000 | 33,013 | 1968* |
| Purbolinggo | 1952-56 | 10,000 | 46,704 | 1963* |
| Raman Utara | 1955-58 | 9,958 | 28,655 | 1968* |
| Rumbia Barat/Sept. | | | | |
| Buminabung | 1960-72 | 9,738 | 20,537 | 1969* |
| Sekampung | 1952-55 | 3,000 | 18,069 | 1955* |
| Seputih Banyak | 1958-61 | 19,180 | 44,752 | 1969* |
| Sept. Mataram | 1962-65 | 38,000 | 43,229 | 1969* |
| Sept. Raman | 1954-59 | 12,630 | 46,915 | 1968* |
| Sept. Surabaya | 1965-70 | 10,000 | 11,045 | |
| Way Jepara | 1957-63 | 11,658 | 46,255 | 1968* |
| Way Seputih | 1954-61 | 10,537 | 57,172 | 1968* |
| | | 163,843 | 413,021 | |
| **North Lampung** | | | | |
| Banjit | 1952-63 | | 19,303 | 1970* |
| Baradatu | 1959-63 | 17,500 | 19,906 | 1970* |
| Negeri Agung | 1965 | 8,500 | 8,542 | |
| Way Abung | 1965-73 | 20,000 | 29,138 | |
| | | 46,000 | 76,889 | |
| Total Lampung | | 252,143 | 541,975 | |

Sources: Tanjungkarang (1973:43-44); Hardjono (1977).
*Projects that are now administrative districts (kecamatan).

Table 3.7
Number of transmigrants, 1950-82

| | 1950-72 | Repelita-I 1969-70 to 1973-74 | Repelita-II 1974-75 to 1978-79 | Repelita-III 1979-80 to 1983-84 target | 1979-80 to end-1982 |
|---|---|---|---|---|---|
| Persons | | | | | |
| Total | 417,500 | 181,700 | 376,900 | 2,100,000 | 1,169,000 |
| Per year | 18,900 | 36,300 | 75,380 | 420,000 | 292,000 |
| Families* | | | | | |
| Total | 100,000 | 46,100 | 87,800 | 500,000 | 286,000 |
| Per year | 4,500 | 9,200 | 17,560 | 100,000 | 57,200 |

Sources: 1950 to 1973-74: Hardjono (1977); 1974-75 to 1982: Directorate-General of Transmigration.
*Assuming 4.2 persons per family.

Table 3.8
Number of persons settled under transmigration program during 1969-70 to
December 31, 1982, by place of settlement

| | Sumatra | | Kalimantan | | Sulawesi | | Maluku | | Irian Jaya | | Total |
| | n (1,000's) | % | n (1,000's) | % | n (1,000's) | % | n (1,000's) | % | n (1,000's) | % | n (1,000's) |
|---|---|---|---|---|---|---|---|---|---|---|---|
| Repelita-I 1969-70 to 1973-74 | 105.2 | 57.9 | 26.6 | 14.6 | 47.7 | 26.3 | 1.7 | 0.9 | 0.5 | 0.3 | 181.7 |
| Repelita-II 1974-75 to 1978-79 | 227.8 | 60.4 | 69.4 | 18.4 | 74.8 | 19.8 | 0.6 | 0.2 | 4.3 | 1.1 | 376.9 |
| Repelita-III 1979-80 to end 1982 | 707.9 | 60.6 | 236.4 | 20.2 | 144.0 | 12.3 | 29.2 | 2.5 | 50.7 | 4.3 | 1,168.2 |

Sources: Repelita-I: Hardjono (1977); Repelita-II and III: Directorate-General of Transmigration.

Table 3.9
Transmigrants and spontaneous migrants from Java,
1950-72 and 1975-80 (thousands)

|  | 1950-72 | | 1975-80 | |
|  | Total | Annual average | Total | Annual average |
|---|---|---|---|---|
| Outflow from Java | 2,068 | 94 | 1,107 | 221 |
| Inflow to Java | -1,065 | -48 | -509 | -102 |
| Net outflow from Java | 1,003 | 46 | 598 | 119 |
| Transmigrants | 418 | 19 | 377* | 75* |
| Spontaneous | 604 | 27 | 221 | 44 |

Sources: 1950-72: Arndt and Sundrum (1977); 1975-80:
Transmigrants, Table 4, Repelita-II: Department of Information, Jakarta; Spontaneous, Population Census, 1980,
Central Bureau of Statistics, Jakarta.
*1974-75 to 1978-79.

Table 3.10
Growth rates of area, production, and yield of wet rice (sawah),
Sumatra, 1951-60 to 1976-80 (percentage per annum)

|  | 1951-60 to 1976-80 | | | 1971-75 to 1976-80 | | |
|  | Harvested area | Produc-tion | Yield | Harvested area | Produc-tion | Yield |
|---|---|---|---|---|---|---|
| 1. Aceh | 1.9 | 3.3 | 1.4 | 1.7 | 1.9 | 0.2 |
| 2. North Sumatra | 3.5 | 4.8 | 1.3 | 0.4 | 0.2 | -0.2 |
| 3. West Sumatra | 2.6 | 3.4 | 0.8 | 1.4 | 5.4 | 3.9 |
| 4. Riau | 3.6 | 4.6 | 0.9 | -0.2 | 3.0 | 3.2 |
| 5. Jambi | 4.1 | 4.8 | 0.7 | 4.1 | 7.3 | 3.2 |
| 6. South Sumatra | -- | -- | -- | 3.5 | 7.6 | 4.1 |
| 7. Bengkulu | -- | -- | -- | 1.2 | 1.7 | 0.5 |
| 8. Lampung | -- | -- | -- | 5.1 | 9.2 | 4.1 |
| 6 & 7 & 8 | 4.6 | 5.2 | 0.6 | 3.7 | 7.3 | 3.5 |
| Sumatra, total | 3.4 | 4.3 | 0.8 | 1.9 | 3.7 | 1.7 |
| Java | 0.4 | 3.4 | 3.1 | 0.6 | 3.7 | 3.2 |

Source: Central Bureau of Statistics: Production of food
crops in Indonesia.
Notes: In the earlier period, Bengkulu and Lampung were part
of the province of South Sumatra. Totals may not add up owing to
rounding.

Table 3.11
Transmigration: Central government development budget allocation
and number of families settled, 1969-70 to 1983-84

| Year | Development budget Rp. (billions) | Total transmigration allocation | | Families settled (thousands) | Cost per family | |
|---|---|---|---|---|---|---|
| | | Rp. (billions) | As percentage of total | | Rp. (thousands) | U.S.$[a] |
| 1969-70 | 123 | 0.85 | 0.7 | 3.9 | 218 | 577 |
| 1970-71 | 161 | 1.04 | 0.6 | 4.4 | 236 | 624 |
| 1971-72 | 242 | 1.36 | 0.6 | 4.1 | 332 | 878 |
| 1972-73 | 314 | 2.32 | 0.7 | 11.3 | 205 | 522 |
| 1973-74 | 344 | 3.66 | 1.1 | 22.4 | 163 | 393 |
| 1974-75 | 616 | 6.65 | 1.1 | 13.3 | 500 | 1,204 |
| 1975-76 | 1,268 | 15.08 | 1.2 | 11.0 | 1,370 | 3,301 |
| 1976-77 | 1,920 | 27.30 | 1.4 | 11.8 | 2,314 | 5,576 |
| 1977-78 | 2,168 | 50.93 | 2.3 | 23.1 | 2,205 | 5,313 |
| 1978-79 | 2,455 | 104.50 | 4.3 | 28.8 | 3,628 | 7,344 |
| 1979-80 | 3,488 | 146.2 | 4.2 | 50.7 | 2,884 | 4,689 |
| 1980-81 | 5,028 | 272.4 | 5.4 | 79.9 | 3,409 | 5,543 |
| 1981-82 | 6,399 | 394.0 | 6.2 | 88.0 | 4,477 | 7,280 |
| 1982-83 | 8,605 | 526.7 | 6.1 | 67.4 | 7,815 | 11,663 |
| 1983-84 | 9,290 | 539.0 | 5.8 | (125.0)[b] | (4,312)[b] | (6,436)[b] |

Sources: Development Budget: Ministry of Finance; families settled:
Directorate General of Transmigration.
[a] Exchange rates used (Rp.):
    1969-70 to 1971-72: 328
    1972-73:            393 (weighted average)
    1973-74 to 1977-78: 415
    1978-79:            494 (weighted average)
    1980-81 to 1981-82: 615
    1982-83 to 1983-84: 670 (weighted average)
[b] Target: recently revised to 150,000.

Table 3.12
Outflow of transmigrants and spontaneous migrants from Java to Sumatra by
province of settlement, 1950-72, 1975-80 (in thousands)

| Area | 1950-72 | | | | 1975-80 | | | |
|---|---|---|---|---|---|---|---|---|
| | Total outflow (1) | Trans-migrants (2) | Spontaneous (3) | Spontaneous: transmigrants ratio--(3)/(2) (4) | Total outflow (1) | Trans-migrants (2) | Spontaneous (3) | Spontaneous: transmigrants ratio--(3)/(2) (4) |
| Lampung | 880 | 213 | 667 | 3.1 | 429 | 30 | 399 | 13.3 |
| South Sumatra | 268 | 82 | 185 | 2.2 | 160 | 59 | 101 | 1.7 |
| Bengkulu | 14 | 9 | 5 | 0.6 | 42 | 29 | 13 | 0.4 |
| Southern Sumatra | 1,162 | 305 | 857 | 2.8 | 631 | 118 | 513 | 4.3 |
| Aceh | 21 | 1 | 20 | 20.0 | 18 | 10 | 8 | 0.8 |
| North Sumatra | 417 | 7 | 410 | 58.6 | 37 | 2 | 35 | 17.5 |
| West Sumatra | 56 | 18 | 38 | 2.1 | 32 | 23 | 9 | 0.4 |
| Riau | 85 | 2 | 83 | 41.5 | 28 | 13 | 15 | 1.1 |
| Jambi | 58 | 5 | 53 | 10.6 | 64 | 61 | 3 | 0.1 |
| Northern Sumatra | 637 | 33 | 604 | 18.3 | 179 | 109 | 70 | 0.6 |
| Sumatra | 1,799 | 338 | 1,461 | 4.3 | 810 | 227 | 583 | 2.6 |
| Other outer islands | 269 | 80 | 189 | 2.4 | 297 | 149 | 148 | 1.0 |
| All Indonesia | 2,068 | 418 | 1,650 | 4.0 | 1,107 | 377 | 730 | 1.9 |

Sources: 1950-72: Arndt and Sundrum (1977); 1975-80: Transmigrants, Table 4, Repelita-II;
Other: Population Census, 1980.

Tunku Shamsul Bahrin

4

# Land Settlement in Malaysia: A Case Study of the Federal Land Development Authority Projects

## INTRODUCTION

Although Malaysia is a relative newcomer in implementing land settlement schemes in Southeast Asia, its style of implementation and overall performance have received worldwide attention. Whereas many of the other Southeast Asian programs can be traced to the early part of this century, the Malaysian program did not begin until the mid–1950s. Within a time span of less than 30 years, large tracts of land have been developed and occupied by previously poor and landless peasants who can now pride themselves on a relatively good income and standard of living, compared with those who remained in the old villages.

Apart from its recent origin, the Malaysian resettlement program also differs in many respects from its other Southeast Asian counterparts. It was never intended as a population redistribution measure, but was essentially aimed at improving the socioeconomic status of the participants. Neither is it being implemented as part of a more comprehensive agrarian reform program. Malaysian land settlement schemes generally use land for growing cash crops, especially rubber and oil palm, rather

Professor, Department of Geography, University of Malaya

than subsistence food crops. The manner of implementation also differs somewhat from other programs. In Malaysia, the settlers are not required to engage in the more arduous task of jungle clearing; this is left instead to private contractors, thus making the projects relatively more capital-intensive.

The purpose of this study is fourfold. First, to discuss the basic policy issues related to land development in Malaysia. Second, to examine the way in which land is being developed for new settlements, with special emphasis on the role and activities of the Federal Land Development Authority (FELDA). Third, to assess the achievements and impact of land settlement projects, and fourth, to suggest measures for improving settlement performance.

## POLICY ISSUES

The need for planned development of land in the various states of Malaysia had been evident for a long time. But it was only in 1955 that the government committed itself to land development as a basic strategy for the improvement of the economic status of the rural poor.

### Land alienation and development

In peninsular Malaysia, all unalienated land in each state is vested in the ruler-in-council, and the alienation and issue of titles to such lands is all done through the ruler. Demand for land had long been outstripping the capacity of most land offices in the country. At the time of independence (August 1957) there were some 200,000 land applications awaiting action.

The slow progress of land alienation had convinced the government of the need for action. A committee was set up to look into the whole process of land alienation in the country and make recommendations for improvements. The report, submitted in 1957, emphatically observed that "the method of land alienation in Malaysia since the war has commonly been such as to cause the most work, the most trouble and confusion, take the most time, cost the most money, create bothersome bottlenecks and produce the poorest economic results for the individual concerned and for the community" (Government of Malaysia 1957: para. 105).

One of the fundamental causes of this situation was the initiation of land applications by individuals rather than by organizations or agencies that could be expected to be in a better position to have an overall view of the selected area. Almost invariably, applications were made for the sake of personal gain, without the least regard to public interest (Government of Malaysia 1957: para. 106). Under these conditions, applicants who had money and knowledge about application procedures were in a more favorable position to obtain land than those who really needed it.

The system under which land alienation was initiated by the applicants and not by the administration obviously left much to be desired. The committee was of the opinion that in a modern state, land alienation should be initiated by the state and haphazard settlement should be avoided. Accordingly, it was recommended that areas of land suitable for alienation should be identified, and an initial appraisal of the land for its economic viability made prior to dividing it into suitable units. It was also thought that appraising the land before receiving any applications for it would make it possible to draw up a proper plan, which would include provision of basic facilities such as roads, schools, village sites, and so on. Such an approach clearly indicated a system of planned settlement.

The government had also set up a working party earlier in August 1955 with the following terms of reference:

a. to assess the needs of the different states for assistance from the federal government in the development of new areas for land settlement, in the light of this assessment; and

b. to make recommendations, with special reference to financial and administrative aspects, on the most suitable organization for providing such assistance.

In its findings contained in the *Report of the Working Party Set Up to Consider the Development of New Areas for Land Settlement* (Government of Malaysia, 1956), the working party was emphatic about the need for planned development in the country, and concluded that with the traditional methods of development and expansion of agricultural lands, either by large estates or by Malay and Chinese smallholders, development on the scale that had prevailed in the early years of the twentieth century would probably not be possible. Under these circumstances, therefore, the working party emphasized the need for "land resources to be carefully assessed and husbanded." Furthermore, the working party was of the opinion that "large areas for new development should be alienated only after being planned."

Some of the suggestions and recommendations of the working party are noteworthy. The emphasis on the vital need for planned and coordinated development of land to ensure that economic development goes hand in hand with social development is laudable. Associated with this is the suggestion that if steps are to be taken to open up new areas, then it is essential that provision of roads, schools, health services, and so on should be an integral part of any plan from the beginning. The working party also considered that development activities must be co-ordinated and controlled to ensure that fragmentation of holdings does not occur, and that settlers have an adequate amount of land and a reasonable standard of living.

The working party also recommended that a suitable organization should be set up to implement such a development program. It was, however, of the opinion that a federal authority with powers of financing and carrying out individual schemes would be too remote from the state and the people who were to be assisted. The working party therefore suggested that the organization for providing federal assistance for land development schemes should be decentralized; that is, local develop-ment authorities, set up by the ruler-in-council for each scheme, should be responsible for the planning and execution of the projects. The FELDA, on the other hand, should be responsible for contributing funds and resources to such schemes as might be approved on mutually agreed terms. In brief, the FELDA was expected to play a passive role in the initation of projects. It was to be involved only when a local authority had decided to carry out a project. This system had a number of weak-nesses, which partially explain the slow pace in opening new schemes during the initial period.

One major flaw in the decentralization system arose as a consequence of the uneven distribution of population between states, as well as be-tween districts within the same state. According to the administrative and implementation structure created, the initiative in starting a land development scheme rested with the local authority. Thus, logically, resettlement had to start in those areas where there was a problem of population pressure. But those areas did not have much land left for development, otherwise the landless population would have taken steps to occupy land and use it, even without approval if necessary. On the other hand, areas with "excess" land did not need land settlement schemes.

By the end of the first Five-Year Plan in 1960, FELDA had sponsored 25 schemes in different parts of the country and had developed 8910 hectares for rubber plantations. The number of families resettled was 1694. These figures, however, were below the set target of 34 schemes, 68,180 hectares of developed land, and resettlement of 14,400 families (Government of Malaysia 1961a). In view of these limited achievements, the government set up a committee to investigate the reasons for the lack of success and to review the role of FELDA. The committee gave the following reasons for the limited success:

a. The lack of a sense of urgency in land development matters on the part of several state governments and their consequent slow response in proposing schemes

b. The lack of basic land use surveys and consequent absence of plans for land development

c. The lack of access to potential development areas

d. A shortage of suitably qualified and experienced staff to supervise and manage land development schemes

e. The necessity for consultation with 12 departments and agencies responsible to eight ministries, at both state and federal levels, at a time when there was no national directive according high priority to land development (Government of Malaysia 1961b)

The committee also felt that the FELDA was unlikely to meet the increased demand for land development. The establishment of a number of agencies implementing land development schemes was therefore proposed. To date, some 15 different agencies are engaged in land development schemes, the FELDA being the largest. In order to understand fully the process of land settlement in Malaysia, especially with regard to the important role played by the FELDA, it is essential to discuss the limited success of the other types of land development schemes planned and implemented during the 1960s. We shall briefly examine two types of such schemes, namely the Group Settlement Schemes and the Fringe Alienation Schemes.

## The Group Settlement Schemes

The Group Settlements are small-scale, FELDA-type schemes that are financed and implemented by the state governments. They came into being with the implementation of the Group Settlement Areas Act, 1961. Except for those implemented in Kelantan, there is little information available on the workings of these schemes. The Kelantan schemes became prominent for political reasons. Unlike the federal government and the other states in the Federation, which were governed by the then Alliance party, Kelantan was governed by the Pan-Islamic party until 1971. Until that time, Kelantan refused to allow the FELDA to open up schemes in the state and at the same time was refused federal grants to implement projects of its own.

The Group Settlement Schemes had a number of deficiencies. First, although it was recommended that the settlements should be established near populated areas, it was discovered that all the areas earmarked were in remote locations because it was difficult to obtain 2000 hectares (the average size of a settlement) near existing towns and villages. Second, since there was no provision for subsistence allowances, the settlers were forced to find alternative sources of income outside the scheme. The result was that the settlers were unable to carry out full-time work on their holdings. Third, because adequate housing facilities were not provided, the settlers tended to live on their agricultural holdings rather than in the prescribed village area. This made it difficult to enforce discipline and supervision. And, finally, the area held by each settler was far too large for the average family to clear and develop, and the tasks were all the more difficult without any financial assistance from the state.

Because of these weaknesses, all states, except Kelantan, quickly abandoned Group Settlement Schemes. Kelantan did manage to open up 25 schemes, with a total area of 32,000 hectares involving approximately 7000 settlers. Although much has been said about the Kelantan projects, it must be stated that the overall performance has been poor, and that during the past few years a good deal of money has been spent rehabilitating them.

## Fringe Alienation Schemes

Fringe Alienation Schemes are implemented by the state governments but financed by federal grants and loans. The idea behind these schemes was to supplement existing uneconomic holdings. They were therefore located near established agricultural settlements.

The fringe schemes were not intended to cover more than 910 hectares, and the participants were to be farmers who already possessed holdings that were not economically viable. In the Malaysian context, uneconomic holdings were defined as those that were less than 3.6 hectares in area. As the schemes were for people already in possession of some agricultural land, they were expected to work in the schemes on a part-time basis while continuing to farm their own holdings. Hence, the participants were expected to commute regularly from their villages. This meant that the schemes could not be situated more than 5 kilometers from the villages.

The government, when it approved the Fringe Alienation Schemes, also decided to allocate 49,560,000 ringgits (M$) as a federal subsidy for the establishment of such schemes for the period 1960–70. The money was to be provided in the form of loans and grants to cover the costs of clearing land. The loans were not to exceed M$815 per hectare to meet the cost of specified items, and interest was to be charged at a rate not exceeding 5 percent per annum, over a period of six years. In addition to the loan, an outright grant was to be made by the federal government equivalent to M$647 per hectare to cover the costs of material and fertilizers. Since no subsistence allowances were to be paid, the loans and grants were the only federal financial commitment.

By the end of 1970, 423 Fringe Alienation Schemes had been established, covering an area of 64,660 hectares with 26,104 participating families (Senftleben 1976). The overall performance of these schemes can be generally described as disappointing. In fact, the federal government was so dissatisfied with the schemes that it had to create a new federal authority, the Federal Land Consolidation and Rehabilitation Authority (FELCRA), in 1966, one of the major functions of which was to rehabilitate and redevelop those fringe schemes that had failed.

The failure of the Fringe Alienation Schemes can be attributed to a number of factors. The requirement that the schemes should not be more than 5 kilometers from the participants' villages was based on the assumption that the participants would not be entirely landless, and would then be able to devote the afternoons to work on their fringe scheme lots. This assumption did not take into account the fact that there was a paucity of land, either contiguous or in close proximity to the villages, for further expansion. Moreover, the mere availability of unutilized land does not necessarily mean that it is suitable for agriculture, because if it were, then it would already have been used for the purpose. The suitable land was therefore located further from the villages, certainly more than 5 kilometers away, which indicated that the very areas that needed fringe schemes were those where land was not available. This is clearly evident from the fact that in Negeri Sembilan and Melaka, some of the schemes are situated more than 30 kilometers from the participants' villages.

The nonresidence of the participants was another factor that had an adverse effect on the development of fringe schemes, and this was aggravated by the fact that the participants had to divide their working time between their previous holdings and the fringe holdings. In the absence of vigilance on the part of the participants, the fringe holdings were subjected to damage from wild animals from the adjoining forests, and to fire hazards, especially during the drought seasons. Part-time work, in addition, was not conducive to adequate maintenance of the young rubber trees, which were in fact neglected due to the participants' divided interest.

Inadequate management and supervision were also partly responsible for the limited success of the fringe schemes. The responsibility for planning and implementing the schemes was given to the district officer and his staff. But their preoccupation with other duties left little time for the administration of the schemes. In addition, the majority of the staff did not have the necessary training and experience for land development work.

## FELDA'S STRATEGY OF IMPLEMENTATION

### Selection of settlers

Since it first began to implement its land development program in the mid–1950s, the government has been aware that the settlers themselves are the most important factor in determining the success or failure of the overall program. Because of the lack of experience, FELDA tried a number of selection systems to ensure that it obtained the right type of settlers.

Prior to the establishment of the Bilut Valley scheme (1959), there was no single or uniform system for the selection of settlers. The general policy guidelines, however, were based on the working party's recommendation that settlers should have the necessary agricultural background or experience for the crop to be grown. As early as 1956 FELDA, in one of its policy statements, admitted that there was no single criterion for selecting persons for development schemes, but indicated that "a family background is probably essential, but the man must also have initiative" (Government of Malaysia 1956).

The preference indicated both by the working party and by the project statements was for applicants with an agricultural background. But while the working party insisted on settlers having actual experience with the crop to be grown in the scheme, FELDA was more flexible and emphasized the need for a general agricultural background. In retrospect, this was a wise move, especially in view of the emphasis on the cultivation of oil palm, which was a limited activity prior to the mid–1960s. FELDA's inclusion of initiative as a characteristic for settlers was important, since it was interested only in those who were "prepared to help themselves." Initiative was certainly one of the vital qualities that a prospective settler was expected to have, but to consider that "the surest sign of initiative is to have saved money for a definite objective," as suggested by the working party (Government of Malaysia, 1956), would have been rather limiting. If having savings had been used as the sole criterion, a high percentage of those who were to be helped by the land development program would have been disqualified. Such a selection or elimination system would certainly have favored those who were already above the poverty level. Given that those without savings were not to be completely left out, evidence of the initiative of such persons had then to be based on the recommendations of the village heads. The experience of Ayer Lanas (Kelantan), however, proved that this system was unreliable, as there was a tendency for recommendations to be given to known troublemakers in the village in order to get rid of them.

During the past 28 years, FELDA has instituted a number of changes in its selection system and procedures.[1] According to its first formalized settler selection system of 1961, prospective participants had to submit their applications on prescribed forms and they had to be:

i. Malaysian citizens or state nationals
ii. Aged 21–50 years
iii. Married, preferably with children

iv. Landless or with rural holdings of less than 0.8 hectares

v. From an agricultural background

vi. Physically fit

Applicants who met the above requirements were first interviewed and then assessed on a points system. The breakdown of this system is shown in Table 4.1. The people to be awarded the most points were those who were landless, around 35 years of age, with a large number of dependents, and physically fit. The maximum score a candidate could obtain was 100, and any candidate obtaining less than 50 points was disqualified.

In 1966 an additional criterion, "without serious criminal records," was added. A maximum of ten points was allotted to applicants who were between 28 and 30 years of age, and the number of points decreased with any rise or fall in age. The family size criterion gave a maximum of five points at the rate of one point per child. Complete landlessness was also awarded a maximum of five points, decreasing to zero for ownership of more than 0.8 hectares. Skills of the applicants played a major role: two points were received for every skill possessed, leading to a maximum of ten points for this criterion. The maximum number of points an applicant could obtain was reduced to 30, and those who obtained less than 15 points were disqualified. In 1967 a further change was made. The maximum number of points a candidate could obtain remained the same, but in order to keep a balance between "suitability" and "need," certain criteria were requantified according to FELDA's requirements.

In 1968 the total number of points assigned was increased to 35, but those who obtained less than 20 points were disqualified, thus indicating a more stringent selection procedure. Those who were under 21 and over 45 were also disqualified. During the period from 1969 to June 1974, the total number of points a candidate could obtain was again brought down to 30, but the disqualification limit of 20 points was maintained. In 1969 the government ruled that only applicants between 18 and 35 years of age would be considered, with the exception of former servicemen, for whom the upper age limit was fixed at 40. The greatest number of points was now allotted to the age factor, and, in response to the government's concern over the high rate of unemployment in the 23–26 age bracket, FELDA gave priority to candidates within this group.

The current settler selection system came into operation in 1974. In contrast to the earlier plans, the present system requires that both husband and wife should be present at the interview. Some extensions and modifications of the earlier criteria have also been made. As before, the selection committee is guided by two major sets of criteria, namely "suitability criteria" (age and skill factors) and "need criteria" (family size and area of land owned).

The age criterion has thus been changed and modified a number of times. The earlier maximum age limit of 50 years was found to be unsuitable from the point of view of the physical capability of the settlers to cope with the arduous task of pioneering, as well as from the point of view of repayment of the loan to FELDA. Rubber plants take at least seven years to mature, and loan repayments have to be made within 15 years after maturity. A settler therefore needs at least 22 years after resettlement to repay FELDA. If he is 50 at the time of resettlement he will be at least 72 before he can clear his debts. The current upper age limit of 35 was therefore considered more appropriate.

The "skills" criterion, too, has undergone some changes. The original "agricultural background" has been extended to include some additional skills, such as business, tailoring, and carpentry. However, the maximum number of points an applicant can obtain is six. Experience in rubber plantations or in oil palm cultivation each secures a maximum of six points, while experience in orchard or vegetable cultivation or animal husbandry each receives one point. Priority is therefore given to those applicants who have the necessary skills to suit the agricultural and trade/service requirements of a FELDA scheme. This has resulted in the selection of settlers from a wide spectrum of backgrounds. Although the majority who apply are agriculturalists and have experience in rubber plantations, a fair percentage from other vocations have also been absorbed into the schemes. Another change introduced in 1974 was the award of a maximum of four points for educational qualifications. The maximum points are normally awarded to those with at least a Lower Certificate of Education (exam taken after the third year in secondary school). The two main reasons for the inclusion of this criterion were (a) to provide employment opportunities for school dropouts and (b) to provide FELDA schemes with a more literate group of settlers, who could participate more meaningfully and constructively in the FELDA development program.

The two "need criteria" (family size and land ownership) are given a maximum of five points each. One point is awarded for every child up to a maximum of five children. The reason for not giving additional consideration for more than five children is the difficulty of maintaining them during the initial period of resettlement when the crops are not yet productive. The ownership of land criterion reflects the government's policy and national objective of giving land to the landless. Applicants without any land of their own are awarded a maximum of five points. From this maximum, the scoring rate is progressively reduced by one point for every 0.2 hectares owned. No points are given to those who possess more than 0.8 hectares of land.

## Physical development of land

Although Malaysia has considerable land resources available for development, the choice of land for settlement is not as simple a matter as it may seem. Almost all land that is suitable for agricultural development and in close proximity to roads and other major communication lines has already been utilized.

As explained earlier, all unalienated land belongs to the state government, and the FELDA is obligated to negotiate with the state government concerned for the release of any land for settlement. When agreement has been reached with respect to location, area layout, suitable crop or crops, premium rent, and survey fees, the state government declares the land a "development area," and upon such declaration the area is vested in the FELDA.

### Settlement size

The extent of land to be developed per scheme is an important consideration. The FELDA prefers the lower size limit of a scheme to be about 1800 hectares for 400 families. Its choice is governed to a large extent by the following considerations:

i. A scheme with 1200–1600 hectares of rubber crop is ideal for management, since the maximum travelling distance for both settlers and staff from the village center would be about 5 kilometers.

ii. A settlement with 400 families would have a population of about 2000 people, which in terms of the government rural development program is a unit that qualifies for the provision of certain essential services such as a clinic, a primary school, and a police post.

iii. With a population of 2000, the investment in the provision of piped water and electricity supply, village roads, and access roads is adequately justified.

iv. A population base of 2000 is adequate to support the development of a small commercial center to service the settlers.

The size of holding per settler family, on the other hand, is governed by income and employment factors. Each settler family is given 4 hectares of agricultural land and a piece of residential lot (0.1 hectares). Thus, taking into account the land needed for community infrastructure, each settlement works out to the FELDA's figure of approximately 1800 hectares. The limit of 4 hectares is based on the premise that the size of holding must be within the handling capacity of the settler and his immediate family.

Another consideration that affects the size of a scheme is the commutable distance to the various plots assigned to settlers. Since the settlers live on their house lots located in the central village, the larger the area of the scheme, the longer will be the commuting distance between the houses and the agricultural lots. But the FELDA is aware that the settlers should not travel more than 5 or 6 kilometers to their respective agricultural lots, as their efficiency will be affected by a longer commuting distance. These considerations govern the maximum size of a single scheme, which is limited to about 2600 hectares for 600 families. The present tendency, however, is to develop larger areas of about 4000 hectares, especially for oil palm and sugar cane, so that processing units can be established within the schemes. Unlike rubber, which is ecologically a suitable peasant crop, oil palm is subject to greater economies of scale. The establishment of the processing units within the schemes also eliminates unique delays in transporting the harvested crop to the plant.

The above size concepts have not been static. In 1961, for example, the government decided that all areas with more than 800 hectares of available land were to be earmarked for development by the FELDA. Such a decision clearly indicates that the FELDA was expected to develop areas as small as 800 hectares. The consultants for the Jengka Triangle development had recommended that settlement units of 100 families per 480 hectares should be planned, as opposed to the FELDA's settlement units of 400 to 600 families. The FELDA disagreed with the recommended size, because it would have resulted either in far higher infrastructure costs at the existing standard or in a reduced standard of services, when the same number of persons could have been settled in larger units and provided with standard FELDA services. The FELDA also felt that if with the same investment a larger area could be developed and a larger number of settler families maintained at an efficient level, then it was economically unsound to accept a smaller area.

Although the FELDA's experience led it to oppose any reduction in the minimum size of the settlement unit, it favored an increase in the maximum size, especially for oil palm projects. According to the FELDA, the internal rate of return on a project of about 6000 hectares worked out at 13.9 percent, and this was expected to be 2 percent higher if the area was increased by another 1600 hectares. This increase is made possible through savings on the infrastructural development, such as access roads. For this reason, at least, the FELDA prefers larger projects. Despite the development of larger blocks of land with the aim of achieving greater economy in processing, the size of the settlement unit of 400 to 600 families was retained by the FELDA. Though the total land area developed in a contiguous block might be 8000 hectares, it would contain four settlement units of approximately 2000 hectares each. As a result of the Pahang Tenggara regional development studies, however, it has been decided to increase the size of settlement units whenever conditions are suitable.

*Site selection*

In the selection of development sites, the FELDA pursues a policy of making an initial technical investigation into the suitability of the land. Accordingly, the major considerations determining the choice of an area for development are:

a. *Ownership of land*. It is necessary to ascertain whether the area is state land (or forest reserve that is to be cleared) free of occupation. The normal policy is to avoid including occupied land within the boundary of a scheme. But sometimes it may be found that within an extensive area of undeveloped and unalienated land there are a few occupied lots that interfere with the proper implementation of the project plan. For example, two main considerations in the siting of a village are that it should be central and built on gently sloping land. These requirements invariably limit the choice of sites, thus compelling the FELDA to acquire occupied lots that happen to be located within the proposed village sites. Similar constraints apply to nursery sites, which require a flat piece of land with a reliable water supply. Should there be any such lots, either the state government is required to acquire the lot and compensate the persons affected, or alternatively, if the persons affected have the necessary qualifications, they can be settled in the scheme or elsewhere.

b. *Soil suitability*. Consideration of the nature and quality of the soil is important if the objective is to raise the settler's income. Any relaxation of standards of soil fertility adversely affects the settler's future as well as the country's economy. Soil suitability clearance is given by the Department of Agriculture, which provides a soil map of the area indicating not only the soil types and their characteristics, but also the particular crops for which the soil is best suited.

c. *Mineral clearance*. It is the government's view that deposits of valuable minerals such as tin, iron, and bauxite are important natural resources, and that steps should be taken to ensure that any economically viable mineral deposits are not left unexploited because of agricultural development. Land is released for development only if the Director of Geological Surveys and the Chief Inspector of Mines have issued a mineral clearance certificate.

d. *Forest clearance*. The Forest Department must also give a clearance certificate for the release of the area after completion of logging. Logging is organized under the direction of the Forest Department, which has its own system of exploiting the resources, and the FELDA is not involved in the process. This ensures that state revenue from valuable timber is not lost as a result of jungle clearing for agricultural development. Forest clearance is given only when the Department is satisfied that the area has been adequately logged.

e. *Accessibility*. One of the criteria adopted by the FELDA in developing a new area is the cost of constructing an access road from an existing main road to the scheme. The cost would be prohibitive if long stretches of access roads had to be built through inaccessible terrain. On the other hand, if the access road is very long and costly, the project must be proportionately larger to justify its construction. Although the cost of constructing the road is not borne by the FELDA, and is not directly chargeable to the cost of the project, alternative uses of government funds have to be considered. Under these circumstances, remote pockets of land suitable for only one settlement unit are not considered for development unless other pressing factors, such as security, demand it. Lately the FELDA has in fact been moving further into the interior, but for reasons of cost effectiveness its projects in such locations have multiple settlement units.

The preliminary investigations require much tact and patience, for they need the cooperation of not less than 12 government departments and agencies responsible to some eight different ministries.

### Pattern of scheme development

Once an area is selected, the program for implementation is set in motion. Prior to 1966, the development of FELDA schemes took place in different phases. Table 4.2 shows the pattern of development of a pre-1966 FELDA scheme for 400 settler families. The first year was devoted to the felling, clearing, and planting of the village area of about 300 acres (120 hectares) and approximately 1000 acres (400 hectares) of the main crop, allowing for 10 percent unplantable area. The remaining land for the main crop was developed in subsequent annual stages of approximately 1000 to 1500 acres (400-600 hectares). The subsidiary crop areas were developed at a later period, as decided by the FELDA, subject to the progress made in the development of land for the main crop.

This pattern, known as "phased development," was evolved by the FELDA through experience gathered from the Ayer Lanas (1958) and Bilut Valley (1959) schemes. This background knowledge aided the FELDA's decision-making with reference to future land clearing and development. A number of reasons were given for carrying out the work in phases. The experience obtained and lessons learned in the first phase (especially regarding terrain, soil variation, water conditions, etc.) could be profitably utilized in the subsequent phases. Another reason for development in phases was staggered forestry clearance, because the Forest Department was not always able to release a large area of 1200–2400 hectares in one season.

Since 1966, a changeover to the development of larger areas has been evident. A number of factors were responsible for this break with earlier practice. The government's desire to accelerate land development made it imperative that larger areas be made available. The emphasis on oil palm also made the development of larger areas desirable in order to realize the benefits of economies of scale. In the past, logging delays had prevented land becoming rapidly available. But with the higher demand for tropical timbers, logging and extraction rates increased, making it possible to obtain larger areas for new schemes. In addition, the increase in management and contractural experience made it possible to develop larger areas at a faster rate. In this connection it is worth noting that in the Second Malaysia Plan period (1971–75), the FELDA cleared in one planting season planned settlements of 2400 hectares and over.

In the early FELDA-financed schemes, such as Ayer Lanas, Sungei Tiang, Batu Lapan, Bukit Tembaga, and Guar Nepai, there was complete settler participation in the initial development of the schemes from felling to planting, as well as in the building of houses. This method, however, was found to be uneconomical in view of the fact that in some schemes the settlers were able to clear only half the required area. While a date for the completion of a task could be stipulated, its actual completion depended entirely on the ability and willingness of the settlers. The result was that in some cases projects had to be extended from six to eight years. Consequently, in 1958, jungle clearing was given out on contract, while ground preparations (lining, holing, terracing, and planting) and house construction continued to be carried out by the settlers.

The contract method was first adopted in the Bilut Valley scheme, Phase I. This method did overcome the problem of the extension of the development period by two years, which would have been inevitable if the work had been done by the settlers. But the result was still far from satisfactory. Although the clearing was done on contract, the planting and associated work had to be carried out by the settlers themselves. The settlers were unskilled and the volume of work involved, from the time the settlers moved into the scheme to the time of planting, was high. In order to maintain the necessary motivation to work in the new environment, the settlers needed to be provided with an incentive in the form of returns, with the least possible delay. The longer the delay in the returns, the greater the insecurity among the settlers and the less their efficiency. In view of the importance of ensuring a good start with proper planting of the main crops, the FELDA decided to extend contract work to include planting, several months' maintenance, and the construction of settlers' houses. This method, which was introduced in all schemes by the end of 1960, was considered more economical in the long run.

It can certainly be argued that the introduction of contract work can bring about a maldistribution of income benefiting the contractor and jeopardizing the generation of rural incomes. But this issue needs to be examined in the context of the financial implications of the extension of the target period by two years. The FELDA also ensures that its investment in agricultural development is not dissipated away from the rural sector. This is achieved by stipulating that whenever possible at least 50 percent of the contracted labor force shall be recruited from among the settlers or their dependants. To ensure that the best contractors are employed at the best price, they are employed by public tender. The prospective tenderers are given first-hand knowledge of the location, type of jungle, terrain, accessibility, availability of labor, and other prevailing conditions in the field by the FELDA officers. This leads to realistic quotations for the various types of work by the tenderers. Furthermore, the FELDA ensures that tendered quotations do not permit the contractor to make more than what the FELDA considers to be a fair profit. This is achieved by encouraging as many suitable contractors as possible to tender, and by rejecting those tenders above the estimated fair price. With the gathering of experience over the years, detailed specifications have been drawn up for the various works, and the FELDA ensures that these works are carried out according to the specifications under strict supervision by the resident staff.

The result of this dependence on contractors is that the pace of development of any scheme largely depends on the capacity of the contractors to meet the schedule of work set out in the contract agreement. The information available shows that very few schemes have been successfully planted as scheduled. Most delays have been due to one or a combination of the following factors: (i) late nursery preparation, (ii) failure to have the field prepared for planting, (iii) adverse weather conditions, and (iv) late timber extraction.

Evidence also shows that any delay in the development work is usually accompanied by substandard or irregular performance by contractors. It must be admitted, however, that very little can be done if the contractors do not have the capacity to carry out the work on time. In many cases, delays are caused by difficult access and a shortage of skilled labor. Occasionally they are due to the awarding of contracts to untried contractors or allowing them to accept work far beyond their normal capacity. The FELDA is of the opinion, however, that the use of untried contractors is a risk that has to be taken in order to foster competition, and to prevent a few already well-established contractors obtaining a monopoly in FELDA development work. Through this policy the FELDA has been able to build up a pool of contractors who are available and ready to respond to the FELDA's enlarged development program.

The contractors also maintain the agricultural area during the period from the establishment of crop to settlers' entry. From the moment of entry the settlers are kept fully occupied with the following tasks: (i) organizing the households; (ii) planting vegetables and other short-term crops in their 0.1-hectare house lot; (iii) maintaining the agricultural area, which involves keeping the planted rows clean and free of detrimental growth by constant weeding; and (iv) carrying out other common tasks within the village and agricultural area.

Before the main crop comes into production, which is about six years for rubber and three years for oil palm, the settlers cultivate minor cash crops as well as maintaining the main crop.

## Settlers' cultural practices

There have been many changes in settlers' cultural practices in the field. In the initial years it was considered that collective work over the whole area would be a good idea, since it would encourage mutual cooperation among the settlers. However, this was found to be unsatisfactory. Subsequently, each settler was allocated his own plot to work on. It was hoped that this would create a pride of ownership among the settlers, and would not only motivate them to work harder, but would also involve other members of their families in the maintenance of their plots. Unfortunately, even this strategy did not bring about the desired result. In fact, very few of the settlers brought along members of their families to help them. The degree of maintenance of plots, therefore, varied over a wide range in every block of the scheme. The consequent result was the introduction of the block method in all schemes in 1962.

This method requires the settlers to work in groups of between 15 and 20 on blocks ranging from 40 to 80 hectares during the first, second, and third year of planting. They carry out weeding, fertilizing, and pest and disease control under the guidance of FELDA staff. Such a procedure serves two purposes. First, it becomes essentially a training period, and second, it ensures that the terrain and the crops are well maintained. With proper maintenance, the trees tend to mature early and to give the expected yield in later years, which is important to the settlers' income. Under this method each settler works in the same block until he is allocated an individual lot within the block he has been working on. Some of the other advantages of adopting the block method can be summarized as follows:

i. Growth and maintenance in each block is uniform.

ii. Expenditure in each block is shared equally by the settlers working on that block.

iii. Costs involved in the rectification of damage from pests, fire, and other natural calamities in any part of the block can be shared equally.

iv. Eviction of any settler, if it become necessary, is easier.

v. Should a settler slacken in his work, the common opinion of the rest of the block members can weigh against him and induce him to work harder.

vi. Sufficient time is available to carry out proper surveys to ensure that individual lots are demarcated in an equitable manner.

Under this method, each settler is allocated by ballot his individual lot. By the time the settlers receive their individual lots the trees are about four years old, and as the settlers usually gain in experience, they are by then capable of managing on their own. From this stage the settlers maintain their holdings individually, with continuous guidance from the FELDA staff.

In the oil palm schemes, the block system has been further extended to include the concept of cooperative land ownership, whereby the settlers are not given or allocated their individual holdings, but have a uniform and equal share in the ownership and profits of the block holding. The inexperience of the settlers with oil palm and the complex organization involved in its cultivation were the two important considerations that led to the adoption of this method.

## Management and administration

The FELDA is one of the largest statutory bodies in Malaysia and is a complex organization. The total staff strength of 18,570 at the end of 1982 is in marked contrast to its ten employees in 1958 (Table 4.3). This increase in staff strength is not only an indication of the vast increases in its activities in opening up new land, but is also a reflection of the diversification of its other services and commercial functions. This growth has been made possible because of the FELDA's flexibility in making organizational changes whenever they are needed. In 1974, for example, the FELDA established a Transport Service Company, since it was felt that it needed to have its own haulage facilities to transport crop output to the mills and ports for export. In 1982, with 168 tankers, 43 cargo lorries, 11 loaders, 37 tractors, and 87 trailers stationed at the Chuping Sugar Cane Project, it is one of the biggest such companies in the country. Other corporations that were established to meet new service requirements include FELDA Stores Corporation, which carries out retail trading in the schemes (by the end of 1982 it had 205 outlets); FELDA Marketing Corporation, established in 1972, which handles the sale of produce from its land schemes, mills, and factories, and maintains offices in London and New York; FELDA Latex Handling Corporation, also established in 1972, which provides storage and export facilities for latex concentrate; and FELDA Mills Corporation, established in 1975 to look after the operation of all FELDA's mills, five rubber factories, and bulking installations. It operates 39 oil palm mills, five rubber factories, two bulking installations, and one cocoa processing factory, making it the largest single processing organization in Malaysia.

Since the settlement scheme is the most important unit of production within the complex FELDA organization, it is necessary to have some understanding of its management structure. As has been indicated earlier, an average scheme has an area of some 1800 hectares. A typical scheme staff of 23 persons consists of the following:

1 manager
1 assistant manager
4 field supervisors
8 field assistants
3 settler development assistants
2 clerks
2 secretaries
1 driver
1 office boy

The manager has overall responsibility for the scheme and, together with some of the other staff, has to be in the scheme well ahead of the arrival of the settlers. The field staff usually supervise the agricultural activities, while the settler development assistants are responsible for the settlers' welfare and social and community affairs, including nutrition, family planning, youth clubs, kindergartens, and the Women's Institute. Adequate field and social workers are essential to the proper administration and smooth development of a scheme. Without adequate and trained field staff, the physical and agricultural work is greatly hampered, and the income of the settlers will eventually be affected. Such weaknesses have been observed to be a major factor in the failure of other types of land development scheme in Malaysia. The FELDA usually makes sure that it has adequate staff, especially at the scheme level.

During the first decade of its existence, the FELDA paid less attention to settlers' welfare. This often led to discontent among settlers. However, recognizing the urgency of taking more responsibility for settlers' welfare and social affairs, a Settler Development Division was created in 1967 which has now become a fully fledged department of the FELDA. The FELDA's Social Development Program operates on the premise that a change in settlers' values, attitudes, and behavior is essential to ensure the fulfilment of both the economic and the social objectives of land settlement. Thus, the FELDA is concerned not only with "economic agricultural holdings," but equally with the development of human resources to encourage achievement-oriented settlers.

The formal establishment of the Scheme Development Committee (SDC) in 1967 provided the FELDA with the required organizational structure and a system for settler participation. Considered as the highest decision-making body of the settlers at the scheme level, the SDC is made up of elected representatives of the settlers. Twenty settlers working in a block, and residing in close proximity within the village area, elect a block leader to represent them on the SDC, which also includes some *ex officio* members such as the local headmaster, the *imam* (religious head), and the police representative. The SDC meetings are chaired by the scheme manager. The vice-chairman, secretary, and treasurer are chosen from among the settlers' block leaders, and it is usually the intention that a settlers' leader will eventually take over from the scheme manager as chairman of the SDC.

The SDC meets every month to discuss progress and problems affecting the development of the scheme. It also coordinates the activities of other settler bodies such as the youth club, the Women's Institute, and the cooperative.

The system of settler representation through the SDC was further extended in 1976 with the establishment of the Regional Federation of Settlers Development Committees and the National Federation of Settlers Development Committees. The vice-chairmen of all SDCs within a region are represented on the regional federation of SDCs. The area controller acts as the chairman of the executive committee of the Regional Federation, with the regional settlers development officer as secretary/ treasurer. The post of vice-chairman and assistant secretary and five other members of the executive committee are filled by settlers. The chairman of the Regional Federation, together with the vice-chairman and assistant secretary, are represented on the National Federation, which is chaired by the FELDA's director-general.

During their quarterly meetings, the Regional and National Federations discuss policies, progress, and problems connected with the development of the schemes. A very important role of the National Federation is to review the FELDA's policies and programs, and to make proposals and recommendations aimed at further improving the administration and management of settlers and their land schemes.

## ACHIEVEMENTS AND ASSESSMENT

### Area developed

The area of land developed and planted by the FELDA makes it the most important government agency in the field of land settlement. This is clearly recognized by the government, as indicated by the area allocated to be developed by the FELDA during the current development period (1981–85) and during the decade of 1971–80 (Table 4.4).

By the end of 1982, the FELDA had implemented 331 schemes with a total of 1,383,528 acres (559,906 hectares) of agricultural land and 93,527 acres (37,850 hectares) of urban and residential land (Table 4.5). Oil palm and rubber were the major crops, occupying some 60.6 and 29.3 percent of the total agricultural area, respectively.

The FELDA has made a number of significant contributions to the development and diversification of agriculture in Malaysia. The area developed and maintained by the FELDA constitutes approximately 12 percent of peninsular Malaysia's cultivated land. Although it has helped to create a community of modern and relatively prosperous rubber smallholders, the expansion in the cultivation of oil palm is its greatest contribution.

Before 1960, oil palm cultivation was comparatively insignificant in Malaysia. But its rapid expansion from 54,634 hectares in 1960 to 1,170,038 hectares in 1982 indicates the current importance of the crop in the national economy. Although the oil palm industry is comparatively new in Malaysia, today it is the second largest user of agricultural land after rubber. This expansion is due both to the replanting of rubber estates with oil palm and to the planting of newly developed land. The switch from rubber to oil palm, especially in estates, started in the early 1960s because of the decline in rubber prices. From the investor's point of view, oil palm is preferred because it has a shorter gestation period. The payback period for rubber is estimated to be 12 to 15 years, whereas for oil palm it is 8 to 10 years.

By the end of 1982, the FELDA had resettled 43,978 settlers on its oil palm schemes, and these are responsible for producing 4,734,605 tons of palm oil, representing nearly 30 percent of Malaysia's total production. The newly established smallholders are playing a significant role in making Malaysia the biggest producer of oil palm in the world. The FELDA has successfully shown that traditional peasant farmers can be turned into modern agriculturalists if given the proper guidance and opportunities.

## Settler intake

Although the FELDA has been highly successful in developing land, its program of placing settlers has been relatively slower. In 1960, the FELDA's intention was to resettle 4,662 families, but it was able to place only 1,981. During the Second Malaysia Plan (1961–65), the FELDA set an ambitious target of 24,000 familes for resettlement, but it was able to settle only 6,083 (Table 4.6). Based on the experience of the previous plan period, it set itself a more practical target of 12,745 families during the

First Malaysia Plan, and was able to settle 11,863. During the 1971–75 plan period, the target was 20,000 families, but the FELDA recruited only 13,779. During the Third Malaysia Plan period, however, the FELDA resettled 15.9 percent more than its target. And during the current plan period, the FELDA has been able to exceed its target figure of 6,000 families annually by 500 and 219 in 1981 and 1982, respectively.

The early shortfalls in settler intake can be largely attributed to delays in the preparatory work, especially in the provision of infrastructure such as roads, water supply, and housing. This was due mainly to contract delays resulting from the employment of inexperienced contractors, the short supply of timber for the construction of houses, and the difficulties in obtaining skilled workers at the remote sites where the majority of the FELDA schemes were located.

Be that as it may, the provision of basic infrastructural facilities, such as administration, community centers and services, offices, public utilities, and commercial and industrial centers, appears to be one of the major factors that attract and retain the settlers in the schemes. Land is also allocated for other amenities such as a marketplace, cooperative building, post office, or stalls, with a view to intensifying the suburbanization process of the scheme community. Table 4.7 shows the extent and distribution of infrastructural facilities in FELDA schemes.

## Settlers' previous occupations

In order to gain a clear understanding of the progress made by the settlers as a result of participating in FELDA projects, an examination of their previous occupations would be useful. Based on information gathered from a census carried out among FELDA settlers in 1976, more than 68 percent of the settlers were agriculturalists or closely connected with agricultural activities before moving to the settlements (Table 4.8). This relatively high percentage is to be expected because of the earlier bias in favor of such applicants in the selection criteria. Also prominent were former servicemen and people engaged as laborers. The relatively high percentage of former servicemen (9.1 percent) can be explained by the fact that 10 percent of places are reserved for them. Among those who were laborers prior to their entry into the schemes (10.9 percent), the majority actually had no fixed vocation and included casual workers and part-time agriculturalists. In addition, there were 4.1 percent who were previously unemployed.

## Settlers' income

At the outset it must be pointed out that during the first few years after entry into the schemes average settlers' income is usually lower than they were receiving previously. This is because the settlers receive only a subsistence allowance of about M$100 per month during the pre-production stage of three to five years (Table 4.9). After this stage, however, the average income increases with the period of residence in the scheme. The last column shows that the increase in real income after 10 to 12 years' residence in a FELDA scheme is between 50 and 74 percent. In interpreting these figures, it is essential to remember that the income figures given in columns 3 to 6 do not refer to the same settlers as entered in 1976, whose pre-entry income is considered (Mariam Omar Din 1981: 34–37). It can be observed that a poor rural farmer of any age who decided to join a FELDA scheme appears to have experienced, after an initial financial setback prior to production of crops, a steady increase in the level of real income of between 50 and 74 percent, compared with farmers of the same age who did not join the FELDA schemes, but who might have been benefiting from other rural development programs during the same period (Mariam Omar Din 1981).

Among other things, the total income earned by a settler is determined by the world market price of the commodity concerned and the size of holding allocated to him. The net average monthly income of a settler in an oil palm scheme organized under the block system was M$624 in 1982, compared with M$642 in 1981. The respective figures for rubber schemes were M$492 and M$402 (Table 4.10).

While the average income of rural workers in Malaysia increased from M$200 per month in 1970 to M$355 in 1980, the comparative figures for the average urban worker were M$428 and M$675, respectively. Although the income of the FELDA settlers in rubber schemes is still well below urban levels, the income of the oil palm settler is definitely comparable. This would therefore suggest that FELDA should review its land allocation policy for future settlers in rubber schemes.

### Settlers' loan repayment

According to Section 8 of the Land Development Ordinance, 1956, the FELDA was required to recover from the settlers any amount it spent on the development of a scheme, including the costs of developing the agricultural holdings, settlers' subsistence allowances, and expenditure on basic services like roads, office buildings, and management. The loan was to be repaid in 15 years, starting from the maturing of the crop, with a 6.25 percent interest rate.

It has been estimated that the FELDA spends approximately M$26,600 to resettle one family. The breakdown of costs is shown in Table 4.11. The settlers are obliged to repay the following costs:

i.    cost of jungle clearing, preparation of land and planting of the main crop, including maintenance by contractors until settlers' entry;

ii.  cost of development of house sites and construction of houses;

iii.  cost of maintenance including materials, subsistence allowance before crop production, fertilizer and chemicals, and tools and equipment during the immaturity period of the main crop.

In addition, the settlers have to pay land rent and premiums after the main crop matures.

The settlers are fully aware that their loan obligations must be met in full before they are issued with titles to their holdings, but repayment of the loan can be difficult, especially when the prices of rubber and oil palm are low. Under such circumstances the FELDA sometimes has to modify its system of loan recovery.

Despite declining commodity prices, the collection of loan repayments can be considered satisfactory. The first batch of settlers fully repaid their loans and were awarded their land titles in 1977, exactly 21 years after the establishment of the FELDA. By the end of 1982, a total of 2,724 settlers, comprising 1,822 rubber settlers and 902 oil palm settlers, had fully repaid their loans. In 1982, the FELDA collected a total of M$75,708,442 from the settlers in the form of loan repayments. During that year the collection rate was 91.2 percent from the oil palm settlers and 67.6 percent from rubber settlers (FELDA, *1982 Annual Report*, p. 16).

The cost of M$26,600 to resettle one family on a FELDA scheme is very high. This seems to be the reason for the common comment that the FELDA settlers are being pampered and spoon-fed, especially when they are not required to do the arduous work of clearing the jungle and planting crops. What is seldom remembered is that when FELDA started its first group projects in the mid-1950s, its system of development was similar to, if not modeled on, the neighboring programs where settlers were brought in at the beginning and were fully responsible for clearing the jungle, constructing their houses, and planting and maintaining their crops. We have already discussed the undesirable results of this system. Those early schemes were characterized by poor jungle clearing, delays in planting, poor crop maintenance, and high dropout rates. Even to this day, some of the early schemes have not been completely rehabilitated.

While the FELDA model may not be considered appropriate for other countries, the so-called pioneering and self-help schemes have been found to be unworkable in Malaysia. Given the increasing trend toward labor shortages in the rural areas of Malaysia, without the kind of capital investment put in by the FELDA, no landless person in Malaysia would now be prepared to undertake the sort of pioneering work that is done by his counterparts elsewhere. It must also be remembered that the Malaysian model has shown satisfactory loan repayment and a relatively low dropout rate of less than 5 percent among settlers, some of whom were actually asked to leave the schemes for disciplinary reasons.

## Population redistribution

Unlike many land settlement programs in other countries, population redistribution does not feature in Malaysia's land development program. It was never the intention of the government to move excess population from one part of the country to another more sparsely populated part. It is for this reason that the place of origin is not taken into consideration in the selection of settlers. It is only considered in the context of the implementation of the quota system, whereby most states insist that at least 50 percent of settler places in schemes located in that state should be reserved for its state "nationals." Nevertheless, resettlement does involve the transfer of people and therefore has an impact on population redistribution.

Table 4.12 gives the origin and state of residence of those persons who were settled between 1957 and September 1983. Numerically, the total migration is much greater, as marriage is a necessary qualification for selection as a settler and having children is given added priority. The data show that intrastate migration is far more widespread than interstate migration, involving 77.7 percent of all FELDA settlers. Only 22.3 percent have been resettled in another state. One of the major reasons for the low incidence of interstate resettlement is the system of selection and emplacement of settlers. As has already been indicated, states usually insist that at least 50 percent of the settlers in each scheme should be their own state nationals. Because the number of applicants from each state (except Pahang) always exceeds the number of places available, the number of allocations to out-of-state residents is usually small. It may be noted, however, that even land-rich states such as Pahang, Johor, and Terengganu have some of their settlers resettled in another state. This is probably for administrative and settlers' convenience, since most of these live very close to state boundaries. It is more convenient, for example to resettle applicants from west Pahang or northern Johor in schemes in Negeri Sembilan than in their own respective states. It may also be noted that as a consequence of the agreed quota system, applicants from Pahang have a better chance of being selected for settlement within Pahang than those from Selangor, Melaka, or Perak, where land available for development is limited. It has even been suggested that many potential settlers have found it convenient in recent years to find employment for a period of five years in Pahang, whereafter they can apply for admittance to the FELDA under that state's quota, for which there is no waiting list, thereby short-circuiting the lengthy delays in placement experienced by applicants from land-poor states (Blair and Noor 1981: 4).

Thus it appears that so far land settlement has not made any great impact on population redistribution in Malaysia. The only exception is in Pahang, which has absorbed 14,572 families from other states, particularly Kedah, Kelantan, Perak, Selangor, and Pinang. As it is planned to open up more land in Pahang, and as fewer applicants are forthcoming from within the state, the out-of-state contribution will definitely increase. Another state that may possibly receive a higher proportion of out-of-state settlers in the future is Negeri Sembilan. What resettlement has achieved during the past two and a half decades, however, is to give potential rural–urban migrants the alternative of remaining in the rural areas rather than migrating to the already crowded major towns. It must be noted, however, that because of the ethnic-biased selection criteria adopted by the FELDA, land development in fact stimulates the mobility of Malays and at the same time directs their movement back into the rural areas (Chan 1983).

Since intrastate migration appears to be the main feature in the pattern of mobility among FELDA settlers, a deeper understanding of this phenomenon would be useful. In the 1976 FELDA settler census, a question was asked concerning the distance a settler had moved from his previous home (Table 4.13). This revealed a clear tendency for more recent settlers to have moved over a greater distance than their earlier counterparts. Of settlers entering FELDA schemes between 1957 and 1961, 76 percent had migrated 50 miles (80 kilometers) or less, as against 60 percent, 31 percent, and 26 percent, respectively, in the three subsequent periods. In sharp contrast, only 6 percent had migrated over 200 miles (320 kilometers) in the first period, as against 7 percent in the fourth period, 24 percent in the third period, and 25 percent in the fourth period. This dramatic swing to longer-distance migration is partly a reflection of the acceleration of FELDA's development program, especially in the more remote areas, which were previously inaccessible (Blair and Noor 1981).

### Second-generation migration

After a period of time, when the original settlers' children have entered the labor market, many of them will inevitably have to move out of the schemes in search of employment. Although no detailed census data are available to illustrate this situation, information is available from a survey of 829 settler households carried out during 1977–78 in several FELDA schemes at different stages of development.

Table 4.14 shows the place of residence of the children of the interviewed settlers. As would be expected, the vast majority of children under 15 years lived with their parents on the scheme. The percentage of nonresident children increases with age, reaching 100 percent for females over 36. This is not surprising, as females who marry are usually expected to follow their husbands. The patterns for the males is quite interesting. About a quarter of male children between the ages of 16 and 20, and more than half of those over 20, had left home at the time of the survey. It would be reasonable to assume that a good percentage of these out-migrants head for the towns (Blair and Noor 1981).

The availability of better educational facilities in the schemes, and the provision of financial and other assistance for more advanced educational and vocational training, encourage them to choose the urban areas for their place of employment and residence. MacAndrews and Yamamoto estimated that between 1957 and 1990 a total of 126, 386 settlers' dependents would enter the Malaysian labor force (Table 4.15). However, a great deal of research still needs to be done on second-generation settlers.

## CONCLUSIONS

After 26 years Malaysia can claim that it has planned and implemented a satisfactory land settlement program that has also become a significant instrument for the economic development of the country as a whole. While land settlement has done something to ameliorate the adverse conditions that existed, it has also had a favorable impact on the national economy. FELDA-type schemes have attracted a great deal of attention from those involved in similar programs elsewhere. This does not in any way mean that the program as it exists today is perfect and in due course will solve all the problems of the rural sector. As observed earlier, by the end of 1982 the FELDA had only been able to resettle 76,782 families, and many more applications are waiting to be processed. A great deal more therefore needs to be done, and new demands and challenges will have to be met.

One of the main issues of importance for the future planning and implementation of land settlement schemes is the availability of land for development. According to the Third Malaysia Plan (1976–80), there are 2 million hectares of land suitable for agricultural purposes awaiting development. This is the area available after due allowance has been made for the requirements of forestry and ecological conservation. In addition, another 800,000 hectares of alienated land suitable for agriculture has yet to be developed for crop production. At the present rate of land development in Malaysia, a time will come in the near future, at most in 20 years, when the existing land area will not have the resilience to adjust itself to the influences of population pressures. This is evident from the growth in landlessness and the steadily increasing demand for land. A long-term strategy for the whole country is therefore vital at this stage. In this connection one of the more important tasks is the preparation of a national master plan for the development of the fast-depleting land resources. This should be based on an in-depth study of the quality and quantity of land available.

Directly related to the issue of opening up new land is the amount of idle land in the already established rural areas. It has been reported that, for one reason or another, there are perhaps 1 million hectares of already alienated land that were previously under cultivation but have now been abandoned. The significance of this vast area of idle land can be realized when we take note that the FELDA, despite its impressive record, has been able to develop only 594,900 hectares in its 26 years of operation. To date, the process of developing new land has never been related to what happens to the land in the original villages. It is quite likely that the transfer of farmers to the FELDA and other schemes contributes to the abandonment of land elsewhere. For long-term land planning purposes it would therefore be pertinent for the government to look at the opening up of new land and the utilization of idle land together. One way to generate a more balanced development is for the government to take over the land left behind by the settlers for redistribution among those left behind. Some kind of compensation could be arranged. In this way, those left behind could hope to increase their landholdings and their income. The settlers, on the other hand, could use the money obtained either to pay back their loan or to help them during the initial years of resettlement.

A second issue is the size of landholdings. It was mentioned at the outset that one of the main aims of the Malaysian land settlement program is to provide the settlers with incomes comparable to those obtained by their urban counterparts. Consequently, the various land development agencies are confronted with the problem of creating economically viable farms. Each settler must be given a farm of sufficient size to ensure an adequate return on his labor and other inputs.

During the past 26 years, however, the FELDA has modified the size of agricultural holdings allotted to its settlers. A 2.5-hectare holding planted with rubber was considered adequate during the formative years of the FELDA. Later, during the 1970s, increases in the size of holdings to 5 and 6 hectares for rubber and oil palm, respectively, were deemed necessary in order to meet the objective of providing the resettled families with a "fair income." Although such changes were necessary, the size of holdings cannot be increased indefinitely in the future for two main reasons. First, the changes in holding size have created inequalities in landholdings among the FELDA's own settlers, and this in turn is likely to create several problems. Adequate steps therefore need to be taken to reduce inequalities in landholdings. This could be done by allocating additional land close to the project, if available, prior to its alienation to other agencies or individuals. In fact, the FELDA has increased the size of holdings in some of the early schemes by developing the reserve areas. Second, land available for development is limited in Malaysia. Under these circumstances an optimum size has to be worked out whereby the limited resources can be used to benefit the maximum number of people without depressing family incomes to the poverty level. This could even require an overall review of the concept of resettlement in the future, in order to meet the changing situation in the country.

Provision for second- and third-generation settlers is another important issue. Recently land development has been widely talked about as a measure to reduce rural–urban migration. Although it was not intended, it is evident that the program in Malaysia has played an indirect role here in that it has made it possible for potential rural–urban migrants to be directed to another rural setting. The exodus to the town has thus to some extent been reduced. But it has also been observed that resettlement can play only a temporary role in combating rural–urban migration. After a generation or two, the schemes will themselves experience overcrowding unless adequate measures are taken. Since only one member of the family can inherit the land, the rest of the second and third generations will have to leave the schemes to look for work elsewhere. Under such circumstances, early action to establish agro-based industries in the schemes or their immediate environs would be necessary. Urban-based industries and activities should be part and parcel of land development planning in Malaysia. In a sense, this would allow the FELDA to play a more significant role in the process of urbanizing the rural areas. If the FELDA-type of land development is to function effectively as an urbanizing agent, then it must offer a socio-economic environment that is different from the traditional rural one. The social, economic, and commercial structure must be different, and it must offer opportunities for competitive endeavors, as are usually found in the urban centers in the country (Chan 1983).

A fourth issue to be considered is the future role of the FELDA staff in the schemes. As more and more settlers complete their loan repayments and are issued titles to their individual holdings, it would be expected that settlers' participation in the management and administration of the scheme would be intensified. The FELDA must necessarily withdraw, although withdrawal need not be total or abrupt. The reduced number of FELDA supervisory staff could take on new roles and functions. One function through which the FELDA could contribute further to the development of the settler communities would be by acting as an intermediary between them and other government agencies. The FELDA could help the settlers obtain better facilities such as credit, health, and education, besides, of course, being responsible for the replanting of their holdings and the processing and marketing of their products.

Overall, it would be reasonable to conclude that the land development program in Malaysia, as planned and implemented by the FELDA, has achieved the objectives formulated in the mid–1950s. It can even be said that the achievements are beyond expectations, especially when viewed against the poor record of land development and settlement in many other developing countries. One of the main factors that has contributed to the achievements of the FELDA is its flexible approach at each phase of development. It is hoped that this flexible approach will continue to be utilized, both in the opening up of new schemes and in dealing with new sets of problems, particularly those concerning second-generation settlers.

## NOTE

1. This discussion is largely based on Bahrin and Perera (1977).

## BIBLIOGRAPHY

Alias, R. M. 1982. "Productivity in Agriculture." *Land Development Digest* (Kuala Lumpur) 5, no. 1 (December): 1–14.

Alladin Hashim. 1980. "FELDA's Continuing Development Tasks." *Land Development Digest* 3, no. 1 (October): 13–35.

———. 1981. "FELDA—The Malaysian Experience." Paper presented at the 8th ARTDO International and Training Conference, Kuala Lumpur.

Bahrin, T. S. 1968. "Land Development in Post-Independence Malaysia: Some Lessons." *Geographica* (Kuala Lumpur) 4: 67–83.

Bahrin, T. S., and P. D. A. Perera. 1977. *FELDA: 21 Years of Land Development.* Kuala Lumpur, Ministry for Land and Regional Development.

Bahrin, T. S., P. D. A. Perera, and H. K. Lim. *Land Development and Resettlement in Malaysia.* University of Malaya, Department of Geography.

Blair, J. A. S., and Nache M. Noor. 1981. "Migration and Land Development in Peninsular Malaysia." *Land Development Digest* 3, no. 2 (August) 1–30.

Chan, P. 1983. "Population Distribution and Development Strategies in Peninsular Malaysia." In *State Policies and Internal Migration: Studies in Market and Planned Economies,* edited by A. S. Oberai.

Fryer, D. W. 1970. *Emerging Southeast Asia.* London: Philip.

Government of Malaysia. 1956. *Report of the Working Party Set Up to Consider the Development of New Areas for Land Settlement.* Kuala Lumpur.

———. 1957. *Report to the Commission on Land Administration.* Kuala Lumpur.

———. 1961a. *Second Five-Year Plan (1961–1965).* Kuala Lumpur.

———. 1961b. *Report of the Special Committee to Review the Role of the FELDA within the National Rural Development Program.* Kuala Lumpur: Ministry of Rural Development.

MacAndrews, C. 1977. *Mobility and Modernisation: The Federal Land Development Authority and Its Role in Modernising the Rural Malay*. Yogyakarta: Gadjah Mada University Press.

Mariam Omar Din. 1981. "FELDA Settler Income Trends." *Land Development Digest* 3, no. 2 (July): 31–49.

Senftleben, W. 1976. *Background in Agricultural Land Policy in Malaysia*. Wiesbaden, West Germany: O. Harrassowitz.

Table 4.1
Settler selection points system, 1961

| Criterion | Maximum points |
|---|---|
| Age of applicant (21-50) | 20 |
| Married, preferably with children | 20 |
| Landless or holding less than 0.8 hectares | 20 |
| Agricultural background | 20 |
| Physical fitness | 20 |
| Total | 100 |

Source: Bahrin and Perera (1977: 56).

Table 4.2
Pattern of development of a pre-1966 FELDA scheme (acres)

| Area | Phase I 1st year | Phase II 2nd year | Phase III 3rd year | Phase IV 4th year | Total |
|---|---|---|---|---|---|
| Central village | 300 | -- | -- | -- | 300 |
| Main crop |  |  |  |  |  |
|   Rubber | 1,000 | 1,100 | 1,100 | -- | 3,200 |
|   Oil palm | 1,000 | 1,500 | 1,500 | -- | 4,000 |
| Subsidiary crops | -- | -- | -- | 800 |  |
| Total |  |  |  |  |  |
|   Rubber | 1,300 | 1,100 | 1,100 | -- | 3,500 |
|   Oil palm | 1,300 | 1,500 | 1,500 | -- | 4,300 |

Source: Bahrin and Perera (1977:33).
2.5 acres = 1 hectare.

Table 4.3
FELDA staff, 1982

| Category | Number | Percent |
|---|---|---|
| FELDA | 7,835 | 42.2 |
| Head office | 725 | 3.9 |
| Area (regional) | 1,167 | 6.3 |
| Scheme | 5,943 | 32.0 |
| Corporation and joint ventures | 10,735 | 57.8 |
| Total | 18,570 | 100.0 |

Source: FELDA, 1982 Annual Report.


Table 4.4
Malaysia: Progress in land development, 1971-80, and
target area, 1981-85 (acres)

| Agency | 1971-80 | | | 1981-85 |
| | Target | Achievement | Percentage | Target |
|---|---|---|---|---|
| Federal programs | | | | |
| FELDA | 903,000 | 923,051 | 102.2 | 370,000 |
| FELCRA[a] | 150,000 | 125,254 | 83.5 | 80,675 |
| RISDA[b] | 250,000 | 77,714 | 31.1 | 38,060 |
| Total | 1,303,000 | 1,126,019 | 86.4 | 488,735 |
| State programs | | | | |
| Peninsular Malaysia | 187,500 | 384,485 | 205.1 | 355,364 |
| Sabah | 167,000 | 142,806 | 85.5 | 140,000 |
| Sarawak | 222,800 | 189,338 | 85.0 | 41,000 |
| Total | 577,300 | 716,629 | 124.1 | 536,364 |
| Joint-venture/public sector | 332,500 | 296,516 | 89.2 | 317,250 |
| Total | 2,212,800 | 2,139,164 | 96.7 | 1,342,349 |

Source: Government of Malaysia, Fourth Malaysia Plan, 1981-
1985. Kuala Lumpur, p. 270.
  2.5 acres = 1 hectare.
  [a] Federal Land Consolidation and Rehabilitation Authority.
  [b] Rubber Industry Smallholders Development Authority.

Table 4.5
Area developed and number of families settled by the
FELDA up to 1982

| Crop | No. of schemes | % | Area (acres) | % | Settlers | % |
|------|------|------|------|------|------|------|
| Agricultural land | | | | | | |
| Oil palm | 194 | 58.6 | 894,997 | 60.6 | 43,978 | 57.3 |
| Rubber | 122 | 36.9 | 432,860 | 29.3 | 32,188 | 41.9 |
| Cocoa | 12 | 3.6 | 41,723 | 2.8 | 438 | 0.6 |
| Sugar cane | 2 | 0.6 | 12,641 | 0.9 | 178 | 0.2 |
| Coffee | 1 | 0.3 | 1,307 | 0.1 | -- | -- |
| Urban/residential land | -- | -- | 93,527 | 6.3 | -- | -- |
| Total | 331 | 100.0 | 1,477,055 | 100.0 | 76,782 | 100.0 |

Source: FELDA, 1982 Annual Report.
2.5 acres = 1 hectare.

Table 4.6
Projected and actual intake of settlers in FELDA schemes

| Plan period | Projected | Actual | % |
|------|------|------|------|
| Second Malaysia Plan (1961-65) | 24,000 | 6,083 | 25.3 |
| First Malaysia Plan (1966-70) | 12,745 | 11,863 | 93.1 |
| Second Malaysia Plan (1971-75) | 20,000 | 13,779 | 68.9 |
| Third Malaysia Plan (1976-80) | 25,500 | 29,566 | 115.9 |
| Fourth Malaysia Plan (1981-85) | 30,000 | 12,719 (by end 1982) | -- |

Source: FELDA, 1982 Annual Report.

Table 4.7
Distribution of infrastructural facilities in
FELDA schemes, 1981

| Facilities | Target | Completed |
|---|---|---|
| Roads | | |
|   Access | 696 miles | 603 miles |
|   Village | 1,327 miles | 1,207 miles |
| Water supply | 193 schemes | 169 schemes |
| Electricity | 194 schemes | 47 schemes |
| Schools | | |
|   Primary | 184 | 154 |
|   Secondary | 47 | 37 |
| Clinics | 187 | 147 |
| Mosques | 188 | 158 |
| Community centers | 194 | 168 |

Source: FELDA, 1981 Annual Report.
Note: 1 mile = 1.6 kilometers.

Table 4.8
Settlers' occupation prior to entry into FELDA schemes

| Occupation | Percentage |
|---|---|
| Padi planter | 36.5 |
| Rubber tapper | 27.2 |
| Laborer | 10.9 |
| Former serviceman | 9.1 |
| Oil palm plantation worker | 4.5 |
| Unemployed | 4.1 |
| Fisherman | 4.0 |
| Trader | 3.7 |
|   Total | 100.0 |
| | (34,936) |

Source: FELDA, Settler Census, 1976, p. 269.

Table 4.9
Settlers' average monthly income (1976) by age and duration of stay in FELDA scheme

| Age group | Average monthly income before scheme entry for those entered in 1976 only (M$) | Settlers' average present monthly income in 1976 by number of years in FELDA (M$) | | | | Percentage increase in real income after 10-12 years |
| --- | --- | --- | --- | --- | --- | --- |
| | | 1-3 years | 4-5 years | 7-9 years | 10-12 years | |
| (1) | (2) | (3) | (4) | (5) | (6) | (7) |
| 20-24 | 113.37 | 106.06 | 174.28 | * | * | -- |
| 25-29 | 149.05 | 115.90 | 186.39 | 230.46 | * | -- |
| 30-34 | 162.05 | 115.32 | 186.79 | 249.78 | 243.50 | 50.3 |
| 35-39 | 164.41 | 108.19 | 185.82 | 268.34 | 285.87 | 73.9 |
| 40-44 | 184.22 | 116.18 | 192.92 | 287.52 | 286.38 | 62.2 |
| Total | 171.72 | 115.40 | 187.95 | 276.26 | 278.53 | 55.5 |

Source: Mariam Omar Din (1981).
*Whenever the number of settlers is less than 50, they are excluded from the analysis.

124

Table 4.10
Settlers' average monthly net income (M$)

| Area (acres)* | 1982 | | 1981 | |
|---|---|---|---|---|
| | Oil palm | Rubber | Oil palm | Rubber |
| 6 | -- | 333 | -- | 458 |
| 7 | -- | 366 | -- | 449 |
| 8 | -- | 430 | -- | 527 |
| 10 | 614 | 412 | 632 | 451 |
| 12 | 758 | 837 | 712 | 756 |
| 14 | 757 | -- | 847 | -- |
| All | 624 | 402 | 642 | 492 |

Source: FELDA, 1982 Annual Report, p. 17.
Home income after deduction of development loan
installments and farm operating costs.
*2.5 acres = 1 hectare.


Table 4.11
FELDA: Cost of resettling one family, 1976 (M$)

| Sources of cost | Oil Palm | Rubber |
|---|---|---|
| Infrastructure development | 5,200 | 5,200 |
| Management and administration | 3,700 | 4,200 |
| Development of agricultural holding (10 acres/4 hectares) | 15,500 | 14,800 |
| Settler's house | 2,200 | 2,200 |
| Total | 26,600 | 26,400 |

Source: Bahrin and Perera (1977: 79).

Table 4.12
Intrastate and interstate migration to FELDA schemes, 1957-83 (number of families)

| Settlement | Origin | | | | | | | | | | | Total | % intra-interstate | Total inter-state |
|---|---|---|---|---|---|---|---|---|---|---|---|---|---|---|
| | Johor | Kedah | Kelantan | Melaka | Negeri Sembilan | Pahang | Perak | Perlis | Selangor | Terengganu | Pinang | | | |
| Johor | 19,195 | 24 | 16 | 124 | 35 | 46 | 67 | 1 | 37 | 56 | 19 | 19,620 | 97.8 | 425 |
| Kedah | -- | 2,138 | 10 | -- | 1 | -- | 10 | 10 | 1 | -- | 23 | 2,193 | 97.5 | 55 |
| Kelantan | -- | -- | 748 | -- | -- | -- | -- | -- | -- | -- | -- | 748 | 100.0 | -- |
| Melaka | 53 | 7 | -- | 1,187 | 56 | 4 | 8 | 3 | 5 | -- | 1 | 1,324 | 89.7 | 137 |
| Negeri Sembilan | 582 | 35 | 31 | 497 | 10,921 | 23 | 160 | 3 | 319 | 10 | 16 | 12,597 | 86.7 | 1,676 |
| Pahang | 1,417 | 2,050 | 1,752 | 745 | 362 | 17,311 | 3,623 | 384 | 2,672 | 766 | 801 | 31,883 | 54.3 | 14,572 |
| Perak | 4 | 25 | 9 | 1 | 4 | 3 | 2,666 | 3 | 28 | 2 | 92 | 2,837 | 92.5 | 231 |
| Perlis | -- | -- | -- | -- | -- | -- | -- | 454 | -- | -- | -- | 454 | 100.0 | -- |
| Selangor | 28 | 43 | 3 | 14 | 6 | -- | 301 | -- | 1,683 | -- | 8 | 2,089 | 80.6 | 406 |
| Terengganu | 3 | 2 | 184 | 1 | 2 | 18 | 1 | -- | 2 | 4,417 | -- | 4,630 | 95.4 | 213 |
| Total | 21,282 | 4,324 | 2,753 | 2,569 | 11,387 | 17,405 | 6,836 | 858 | 4,747 | 5,254 | 960 | 78,375 | 81.7 | 17,502 |

Source: Compiled by author from official records.

126

Table 4.13
Settlers' migration by distance, 1957-76

| Distance (miles) | 1957-61 No. | % | 1962-66 No. | % | 1967-71 No. | % | 1972-76 No. | % |
|---|---|---|---|---|---|---|---|---|
| Less than 26 | 1,137 | 44.6 | 1,837 | 28.5 | 1,419 | 12.1 | 1,446 | 10.3 |
| 26-50 | 795 | 31.2 | 2,032 | 31.5 | 2,168 | 18.5 | 2,193 | 15.6 |
| 51-75 | 112 | 4.4 | 1,099 | 17.0 | 1,809 | 15.4 | 1,546 | 11.0 |
| 76-100 | 93 | 3.6 | 489 | 7.6 | 1,448 | 12.4 | 1,541 | 10.9 |
| 101-150 | 187 | 7.3 | 405 | 6.3 | 1,415 | 12.1 | 2,685 | 19.1 |
| 151-200 | 67 | 2.6 | 112 | 1.7 | 656 | 5.6 | 1,170 | 8.3 |
| 201-250 | 34 | 1.3 | 53 | 0.8 | 486 | 4.1 | 779 | 5.5 |
| 251-400 | 108 | 4.2 | 345 | 5.3 | 1,619 | 13.8 | 1,946 | 13.8 |
| Over 400 | 14 | 0.5 | 79 | 1.2 | 694 | 5.9 | 785 | 5.6 |
| Total | 2,547 | 100.0 | 6,451 | 100.0 | 11,714 | 100.0 | 14,091 | 100.0 |

Source:  Blair and Noor (1981).
Note:  1 mile = 1.6 kilometers.

Table 4.14
Age-sex distribution of settlers' children by residence, 1977-78

| Age group (years) | Male | | | Female | | |
|---|---|---|---|---|---|---|
| | Resident | Non-resident | Non-resident (%) | Resident | Non-resident | Non-resident (%) |
| 0-5 | 537 | 13 | 2.4 | 462 | 7 | 1.5 |
| 6-10 | 497 | 19 | 3.7 | 469 | 21 | 4.3 |
| 11-15 | 370 | 51 | 12.1 | 362 | 42 | 10.4 |
| 16-20 | 217 | 76 | 25.9 | 160 | 88 | 35.5 |
| 21-25 | 55 | 62 | 53.0 | 39 | 84 | 68.3 |
| 26-30 | 6 | 51 | 89.5 | 12 | 41 | 77.4 |
| 31-35 | 1 | 18 | 94.7 | 4 | 19 | 82.6 |
| 36 and over | 2 | 13 | 86.7 | -- | 10 | 100.0 |
| Total | 1,685 | 303 | 18.0 | 1,508 | 312 | 20.7 |

Source:  Blair and Noor (1981).

Table 4.15
Labor force of dependents in FELDA schemes, 1975-90

|  | 1975 | 1980 | 1985 | 1990 |
|---|---|---|---|---|
| Working age population[a] | 16,631 | 53,129 | 124,281 | 205,173 |
| Participation rate[b] (%) | 62.6 | 62.7 | 62.1 | 61.6 |
| Labor force | 10,411 | 33,312 | 77,179 | 126,386 |

Source: MacAndrews (1977), as reproduced by Chan (1983).
[a] The working age population estimated on the basis of an average figure of six children per family.
[b] Participation rate is taken from the Mid-Term Review of the Second Malaysia Plan 1971-75, p. 66. Kuala Lumpar, Government Press, 1979.

Cayetano Paderanga, Jr.                                    5

# Land Settlements in the Philippines

## INTRODUCTION

The Philippines have already had quite a substantial period of land settlement. Since the pacification of the Muslim south, a southward migration has begun. At the same time another migration was going in the opposite direction, toward the sparsely populated regions of Cagayan Valley. This process included both government-sponsored and spontaneous population movements (Pelzer 1945).

Among the various objectives of government-assisted resettlement programs are an increase in agricultural production and an acceleration of both national and regional development by improving the quality of life of the poor. This involves the distribution of publicly owned agricultural land to the landless families. Resettlement has also been used by the government to encourage migration to sparsely populated regions and to develop the hinterlands by building new communities where the standard of living of settler families may be upgraded (Ministry of Agrarian Reform 1979).

The author is an assistant professor of the University of the Philippines, and a Visiting Fellow at the Economic Growth Center, Yale University.

During the earlier part of the period under review, the land settlement program was typically rural in character. Settlers were moved from areas where high person–land ratios and strained landlord–tenant relationships had resulted in widespread agrarian unrest, to areas that the government perceived to be sparsely populated (at least by the standards of settled farming that were predominant in the pacified Christian areas). A good example of this program was the resettlement of landless farmers from troubled central Luzon in the large unfarmed areas of central and southern Mindanao. In the latter part of the period, a second type of settlement program appeared. This was the resettlement of landless families from the (perceived) overcrowded areas of metropolitan Manila to outlying towns and provinces or other parts of the country.

The purpose of this study is threefold. First, to determine the extent to which the aims of the settlement program have been met. Second, to identify unintended effects of the program and to see how they influenced the ultimate attainment of these goals. Third, to assess the impact of the program on national development with a view to learning lessons for the design of similar programs in the future.

## ECONOMIC POLICIES AND LAND SETTLEMENT, 1900–75

The first three-quarters of the century was characterized by profound changes in the Philippine economy. Over the period 1900–75, the population increased by more than five times and the number of commercial and industrial establishments by almost 20 times. This was accompanied by a radical change in the structure of the economy, as it changed from a largely agricultural to an industrial base. The agricultural sector shrank from a share of 55 percent to merely 27 percent of estimated total output. These broad changes are summarized in Table. 5.1.

The broad economic changes were accompanied by changes in the spatial distribution of population. These changes were influenced both by historical forces and by government policy. Government policy in each period tended to favor some regions over others, and this became imprinted on the socioeconomic landscape. Among these policies were explicit population redistribution programs and changes in policies regarding land ownership and transfer, as well as broad macroeconomic and trade policies with indirect but nevertheless strong population distribution effects.

### The colonial period, 1900–1935: Changes in trade policy and the opening of the frontier

At the turn of the century, the level of economic activity in the country was relatively low and the pattern of settlements was generally dispersed. The island of Mindanao was virtually unexplored, and 400 years of Spanish rule had left a traditional agricultural economy oriented toward the production of export crops. This was the setting in which the special trade relationship between the Philippines and the United States developed.

Three major elements of United States policy at that time are of particular interest. First, U.S. policymakers wanted to integrate the Philippine colony into the U.S. market. This was done by systematically lowering the barriers to trade between the two countries. Because of historical antecedents and by virtue of the Philippine economy's comparative advantage, the result was a very strong encouragement of the production of primary products.

The second thrust of the U.S. colonial government was an attempt to rationalize land ownership. During the Spanish era the communal ownership of land dating from pre-Hispanic times had slowly evolved toward formal private ownership, aided by the initial introduction of the *encomienda* system, whereby large tracts of land were entrusted to favored individuals (*encomenderos*) by the royal government in exchange for tribute in the form of labor, goods, and cash. Over time, private individuals gained more formal control over the parcels of land. However, the process of acquiring land was not well defined apart from the outright grants from the crown or purchase from other individuals. The mixture of the remnants of the Spanish system with a different method of land management and registration under the United States led to friction between landowners and tenants, and conflicting claims to ownership of land.

Under the United States, new laws regulating the possession and ownership of land were passed. These laws provided for the disposition of public land and introduced the homestead concept. The possession and registration of private land was also affected. The Philippine Bill of 1902 set out more specific conditions relating to the disposition of public land. This opened up huge areas that had for various reasons been closed to private exploitation under the Spanish regime. The opening up of land was facilitated by the introduction of systematic registration of land titles under the Land Registration Act of 1902.

The third element of U.S. colonial policy was the pacification and amalgamation of the non-Christian population, especially the Muslims in the south. A major strategy used to pursue this objective was to encourage people from the north and central parts of the country to settle in the frontier regions.

Table 5.2 shows the population density of the frontier regions relative to other regions in 1903. The glaring imbalance in population densities also led to a series of projects to resettle people in the underpopulated areas.

*The initial opening and settlement of the frontier*

There were hardly any Christian Filipinos in Mindanao at the turn of the century, except in a narrow strip of Visayan settlements on the northern coast of Misamis Oriental and Misamis Occidental. Mindanao's population consisted primarily of various Muslim groups and of pagan mountain tribes such as the Bagobos, Manobos, Bilaans, and Bukidnons. During the earlier part of the century, government land settlement policy consisted of encouragement rather than direct participation. The initial response of the Filipinos to the new land policy was disappointing, however.

Apart from the legal changes introduced by the new laws, the government therefore set up the Interisland Migration Division of the Bureau of Labor to assist and guide program families. This office operated from 1918 to 1939. Although its record is a mixed one, it was a manifestation of the government's encouragement of frontier settlements. After 1912, the number of homestead applicants grew slowly but steadily, no doubt affected by the other land policy changes mentioned above. From 1919 to 1925, applications increased annually from 5000 to 10,000, averaging 12,000 per year between 1926 and 1930 before declining to 7000 per year in 1934, the year before the establishment of the Commonwealth Government.

*Direct government resettlement programs*

Direct government land settlement programs started when the government adopted a policy of active encouragement of migration in 1913. It established agricultural colonies that offered free transportation, financial assistance, and town sites. From 1913 to 1917, nine such colonies were founded, covering a total area of 21,760 hectares, seven in Mindanao and one each in the Visayas (Bohol) and Cagayan Valley (Pelzer 1945).

Policymakers sought to direct homesteaders from congested areas of the Visayas into the interior and southern parts of Mindanao. They also hoped that it would lead to the amalgamation and Filipinization of the Muslims and pagans in these areas (Pelzer 1945). These colonies were by and large unsuccessful, however. A lack of funds, ill-chosen sites, and unwise selection of settlers combined to make the total number of migrants small. By 1917 the government, discouraged by the high costs and lack of success, retreated from its policy of sponsored colonies. The program was replaced by one that merely encouraged the movement of migrants who could support themselves for at least six months in the settlement area. Apart from transportation and guidance regarding the final destination, no other support was offered.

The quantitative impact of these early programs was negligible. Up to 1935, only 30,000 to 35,000 persons had been relocated by the government-sponsored programs. The main reason given for this failure was the lack of infrastructure in the island of Mindanao, especially the absence of a road network. Simkins and Wernstedt (1971) argue that the program had no noticeable effect on the crowded conditions in Luzon and the Visayas, which they were designed to relieve. The figures understate the final effect, however, since they do not include those who migrated spontaneously.

## The Commonwealth period: 1935–46

The Commonwealth Government maintained the policy of encouraging settlement in sparsely populated areas. Conscious of past mistakes, it concentrated on building up infrastructural support in Mindanao and other frontier regions. Funds originally alotted for direct expenditure on agricultural colonies were diverted to road construction and the public land survey (Pelzer 1945: 135). The government also passed Commonwealth Act no. 441, which set up the National Land Settlement Administration (NLSA), with the following objectives:

a. to facilitate the acquisition, settlement and cultivation of public and private land;
b. to afford an opportunity to own farms to tenant farmers and small farmers from congested areas, and to trainees who had completed the prescribed military training;
c. to encourage migration to sparsely populated regions, and to facilitate the amalgamation of the people in different regions;
d. to develop new cash crops more suited to the U.S. market.

The NLSA initiated three major settlement projects: Koronadal Valley and Allah Valley in Cotabato, and the Mallig Plains in Cagayan Valley. About 8300 families were directly resettled by this office at the cost of 11 million pesos, before it was replaced by another government agency in 1950.

Specific requirements for settler selection were laid down. A settler had to be:

a. a Filipino or American of legal age, preferably under 40, married and with children;
b. "fit for a pioneering life," with some agricultural experience;
c. of good character and reputation; and
d. qualified to apply for public lands under the Public Lands Act.

When news of the NLSA spread, however, many families moved to the settlement districts at their own expense. Faced with the actual presence of families, the administration found it difficult to turn back these settlers.

The new roads connected the important towns of northern Mindanao with Davao and Cotabato, where the main settlement areas were, and the information that flowed back to the settlers' former homes induced a long-term voluntary stream southward from the Visayas and led to a rapid growth of population in Mindanao.

## Immediate post-independence period: 1946–60

Independence dictated a different set of priorities. Whereas colonial policy dictated close integration between the Philippines and the United States, political autonomy now decreed that the economy should stand on its own as much as possible. The era of free trade between the two countries was also drawing to a close, although "special relations" were expected to persist for some time. For the Philippines, this implied that a larger proportion of the industrial products it consumed would have to be generated from within. The unifying aim was industrialization, with import substitution as the main strategy to be followed.

The main policies used to implement this strategy were exchange and import controls. Rather than adjusting the overvalued peso, policymakers regarded it as an instrument to direct capital funds to preferred industries at subsidized rates. To maintain the official rate, the use of foreign exchange had to be controlled and a system of priorities instituted. Import substitution industries such as textiles and appliance manufacturing were favored.

Tax incentives and a comprehensive restructuring of tariffs were also used to achieve the overall objective. Industries classified as "new and necessary" were typically exempted from taxes for limited periods of time. Selective credit instruments, including long-term financing institutions set up by the government, also discriminated in favor of "new and necessary" industries. The final policy of the period was to raise the minimum wage in response to agitation in the urban areas, where standards of living and skill levels were higher. Its unintended result was to discourage labor-intensive industries and further bias investment toward capital-intensive, import substitution industries.

Hidden among these policies was a very strong disincentive to the agricultural sector. The overvalued peso, together with the bias of foreign exchange controls toward import substitution, effectively penalized the export-oriented agricultural cash crops on which the growth of the agricultural sector had been based before independence. At the same time the ability of the agricultural sector to shift forcefully to the production of food for the domestic market was effectively choked by the bias against the sector contained in the selective credit instruments and the official policy of subsidized importation of "essential" commodities, including food products, aimed at lowering food prices to the vocal urban sector (especially the price of rice during biennial election years).

Partly as a result of this unintended bias against the agricultural sector, production techniques hardly changed for many years (Crisostomo and Barker 1972). Until 1960 almost all agricultural growth came not from increased productivity but from increases in the area of land under cultivation. And such increases were possible only because of the intensification of the settlement of the frontier region, especially Mindanao. Table 5.3 shows the relative growth rates of agricultural output and cultivated area for different periods.

World War II interrupted the settlement activities of the government, but they resumed soon after. In the Mindanao frontier areas, applications accelerated sharply immediately after liberation, as newly arrived migrants squatted on former Japanese plantations (Simkins and Wernstedt 1971). In 1950 the Agricultural Machinery and Equipment Corporation, whose function was to supply farmers with agricultural machinery and equipment at cost, with payment by installments, was merged with the Rice and Corn Production Administration (RCPA) to form the Land Settlement Development Corporation (LASEDECO). This new institution became the implementing agency of the government's resettlement program.

The resurgence of agrarian problems manifested by the communist-oriented *Hukbo ng Bayan Laban sa Hapon* (National Army against the Japanese), later known as the *Hukbalahap*, or Huks, necessitated more reshuffling of government agencies. In 1954, the National Resettlement and Rehabilitation Administration (NARRA) replaced the LASEDECO. Within a period of nine years this agency resettled 20,500 families at a cost of 44.5 million pesos.

## Closing the frontier: 1962 and beyond

The second major objective of the government resettlement program was the alleviation of the agrarian problems in the more densely populated areas of central Luzon and the Visayas, which also had a high tenancy rate. Even when frontier development was the predominant aspect of the settlement program, laws governing agrarian relations were continually being promulgated in response to the increasing strain between landlords and tenants. During the colonial and Commonwealth periods, the most important such laws were the Rice Share Tenancy Act (1933) and the Tenancy Act (1934), which laid down the rights of tenants and landlords, and Commonwealth Acts 461 (1939) and 604 (1940), which set up arbitration and litigation procedures to implement the previous laws. The Court of Agrarian Relations was set up in 1955, and on August 8, 1963, all existing laws relating to agrarian relations were codified under the Agrarian Land Reform Code. This was further amended in 1971. Apart from outlawing share tenancies and regulating land ownership and agrarian relations, this law created the Land Authority. One of the Authority's functions was to administer the land resettlement program as part of the general program of land reform. By 1983, the Bureau of Resettlement of the Ministry of Agrarian Reform had been able to develop 736,969 hectares of land and resettle 52,728 families. This last figure, however, included the settlers inherited from previous agencies. The number of settler families in settlements opened between 1963 and 1983 amounted to 20,225—still a very respectable number.

The change in machinery introduced in 1963 was due to the narrower thrust of government resettlement programs; the partial alleviation of agrarian problems had become the main objective. It implied an increasing perception of the exhaustion of the frontier, the occupation of which had been a major impetus of resettlement programs since the turn of the century. The decreasing rate of expansion of the cultivated area, leading to a deceleration in the growth of agricultural output, supported this impression. A 1974 study was skeptical of this, however. An inventory of Philippine land use indicated that an additional 8.6 million hectares was still available for agricultural use.

## The regional awareness period: The 1970s

Toward the end of the 1960s, enunciated policy shifted from import substitution to export promotion. At this time, the government began to display a conspicuous awareness of the spatial dimension of development. An indirect effect of the shift in policy was the renewed encouragement of traditional exports. Explicit consideration of the regional aspects of development was also incorporated into investment and other priorities.

Major indications of this change in emphasis were the various investment and export incentive acts of the late 1960s and early 1970s, especially the Investment Incentives Act of 1967, which also created the Board of Investment (BOI). The BOI explicitly included regional dispersal as one of the criteria for the granting of loans. Other criteria included export promotion and employment creation, both of which have had strong effects on regional development. Also included in the act was the revision of the tariff structure to remove the bias toward import substitution. The government also undertook a massive national infrastructure program that was expected to have strong positive effects on regions away from the Central Industrial Region (CIR). Finally, the gov-

ernment forcefully encouraged agriculture in order to attain self-sufficiency in food. Among other things, there was a reassessment of the
policies that had been penalizing the agricultural sector.

The government's land policy during this last period may be characterized as one of consolidation. The emphasis has been on strengthening and institutionalizing of changes in land policy. The Department
of Agrarian Reform was upgraded to a ministry. Since 1972, 16 new land
settlement areas have been opened, with a total of 238,443 hectares;
13,285 new settler families are under the ministry's Bureau of
Resettlement.

## CASE STUDIES

In order to highlight the processes and the problems of land settlement, we shall briefly discuss two resettlement projects: (1) the settlement of the Digos-Padada Valley in Davao Province; and (2) the Central
Palawan Resettlement Project. Since these settlements started at different times, no direct comparisons are implied.

### Settlement of the Digos-Padada Valley

The Settlement of the Davao Province, was studied by Simkins and
Wernstedt (1971). The major objective of this study was to assess the
socioeconomic impact of the immigration on the Digos-Padada region.

The Digos-Padada Valley consists of a relatively large alluvial plain
and piedmont area along the western shore of Davao Gulf. The lowland
begins approximately 50 kilometers along the shores of the gulf. Spontaneous migration into Davao Province started at the beginning of the
twentieth century. Migrants were mainly attracted by earlier migrants
to government projects and nearby places. The promise of land through
the Public Lands and Homestead Acts was incentive enough for this
spontaneous migration to proceed.

The volume of migration into Davao Province accelerated between
1918 and 1930, during which the province attained a population growth
rate of 4.9 percent per year at a time when the country's population was
growing at 2.1 percent per year and the southern part of Mindanao had
an annual growth rate of 3.8 percent. The pattern of new settlements
followed the one set earlier, with expansion occurring in belts around
the old established towns. Migration into the area continued to be heavy
from 1948 to 1960, after a brief hiatus during World War II (1941–45).
Over the years, however, the expanding belts started spilling into less
and less desirable land, and homesteads became difficult to come by.
Large-scale in-migration virtually ceased after 1960, when crude popu-

lation density reached 250 persons per square kilometer, although there was still considerable movement within the valley.

*Origins and characteristics of migrants*

Although all regions of the country contributed settlers, over 60 percent of the total movement into the valley came from the central Visayan province of Cebu (Table 5.4).

The occupation of the Digos-Padada Valley was dominated by agriculturists. After the initial sparse settlement by the indigenous tribes came the large U.S. and Japanese corporations, which blocked out large tracts of land for plantation development. The plantations started the migration process by providing temporary employment (and often the cost of moving whole families) for migrants. Settlers usually worked on the plantations until they were able to purchase their own land. Despite the initial push of the large plantations, historical developments (the expulsion of the Japanese after World War II and the various limitations on ownership of large tracts of land) led to the pattern of small subsistence farms that now characterize the valley.

Simkins and Wernstedt noted that the presence of relatives or friends already in the Digos-Padada Valley had some influence on prospective migrants. Nearly 90 percent of migrants reported acquaintances already present in the valley at the time of their arrival, and about 70 percent were actually encouraged to move to the settlement. Besides the information links between migration source areas and destinations, previous arrivals also provided financial and other assistance to new settlers.

The new settlers in the valley were mostly young upon arrival. Their median age at the time of departure from their homes was 23 years. Other data led the authors to conjecture that a substantial proportion of migrants consisted of families. By 1960 the age pyramid of the migrants and their descendants was already similar to that of the Philippines as a whole, except for the base and apex. The valley had a higher proportion of persons 15 years and below and a lower proportion of persons 55 years and above. This is probably a result of the relative newness of the settlement and the selectivity of the migration process in favor of young adults and their families.

The migrants also appear to have been better educated than the average Filipino, and this difference is even greater when the comparison group is the source province of Cebu. The median number of school years completed for migrants into the Digos-Padada Valley was higher than for the Philippines as a whole or for Cebu, and the proportion of illiterates much lower (Table 5.5).

Since migration was largely self-financed, no significant prior screening was carried out. Government agencies vainly tried to establish criteria for selection. But often, faced with an accomplished move, they had no choice but to approve applications for land.

*The migration process*

The settlement of the Digos-Padada Valley was spontaneous and unofficial rather than sponsored. Migrants financed their own transfer with some help from relatives. Money for the trip itself did not seem to be a great problem. A large number of inter-island ships plied between Luzon, the Visayas, and Davao City, and passage was relatively cheap. The cost of transportation itself was, therefore, relatively unimportant. The most common means of financing the transfer was through the sale of land, livestock, or crops, and financial assistance from family members. Borrowing and sponsorship by prospective employers were of minor importance (Simkins and Wernstedt 1971).

According to Simkins and Wernstedt, the selection of specific destinations within the Digos-Padada Valley was mainly influenced by the availability of land, the accessibility of markets and roads, the availability of water, and the location of relatives and friends who had previously settled in the valley.

Availability of land was of little concern at the start, but as the valley filled up it became progressively more crucial in the choice of location.

The main crops of the valley are corn, coconuts, rice, and others that are often cultivated in combination with corn. The predominance of corn is a reflection of the origin and resources of most migrants to the valley, as well as the character of the area itself and the absence of infrastructure at the start of settlement. The gestation period for coconuts is a minimum of six years, and settlers rarely arrived with funds for more than six months or a year. It was therefore natural for the settlers to fall back on the commodity that was most familiar to the majority of them.

The migration to the Digos-Padada Valley is described by Simkins and Wernstedt (1971: 95) as among the more successful migrations as measured in economic terns. While the quality of housing of migrants is essentially the same as it was in the home province, ownership has now risen to 93 percent. Occupational changes have also been beneficial. Almost all agricultural laborers interviewed finally had access to land, and among unskilled laborers three-quarters were now farmers. Perhaps most important was the increase in the size of farms from an average of 2.6 hectares prior to migration to an average of 4.2 hectares after migration (Table 5.6).

## Settlement in Palawan Province

The Central Palawan Resettlement Project studied by James (1978) was opened up in 1950 by the Land Settlement Development Corporation (LASEDECO); the work was taken over in 1954 by the National Resettlement and Rehabilitation Administration (NARRA).

Palawan is the least densely populated province in the Philippines. It covers 14,895 square kilometers or almost 1.5 million hectares. As of 1976, less than one-quarter of the area released for agriculture was occupied, and substantial room for future expansion existed. A major government resettlement project covered 25,000 hectares, and four more large settlement sites were under consideration. The main objectives of this resettlement project were those pursued by LASEDECO, that is, the resettlement of people from "overcrowded" areas, the settlement of frontier areas, and an increase in agricultural output.

The study area was chosen because self-financed and government-sponsored settlers lived in close proximity to each other. Interviews with 100 settlers, evenly divided between self-financed and government-sponsored, and supplemented by meetings with key informants (community leaders, public land surveyors, local extension workers, etc.), were the main data-gathering technique used. Available secondary data on the area provided by various government agencies were also used.

*Origins of settlers and reasons for migrating*

The majority of the settlers (53 percent) were Ilocanos (a regional grouping occupying the northern part of Luzon, the biggest island in the Philippines, which also contains metropolitan Manila). The next major group came from other Luzon provinces, while Visayan settlers constituted only about one-fifth of the total. This breakdown is interesting, because Palawan is nearer to the Visayas than to the Ilocano-speaking provinces.

The migrants came from predominantly overcrowded regions characterized by high population density, a high rent–wage ratio, minuscule farm sizes, high tenant–land ratios, and low agricultural incomes. In contrast, Palawan had low population density, a low rent–wage ratio, abundant public land, and a relative scarcity of labor. The survey in 1978 found, for example, that rice harvesters in Palawan earned on average 50 percent more than those in Pangasinan (an Ilocano-speaking province of northern Luzon). The survey also found that landowners earned on average 42 percent of the total output by way of rent in the source areas, compared to 36 percent in Palawan. James's study also observed significant changes in land ownership in terms of average farm sizes and land tenure (Table 5.7). Prior to migration, almost three-quarters owned no land, and those who did own land had on average only 2.57 hectares. Following migration to Palawan, 93 percent owned land, with an average farm size of 8.6 hectares.

The main attraction to Palawan was, therefore, the availability of land. Fifty-nine percent cited landlessness as the major reason for migrating, and three-quarters mentioned land availability as the reason for selecting Palawan.

Financing the move differed between government-assisted and self-financed settlers. Forty-six of the 50 government-assisted settlers were moved at government expense, while only ten reported receiving aid from relatives or friends. Twenty-seven claimed that they would never have moved without government assistance. In contrast, 38 of the self-financed settlers mentioned having received assistance from relatives or friends.

### The settlement process

Very few of the settlers arrived in Palawan with enough resources to transform virgin forest into cultivable farms on their own. Given their circumstances, an initial crop failure would have been catastrophic for the individual settlers. The process of "recontracting" or "exchange labor" therefore arose (James 1978). Under this arrangement settlers worked on other lots, or others assisted them in developing their own.

James's study also contains valuable information on the comparative costs of establishing a 5-hectare rice farm in the Palawan area for government-assisted and self-financed settlers. Table 5.8 shows the cost estimates for the two alternative systems. The author finds the cost of government settlement to be "discouragingly high." He also notes that this does not include administrative or infrastructural costs. Further, only 1 percent of the interest-free, long-term assistance loans had been repaid by 1978. As a result, infrastructural development in the resettlement area was extremely poor.

The major conclusions drawn by the study are the following: (a) planned (government-assisted) settlement has involved much higher costs than spontaneous settlement through the homesteading system, yet its accomplishments are much smaller in terms of settlers' incomes and farm development; and (b) the difference in results is due partly to the higher level of skills possessed by self-financed settlers and the greater facility with which they adapt institutionally to the new environment and partly to the negative incentive features inherent in the grants offered to government-sponsored settlers.

## ASSESSMENT OF PROGRAM ACHIEVEMENTS

An attempt is made in this section to discern an ultimate coherence in the disparate settlement projects carried out in the first three-quarters of this century. The historical perspective provides the framework for an analysis of the overall effects on social and economic development, even though these projects were initiated in response to different problems over the years.

Quite frequently, individual projects had multiple objectives such as the following: development of the frontier area (which was especially important during the early part of the century), growth of agricultural output, alleviation of agrarian problems in overcrowded agricultural regions, pacification and assimilation of minority groups, and decongestion of overcrowded cities, especially metropolitan Manila (this objective became more important in the later period). This list provides a convenient framework for assessing the program's effect on national development.

## Development of the frontier area

The earliest resettlement projects had the colonization of the frontier as their major objective. It was considered that the unexplored areas of Mindanao, Palawan, and Cagayan Valley had resources that were underutilized. The initial projects therefore sought to achieve a major shift of population, with the aim of changing the economic and demographic character of the frontier area. From this point of view, the settlement program was very successful. Table 5.9 shows some of the crude estimates of the volume of net migration into the different regions of the country. During most of the period 1900–75, the frontier regions of Mindanao shows a steady increase in population growth that can be explained only by massive rates of in-migration. The record for Cagayan Valley during the same period is mixed.

Within Mindanao itself, however, there have been regional variations in population growth. During the earlier periods of this century, the northern Mindanao provinces of Misamis, Surigao, and Agusan were the fastest-growing areas of the country. Census figures from 1903 to 1948 show that these provinces had a slight edge over the rest of Mindanao. From 1948 until 1970, however, western, southern, and central Mindanao started to outstrip the northern parts of the island, with figures even indicating net out-migration for Misamis. During the period 1948–60, southern Mindanao, which consists of Davao and parts of Cotabato, was growing at almost 10 percent per annum, twice the rate of growth for Mindanao as a whole, which was in turn growing twice as fast as the country as a whole. Vandermeer and Agaloos (1962) ascribe the later boom in the southern areas of Mindanao to the initial absence of a good transport network in these areas. They point to the rapid settlement of the southern provinces, especially Davao and Cotabato, after the building of the two major highways connecting the important settlements of Davao and Cotabato with each other and with Cagayan de Oro in northern Mindanao. These findings are corroborated by Pelzer (1945: 235) and Wernstedt and Simkins (1965: 115); the latter also suggested that a substantial role was played by the flow of information between origin and settlement areas.

The ultimate effect of these migrations was to change totally the demographic profile of the Philippines. This is manifested in the increasing proportion of the population living on the island of Mindanao and the relative changes in population density. From about one-seventh of the average population density of the country's traditional agricultural region at the beginning of the century, Mindanao's density rose to about one-half by 1975 (Table 5.10). This meant that the notion of Mindanao as a safety valve for overcrowding in other parts was rapidly being eroded. It also meant that a larger proportion of the labor force now resided in the "frontier" regions.

### Agricultural output

The change in the distribution of population and the labor force affected the distribution of output. The frontier regions started to account for an increasingly larger proportion of total output. This is reflected in the increasing share of frontier regions in total employment and the number of industrial establishments (Table 5.11). The most profound changes, however, were in the distribution of agricultural output. This was, perhaps, a natural consequence, because the settlement program and its corresponding migration stream were for most of the period predominantly agricultural in character. The distribution of agricultural output reflects the growing importance of the newly opened regions to the agricultural production of the Philippines (Table 5.12). These figures even understate the growth of agricultural output in the frontier region by using 1939 as the base year, although the base was already much larger than in 1903. Data for earlier years are incomplete.

The increase in agricultural output is the second major benefit of the frontier migration. Just as it provided land to migrants from overcrowded regions, the frontier also supplied the additional food for a rapidly growing population. The 1974 ILO report, for example, points to expansion of the cultivated area as a major factor in the growth of agricultural output (p. 453). In fact, one should go back as far as the colonial period in order to appreciate fully the effect of land settlement on agricultural output. When land expansion decelerated between 1960 and 1965, the growth of agricultural output also slowed down.

The actual impact of frontier migration is even greater when it is taken in the context of the country's economic structure. For most of the colonial period, the Philippines enjoyed rapid export-led economic expansion under the aegis of free trade with the United States. This growth was largely based on primary product exports to the U.S. market (Paderanga and Pernia 1983). While the traditional agricultural region supplied most of the exports during the early period, the frontier areas also contributed by increasing production of staple commodities, thereby releasing land in other places for cash crops.

## Alleviation of agrarian problems

The results of the land settlement program in terms of alleviating agrarian problems in overcrowded or high-tenancy areas were mixed at best. The possible effects on overcrowded areas are both economic (agrarian) and political. The government's land settlement program enjoyed a brief period of success as Ramon Magsaysay, first as the secretary of national defense and later as president, promised "land for the landless" in the hope of undercutting the appeal of the dissident Huks in the middle of the 1950s. On the whole, however, the impact of the government's settlement program on agrarian unrest was negligible, and just a decade later, in the 1960s, agrarian problems again featured prominently in the appeal of the New People's Army (NPA) to the people.

The settlement program had no perceptible effect on the proportion of land cultivated by tenants. The ILO (1974) study, for example, reports that the percentage of farms cultivated by tenants was 73 percent for all crops taken together (75 percent for palay rice: p. 462). Comparing these figures with those given in the 1939 census for the same area (Table 5.13), it can be seen that the situation had actually deteriorated over the years. Even more discouraging was the perceived reversion of the pattern of land ownership in the frontier areas to that prevailing in the regions of origin. Krinks (1974: 11) provides data that appear to indicate a rise of tenancy in Mawab in Davao Province (which was settled about the same period as the Digos-Padada Valley).

One cannot conclude, of course, that resettlement was a complete failure as far as solving the agrarian problems in the origin areas was concerned. For one thing, present tenancy ratios in these areas could conceivably have been much higher without the out-migration that they experienced in the previous decades. The ultimate reasons for the persistently high tenant-farmer ratios may be found in the high population growth rates of the country and the absence of technological and structural changes that might have (a) freed labor from the farms, and (b) created employment opportunities outside the farms. Neverthelesss, the evidence suggests that land settlement programs alone cannot be expected to solve agrarian problems. At best, they are palliatives that buy time so that correct policies can operate fully.

## Pacification and assimilation of minority groups

It was thought that an influx of Christian settlers into the frontier regions would lead to the assimilation of cultural minorities, or at least reduce the threat of raids or warfare against other regions. The pacification of minority (especially Muslim) areas seemed to meet with success at the start. For three or four decades after the start of the settlement program in 1913, these areas rapidly became "Christianized." As a result of this, together with increases in economic output, these areas became more easily governable, first by the U.S. colonizers and later on by an indigenous government. As the frontier areas rapidly filled up, however, conflicts between the original tribal inhabitants and the settlers started to appear. Early friction returned (Vreeland et al. 1976), because of both cultural differences and conflicts over land. These conflicts became acute as the land available for homesteads became scarcer. At the same time, the roads built deep into the hinterlands in the 1950s and 1960s to accompany the expanded logging operations brought new settlers into competition with indigenous groups using different farming techniques (traditionally slash and burn, as contrasted with the more settled farms of the new arrivals; see, for example, Nance 1977). Land disputes contributed to the problems, which culminated in the violent uprising led by Muslim separatists in the early 1970s. Thus, the goal of pacifying cultural minorities was not attained. It now seems that with proper delineation of areas and planning to ensure the observance of cultural differences, settling the frontier could have been carried out more smoothly.

## CONCLUSIONS AND POLICY IMPLICATIONS

The main conclusion that can be derived from the Philippine experience is that a land settlement program alone cannot solve social and economic problems. The preceding section discussed the changes land settlement has brought about. Comparing these with the stated aims, it is clear that the program typically fell short, except perhaps in the case of population redistribution and growth of agricultural output. Nevertheless, the changes that are traceable to land settlement indicate that, in conjunction with other policies, it can be a significant tool for countries still blessed with this option.

One area in which land colonization can still play an important role is in increasing agricultural output. The ILO mission report of 1974 shows that even on the most conservative estimates, a substantial amount of unused agricultural land still remains to be exploited. Given the deceleration in the growth of agricultural output in the late 1970s and early 1980s (NEDA, *National Income Account*, various years), land settlement can contribute to increased agricultural output, even if this means reverting to the old pattern whereby output was increased by bringing more land under cultivation.

But land settlement cannot be seen as the only option here. Other instruments for increasing agricultural output must be considered. There is, for example, intensified cultivation, which would entail investment in rural infrastructure (irrigation, rural roads, etc.). The optimal mix will depend on prevailing prices and conditions. Table 5.14 shows the benefit-cost ratios estimated by both the World Bank and the Bureau of Resettlement, Ministry of Agrarian Reform (MAR). The benefit-cost ratios for irrigation of rice land are higher than those for land resettlement, although the latter still has a ratio greater than one if MAR estimates are used. As the land area fills up, however, resettlement costs increase rapidly.

The prospects for the medium term, given the availability of unexploited land, would point to a moderate pursuit of land colonization in combination with infrastructural development in settled areas.

The continued use of land settlement as an instrument for achieving increased agricultural production will also automatically fulfill the goal of population redistribution. But rather than emphasizing the numbers involved, this goal should be embedded in a more general analysis of regional development. Population transfer, of course, could be tied to the balancing of densities between the sparsely populated frontier areas and densely populated ares (Pernia and Paderanga 1981). However, this balance should be pursued in conjunction with the overall goals of regional development, if the origin area problems are not to be repeated in the settlement areas. The delineation of target destinations, therefore, should involve consideration of the potential for area development, which in turn will entail looking at available (or potential) physical infrastructure such as roads and irrigation, as well as such things as credit, marketing, and health facilities. The case studies (e.g., Digos-Padada) show that a minimum of these infrastructural facilities are required, and information about them must filter back to the areas of origin before public settlement projects can induce the spontaneous movements, which have been numerically more significant. Considerations of interregional development may also require investment in infrastructure in the origin areas. The choice of projects flowing out of this holistic exercise may turn out to be radically different from that coming out of a mechanical balancing of population densities (no matter how broadly defined) or out of a response to a narrow interpretation of agrarian problems in congested areas.

The solution to agrarian problems cannot be found in a mere transfer of tenants or surplus population. The plethora of agrarian programs and laws introduced by the government during three-quarters of a century of land settlement attest to this. Recent studies also show that land tenancy is the result of a complex combination of environmental and institutional factors such as property rights, inheritance laws, and other aspects of the prevailing socioeconomic structure (see, for example, Bardhan 1977; Braverman and Stiglitz 1982). The haphazard introduction of land settlement projects is not likely to be a lasting solution to the tenancy problem.

The poverty and maldistribution of income often identified with tenancy may also be substantially influenced by broad macroeconomic policies (such as import substitution) that penalize the agricultural sector, as discussed earlier (Power and Sicat 1971). In the economic atmosphere that prevailed after World War II, agriculture was unable to invest in infrastructure that would have raised labor productivity in this sector. At the same time, dependence on a slow-growing, protected domestic market prevented the industrial sector from absorbing the surplus labor from farms, which was in any case being augmented by a high population growth rate. The upshot was a growing rural (and industrial) reserve army that greatly limited the power of tenants and farm workers to bargain with the landlords. Unless these and other more basic conditions are altered, it is doubtful whether land settlement will have any long-lasting impact on agrarian problems. What the land colonization program can do is to give tenants and landless rural workers temporary help until the effects of more basic changes begin to be felt.

One of the first objectives of the settlement program, and one that appeared to be achieved at first, the pacification of cultural minorities, now looks to be one of the more palpable failures of the program. The rectification of the grievances that led to the Muslim uprising and other related problems in the early 1970s is now beyond the scope of the program. What is still under the control of program administrators is the design and implementation of present and future projects. A recognition of the complexity of the situation that a settlement program is asked to address should lead to the avoidance of "single-issue" projects (which treat only decongestion of overcrowded areas, for example). Embodied within a broader scheme of regional development, agricultural growth, and other goals, land resettlement should automatically consider the effects of all projects in the receiving areas. This includes the possible effects of the projects on indigenous populations. The proper delineation of reserved areas for minorities and procedures for cooperation should be an essential part of all settlement plans.

Finally, the most important lesson to emerge from this analysis may only be indirectly related to land settlement schemes. A significant cause of the problems that land settlement programs are called to address are the broad macroeconomic and trade policies that have had such a tremendous impact on the demographic configuration of the Philippines. These same policies also tend to negate the long-term benefits that could be expected from the various settlement projects. Unless changes are made in these more fundamental policies, the ultimate benefits from land settlements will be negligible.

## Policy recommendations

Land settlements should be embodied within a national settlements policy that encompasses and coordinates all major macroeconomic policies, including trade, agricultural, and industrialization policies. Within this overall policy, goals relating to regional development and the national urban system should be spelled out. Infrastructural development in the regional centers and even in smaller centers should be included. Once the broad policies are corrected to reflect the true resource endowments of the country, land settlement projects may then be designed to augment the natural growth processes in those areas where they are needed. More specifically, land settlement should be considered in the following context:

i. A more coordinated and integrated national settlements policy, which includes all the regional plans and infrastructure programs and which considers the influence and design of broad (and seemingly unrelated) macroeconomic policies.

ii. A systematic inventory of land and other resources, which should be carried out as part of regional policy determination in all regions. This would mean that land resettlement would be subsumed under a more general scheme of regional development policy.

iii. An assessment of the need for physical and other infrastructure investments in resettlement projects, in order to exploit fully the potential of the projects for (a) increasing output, and (b) alleviating poverty and the maldistribution of income.

iv. A mandatory consideration of cultural and other differences in planned resettlement areas.

v. A systematic examination of macroeconomic and trade policies for their unintended effects on the objectives of land resettlement. Programs that tend to raise agricultural productivity may in fact have much more beneficial effects and provide a better solution to agrarian problems than the piecemeal palliatives offered by resettlement projects. Other policies, by increasing industrial employment, may also raise the opportunity cost of agricultural labor and contribute to the solution of agrarian problems.

vi. The need for better coordination of policies, since land colonization affects and is affected by other policies. This coordination can perhaps be best achieved by using the national settlement policy as a necessary part of the planning process.

## ACKNOWLEDGMENTS

The assistance of Diana H. Good, who started the initial survey of the literature, and the help of Ms. Paz Bassig of the Bureau of Resettlement, Ministry of Agrarian Reform of the Philippines, in the preparation of this chapter, are gratefully acknowledged.

## BIBLIOGRAPHY

Bardhan, P. K. 1977. "Variations in Forms of Tenancy in a Peasant Economy." *Journal of Development Economics* (Amsterdam) 4 (June): 105–18.

Braverman, A., and J. F. Stiglitz. 1982. "Sharecropping and the Interlinking of Agrarian Markets." *American Economic Review* 72 (September) 695–715.

Brown, G. T. 1979. "Agricultural Pricing Policies in Developing Countries." In *Distortions of Agricultural Incentives*, edited by T. W. Schultz, pp. 25–36. Bloomington, IN: Indiana University Press.

Crisostomo, C., and R. Barker. 1972. "Growth Rates of Philippine Agriculture, 1948–1969." *Philippine Economic Journal* (Quezon City) (First semester): 88–148.

Demko, G. J., and R. J. Fuchs. 1979. *Population Distribution Policies in Development Planning: An Overview*. Report prepared on the basis of the UN/UNFPA Workshop on Population Distribution Policies in Development Planning, Bangkok (September).

Department of Agrarian Reform. 1977. *Resettlement Program of the Department of Agrarian Reform*. Quezon City: Public Information Division.

Fernandez, C. A. 1972. "Blueprints, Realities and Success in a Frontier Resettlement Community." *Philippine Sociological Review* (Manila) 20, nos. 1 and 2 (January and April): 176–85 and 272–73. (Special issue entitled: "View from the Paddy: Empirical Studies of Philippine Rice Farming and Tenancy.")

Gilbert, A. G., and D. E. Goodman. 1976. "Regional Income Disparities and Economic Development: A Critique." In *Development Planning and Spatial Structure*, edited by A. Gilbert, pp. 113–42. London: J. Wiley.

Golay, F. H. 1961. *The Philippines: Public Policy and National Economic Development*. Ithaca, NY: Cornell University Press.

Hermoso, V. P. 1983. *The Development of the Philippine Space Economy: 1900–1975*. Ph.D. dissertation, University of the Philippines.

Huke, R. E. 1963. "Mindanao . . . Pioneer Frontier?" *Philippine Geographical Journal* (Manila) 7, no. 2: 74–83.

Huke, R. E. et al. 1963. *Shadows on the Land: An Economic Geography of the Philippines*. Makati, Rizal, Philippines: Bookmark Inc.

International Labour Office. 1974. *Sharing in Development: A Programme of Employment, Equity and Growth for the Philippines*. Geneva: ILO.

James, W. E. 1978. "An Economic Analysis of Public Land Settlement Alternatives in the Philippines." Department Paper no. 78–30. Los Banos, Laguna, Philippines: International Rice Research Institute.

Katzman, M. T. 1978. "Colonization as an Approach to Regional Development." *Economic Development and Cultural Change* 26, no. 4 (July): 709–25.

Kim, Y. 1972. *Net Internal Migration in the Philippines, 1960–1970*. Manila: Bureau of Census and Statistics.

Krinks, P. 1974. "Old Wine in a New Bottle: Land Settlement and Agrarian

Problems in the Philippines." *Journal of Southeast Asian Studies* (Singapore) 5 (March): 1–17.

Mabogunje, A. K. L. 1981. "Objectives and Rationales for Regional Population Redistribution in Developing Countries." In *Population Distribution Policies in Development Planning*. Population Studies no. 75, pp. 19–29. New York: United Nations Department of International Economic Affairs.

Madigan, F. C. 1963. "The Early History of Cagayan de Oro." *Philippine Studies* (Manila) 2.

Ministry of Agrarian Reform. 1979. *Primer on Agrarian Reform*. Manila: National Media Production Center.

Nance, J. 1977. *The Gentle Tasaday: A Stone Age People in the Philippine Rain Forest*. New York: Harcourt-Brace.

National Housing Authority. Research Department. 1982. *Squatter Population Growth in Metro Manila (1978–1981)*. Quezon City.

Paderanga, C., Jr., and E. M. Pernia. 1983. "Economic Policies and Spatial and Urban Development: The Philippine Experience." *Regional Development Dialogue* (Nagoya) 4, no. 2: 67–86.

Pascual, E. M. 1966. "Internal Migration in the Philippines." In *First Conference of Population, 1965*. Quezon City: University of the Philippines Press.

Pelzer, K. J. 1945. *Pioneer Settlement in the Asiatic Tropics*. New York: American Geographical Society.

Pernia, E. M. 1976. "Urbanization in the Philippines: Historical and Comparative Perspectives." Papers of the East-West Population Institute, no. 40. Honolulu: East-West Center.

———. 1977. "Urbanization and Economic Development in the Philippines." Discussion Paper no. 77–3. Manila: Institute of Economic Development and Research, School of Economics, University of the Philippines.

Pernia, E. M., and C. Paderanga, Jr. 1981. "Urbanization and Spatial Development in the Philippines: A Survey." In *Survey of Philippine Economic Development Research*, vol. 1. Manila: Philippine Institute for Development Studies.

Power, Jr., and G. P. Sicat. 1971. *The Philippines: Industrialization and Trade Policies*. London: Oxford University Press for OECD.

Renaud, B. 1981. *National Urbanization Policies in Developing Countries*. Baltimore, MD: Johns Hopkins University Press.

Rocamora, J., and C. Panganiban. 1975. *Rural Development Strategies: The Philippine Case. Final Report*. Quezon City: Ateneo de Manila University, Institute of Philippine Culture.

Simkins, P. D., and F. L. Wernstedt. 1968. "The Growth and Internal Migrations of the Philippine Population, 1948 to 1960." *Journal of Tropical Geography* (Singapore) 17: 197–202.

———. 1971. "Philippine Migration: The Settlement of the Digos-Padada Valley, Davao Province." Yale University Southeast Asia Studies, Monograph Series, no. 16. New Haven, CT.

Simmons, A. B. 1981. "A Review and Evaluation of Attempts to Constrain Migration to Selected Urban Centres and Regions." In *Population Distribution Policies in Development Planning*, Population Studies no. 75, pp. 87–100. New York: United Nations Department of International Economic Affairs.

Vandermeer, C., and B. C. Agaloos. 1962. *Twentieth Century Settlement of Mindanao*. Papers of the Michigan Academy of Science, Arts and Letters, vol. 47.

Vreeland, N., G. B. Hurwitz, P. J. Philip, W. Moeller, and R. S. Shin. 1976. *Area Handbook for the Philippines*. Washington, D.C.: U.S. Government Printing Office.

Wernstedt, F. L., and P. D. Simkins. 1965. "Migrations and the Settlement of Mindanao." *Journal of Asian Studies* (Ann Arbor) 25: 83–103.

Wernstedt, F. L., and P. Spencer. 1967. *The Philippine Island World: A Physical, Cultural, and Regional Geography*. Los Angeles, CA: University of California Press.

World Bank. 1973. *Philippine Agricultural Sector Survey*. Washington, D.C.

Table 5.1
Percentage distribution of output, industrial employment, and
population by broad regional grouping, 1903 and 1975

|  | 1903 | 1975 |
|---|---|---|
|  | Output | |
| Broad economic sector | | |
| Primary | 55.0 | 26.6 |
| Secondary | 13.4 | 33.2 |
| Tertiary | 31.6 | 40.2 |

|  | 1903 | | 1975 | |
|---|---|---|---|---|
|  | Industrial employment | Population | Industrial employment | Population |
| Broad region[a] | | | | |
| National capital[b] | 6.5 | 4.9 | 47.4 | 21.8 |
| Metropolitan periphery | 23.1 | 22.2 | 16.2 | 21.8 |
| Traditional agricultural | 67.1 | 59.6 | 22.2 | 39.5 |
| Frontier | 3.3 | 13.3 | 14.2 | 26.3 |

Sources: For 1903 output, see R. Hooley, "Long-Term Economic Growth in the Philippines, 1902-61." In Conference on Growth of Output in the Philippines. Los Banos: International Rice Research Institute, 1966. For 1975 output, see National Economic Development Authority (NEDA). The National Income Accounts, CY 1946-75. Manila, 1978. For 1903 industrial employment and population, see the 1903 Population and Economic Censuses. For 1975 industrial employment, see 1975 Census of Establishments. For 1975 population, see 1975 Population Census.

[a] The broad regions are metropolitan Manila, national capital region (NCR); metropolitan periphery (MP), central Luzon and Southern Tagalog; traditional agricultural region (TAR), Ilocos, Bicol, eastern Visayas, western Visayas, and central Visayas; frontier region (FR), Cagayan Valley, northern Mindanao, western Mindanao, central Mindanao, and southern Mindanao.

[b] Includes the rest of Rizal Province.

Table 5.2
Population and density by region, 1903

| Region | Population | Population density* |
|--------|-----------|---------------------|
| National capital | 370,851 | 191 |
| Metropolitan periphery | 1,697,432 | 27 |
| Traditional agricultural | 4,552,911 | 48 |
| Frontier | 1,014,232 | 7 |

Source: Census of the Philippines, 1903.
*Number of persons per square kilometer.


Table 5.3
Some indicators of agricultural growth, 1950-70

| | 1950 | 1960 | 1965 | 1970 |
|---|------|------|------|------|
| Net value added (millions of pesos) | 3,629 | 5,870 | 7,131 | 8,918 |
| (Percentage annual increase) | -- | 4.9 | 3.9 | 4.6 |
| Yield per hectare (pesos) | 978 | 1,051 | 1,197 | 1,408 |
| (Percentage annual increase) | -- | 0.7 | 2.6 | 3.6 |
| Cultivated area (thousand hectares) | 3,711 | 5,580 | 5,958 | 6,335 |
| (Percentage annual increase) | -- | 3.4 | 1.4 | 1.2 |

Source: Adapted from ILO (1974: Table 91).


Table 5.4
Origins of migrants to Digos-Padada Valley (percentages)

| Island of birth | Source of data | |
|-----------------|----------------|------------------|
| | Interview | Government files* |
| Bohol | 12.3 | 8.4 |
| Cebu | 60.8 | 64.8 |
| Leyte-Samar | 4.7 | 5.3 |
| Luzon | 6.4 | 8.0 |
| Mindanao | 5.5 | 4.5 |
| Negros | 5.2 | 4.5 |
| Panay | 4.9 | 4.3 |

Source: Simkins and Wernstedt (1971).
*From land applications filed by settlers.

Table 5.5
Educational attainment: Persons 20 years or older, 1964-65 migrant
survey (percentages)

| Grades completed | Philippines | Cebu Province | Digos-Padada Valley |
|---|---|---|---|
| None | 29.9 | 36.5 | 9.0 |
| 1 | 2.4 | 2.4 | 2.7 |
| 2 | 6.1 | 7.2 | 8.5 |
| 3 | 7.7 | 8.4 | 11.1 |
| 4 | 13.5 | 13.3 | 19.6 |
| 5 | 7.7 | 6.4 | 10.1 |
| 6 | 12.1 | 7.6 | 16.4 |
| 7-10 | 14.8 | 11.1 | 17.1 |
| 11 or more | 6.9 | 6.8 | 5.4 |

Source:  Simkins and Wernstedt (1971).

Table 5.6
Total number of hectares farmed per farm family in
Digos-Padada settlement

| Hectares | Prior to migration | | After migration | |
|---|---|---|---|---|
| | No. | % | No. | % |
| Less than 1 | 13 | 3.1 | 15 | 2.0 |
| 1.0-1.9 | 104 | 24.8 | 100 | 13.6 |
| 2.0-2.9 | 168 | 40.1 | 186 | 25.2 |
| 3.0-3.9 | 73 | 17.4 | 138 | 18.7 |
| 4.0-4.9 | 27 | 6.4 | 78 | 10.6 |
| 5.0-7.5 | 21 | 5.0 | 133 | 18.0 |
| More than 7.5 | 13 | 3.1 | 87 | 11.8 |

Source:  Simkins and Wernstedt (1971).

Table 5.7
Average area owned by settlers, Palawan Resettlement Project, 1978

| | Before migration | | After migration | |
|---|---|---|---|---|
| Type of settler | No. of owners* | Average area | No. of owners* | Average area |
| Government-assisted | 11 | 2.64 | 49 | 8.01 |
| Self-financed | 17 | 2.53 | 44 | 9.34 |
| All | 18 | 2.57 | 93 | 8.64 |

Source: James (1978).
*From a sample of 100.


Table 5.8
Estimated costs of establishing a 5-hectare rice farm through government-assisted and self-financed settlement

| | Estimated cost in pesos (1978 prices) | | |
|---|---|---|---|
| Item | World Bank | Bureau of Resettlement | Self-financed settlers |
| Land survey | 370 | 425 | 600 |
| Land clearing | 9,421 | 1,225 | 4,836 |
| Direct assistance | 12,811 | 26,600 | 6,871 |
| Housing | 4,710 | 10,000 | 864 |
| Work animal | 1,130 | 2,000 | 1,433 |
| A year's subsistence rations | 5,652 | 6,000 | 2,568 |
| Medical assistance | 565 | 1,200 | 572 |
| Seeds and seedlings | 377 | 1,500 | 86 |
| Chemicals and fertilizers | 377 | 3,000 | 415 |
| Farm implements/hand tools | none | 900 | 222 |
| Land preparation | none | 1,500 | (by settler) |
| Moving and transportation | none | 500 | 711 |
| Total costs without infrastructure | 22,602 | 28,250 | 12,307 |

Sources: World Bank (1973); ILO (1974); mimeo., Settlers' Affairs Division, Bureau of Resettlement, Ministry of Agrarian Reform, August 24, 1977; and James (1978).

Table 5.9
Estimated net migration by region, 1903-75

| Region | Period | | | | | |
|---|---|---|---|---|---|---|
| | 1903-18 | 1918-39 | 1939-48 | 1948-60 | 1960-70 | 1970-75 |
| Central industrial | -62,824 | 138,356 | 231,196 | 336,750 | 1,111,334 | 587,139 |
| National capital region | 14,598 | 268,520 | 372,752 | 261,452 | 661,140 | 445,055 |
| Central Luzon | -64,406 | -43,981 | -47,209 | -44,420 | 237,699 | 101,491 |
| Southern Tagalog | -13,016 | -86,183 | -94,347 | 119,719 | 212,495 | 40,594 |
| Traditional agricultural | -123,247 | -684,455 | -391,181 | -1,686,369 | -1,847,083 | -594,273 |
| Ilocos | -36,602 | -406,594 | -133,504 | -310,522 | -297,079 | -160,257 |
| Bicol | -29,809 | 43,545 | 47,669 | 15,817 | -232,901 | -208,770 |
| Western Visayas | -116,361 | 83,629 | -82,372 | -485,447 | -550,581 | -3,194 |
| Central Visayas | -32,978 | -350,787 | -229,395 | -462,779 | -383,878 | -90,722 |
| Eastern Visayas | 92,504 | -54,248 | 6,422 | -443,437 | -382,644 | -131,330 |
| Frontier | 186,070 | 546,099 | 159,985 | 1,349,619 | 735,749 | 7,134 |
| Cagayan Valley | -13,894 | 17,632 | -85,290 | 110,567 | 63,517 | -6,629 |
| Western Mindanao | 65,238 | 106,525 | 37,771 | 276,519 | 39,737 | -95,549 |
| Northern Mindanao | 52,962 | 149,507 | 73,034 | -1,352 | 195,758 | 74,761 |
| Southern Mindanao | 19,225 | 130,576 | 35,744 | 539,270 | 368,650 | 190,712 |
| Central Mindanao | 62,540 | 141,860 | 98,726 | 424,616 | 68,086 | -156,161 |

Sources: Population Censuses 1903, 1918, 1939, 1948, 1960, 1970 and 1975.

Table 5.10
Population density by region, 1903-75 (per square kilometer)

| Region | 1903 | 1918 | 1939 | 1948 | 1960 | 1970 | 1975 |
|---|---|---|---|---|---|---|---|
| Central industrial | 31 | 42 | 67 | 83 | 123 | 183 | 219 |
| National capital region | 191 | 265 | 549 | 852 | 1,334 | 2,147 | 2,691 |
| Central Luzon | 45 | 57 | 87 | 102 | 141 | 204 | 239 |
| Southern Tagalog | 19 | 26 | 38 | 43 | 64 | 91 | 105 |
| Traditional agricultural | 48 | 63 | 90 | 105 | 130 | 156 | 173 |
| Ilocos | 48 | 64 | 80 | 90 | 113 | 139 | 152 |
| Bicol | 37 | 48 | 76 | 95 | 134 | 168 | 181 |
| Western Visayas | 54 | 67 | 107 | 125 | 152 | 179 | 205 |
| Central Visayas | 75 | 99 | 131 | 142 | 169 | 203 | 227 |
| Eastern Visayas | 31 | 46 | 68 | 82 | 95 | 111 | 121 |
| Frontier | 7 | 11 | 21 | 27 | 48 | 70 | 80 |
| Cagayan Valley | 9 | 12 | 20 | 21 | 33 | 46 | 53 |
| Western Mindanao | 10 | 17 | 32 | 41 | 72 | 100 | 110 |
| Northern Mindanao | 8 | 13 | 25 | 33 | 46 | 69 | 82 |
| Southern Mindanao | 4 | 7 | 14 | 18 | 43 | 69 | 86 |
| Central Mindanao | 5 | 10 | 22 | 31 | 62 | 87 | 93 |
| Philippines | 25 | 34 | 53 | 64 | 90 | 122 | 140 |

Sources: Population Census, 1903, 1918, 1939, 1948, 1960, 1970, and 1975.

Table 5.11
Percentage distribution of employment and number of industrial
establishments by region: 1903, 1948, 1971-72

| Region | Employment | | | Establishments | | |
|---|---|---|---|---|---|---|
| | 1903 | 1948 | 1971-72 | 1903 | 1948 | 1971-72 |
| Central industrial | 32.1 | 23.7 | 23.8 | 25.1 | 22.6 | 23.0 |
| National capital region | 6.8 | 6.2 | 5.9 | 1.6 | 2.3 | 3.5 |
| Central Luzon | 12.2 | 7.9 | 8.8 | 10.1 | 8.7 | 8.0 |
| Southern Tagalog | 13.2 | 9.6 | 9.1 | 13.4 | 11.6 | 11.5 |
| Traditional agricultural | 60.2 | 54.7 | 43.6 | 66.4 | 56.8 | 43.5 |
| Ilocos | 12.8 | 10.9 | 9.4 | 23.6 | 13.1 | 9.0 |
| Bicol | 8.5 | 8.4 | 9.4 | 7.8 | 8.8 | 9.1 |
| Western Visayas | 15.9 | 13.1 | 9.7 | 9.8 | 11.0 | 8.1 |
| Central Visayas | 13.8 | 12.7 | 6.8 | 17.6 | 14.1 | 9.3 |
| Eastern Visayas | 9.2 | 9.5 | 8.2 | 7.6 | 9.9 | 8.0 |
| Frontier | 7.7 | 21.7 | 32.7 | 8.6 | 20.5 | 33.5 |
| Cagayan Valley | 3.9 | 4.3 | 8.5 | 3.9 | 5.1 | 6.5 |
| Western Mindanao | 0.5 | 3.9 | 4.9 | 0.5 | 3.2 | 6.2 |
| Northern Mindanao | 3.0 | 5.7 | 5.2 | 4.0 | 5.7 | 6.7 |
| Southern Mindanao | 0.3 | 2.6 | 6.8 | 0.2 | 2.2 | 7.1 |
| Central Mindanao | 0.0 | 5.2 | 7.2 | 0.0 | 4.4 | 7.1 |
| All | 100.0 | 100.0 | 100.0 | 100.0 | 100.0 | 100.0 |

Source:   Economic censuses, 1903, 1948, and 1971-72.

Table 5.12
Percentage distribution of agricultural output by region, 1939, 1960, and 1971

| Region | 1939[a,b] | 1960[a] | 1971[c] |
|---|---|---|---|
| Central industrial | 29.2 | 24.9 | 22.3 |
| National capital region | 6.9 | 0.6 | 0.5 |
| Central Luzon | 12.1 | 11.7 | 11.6 |
| Southern Tagalog | 10.1 | 12.6 | 10.3 |
| Traditional agricultural | 50.0 | 43.8 | 40.3 |
| Ilocos | 9.1 | 10.6 | 9.3 |
| Bicol | 16.8 | 8.3 | 7.0 |
| Western Visayas | 19.2 | 11.9 | 12.0 |
| Central Visayas | 2.5 | 6.6 | 5.7 |
| Eastern Visayas | 2.5 | 6.3 | 6.3 |
| Frontier | 20.7 | 31.3 | 37.4 |
| Cagayan Valley | 1.8 | 6.0 | 6.4 |
| Western Mindanao | 7.2 | 4.3 | 4.8 |
| Northern Mindanao | 4.6 | 7.9 | 7.1 |
| Southern Mindanao | 1.9 | 4.6 | 8.4 |
| Central Mindanao | 5.2 | 8.5 | 10.6 |
| All | 100.0 | 100.0 | 100.0 |

Source: Economic and agricultural censuses, 1939, 1960, and 1971.
[a] Value of production.
[b] Excludes forestry, logging, and fishing.
[c] Value added.

Table 5.13
Percentage of farm area and cultivated area operated by tenants, 1939

| Province | Percentage operated by tenants | |
|---|---|---|
| | Farm area | Cultivated area |
| Bulacan | 60.5 | 66.5 |
| Nueva Ecija | 57.3 | 67.8 |
| Pampanga | 52.9 | 67.0 |
| Cavite | 54.7 | 58.5 |
| Tarlac | 45.3 | 52.4 |
| Laguna | 41.3 | 44.3 |

Source: Census of the Philippines, 1939.

Table 5.14
Estimates of relative costs of land settlement and irrigation

| | Cost in pesos in 1970 prices | | | | | Benefit-cost ratio | |
| | Per hectare | Per man-day | | Per metric ton | | Palay rice | Maize |
| | | Palay rice | Maize | Palay rice | Maize | | |
|---|---|---|---|---|---|---|---|
| Land settlement | | | | | | | |
| World Bank estimates | 3,500 | 109 | 55 | 4,300 | 3,200 | 0.76 | 1.12 |
| Bureau of Resettlement estimate | 2,500 | 78 | 39 | 3,100 | 2,300 | 1.08 | 1.56 |
| Irrigation | 1,200 | | | | | | |
| Traditional[a] ( 0 N) | -- | 52 | -- | 1,800 | -- | 1.61 | -- |
| Traditional[a] (15 N) | -- | 48 | -- | 1,600 | -- | 1.69 | -- |
| HYV[b] (30 N) | -- | 34 | -- | 850 | -- | 3.23 | -- |
| HYV[b] (60 N) | -- | 31 | -- | 790 | -- | 3.33 | -- |

Source: ILO (1974: 448).
Figures followed by the letter N stand for the number of kilograms of nitrogen
fertilizer applied annually per hectare.
  a Traditional seed varieties.
  b High-yielding varieties.

Eishetu Chole and Teshome Mulat    6

# Land Settlement in Ethiopia: A Review of Developments

## INTRODUCTION

Ethiopia, with a total land area of 1.24 million square kilometers and a population (in 1983–84) of nearly 35 million, is the seventh largest and third most populous country in Africa. When viewed on an aggregate basis, this gives a population density of about 28 persons per square kilometer, certainly a favorable person–land ratio. A closer look at land use and population settlement patterns, however, reveals that this general picture camouflages some very real problems.

As Table 6.1 shows, only 14.8 percent of the country's land area is under cultivation, whereas more than 50 percent consists of grazing and browsing land. Moreover, nearly 19 percent of the land is currently unutilizable. A very large proportion of the population lives in areas that taken together represent a very small fraction of the country's total land area.

There are three climatic zones in Ethiopia, classified on the basis of the relation between altitude and temperature, rainfall, and vegetation. First, there is the *Kolla* zone, embracing lands below an altitude of

From the Institute of Development Research, Addis Ababa University.

1500 meters above sea level, with high temperatures throughout the year (average monthly temperatures of 20°C amd higher) and associated, generally, with low vegetation density. Second, covering all lands of 1500–2500 meters above sea level, with medium temperatures (average monthly temperatures of 20°C and higher) and associated, generally, with low vegetation density. Second, there is the *Weynadega* zone, covering all lands of 1500–2500 meters above sea level, with medium temperatures (average monthly temperatures of 20°C for the hottest months) and where rain-fed agriculture is practiced. Third, the *Dega* zone consists of the highland areas with altitudes of 2500 meters and more above sea level and low temperatures throughout the year.

The population settlement patterns follow these physiographical divisions of the country. Most of the population practice rain-fed agriculture and are located in the *Dega* and *Weynadega* zones. In the plateau regions of Eritrea, Tegre, and Wallo, nucleated settlements (characterized by compact groupings of huts situated mainly on elevated ground near farms) are common. Closely spaced groups of huts characterize the settlement patterns in parts of the Gondar, Gojam, Shoa, and Gamo-Gofa plateau regions. Elsewhere in the highland areas, scattered settlements and widely spaced groups of huts are typical. More than 78 percent of the Ethiopian population live in the *Dega* and *Weynadega* zones (NRDC/CPSC 1984: 26). Because the highland zones are endowed with good volcanic soil, favorable temperatures, and high rainfall, they have traditionally been suitable for settled agriculture.

The lowlands (Kolla zone), on the other hand, have a very low population density. With a harsh climate characterized by high temperatures throughout the year, irregular and insufficient rainfall, scanty and shrubby vegetation, and the widespread existence of such debilitating hazards as malaria and the tsetse fly, these lands cannot support large populations except in irrigated areas. The Kolla zone covers about 60 percent of the land area of the country and supports a mainly nomadic population that accounts for nearly 10 percent of the total population of Ethiopia (UNDP/RRC 1983).

The settlement pattern of the country is thus highly lopsided. An obvious consequence of this concentration of a substantial majority of the population in the highlands has been to create immense pressure on the land, giving rise to land fragmentation (with obvious adverse effects on productivity) and even outright landlessness.

This already bad situation has been made even worse by the recurrent droughts that have hit the country since 1972–73. While the immediate effect of this disaster was to focus public attention on relief aid for the survivors, it also encouraged policymakers to think in terms of long-term solutions, most notably concerning the resettlement of those for whom there was no hope of making a livelihood on the lands that they had hitherto occupied.

The purpose of this study is to examine Ethiopia's experience with respect to resettlements, and especially to draw up a balance sheet of the record of the last decade in terms of the costs involved, as well as the results achieved. The problems, the organizational forms, and the performance of planned settlements are reviewed in order to draw some lessons for future settlement programs.

## LAND ADMINISTRATION AND SPONTANEOUS SETTLEMENTS

Although population settlements have a long history in Ethiopia, the important developments relevant to this study can be traced to the period of World War II and the emergence of an independent state. More recent developments relating to planned settlements are discussed later.

### Land administration

Following Memelik's establishment of a unitary state, large tracts of land, particularly in the southern regions, were designated government land. After the expulsion of the Italian occupation forces in 1941, these constituted the bases for settlement programs. Emperor Haile Selassie distributed land to patriots, prewar soldiers, public servants, landless and unemployed persons, civil servants with more than five years of service, and others in return for meritorious service to the government on the basis of his "land grant orders" (Wood 1977: 56). Several of these "land grant orders" were issued as early as 1942. But the supreme power of the monarch in matters of land administration was enshrined in the 1930 Constitution (Article 15) and in the Revised Constitution of 1955 (Article 31). The monarch used his powers not only to dispense "government land" in the above fashion, but also to change the status of landholdings from one form to another. For example, he made as many as five authorizations for the conversion of temporary usage rights to land into freehold usages (Wood 1977: 60).

This exercise by the monarch of his powers relating to land administration did not always result in beneficial settlement patterns. Often political considerations were given more weight than long-term economic gains. Many grantees did not themselves settle on the land but kept title to it. Others used their ownership privileges to maintain tenants and extract surpluses. Often the beneficiaries of the grantee system were landowners. The system therefore had the effect of accentuating the existing inequality of incomes and bolstering the relative powers of

the landed gentry. The landlord-dominated parliament failed to introduce any reform in agriculture, which remained backward and faced
declining productivity.

The Ministry of Land Reform and Administration, established in 1966,
was entrusted with the task of formulating appropriate land reform
policies. Among its priority considerations was the adoption and implementation of settlement and resettlement programs (Imperial Ethiopian Government 1968: 425–26). The government appeared to attach
great significance to the issue of settlements, both as an approach to
solving the problems of a too high labor–land ratio in the northern
plateau regions, and as a way of modernizing agriculture and increasing
agricultural productivity in the economy as a whole.

A 1971 report by a consultant for the Harvard Advisory Group advocated the abrogation of the land grant system, and proposed a comprehensive planned utilization of government lands through an
appropriate settlement policy. Key elements in this policy were support
to individual initiative and low-cost settlement programs (MacArthur
1972). Another problem identified by this report—of which immediate
control was advised—was that of the excessive "spontaneous settlements" taking place on government land at the time. An earlier study
by the Planning Commission Office had also concluded that spontaneous
and unorganized settlements were not a very satisfactory means of improving agriculture, that publicly supported land settlement schemes
for small farmers were costly, and that large-scale land development by
commercial interests constituted the most viable proposition from the
point of view of raising agricultural productivity, increasing export earnings, and even expanding employment (Planning Commission Office
1971).

Although the Ministry of Land Reform and Administration, as well
as the Third Five-Year Development Plan, saw settlements as an important development strategy, several soil studies showed that government land that could be effectively used for settlements was rather
limited. Large areas of government land were located in arid regions
with little prospect of irrigated agriculture. Other areas were located in
remote regions and contained forest and swampy land that could prove
costly to develop. The government was, however, unable to produce a
working land use policy and program before its overthrow in 1974.

## Spontaneous settlements

Since 1942, spontaneous movements involving millions of people have
taken place, caused by a number of factors. The population has been
increasing at relatively high rates throughout the country, including the
northern plateau regions, which already had high population densities.

At the same time there have not been any appreciable changes in agricultural technology. In fact, a worsening land productivity situation has been observed over the years. The communal land ownership patterns in the northern regions were not particularly encouraging to private initiative, so individuals could escape total economic and social stagnation only through emigration. There were large-scale evictions of tenants from the land, as a result of commercialization and mechanization in the central regions. The improvements in transportation and communications, and the government's land grant system, by which a large number of grantees were encouraged to settle in new areas, may also have contributed to increased migration and resettlement.

The absence of any official registration makes it difficult to measure accurately the extent of resettlement since the 1940s, but it is thought to be considerable. A study carried out in 1975 observed that "spontaneous resettlement has become a widespread feature in Ethiopia during the last three decades" (Wood 1977: 77), and the same study concluded that "numerically it is certain that millions of people have been involved in some degree of resettlement since the Italian occupation" (p. 84). An impression of the number of persons involved in resettlement can also be obtained by looking at the amount of land distributed under the land grant system. It is estimated that 48,280 *gashas* (about 1,931,200 hectares) of land was distributed to individuals and groups under that system between 1942 and 1971 (Asfaw 1975). Since spontaneous resettlement on an even larger scale is known to have taken place outside this system, the overall volume of resettlement must have been considerable indeed.

Another indication of the volume of resettlement is given by a 1971 study under the USAID program, which reported that the area under cultivation in the country as a whole had increased by as much as 20 percent between 1966 and 1970 alone (Wood 1977: 84). Since overall labor–land ratios changed little during this short period, most of this increase in land use must have been associated with a net increase in labor utilization or an expansion of spontaneous settlement or both. There were also numerous cases of tenant evictions due to the mechanization and commercialization of agriculture. In the Chilalo Agricultural Development Unit (CADU) Project area, for example, it was recorded that in 1971 alone as many as 550 tenants (or 25 percent of those farming in the area in the mid–1960s) were evicted, "most of them leaving . . . in search of new lands" (Ministry of Land Reform and Administration 1972).

Much earlier resettlement involved short-distance migration. With a buildup of population pressures and a decline in land fertility in traditional farming areas, the only escape appears to have been resettlement. In later years many resettlements involved long-distance migration, and were associated with the resettlement of "outsiders" or nonlocal population groups. It is not unusual to observe, however, the simultaneous resettlement of short-distance and long-distance migrants in the same general area. One recent study of resettlements in southwestern Ethiopia found that long-distance migrants to the area tended to resettle in cities, while short-distance migrants tended to come from and resettle in rural areas (Wood 1977: chap. 11). There were also observed differences in age structure, literacy rates, and motivation between long-distance and short-distance migrants. Long-distance migrants tended to be younger, often single, with relatively more literates among them; they often chose to migrate because of rising aspirations and general dissatisfaction with their home area. In contrast, short-distance migrants were found to be relatively older, married and with families, mainly illiterate, and motivated to resettle in response to "environmental problems (erosion, irregularity of rainfall, predations by wild animals, etc. and problems associated with the systems of tenancy and land taxation" (Wood 1977: 327).

## PLANNED SETTLEMENTS

### Historical background

Planned settlements were introduced into Ethiopia only recently and appear to have been given a new impetus after the overthrow of the monarchy in 1974. The First Five-Year Development Plan (1957–61) does no more than mention the need to use settlement programs to improve agricultural productivity and techniques (Imperial Ethiopian Government 1958: 70). The Second Five-Year Development Plan (1963–67) saw no new developments in the field of planned settlements, either. The need for land reform was appreciated, and it was recommended that quantitative studies and land measurement should be undertaken to pave the way for an effective land settlement program in future years. The Second Five-Year Plan sets as its priorities the improvement of landlord–tenant relations, the introduction of progressive taxation, the abolition of out-of-date holdings, and the introduction of cadastral survey and land registration; planned settlements were not priority considerations in its agricultural development strategy (Imperial Ethiopian Government 1962: 326–29).

In the Third Five-Year Development Plan (1968–73), settlements were viewed in the context of a regional development strategy aimed at relieving population pressures in the northern plateau regions, and raising agricultural productivity through the use of underdeveloped land resources and the application of improved land management practices (Imperial Ethiopian Government 1968: 373–74).

This was the general picture at the national level. At the local level, however, the first known planned settlement scheme was started in 1958 (known as the Abella and Belle settlements) by the governor of the Sidamo region; the aim was to bring under cultivation lowland areas that were only in marginal use for hunting and grazing and to which there were no strong traditional claims. A further aim of the settlements was to resettle "surplus" population from the overcrowded Welamo Highlands and subsequently from other similar areas as well. These settlements were later passed on to the Welamo Agricultural Development Unit (WADU) when it was established in 1970 under the Ministry of Agriculture to implement a regional development program for the Welamo subprovince (Simpson 1975: 4–36; Wood 1977: 75). Several other planned settlements have followed these, sponsored or created by diverse government agencies and private organizations. These early settlements were conceived as low-cost, labor-intensive projects in which government inputs were kept to a minimum. They were made possible by the active participation of the relevant government departments in the effective control of malaria and trypanosomiasis, careful selection of the settlers, and provision of a demonstration program as part of the Agricultural Extension Service.

A real leap in planned settlement took place, however, with the establishment in August 1974 of the Relief and Rehabilitation Commission (RRC), a direct consequence of the 1972–73 famine that claimed many thousands of lives. Although settlements did not constitute a priority of the commission at the time, it later undertook settlement activities as long-term solutions to persistent drought and population displacement problems (PMAC 1974).

A significant milestone in facilitating the process of settlement was the 1975 Proclamation, which nationalized rural lands (PMAC 1975). The public ownership of rural lands made it possible for the government to resettle people as needed without being hampered by considerations of tampering with private property. In addition, it cleared the ground for setting up peasants' associations, institutions which, as discussed later, were not without their significance to settlement programs.[1]

The next important development was the establishment in 1978 of a Settlement Authority as an autonomous unit within the Ministry of Agriculture and Settlement (Ministry of Agriculture and Settlement 1978: 2). The priorities of the Settlement Authority were the settlement of unemployed persons, displaced groups, landless peasants, and nomads, in that order. According to its planned programs, the Settlement Authority was to provide settlers with agricultural inputs on a credit basis, repayable loans for setting up cooperative shops, a water supply, health care, and education. The schemes, on achieving self-reliance (which was expected to be attained within three years of establishment), were to be owned and managed by the settlers themselves. The Settlement Authority set itself the target of settling 20,000 families per year. Actual performance was short of the mark and constrained by developments that led to a further reorganization of the settlement programs.

Proclamation no. 173 of 1979, which set up a new Relief and Rehabilitation Commission (henceforth RRC), repeated the order that established the former RRC as well as the proclamation that created the Settlement Authority (PMAC 1979a). In fact, the new commission was to bring under one organization tasks hitherto carried out by three different institutions, namely the Awash Valley Authority, the Settlement Authority, and the former RRC. It was to be an autonomous body accountable to the office of the chairman of the Council of Ministers and was given wide-ranging powers and duties in the settlement field. As of 1983 there were 85 settlements under the RRC.

## Objectives of planned settlement programs

The objectives of the early planned settlements were to put idle land and water resources to developmental use, to accommodate landless peasants in settlements, and to provide income-generating activity to unemployed persons and farmers suffering from the ill effects of drought and overcrowding. Similar objectives are indicated in the current settlement programs. Some settlements in Awash, Wabishebelle, and Gambeila have the additional aim of settling nomads. Other settlements in the Gondar and Harar regions have the aim of maintaining farming activity in private and state farms abandoned as a result of war, the nationalization programs, or internal disturbances. The Tedelle settlements in the central region are primarily intended for the settlement of the urban unemployed.

The settlement programs are therefore directed at three target groups. First, there are the urban unemployed of working age and in need of productive employment. As in most underdeveloped countries, the problem of urban unemployment in Ethiopia is assuming alarming proportions. In 1973 an ILO Employment Advisory Mission to Ethiopia estimated open urban unemployment to be between 5 and 10 percent of the urban labor force, and concluded that it was "not a really serious problem, at least in comparison to the rest of tropical Africa" (ILO/UNDP 1973: 2). However, an ILO mission that visited the country nine years later cited a report that stated that this figure had gone up to nearly 20 percent by 1978 (ILO/JASPA 1982: 257). While these figures, as estimates, do not suggest anything beyond a general order of magnitude, they do at least indicate that the problem has been worsening.

The second target group of planned settlement programs consists of those who have been displaced due to disasters such as drought. These, by and large, are inhabitants of the highland regions of the country, which have in any case extremely low soil fertility due to overuse. The climatic changes that have been causing recurrent droughts have accentuated this problem, leaving thousands of families without even the minimal sources of livelihood.

Opinion is divided, however, on the advisability of settling people with "bad" agricultural practices in new areas in the south of the country. The fear is that this could soon lead to a similar deterioriation of agricultural land in the new areas. There is also the argument that the best way to tackle the problem of land misuse in the plateau regions is to keep the population there and raise the productivity of the land through land reclamation and rehabilitation programs. While such views have found acceptance among policymakers, it is believed that some settlements in new areas would still be required. The land–labor ratio in some of the plateau regions is too low, and improved agricultural practices, however well planned and executed, may not provide adequate incomes for all. One way of bringing new land under cultivation is through settlements. And if the settlements are carried out in a planned way, this will reduce the chances of "exporting" agricultural malpractices into new areas.

The third target group is the nomads. Although nomads constitute no more than 10 percent of the total population, they occupy about 61 percent of the total land area. They are diverse, belonging to some 25 ethnic groups. A recent study identifies two types of nomads in Ethiopia: pastoral nomads, who inhabit much of the lowlands in the north and east, and "nomadic hunters-cultivators," who are concentrated in the southwestern part of the country (UNDP/RRC 1983: 6–9). The earliest recorded planned settlements for nomads were located in the Awash Valley under the old Awash Valley Authority, which in 1966 settled 20 Afar nomads on 100 hectares of land in the Dubti area and 72 Afars in the Amibara Pilot Settlement Scheme (Awash Valley Authority 1971: 33–38). However, a more concerted effort to settle nomads was made more recently by the Relief and Rehabilitation Commission. In 1983 the RRC settled some 7000 nomads in some 15 settlement sites; these account for 21 percent of all settlers and 18 percent of all settlements in the country. Recurrent droughts and dislocations, and the government's priority concerning the planned settlement of nomads have contributed to this development. As we shall see later, however, the settlement of pastoralists is an expensive program. Apart from providing for training and easing the way for a change of lifestyle, the infrastructural requirements for irrigated agriculture are much higher than for rain-fed agriculture.

## Typology of settlements

There are several ways of classifying settlement schemes in Ethiopia. Simpson's study suggests a three-way classification: high-, medium-, and low-input settlements (Simpson 1975: 143). According to this classification, a high-input settlement is one with a full-time resident extension agent, while a low-input settlement has none. A medium-input settlement has only part-time services from extension agents.

Van Santen's classificatory system, while adopting Simpson's three-way classification, also attempts to group settlements on the basis of sponsor types and settler types (peasants, pastoralists, unemployed, etc.), and according to whether the agriculture practiced is irrigated or rain-fed (Van Santen 1978).

Although a similar basis is used in the classificatory system adopted by the 1980 FAO report (FAO/UNDP 1980: 30–59), the inputs are more concretely defined, and settlement objectives and benefits are elaborated to help differentiate settlements. This report identifies five settlement types in the country: self-help subsistence, improved subsistence, modern smallholder farming, production-oriented large-scale mechanized farming, and rehabilitation (leper) settlement schemes.

The major activity of the RRC is relief work, involving the provision of food and maintenance aid through distribution centers established in various disaster areas and in relief centers. Another related major activity of the commission is the organization and management of "rehabilitation centers." Relief activity ceases after some time and a rehabilitation program follows, aimed at helping the affected population to start working on the land or to get involved in other productive activities. In 1983–84 there were 26 such rehabilitation programs involving some 60,000 persons (RRC 1984b). The commission normally provides food, seeds, oxen, farm equipment, and other necessary material and services for the implementation of such programs.

Although some rehabilitation programs eventually end up as planned settlement schemes, these should not be confused with the "regular settlements" of the commission, which are based on the "settlement model" conceived in its paper, *Settlement Policy* (RRC 1981). The regular settlements are grouped into two categories: settlements under budget, and settlements under technical aid (Table 6.2). The settlements under budget depend totally on the commission, which covers all aspects of settlement cost through government-approved budgetary provisions. Those under "technical aid" are settlements that have attained some degree of self-sufficiency but are provided with technical personnel, including a farm manager, a cooperative organizer, tractor operators, and so on.

Another classification system currently used by the RRC is based on the nature and intensity of input usage. Settlements are basically grouped into low-cost and special. A low-cost settlement, as the name suggests, aims at making the scheme operational with minimum cost to the government, and usually tends to be labor-intensive. Settlers are provided with seeds, oxen, technical support, credits, supplies, and other inputs under a budgetary provision from the government for up to three years, by which time they are expected to develop into a self-supporting producers' cooperative. The land selected for settlement is free of trypanosomiasis, to make it possible to sustain oxen-based ploughing practice, and settlers are expected to meet objective selection criteria and undergo training (Kassaye 1978: 3–4).

The low-cost settlement model specifies a land area of 2.5 hectares per family for rain-fed agriculture and 1.5 hectares per family for irrigated agriculture (Ministry of Agriculture and Settlement 1978: 3–4). A settlement under this scheme consists of 250 families in an area of 625 hectares for rain-fed agriculture and the same number of families in 375 hectares of land for irrigated agriculture.

The special settlement scheme, on the other hand, is relatively high-cost in that it involves trypanosomiasis and malaria control programs, makes use of advanced agricultural machinery and skilled labor, and aims at producing surplus for the domestic and foreign markets. The special settlement model also assumes a provision of 2.5 hectares per family for rain-fed agriculture and 1.5 hectares per family for irrigated agriculture. A settlement under this scheme consists of 500 families.

Recently the RRC has started exploring the possibility of placing drought victims and displaced persons with established producers' co-operatives. The government would subsidize such cooperatives to defray the extra costs incurred in accommodating additional persons. This scheme is not expected to involve many persons, however, and therefore may not significantly reduce the need for new settlements.

## Institutional arrangements

### Administrative organization of the RRC

The Relief and Rehabilitation Commission is headed by a commissioner who is advised by an advisory council that includes representatives from the various ministries, the All-Ethiopian Peasants' Association, and other mass organizations designated by the government.

The commissioner is assisted by two deputies, one responsible for settlement work and another responsible for support services (transport, finance, etc.). Each deputy commissioner has four departments under his purview. In addition, the commission has a branch office in each administrative region of the country, headed by a branch representative. The same arrangement is repeated at the *awraja* (provincial) level.

*The settlement process*

According to the RRC, the settlement process starts with the identification and selection of a target group. Steps are then taken to make the group familiar with the advantages of participating in a settlement program. Once heads of families register, a feasibility study of the selected site is conducted. This includes a study of its location, climate, geology, soils, topography, vegetation, water resources, communications, and land use. This is carried out by a study team made up of an agronomist, an agricultural engineer, an agricultural economist, a geographer, an animal husbandry expert, and a sociologist. The feasibility study also includes drawing up a general plan that focuses on how and when the various targets are to be realized. There is also a detailed plan that sets up a work schedule for every operation and quantifies the necessary material, financial, and manpower requirements for the fulfillment of the operation. The planning stage of the program is then completed and the implementation starts; the final stage involves assessing the program and making modifications as it is implemented.

Such in brief are the major outlines of the settlement process. The RRC is entrusted with the task of settler selection. The ministries of Agriculture, Interior, and Labour and Social Affairs, as well as the All-Ethiopian Peasants' Association, are expected to participate in recruitment and in persuading people to resettle. In principle no one is chosen for a settlement program unless he/she volunteers for it. Despite this provision, however, there are cases of involuntary resettlement (NRDC/CPSC 1984: 80). In addition, other people who satisfy set criteria (which include willingness to work in agriculture, acceptance of the principles of cooperative production, belonging to the 18–45 age group, good health, and a willingness to live by the RRC rules and regulations) are considered for the settlement programs.

The selection of settlement sites is determined by a committee composed of representatives from relevant ministries, with the RRC acting as coordinator. The detailed planning of the site is the responsibility of the RRC. But there is substantial evidence that the establishment of settlements is in fact seldom preceded by the kind of elaborate planning implied in the outline above (RRC 1981: 3–8).

*The settlement model*

In RRC special settlement schemes, one settlement unit is composed of 500 families, and for administrative and management purposes five such units make one project area, with an office to coordinate its activities (RRC 1981). The settlers, who are at first accommodated in common shelters, later construct their own dwellings. Each settler is given a homestead plot of 1000 square meters.

Until such a time as the settlers attain self-sufficiency they are provided with food, clothing, and other essentials. Self-sufficiency in food is expected to be attained after only two crop seasons. Complete food aid is given during the first crop season, but thereafter it is anticipated that food aid will cover the difference between actual production and food requirements. Expenses incurred for livestock development are expected to be repaid. However, money expended on investments for development works, including buildings constructed for livestock development, is not repayable. There is no indication of the number of installments in which the expenses incurred for livestock development have to be paid, or why certain expenses are repayable and others not.

Settlers are organized into producers' cooperatives called *Welbas*.[2] Within the first year it is anticipated that the settlers will be introduced to the basic principles of cooperative farming, and the leaders of the cooperatives will be given some education in cooperative management, job assignment, and income allocation.

Each settlement unit is expected to have a unit manager (who is an agriculturalist), a cooperative organizer, a home economist, a junior mechanic, and an assistant administrator. According to the plan, 14 skilled persons are assigned through the RRC to each settlement. They often come from the relevant ministries to help establish the settlement cooperatives. Over a three-year period, settlers are given training in the fields of agriculture (crop production, animal husbandry, agricultural technology, etc.), cooperative management (accounting, management, organization and administration, etc.), health, and home economics.

A settlement project is expected to achieve self-sufficiency in three years. In addition to the evaluations that are made during the first two years of the project's life, at the end of the third year a team of experts from the RRC and the Ministry of Agriculture determines whether or not self-sufficiency has been attained. If the conclusion is positive, the Ministry of Agriculture takes over administrative control (the settlement being a producers' cooperative); if not, the RRC runs the project for a few years more.

*The organization and management of settlements*

The organization and management of settlements has been subject to some degree of evolution over time and tends to show regional variations. An attempt will be made, however, to outline its basic features. As pointed out earlier, there is one office to coordinate the operations of every five settlement units. This office is manned entirely by personnel provided by the government.

At the settlement unit level, however, there are two parallel levels of management, one made up of government-supplied personnel and the other of the settlers themselves. The main task assigned to government personnel (14 in all, including a unit manager and other technical personnel) is to train counterparts from the settler population, so that by the end of a three-year period the settlement unit is able to manage its own affairs totally, thereby making it possible for the government personnel to be withdrawn. There is therefore a parallel management structure run by the settlers themselves.

Prior to 1979, when the government issued guidelines regarding the formation and management of cooperatives, the settlers had farmed on an individual basis. As pointed out earlier, however, the guidelines required settlement units to be organized as producers' cooperatives (Welbas). In 1982 a proclamation was issued that stipulated that "a settlement shall be regarded as a kebele peasant association" (NRDC/CPSC 1984: 45). In effect, what this meant was that a settlement unit could constitute itself into a peasants' association as well as a cooperative.

However, this has not meant establishing two separate leadership structures. A cooperative is expected to have a general assembly, an executive, a development committee, an inspection committee and several work teams, as detailed in the government *Guidelines* (PMAC 1979b: 49). A peasants' association, on the other hand, is expected to have a general assembly, an executive committee, an inspection committee and a judicial tribunal. Thus, while the development committee is unique to the cooperative and the judicial tribunal unique to the peasants' association, the other organs are common to both organizations. In practice, therefore, one does not have one structure of management for the cooperative and another for the peasants' association. What is usually found is in fact an amalgam of both, giving rise to a single hierarchy of leadership. The intention is for all peasants' associations eventually to tranform themselves into cooperatives.

## Some socioeconomic characteristics of the settler population

The age distribution of settler household heads for 24 settlements shows that, on average, only about 22 percent fall in the age group 50 and above (Table 6.3). The selection procedure used thus obviously ensures that settlements are well populated by persons of prime working age.

The age distribution for the settler population (as distinct from the distribution of household heads) varies between settlements. The data in Table 6.4 show that the percentage of the population under 15 in the settlements is below the national average. This is in part explained by the relatively low female-to-male ratio and the high proportion of unmarried men among settlers.

The data show that, on average, about 97 percent of all household heads are males. But the sex distribution of the settlement population as a whole gives an average of 42 percent for females, which is low compared with the national average. According to the CSO's *Statistical Abstract*, about 50 percent of the total population in rural areas consists of females. In urban areas the figure is even higher—about 53 percent.

The ratio of males to females in the settlement population also shows considerable variability between settlements. In the Gode settlements in the Harar region, females constitute only 26 percent of the population. But even the highest figure of 46 percent observed in the Bale region is far below the national average. These imbalances in the sex distribution, as shown in Table 6.5, affect the demographic structure of the population in the settlements where, as we have seen, the ratio of children to settlement population is below the national average.

There are other ramifications. Many RRC reports show that there are serious social problems, particularly in settlements that are far away from population concentrations and where the sex ratios are highly unbalanced. Such conditions affect the productivity of settlers and are mentioned as the main cause for their discontentment. The root cause of such problems is reported to be the failure to transport to the new settlement sites members of the family, either with the household heads or soon after they are settled. The healthy and active work environment that prevails in the Assosa settlements (where settlers live with their families) is contrasted with the Gode settlements, where most settler family members have not yet been taken in. The RRC views these problems as temporary and is at present engaged in providing transport and supplies to correct the situation.

But in some settlements the much needed social stability is also adversely affected by a relatively high proportion of unmarried settlers. Table 6.6 shows that about 16 percent of persons aged 15 and over in settlement sites are unmarried, which is higher than the national average for the rural population.[3] The proportion also varies widely between settlement sites.

Another factor to consider is the literacy rate among settlers. The attainment of high literacy rates has been a priority government program, and campaigns have been launched (called "rounds") ten times in the past five years. The results obtained have generally been impressive, particularly in organized population centers, including the settlements. Although the data on participation in literacy programs (Table 6.7) include nonsettlers, literacy campaigns were conducted in all settlements, and it would appear that a 100 percent literacy rate was obtained for all settlers in the relevant age groups (5 years and above). It would be necessary to examine the content and use of the literacy program in order to appraise its relevance for development, but that falls outside the scope of this study.

It would also appear reasonable to consider here the occupational profile of the settlers prior to their settlement in new areas. This is a significant factor, since the work and living experiences of the settlers prior to settlement determine, to a varying extent, their adaptation to a new and settled life in the settlements. Table 6.8 shows that peasants dislocated by drought constitute the majority of the settlers. Peasants displaced as a result of overcrowding make up 10.8 percent of all settlers, nomads about 21.1 percent, and urban unemployed 10.9 percent, while farm laborers and charcoal burners make up 9.6 percent. While this is the general picture, the share of each type of settler in the totals varies among regions. Thus, most nomads are settled in Wallo, while most urban unemployed are located in the settlements of the Shoa region.

## ASSESSMENT OF PROGRAM ACHIEVEMENTS

About 95 percent of all settlements today have been run by the RRC for over three years—more than three years' maximum period prescribed in the *Settlement Policy* document. The extension of the period beyond the planning provisions obviously has cost implications for the RRC. Further, land allocated for settlement programs includes "choice land," with satisfactory moisture and soil conditions, and large sums are absorbed by heavy settlement establishment costs. The government therefore expects the settlement schemes to yield high levels of land and labor productivity. Actual performance is much below expectations, however.

### Settlement productivity

Recent settlement survey results are reported in Table 6.9, together with planned production levels.

The data show that, irrespective of the type of settlement, settlement yields are consistently lower than expected. The relatively low productivity of settlements, an issue over which the RRC has shown concern, has been corroborated by other reports. Production data reported in the NRDC/CPSC *Annual Plans* since 1978 relating to different farm organizations (such as state farms and producers' cooperatives) show that settlements have consistently lower levels of land productivity. This broad conclusion appears to hold true both for overall production and for individual crops.

The data in Table 6.9 also show that there are significant differences in land productivity between low-cost settlements and the high-cost, so-called special settlement schemes. For all crops taken together, higher levels of land productivity are indicated for the low-cost settlements than for the special settlement schemes. Even in the case of individual crops where the special settlements appear to have a productivity edge, the differentials are not significant. When the land productivity figures are adjusted for differences in labor inputs, the low-cost settlements have significantly higher productivity levels than the special schemes (Table 6.10). This finding has important policy implications. The relatively high cost outlay for special settlements could only be justified by the achievement of commensurately high levels of labor and land productivity. In this case, however, the analysis would suggest the adoption of low-cost settlements, and this constitutes an important policy option for the RRC.

The variations in land productivity among settlements depend on several factors. It has already been indicated that due to the pressures of war and drought-induced population dislocations, settlements tend to be established with little time for preparations and planning. Thus settlements that have been in existence for a relatively long time are likely to have higher land and labor productivity than newly established ones. The location of settlements is another important factor. The closer a settlement is to the capital city or to a similar center of population concentration, the more productive it is likely to be, *ceteris paribus*. The relative ease of getting technical and material support, high demand for agricultural products, low transportation costs, and other marketing advantages usually tend to raise the levels of land productivity. A number of other variables also influence land productivity, such as type of settlement, types of settlers, and degree of government participation. In order to assess the precise relationship between land productivity and these factors, a regression equation is estimated by the ordinary least squares (OLS) method using survey data.

The semilog transformation gave the best statistical fit. The regression results presented in Table 6.11 show that settlements occupied by drought victims are over 250 percent less productive than settlements occupied by jobless people mainly from the cities. Agricultural laborers and charcoal burners (prior to settlement) are also, respectively, 57 percent and 64 percent less productive than the urban unemployed. These results do not conform to the expectation that those previously urban unemployed are likely to be the least productive in agriculture. The reason may be that settlements occupied by jobless persons tend to be located close to urban centers and receive (as a result, perhaps) closer government attention as well as other support.

The results also show that settlements occupied by victims of land overcrowding have relatively higher productivity than settlements occupied by the urban unemployed. These victims of land overcrowding are agriculturalists with years of work experience in environmentally degraded areas. It is therefore expected that they would perform well when given better land.

The distance of settlements from the settler's place of origin is also an important factor in determining land productivity, although the elasticity measured is very small. The size of the coefficient of the distance variable indicates that the yields of settlements improve by 0.1 percent on average for every kilometer away from the settler's place of origin. This is perhaps due to the fact that settlers who have traveled long distances are more likely to work hard on the new sites because their chances of returning to their old homes are small.

The regression results indicate that, on average, the special settlement schemes are 73 percent less productive than the low-cost schemes. It is also interesting to note that settlements tend to be relatively more productive when they are totally dependent on government finance than when they receive limited government support. Settlements maintained by government budgetary appropriation are 32 percent more productive than those receiving partial government aid. This result casts doubts on the viability of the settlement maturing process observed in the current RRC practice. The indication that settlements fail to sustain productivity once excessive government support is removed has to be viewed with some concern when considering the development of an appropriate policy for settlement programs in Ethiopia.

## Settlement infrastructure and costs

The "regular settlements" are in general an expensive operation. Pre–1974 planned settlements (except, perhaps, for the Dubti and Amibara schemes in the Awash) had been of the "low-cost" type. Their objective being basically the attainment of small, private subsistence farms, the costs to the government had to be kept low, and were often limited to the provision of food and seeds for a single crop year only. Such settlements were not many, however.

There were many factors that gave rise to the development of high-cost settlements in the post–1974 period. Many large-scale settlement programs were needed within a very short period. Drought, war, local disturbances, and other human-induced calamities caused the displacement of large numbers of persons. In 1980 about 5.2 million persons were victims of the effects of war and drought (RRC 1984c: 61). In 1983 the number of persons requiring government relief and rehabilitation support was estimated at 7 million (RRC 1984c: 63). In order to accommodate a large proportion of the population, existing settlements had to be expanded considerably and new ones had to be established within a short span of time. Table 6.12 shows the rate of growth of settlements during the period 1978–82.

The type of settlement model adopted also affects the costs of the settlements. Various items of economic and social infrastructure are needed, and in the typical settlement site the construction of a settler's village with warehouses, garages, public shops, a school, a cooperative office block, and so on requires considerable financial and other resources. The various facilities provided at settlement sites (Table 6.13) give an indication of cost magnitudes.

Apart from the direct provision of services such as land preparation, well digging, and so on, there is also extensive participation by various government departments in the provision of training programs for settlers and their families. In 1983–84, for which data have been compiled, it was planned to train some 6000 settlers in various fields, including home economics, cooperative management, dairy development, water and soil conservation, vegetable and fruit farming, maintenance of agricultural implements and equipment, and plant protection and development (RRC 1984a: 32). There were in the same year 755 children enrolled in kindergartens and 3168 in primary schools, and some 8000 adults in literacy classes (various reports from RRC archives). All these indicate the high costs incurred in the process of establishing and expanding settlements.

The development of new settlement sites and the expansion of some existing ones involve expensive land clearance, infrastructural development, and related activities. Apart from transporting large settler populations over long distances, food, shelter, medical care, and farm inputs have to be provided for the settlers and their families up to the time when the settlement schemes are fully developed as producers' cooperatives.

Complete data for the calculation of settlement costs are not available at present. The scanty information available is nonetheless indicative of the high costs involved. A 1983 estimate puts the costs of food, clothing, and household material alone at 1403 birr per settler per annum (RRC/CPSC 1983: 119–20).

The estimates in Table 6.14 are compiled from available data and show that government expenditure on settlements has been increasing over time. The costs per settler or per hectare have been declining, however. These costs seem high when compared with costs in traditional farming or with earlier settlements. The peasant agricultural farms (peasants' association farms) are estimated to have cost 230 birr per hectare in 1978 (Ministry of Agriculture and Settlement 1978). This estimate relates to the nonlabor costs incurred by the farmer in running the farm. A 1981 estimate puts the cost of production per hectare in Arssi Rural Development Unit area at 320 birr (Arssi Rural Development Unit 1982b: 5). The farms in this area receive technical and material support from the development unit. Settlement schemes of the pre–1974 period were known to have cost in the range of 50–500 birr per hectare in 1979 (FAO/UNDP 1980). This refers to total development costs, including all costs over the entire development period of the scheme. These figures therefore suggest that the establishment of a settlement at the present time is an expensive activity. Moreover, the cost figures in Table 6.14 refer only to government expenditure; if private costs were also included, the total cost would be even higher.

## Some additional settlement problems

High settlement costs and low levels of agricultural productivity constitute serious problems for the settlement schemes in Ethiopia. But there are other problems for which solutions have to be found if the multi-faceted approach to rural development is to be viable.

As discussed earlier, failure to complete the establishment phase of a settlement program on time and according to plan leads to a considerable increase in settlement costs to the government. In 1984 about 47 settlements were being financed by government budgetary provisions, although almost all of them had been with the RRC for more than three years. Another 28 settlements were also receiving "technical aid" from the government, although this is a relatively less expensive activity.

Many settlements also face serious problems of organization and management, despite years of association with the RRC. Although settlements are modeled on producers' cooperatives, there are still several settlements that have not attained this goal. Of the 85 settlements surveyed in 1984, 56 have formed producers' cooperatives, while 23 have not developed beyond peasant associations. There are six settlements that have remained unorganized for many years.

It can also be observed that many settlements still lack the requisite economic and social infrastructure. The list in Table 6.15 is not exhaustive and includes only the major items of infrastructure to be found in a model settlement scheme. Yet it demonstrates clearly that a significant proportion of the settlements do not contain or have no access to some of these facilities.

Various settlement evaluation reports produced by RRC teams in 1984 also show that the use of tractors in settlements faces serious problems of misuse and misapplication. In the 50 settlement sites reporting tractor use, very few kept all their tractors in working order. In the two settlements where all tractors were said to be working, it was reported that they were old and in a state of deterioration. The ratio of tractors out of use to the total number of tractors in settlements varied considerably between the settlements. On average, 60 percent of all tractors in settlements were out of use, which indicates a high rate of equipment disuse. Old age apart, maintenance problems, lack of spare parts, fuel shortages, and lack of trained personnel were cited as the major reasons for lack of use of tractors in settlements.

Many settlements face additional problems, such as shortages of necessary inputs and spares, better adaptation difficulties, and problems of management and organization (Table 6.16). In some cases settlement sites are selected without prior studies as to the suitability of land and moisture conditions for permanent crops. Many settlements contain settlers separated from their families by time and distance, which is known to have adverse effects on settler work performance. Still other settlements are located far out of easy reach, near the border regions or in disturbed areas, and face serious security problems. The settler selection procedure is not always applied (as prescribed), so that settlement agriculture suffers because of ill-adapted settlers. Although settlements bring together diverse populations for the common objective of nation building, they sometimes constitute hotbeds of tribal and social conflict.

One other major problem, common to most settlements, is the problem of settler retention. It is observed that a large number of settlers leave the settlement sites soon after settlement. Several factors account for the high but variable rate of settler abandonment of the settlements. The distance of a settlement from the original home of the settler, for example, is important in determining the likelihood of his/her remaining in the settlement. The longer the distance, the harder the settler will work in order to succeed in the settlement area. Another important factor is the presence of the settler's family in the settlement. If the settler moved with all his/her family members, there is more incentive to stay and succeed in the new area. Transportation difficulties and poor knowledge of the alternatives will also adversely affect settlers' mobility and tend to force them to remain. The settler's background will also be important in determining success. Settlers with a farming background will be expected to adapt and settle better in new areas than nomads or urban unemployed. The type of settlement and the "maturity" of the settlement are additional factors that are expected to affect the rate of settler retention.

In order to assess the influence of these various factors on settler retention, a regression equation was estimated using survey data.[4]

The regression results presented in Table 6.17 show that the type of settlement and occupational characteristics of the settlers prior to settlement are not important factors in determining the rate of settlement abandonment. It was found, however, that those settlers previously engaged in wage employment in agriculture were more prone to leaving the settlement sites than nomads. Another factor that was found to have some influence on settler retention was the degree of "completeness" of the settler household, although the coefficient is significant only at the 10 percent level. The results also indicate that the older a settlement site is, the less it is afflicted by the settlement abandonment problem. Likewise, the more distant a settlement is from the place of origin of the settlers, the less is the degree of settlement abandonment.

## CONCLUSION AND RECOMMENDATIONS

The distribution of population in Ethiopia is extremely uneven. While the plateau regions have relatively high population densities, accompanied by overuse of land and environmental degradation, the lowlands, wich have great potential for irrigated agriculture, are extremely underpopulated. A measure of population relocation is therefore desirable. Other objectives of such a relocation are an effective use of land and water resources, the settlement of nomads, a reduction in urban unemployment, and the development of agriculture for cash crop production, including exports. If these objectives are to be achieved, the coordination and systematization of the movement and resettlement of a large number of people are essential.

The settlement programs, however, are too costly and face serious problems of mismanagement and low land and labor productivity. The inability to allow sufficient time to prepare, plan, and implement settlement programs is a cause of waste and high costs. But this situation is expected to improve as political stability increases and as the nation weathers the harsh effects of drought and related natural calamities. It may then be possible to make a more judicious selection both of settlement lands and of settlers than at present.

The simultaneous operation of alternative settlement models has its own advantages. The results of this study show that the low-cost settlements are in general more cost-effective and more efficient than the special settlement schemes. Even so, the identification and application of further cost-reducing measures are essential for making the low-cost settlement option a viable proposition in future settlement programs. Settlement costs must be brought down to the cost levels of producers' cooperatives and other competing forms of agricultural organization. Among such cost-reducing measures may be included the careful selection of settlement lands and settlers and the proper execution of settlement programs.

The problem of low labor and land productivity in settlements can also be overcome in the long run and with the adoption of appropriate measures. The introduction of incentives, the provision of inputs and training, and the guarantee of favorable prices for settlement-produced goods and services may all contribute to improved productivity. The adoption of low-input settlement schemes and favorable marketing arrangements are also important considerations that may be taken into account in trying to solve the "low productivity" problem.

Some aspects of the observed problems in settlements, on the other hand, can be solved quickly and without difficulty. The transportation of dependents (families) of settlers will go a long way toward overcoming the uncertainties and social problems encountered in some settlements.

This, together with improved geographical mobility (through the provision of access to centers of population concentration near the settlement sites), is expected to bring about the desired social cohesion, contentment, and stability.

The general question of the management of settlements also needs to be looked into. According to the present practice, settlers are made totally dependent on the government, which provides free food, transportation, inputs and equipment, training, and technical services. This system is in part responsible for the high cost of settlements. It also imparts an unnecessary sense of total dependence on the government. An alternative system might be considered in which voluntary settlements are emphasized, and a partnership arrangement between settlers and the government is introduced for the sharing (based on proper costing of settlement activity) of settlement costs and other responsibilities.

## NOTES

1. The law provides for the establishment of a peasants' association on every 800 hectares. These associations, run by elected officials, are responsible for the administrative, economic, and political affairs of their localities.

2. Some 3 percent of the peasantry belong to agricultural cooperatives. There are three stages in the development of the cooperative. The first stage is called *Malba*. At this stage about 2000 square meters of land per household is allotted to members as family plots, the means of production are privately owned by members who may rent these to the cooperative, and all members are obliged to work on the collective land. The second stage, called *Welba*, is reached when the *Malba* members have gradually reduced their family plots to 1000 square meters per family and when all means of production are socialized through cooperative purchases and through buying from members. The third and final stage, known as *Wellands*, is reached when a minimum of five *Welbas* join together; the country does not yet have any, but they are expected to function as specialized agro-industrial systems.

3. Based on the prevailing practices, all those aged 15 and over are assumed to be eligible for marriage.

4. There are problems in the measurement of some of the variables used in the regression. The sense of "completeness" of the household at the settlement site can be measured in two ways from the available data: either by the ratio of married (or unmarried) settlers to the total number of settlers, or by the ratio of dependents to household heads in each settlement. The latter measure is found to be the better statistical index.

## BIBLIOGRAPHY

Arssi Rural Development Unit. 1982a. *Rural University, Land Utilization Practices and Livestock Survey, 1978*. Asela, Ethiopia.

————. 1982b. *Cost of Production of Major Crops*. ARDU Publication no. 20. Asela (February).

Asfaw, L. 1975. *The Role of State Domain Lands in Ethiopia's Agricultural Development*. LTC No. 106, Land Tenure Center, University of Wisconsin (April).

Awash Valley Authority. 1971. *Awash Valley Development, 1966–1971*. Addis Ababa: Artistic Printers.

Food and Agriculture Organization of the United Nations/United Nations Development Program. 1980. *Assistance to Settlement: Ethiopia Rural Settlement Schemes*. Ag: DP/ETH/75/025 Technical Report 1. Rome: FAO.

Imperial Ethiopian Government. 1958. *Five-Year Development Plan, 1957–1961*. Addis Ababa: PCO.

————. 1962. *Second Five-Year Development Plan, 1963–1967*. Addis Ababa: Berhanena Selam Printing Press.

————. 1968. *Third Five-Year Development Plan, 1968–1973*. Addis Ababa: Berhanena Selam Printing Press.

————. Ministry of Planning and Development. 1969. *Regional Aspects of National Planning in Ethiopia*. Part 1. Addis Ababa: Planning Office.

International Labour Office/Jobs and Skills Programme for Africa. 1982. *Socialism from the Grassroots: Accumulation, Employment and Equity in Ethiopia*, vol. 1. Addis Ababa: JASPA.

International Labour Office/United Nations Development Program. 1973. *Report to the Imperial Ethiopian Government of the Exploratory Employment Mission*. Geneva: ILO.

Kassaye, L. 1978. *Organization and Management Manual for Special Settlement Schemes*. Addis Ababa: Ministry of Agriculture and Settlement (July).

MacArthur, J. D. 1972. *The Development of Policy and Planning for Land Settlement in Ethiopia*, (chaps. 1, 4, and 5.) Addis Ababa: Ministry of Land Reform and Administration.

Ministry of Agriculture and Settlement. 1978. *The Settlement Authority at a Glance*. UNDP/FAO Project ETH/75/025. Addis Ababa: Artistic Printers.

————. 1978. *Land Utilization, Cost of Production and Farm Implements*. Addis Ababa.

Ministry of Land Reform and Administration. 1969. *A Policy-Oriented Study of Land Settlement*, 2 vols. Addis Ababa (December).

————. 1970. *Seminar Proceedings on Agrarian Reform*. Addis Ababa.

————. 1972. *Draft Policy of the Imperial Ethiopian Government on Agricultural Land Tenure*. Addis Ababa (August).

National Revolutionary Development Campaign/Central Planning Supreme Council (NRDC/CPSC). *Annual Plan* (in Amharic). Addis Ababa (published yearly since 1978).

Planning Commission Office. 1971. *Environmental Problems, Policies, and Action in Ethiopia*. Addis Ababa: PCO.

Provisional Military Administrative Council. 1974. "An Order to Establish a Relief and Rehabilitation Commission for Areas Affected by Natural Disaster." *Negarit Gazeta* (Addis Ababa), August 29.

————. 1975. "Proclamation No. 31 of 1975: A Proclamation to Provide for the Public Ownership of Rural Lands." *Negarit Gazeta*.

―――. 1979a. "Proclamation No. 173 of 1979: To Establish a Relief and Rehabilitation Commission." *Negarit Gazeta.*
―――. 1979b. *Guidelines for Peasants' Producers' Co-operatives* (in Amharic). Addis
Ababa: Artistic Printers.
Relief and Rehabilitation Commission. 1981. *Settlement Policy.* Addis Ababa
(July).
―――. 1984a. *1983/1984 Budget Year: Nine Months' Performance Evaluation Report*
(in Amharic). Addis Ababa (April).
―――. 1984b. *Rehabilitation and Programmes.* Addis Ababa.
―――. 1984c. *Ten Years of the Revolution (1974–1984).* Addis Ababa.
―――. No date. *Settlement/Resettlement Programmes.* Addis Ababa.
Relief and Rehabilitation Commission/Central Planning Supreme Council. 1983.
*Settlement Study Technical Committee Report.* Addis Ababa.
Simpson, G. 1975. *A Preliminary Survey of Settlement Projects in Ethiopia.* Addis
Ababa: IDR.
State Farm Development Authority. 1984. *State Farm Development Authority.* Ad-
dis Ababa.
Tegegne, T., and N. Tennassie. 1984. *Rural Poverty Alleviation: The Case of Ethiopia.*
Addis Ababa: IDR.
United Nations Development Program/Relief and Rehabilitation Commission
(UNDP/RRC). 1983. *A Study of Nomadic Areas for Settlement.* Study reports,
vols. 1–3. Addis Ababa.
Van Santen, C. E. 1978. *Six Case Studies of Rural Settlement Schemes in Ethiopia.*
Addis Ababa: Ministry of Agriculture and Settlement.
Welamo Agricultural Development Unit (WADU). 1982. *Annual Report.* Addis
Ababa.
Wetterhall, H. 1972. *Government Land in Ethiopia.* Draft report. Addis Ababa:
Ministry of Land Reform and Administration (June).
Wood, A. P. 1977. *Resettlement in Illubabor Province, Ethiopia.* Ph.D. diss., Uni-
versity of Liverpool, England.

Table 6.1
Land use in Ethiopia

| Land use | Area (hectares) | Percentage |
|---|---|---|
| Cropped land | | |
|   Annual crops | 16,413,140 | 13.1 |
|   Perennial crops | 2,074,050 | 1.7 |
| Grazing and browsing land | 63,725,700 | 51.0 |
| Forest, woodland, bushland, shrubland | | |
|   Forests | 4,473,520 | 3.6 |
|   Others | 10,135,470 | 8.1 |
| Currently unproductive land | 4,719,740 | 3.8 |
| Currently unutilizable land | 23,292,380 | 18.7 |
| Total | 124,834,000 | 100.00 |

Source: UNDP, FAO. Ethiopia: Land Use, Production, Regions and Farming Systems Inventory. Vol. I: Report, p. 35. Rome, 1984.

Table 6.2
Types of settlement under the Relief and Rehabilitation Commission, 1983

| Region | Types of settlement | | Support status | | Forms of agriculture | | |
|---|---|---|---|---|---|---|---|
| | Special | Low-cost | Under budget 1984 | Having technical aid only | Irrigated | Rain-fed | Both |
| Bale | 12 | – | 12 | – | – | 12 | – |
| Eritrea | 1 | – | 1 | – | – | – | 1 |
| Gamo-Gofa | 3 | – | – | 3 | – | 3 | – |
| Gondar | 1 | 3 | 1 | 3 | 4 | – | – |
| Harar | 8 | – | 7 | 1 | 7 | – | 1 |
| Kefa and Illubabor | 1 | 3 | 2 | 2 | – | 4 | – |
| Shoa | 11 | 9 | 8 | 12 | 4 | 13 | 3 |
| Sidamo | 3 | 1 | 3 | 1 | – | 4 | – |
| Walaga | 23 | 2 | 19 | 6 | – | 25 | – |
| Wallo | 2 | 2 | 4 | – | 4 | – | – |
| Total | 65 | 20 | 57 | 28 | 19 | 61 | 5 |

Source: Compiled by author from unpublished official records.

187

Table 6.3
Percentage distribution of household heads by age in
24 settlements, 1983

| Settlement | n | Age group | | |
|---|---|---|---|---|
| | | 18-30 | 31-49 | 50+ |
| Assosa | | | | |
| No. 1 | 477 | 29.1 | 38.0 | 32.9 |
| 2 | 502 | 19.7 | 46.0 | 34.3 |
| 3 | 498 | 18.9 | 47.0 | 34.1 |
| 4 | 485 | 21.9 | 48.2 | 29.9 |
| 5 | 458 | 30.1 | 43.7 | 26.2 |
| 6 | 467 | 37.7 | 34.9 | 27.4 |
| 7 | 484 | 26.9 | 44.8 | 28.3 |
| 8 | 484 | 25.2 | 43.2 | 31.6 |
| 9 | 491 | 25.4 | 42.8 | 31.8 |
| 10 | 469 | 22.0 | 34.8 | 43.2 |
| 11 | 487 | 26.7 | 43.9 | 29.4 |
| 12 | 394 | 47.0 | 33.0 | 20.0 |
| 13 | 411 | 22.1 | 59.6 | 18.3 |
| 14 | 379 | 27.2 | 33.0 | 39.8 |
| 15 | 424 | 32.1 | 47.2 | 20.7 |
| 16 | 415 | 29.2 | 42.2 | 28.6 |
| Bewel | 163 | 27.6 | 57.7 | 14.7 |
| Erer | 481 | 54.1 | 37.8 | 8.1 |
| Fafen | 484 | 65.5 | 30.8 | 3.7 |
| Haligen | 288 | 11.5 | 8.4 | 4.5 |
| Jerere | 406 | 53.2 | 38.4 | 8.4 |
| Korahe | 496 | 54.4 | 40.4 | 5.2 |
| Maikadra | 425 | 86.4 | 13.4 | 0.2 |
| Welwel | 425 | 51.8 | 39.3 | 8.9 |
| Mean | | 35.2 | 42.7 | 22.1 |
| (standard deviation) | | (17.7) | (12.7) | (12.6) |

Source: RRC, Evaluation of Settlements by Group 1
(in Amharic), Addis Ababa (1984).

188

Table 6.4
Age distribution of total settlement population, 1983

| Region | Number of settlements | Age group (percentages) | | |
|---|---|---|---|---|
| | | 0-5 | 6-14 | 15+ |
| Gamo-Gofa | 3 | 22 | 15 | 63 |
| Gondar | 3 | 16 | 8 | 76 |
| Harar | 6 | 8 | 10 | 82 |
| Kefa and Illubabor | 3 | 29 | 20 | 51 |
| Shoa | 17 | 27 | 14 | 59 |
| Sidamo | 3 | 17 | 30 | 53 |
| Walaga | 25 | 19 | 18 | 63 |
| Wallo | 2 | 8 | 13 | 79 |
| Total | 62 | 20 | 16 | 64 |
| Average | | | 36 | 64 |
| National average* | | | 46 | 54 |
| Rural average | | | 46 | 54 |
| Urban average | | | 43 | 57 |

Source: RRC, "Number of Settlers by Age and Sex Groups" (in Amharic), Addis Ababa (1984).
    *The national figures are taken from the Central Statistical Office (CSO), Statistical Abstract, 1980.

Table 6.5
Sex distribution of household heads and total settlement population, 1983

| Region | Number of settlements | Household heads | | | Total settlement population | | |
|---|---|---|---|---|---|---|---|
| | | | | Percentage | | | Percentage |
| | | n | Male | Female | n | Male | Female |
| Bale | 12 | 4,867 | 97 | 3 | 16,716 | 54 | 46 |
| Gamo-Gofa | 3 | 1,058 | 99 | 1 | 5,718 | 63 | 37 |
| Gondar | 4 | 1,076 | 98 | 2 | 3,012 | 62 | 38 |
| Harar | 7 | 2,799 | 98 | 2 | 7,857 | 74 | 26 |
| Kefa and Illubabor | 3 | 835 | 96 | 4 | 3,433 | 57 | 43 |
| Shoa | 18 | 4,278 | 97 | 3 | 14,472 | 56 | 44 |
| Sidamo | 3 | 657 | 92 | 8 | 3,735 | 57 | 43 |
| Walaga | 25 | 9,289 | 97 | 3 | 30,548 | 56 | 44 |
| Wallo | 3 | 1,833 | 90 | 10 | 6,407 | 62 | 38 |
| Total | 78 | 26,692 | 97 | 3 | 91,898 | 58 | 42 |

Source: RRC, "Number of Settlers by Age and Sex Groups", Addis Ababa (1984).

189

Table 6.6
Unmarried settlers in 56 settlements, 1983

| Region | Number of settlements where unmarried settlers over age 15 are indicated | Number of settlers of age 15 and above | Unmarried settlers of age 15 and above | Percentage unmarried (to total "eligibles") |
|---|---|---|---|---|
| Gamo-Gofa | 3 | 3,590 | 41 | 1.4 |
| Gondar | 3 | 1,637 | 260 | 13.0 |
| Harar | 5 | 2,532 | 1,684 | 66.7 |
| Kefa and Illubabor | 3 | 1,756 | 154 | 8.9 |
| Shoa | 15 | 7,769 | 591 | 8.7 |
| Sidamo | 2 | 587 | 39 | 6.6 |
| Walaga | 25 | 18,809 | 2,455 | 13.8 |
| Total | 56 | 36,680 | 5,224 | 15.8 |

Source: RRC, "Number of Settlers by Age and Sex Groups," Addis Ababa (1984).

Table 6.7
Total number of participants in literacy programs (in all "rounds")

| Region | Number of settlements | Number of participants in different levels of literacy programs | | | | Total settlement population of age 5 and above |
| --- | --- | --- | --- | --- | --- | --- |
| | | Beginners | Follow-up | Post-literacy | Total | |
| Bale | 12 | 16,258 | 311 | 3,538 | 20,107 | 4,021* |
| Gamo-Gofa | 3 | 3,327 | 623 | 1,373 | 5,323 | 4,468 |
| Gondar | 4 | 4,632 | 1,328 | 2,004 | 7,964 | 1,810 |
| Harar | 8 | 5,556 | -- | 2,345 | 7,901 | 5,739 |
| Kefa and Illubabor | 4 | 1,367 | 97 | 108 | 1,572 | 2,458 |
| Shoa | 20 | 39,136 | 2,784 | 16,695 | 58,615 | 9,537 |
| Sidamo | 4 | 37,666 | -- | 8,818 | 46,484 | 3,137 |
| Walaga | 25 | 39,774 | 1,617 | 21,599 | 62,990 | 24,829 |
| Wallo | 4 | 7,700 | 6,374 | 9,583 | 23,657 | 5,206 |
| Total | 84 | 155,416 | 13,134 | 66,063 | 234,613 | 61,205 |

Source: RRC, Results of the Literacy Campaign, 10th Round, 1984, p. 5.
*An estimate based on age-group proportion of total population for all observed sites.

191

Table 6.8

Percentage distribution of settlers (household heads) by occupation prior to settlement, 1984

| Region | Number of settlements | Total number of (settler) household heads | Occupation prior to settlement | | | | | |
|---|---|---|---|---|---|---|---|---|
| | | | Urban unemployed | Victims of land over-crowding | Nomads | Farm wage laborers | Charcoal burners | Drought victims |
| Bale | 12 | 5,203 | -- | -- | -- | -- | -- | 100.0 |
| Gamo-Gofa | 3 | 1,130 | 34.8 | 65.2 | -- | -- | -- | -- |
| Gondar | 4 | 1,139 | -- | -- | -- | 62.7 | -- | 37.3 |
| Harar | 8 | 3,753 | -- | -- | 30.8 | -- | -- | 69.2 |
| Kefa and Illubabor | 4 | 1,267 | -- | -- | 32.2 | 67.8 | -- | -- |
| Shoa | 20 | 6,267 | 47.3 | 22.0 | 5.1 | 6.8 | 18.8 | -- |
| Sidamo | 4 | 754 | 20.3 | -- | 79.7 | -- | -- | -- |
| Walaga | 25 | 9,246 | 1.3 | 15.7 | 1.2 | -- | -- | 81.8 |
| Wallo | 4 | 4,422 | -- | -- | 100.0 | -- | -- | -- |
| Total | 84 | 33,181 | 10.9 | 10.8 | 21.1 | 6.0 | 3.6 | 47.6 |

Source: RRC, "Settlers' Occupation Prior to Settlement" (typed tables), Addis Ababa (1984), 10 pp.

Table 6.9
Land productivity in settlement schemes, 1983

| Crop | Planned production per hectare (kg)[a] | Average yeild (kg/hectare)[b] | | |
|------|------|------|------|------|
| | | All settlements | Special settlement schemes | Low-cost settlement schemes |
| Chillies | 1,200 | 374 (346) | 346 (286) | 596 (601) |
| Cotton | -- | 1,142 (990) | 1,352 (1,190) | 970 (748) |
| Ground nuts | 500 | -- | -- | -- |
| Maize | 2,167 | 1,355 (874) | 1,351 (698) | 1,324 (1,413) |
| Sorghum | 2,000 | 1,204 (696) | 1,252 (639) | 1,091 (861) |
| Teff | 800 | 677 (415) | 501 (428) | 364 (331) |
| All production | 1,460 | 1,250 (1,141) | 1,144 (704) | 1,440 (1,849) |

Source: RRC, Settlement Policy, "Area Cultivated and Yield 1978-1983" (typed tables) (1984).
[a] Target production for the third year of settlement.
[b] The figures in parentheses are standard deviations.

Table 6.10
Settlement productivity by settlement types, 1983

| Crop | Average yield per hectare (in kg) adjusted for variations in labour inputs* | | |
|---|---|---|---|
| | All settlements | Special settlement schemes | Low-cost settlement schemes |
| Chillies | 1.4 (2.5) | 1.0 (1.1) | 4.4 (5.9) |
| Cotton | 4.2 (3.4) | 2.7 (2.9) | 5.4 (3.3) |
| Maize | 4.1 (4.2) | 3.2 (1.8) | 7.9 (9.2) |
| Sorghum | 4.2 (3.6) | 3.1 (1.7) | 6.7 (5.8) |
| Teff | 1.4 (1.3) | 1.3 (1.1) | 1.8 (1.9) |
| All production | 3.9 (3.2) | 2.7 (1.7) | 6.7 (4.4) |

Source: RRC, "Area Cultivated and Yield, 1978-1983" (typed tables) (1984).
*Figures in parentheses are standard deviations.

Table 6.11
Regression results: The determination of settlement productivity

| Variable number | Independent variables* | Regression Coefficient | T-value |
|---|---|---|---|
| 00 | Intercept | 0.18996 | |
| 01 | Lumpen (unemployed from cities) | L | L |
| 02 | Victims of land overcrowding | 0.26636 | 1.52586 |
| 03 | Nomads | 0.12393 | 0.50489 |
| 04 | Agricultural laborers | -0.56555 | -2.44191 |
| 05 | Charcoal burners | -0.64156 | -2.11961 |
| 06 | Drought victims | -2.52182 | -5.26472 |
| 07 | Settlement distance from place of origin of the settler (in km) | 0.00133 | 2.91439 |
| 08 | Years since establishment of settlement | 0.00555 | 0.17628 |
| 09 | Special settlement schemes | -0.73082 | -3.77883 |
| 10 | Low-cost settlement schemes | L | L |
| 11 | Irrigated settlement | -0.17932 | -0.82842 |
| 12 | Rain-fed settlement | L | L |
| 13 | Settlement on government budget | 0.31699 | 2.29464 |
| 14 | Settlement on government "technical aid" | L | L |

Source: Compiled by the author.
Dependent variable = log (value of gross production/number of settlers x area cultivated).
Number of observations = 54.
Multiple correlation = 0.87784.
Standard error of estimate = 0.30053.
F-value = 8.39811.
*Variable numbers 1-6, 9, 11, and 13 are dummies measured with values of 1 and 0. L indicates the variable left out of the regression.

Table 6.12
Planned settlement growth, 1978-82

_____

Settlement variables    1978      1979      1970      1981      1982

Table 6.12
Planned settlement growth, 1978-82

_____

| Settlement variables | Levels in various years* | | | | | Rate of growth per annum (1978-82) |
|---|---|---|---|---|---|---|
| | 1978 | 1979 | 1980 | 1981 | 1982 | |
| Settlers (household heads) | 18,989 | 19,855 | 31,975 | 37,929 | 38,813 | 32 |
| Settlement population | 60,646 | -- | 106,721 | 103,719 | 108,834 | 20 |
| No. of settlements | 51 | -- | 67 | 87 | 88 | 16 |

_____

Source: CPSC, Agriculture: 10-Year Indicative Plan (1985-1997) (in Amharic), p. 48. Addis Ababa: CPSC, July 1984.

*The data presented in this table indicate the total number of settlers under the RRC. They do not tally with the earlier figures largely because the latter are based on specific survey results and do not include those who have already left.

Table 6.13
Various facilities provided at settlement sites, 1983

| Region | School | Kinder-garten | Clinic | Office | Public shop | Ware-house | Garage | Mill | Cottage indus-tries | Meeting hall, Market hall | Silo | Total |
|---|---|---|---|---|---|---|---|---|---|---|---|---|
| Bale | 5 | 3 | 4 | 4 | 1 | 13 | 2 | 10 | 18 | -- | 20 | 80 |
| Gamo-Gofa | 2 | 3 | 3 | 3 | 3 | 3 | 3 | 3 | -- | 1 | 8 | 32 |
| Gondar | 4 | 2 | 3 | 3 | 3 | 4 | 1 | 8 | -- | -- | -- | 28 |
| Harar | 8 | -- | 8 | 8 | 8 | 10 | 8 | 10 | 9 | 5 | 2 | 76 |
| Kefa and Illubabor | 3 | 3 | 4 | 3 | 3 | 6 | 1 | 5 | -- | -- | -- | 28 |
| Shoa | 8 | 1 | 13 | 14 | 16 | 28 | 14 | 21 | 3 | 1 | 30 | 149 |
| Sidamo | 1 | -- | 1 | 3 | 2 | 3 | 2 | 6 | 8 | 1 | -- | 27 |
| Walaga | 13 | 1 | 18 | 16 | 17 | 22 | 13 | 24 | 7 | 3 | 27 | 161 |
| Wallo | 3 | -- | 4 | 3 | 5 | 8 | 2 | 2 | -- | -- | -- | 27 |
| Total | 47 | 13 | 58 | 57 | 58 | 97 | 46 | 89 | 45 | 11 | 87 | 608 |

Source: RRC, "Social and Economic Infrastructure at Settlement Sites" (typed data) (1984).

Table 6.14
Some settlement cost estimates, 1978-82

| Item | Expenditures in birr* | | | | | Percentage rate of growth per annum (1978-82) |
| --- | --- | --- | --- | --- | --- | --- |
| | 1978 | 1979 | 1980 | 1981 | 1982 | |
| Total expenditures on settlements | 34,395,000 | 49,203,000 | 77,436,000 | 71,269,000 | 37,047,000 | 11.3 |
| Total expenditures on settlements per household head | 1,811 | 2,478 | 2,422 | 1,879 | 954 | -9.3 |
| Total expenditures on settlements per hectare | 573 | 729 | 712 | 655 | 341 | -7.8 |

Source: CPSC, Agriculture: 10-Year Indicative Plan (1985-1997), Part I (in Amharic), pp. 48, 76. Addis Ababa: CPSC, July 1984.
*Figures indicated here refer only to government expenditures, and do not include private costs.

Table 6.15
Frequency of settlements without access to items of social and economic infrastructure, 1983

| Social and economic infrastructure | Number of settlements not containing or not having access to the facility | Percentage of total settlements not containing or not having access to the facility |
|---|---|---|
| School | 30 | 36 |
| Kindergarten | 68 | 81 |
| Clinic | 9 | 11 |
| Office | 23 | 27 |
| Public shop | 28 | 33 |
| Warehouse | 16 | 19 |
| Garage | 34 | 40 |
| Mill | 10 | 12 |
| Cottage industry | 36 | 43 |
| Meeting hall, market hall | 73 | 87 |
| Silo | 69 | 82 |

Source: RRC, "Social and Economic Infrastructure at Settlement Sites" (typed data) (1984).

Table 6.16
Some settlement problems

| Problems | Number of settlements by region | | | | | | | | |
|---|---|---|---|---|---|---|---|---|---|
| | Walaga | Shoa | Bale | Harar | Wallo | Kefa and Illubabor | Sidamo | Gamo-Gofa | Gondar |
| Lack of spare parts, pesticides, improved seeds, fertilizers, fuel, etc. | 25(100) | 16(80) | 12(100) | 8(100) | 4(100) | 3(75) | -- | 3(100) | 3(75) |
| Animal diseases, rodents, human diseases, etc. | 9(36) | 4(20) | -- | -- | -- | 3(75) | -- | -- | -- |
| Management problems, shortage of skilled manpower, etc. | 25(100) | 20(100) | 12(100) | 8(100) | 4(100) | -- | -- | -- | 3(75) |
| Shortage of cultivable land, soil problems, etc. | 16(64) | 11(55) | 12(100) | 1(13) | 4(100) | 1(25) | -- | 3(100) | -- |
| Transportation problems | 25(100) | 20(100) | -- | 6(75) | 4(100) | 1(25) | -- | -- | -- |
| Underdeveloped infrastructure (cooperatives, public shops, warehouses, clinics, kindergartens, etc.) | 11(44) | -- | 11(92) | 6(75) | 4(100) | 2(50) | -- | 3(100) | 1(25) |
| Security problems | -- | 4(20) | -- | -- | -- | -- | -- | -- | 3(75) |
| Social (tribal) conflicts | -- | 3(15) | -- | -- | -- | -- | -- | -- | -- |
| Settlers with adaptation problems | 16(64) | 2(10) | -- | -- | 1(25) | -- | -- | -- | -- |
| Family problems (e.g., settlers' families not with the settlers) | 25(100) | -- | -- | -- | -- | -- | -- | -- | -- |
| Water shortages | 25(100) | 20(100) | -- | -- | 2(50) | -- | -- | 1(33) | 3(75) |

Source: RRC, various settlement evaluation reports (1984).
Figures in parentheses are percentages of the total number of settlements in each region.

Table 6.17
Regression results: Determination of settlement "abandonment"
rates

| Variable number | Independent variables | Regression coefficient* | T-value |
|---|---|---|---|
| 00 | Intercept | 3.79939 | -- |
| 01 | Urban unemployed | 0.52681 | 0.69410 |
| 02 | Victims of land overcrowding | 0.29432 | 0.41427 |
| 03 | Nomads | L | L |
| 04 | Agricultural (wage) laborers | 2.16661 | 2.31123 |
| 05 | Charcoal burners | 0.41347 | 0.44259 |
| 06 | Drought victims | 0.32520 | 0.35445 |
| 07 | Dependants/household heads | -0.00185 | -1.61990 |
| 08 | Distance of settlement from place of origin of the settler (in km) | -0.00203 | -1.43767 |
| 09 | Years since establishment | -0.21639 | -1.89022 |
| 10 | Special settlement schemes | -0.10390 | -0.16249 |
| 11 | Low-cost settlement schemes | L | L |

Source: Compiled by the author.
Number of observations = 45.
Multiple correlation = 0.58405.
Standard error of estimate = 1.31963.
F-value = 2.47084.
Dependent variable = log (percentage of settlers left).
*Variable numbers 1-2, 4-6, and 10 are dummies measured with values of 1 and 0. L indicates the variable left out of the regression.

Tod A. Ragsdale and Abdullahi Scek Ali  7

# A Case Study of the Resettlement of Nomads in Somalia

## INTRODUCTION

This study provides a comprehensive profile of the resettlement program in Somalia and assesses the demographic and socioeconomic implications of settling Somalia's nomadic population. It is divided into five sections.

Section I presents a brief background to Somalia and describes the 1974 drought and the resultant international relief efforts that led to the establishment of the SDA (Settlement Development Agency) and CDP (Coastal Development Project) resettlement programs. Section 2 discusses the primary objective of Somalia's resettlement program and examines alternative resettlement strategies. Section 3 gives a general description of the three agricultural and three fisheries settlement projects, and of their administrative and sociopolitical structure. It also provides information on the cultural, socioeconomic, and demographic characteristics of the former nomad populations; their access to basic social and educational services; the extent of the settlers' integration

From the University of North Carolina at Chapel Hill and the Ministry of Agriculture, Mogadishu.

with previously existing populations at the resettlement sites; and the settlement schemes' occupational and income structure. Section 4 assesses the availability of infrastructure and social services, the retention of settlers in settlement areas, and the success of the SDA/CDP resettlement programs in meeting their primary objectives. Section 5 brings together the major findings of the study and highlights their policy implications.

The data in many of the tables presented here should be treated with some caution.[1] Particular factors influencing the quality of the available data are (a) the mobility of the resettlement population itself, which creates considerable difficulties in collecting generalizable data on the resettlement schemes and (b) the lack of skilled manpower to collect, organize, and produce the various statistics needed for the effective monitoring of the schemes.

Despite these reservations, the data presented here, collated from official records and documents, and produced in tabular form for the first time, will indicate at least the broad parameters of the socioeconomic characteristics of the resettlement schemes in Somalia.

## GENERAL BACKGROUND

Somalia's population is around 6 million (of which over two-thirds are nomads) in an area of about 637,657 square kilometers. Geographically, it is a land of rolling savannah, with high areas in the north. The country's only rivers of size are the Juba and Shabeelle in the south. Both rise in the Ethiopian highlands, and the land between them is the most fertile and well irrigated in the country.

The climate is dry and hot, though in some northern highland areas temperatures can drop below freezing. Most of the country is classified as arid or semiarid, and rainfall is generally low and irregular. The rainfall pattern varies throughout the country and by season; cyclical droughts are common. The time of arrival and sufficiency of rain are overriding factors in determining whether or not grazing will be adequate for the large nomadic herds.

The *Dabadheer* or "Long-Tailed Drought" that lasted from April 1973 until June 1975 is believed to have been a continuation of the great Sahelian drought that devastated vast areas of north Africa (Kamrany and Nake 1977) and is generally considered by the populations affected to be the worst in living memory.

The 1974 drought resulted in a mass exodus of nomads from the rural areas to the towns in search of water and food. During the drought's most desperate period in March 1975, they moved into some 20 relief camps at rates of up to 5000 a day. By the arrival of the seasonal rains in June, the total population of these camps was estimated at nearly

300,000. Overall, the drought affected nearly 700,000 nomads in half the country's 16 regions. More than 20,000, mostly children and the elderly, are thought to have died. Further, the drought claimed more than 5 million animals, nearly half of Somalia's sheep and goats, a third of its cattle, and up to 120,000 tons of food grains.

With the rains, most of the drought-stricken nomads returned to the rural areas to rebuild their herds. Those who remained behind (some 120,000) continued to be assisted by teams of doctors, veterinarians, army engineers, and student volunteers. At this time the Somali government decided to resettle the remaining relief camp population in permanent agricultural and fishing settlements. Some 15,000 were transferred to three fishing settlements and 105,000 to three agricultural settlements.

Establishing permanent settlements for over 100,000 people was a formidable task. Initially the settlers had to be provided with all their basic requirements: food, shelter, water, and, additionally, health and education facilities. This task was at first accomplished by an inter-agency committee representing many government ministries. However, because of the complex nature of the work, it was decided to create two independent agencies to be responsible for the development of the settlements. Thus in 1976 the Settlement Development Agency (SDA) and the Coastal Development Project (CDP) came into existence.

During the initial period from 1975 to 1977, the settlements were run primarily as an extension of the relief camps. While providing the settlers with such relief help as makeshift housing (military tents) and emergency rations, the agencies set out to upgrade medical facilities, build schools and administrative centers, dig wells, and erect food storage facilities. To alter the destitute character of the camps, land clearing began immediately, and crops were being cultivated at the agricultural settlements before the end of 1975. This period was nevertheless one of profound readjustment for the former nomad settlers, as well as for the new agencies, with many settlers leaving, and presumably returning to their herds and pasture lands. The settlements as a whole lost some 40 percent of their population. In 1976, the arrival of modern boats and the construction of permanent housing and processing facilities did much to stabilize this drift at the fishing settlements. Primarily because much-needed agricultural equipment did not arrive until 1979, this stabilization occurred much later at the agricultural settlements.

## THE RESETTLEMENT PROGRAM

The policy of resetting Somalia's nomadic population predated the 1974 drought. However, the international aid extended to Somalia in response to the drought brought this policy into greater focus and added

momentum to its implementation. The major objective of the resettlement policy as it has evolved since 1974 had been to attain a major
redistribution of Somalia's population so as to reduce the ecological
deterioration of the rangelands and to redirect urban growth into productive rural enterprises. By developing large-scale turnkey irrigation
schemes and coastal and deep-sea fishing, the Somali government hopes
to diversify the national economy in order to achieve greater national
self-sufficiency and reduce the country's growing trade deficit.

Secondary but no less important goals of this population redistribution
are the provision of social services to Somalia's largely nomadic population, the restructuring of the country's traditional "tribal" society, and
since early 1983 the resolution of Somalia's war refugee problem.

## Reduction of the ecological deterioration of the rangelands

The 1974 drought brought a new awareness of the deterioration of
Somalia's rangelands. There was speculation that the drought might to
some extent have resulted from long-term changes toward desertifica-
tion, but the evidence also indicated that some other factors were responsible, perhaps the main one being the increasing pressure of
livestock population growth on the rangelands. An FAO survey in 1967
found that the national herd had increased almost three times since the
late 1950s, despite progressive depletion of pasture land; and an ILO
mission in 1971 estimated that the total number of animals had risen by
40 to 60 percent in the preceding five years (Cassanelli 1982; Kaplan
1977a). This increase was due both to new market demand in the Gulf
States and to successful veterinary campaigns by the government (especially against rinderpest).

The 1974 drought proved that the overgrazing of the pasture lands
had indeed become untenable and that serious and painful readjustments would be necessary to maintain Somalia's pastoral economy. The
fewer people there were who were directly dependent on livestock, it
was felt, the more manageable the necessary readjustments would be.
Population redistribution was therefore viewed as complementary to the
introduction of new programs of rangeland management and as a necessary precondition for a planned decrease in the size of the national
herd.

To achieve the government's goal of a zero growth rate for the nomadic
population, approximately 50,000 pastoralists would have to be absorbed
annually into other sectors of the economy. It was expected that agriculture would absorb about 86 percent of this displaced population and
maritime commercial fishing much of the rest (ILO 1977).

## Slowing urban growth

As elsewhere in the developing world, Somalia's urban centers have grown at a tremendous rate in recent years. Mogadishu's population, for instance, has been growing at about 25 percent per year since 1971 (Somali Democratic Republic, SDR 1981). Shortages of food and housing and lack of employment opportunities for the fast-growing urban population are major problems in Somalia.

The irony is that urban growth has occurred alongside continuing acute shortages of manpower on productive rural development projects, especially large-scale irrigation schemes.

## Diversification of the national economy through development of economic resources

At present livestock and animal products account for about four-fifths of Somalia's export revenues, while perhaps as much as 80 percent of the population is engaged in pastoral and related activities (SDR 1981). The 1967 closing of the Suez Canal and loss of protection on Italian markets relegated banana production to second place in export earnings. Because of past and present reliance on these two commodities alone, Somalia's balance of payments situation remained structurally weak during the late 1970s, and climatic and other factors led to sluggish growth of these exports. The difficulties experienced by the economy between 1976 and 1980, as well as the international increase in oil prices, are reflected in a marked deterioration in Somalia's balance of payments. On the other hand, with the increase in excess demand for capital goods and food commodities, the growth of imports has far outpaced that of exports. As a consequence the deficit in the trade balance increased rapidly from U.S. $71 million in 1977 to U.S. $176 million in 1980 (SDR 1981).

A desire to achieve self-sufficiency in food production and to reduce Somalia's balance of payments deficit led the government in 1981 to set four objectives for the agricultural sector:

i. to increase the gross value of agricultural output by achieving an average annual growth rate of 6.2 percent at 1980 constant prices;

ii. to expand production of the main food grain crops, sorghum and maize, with a view to progressively decreasing imports of these commodities;

iii. to achieve self-sufficiency in sugar, fruit, and vegetable production; and

iv. to diversify agricultural production by encouraging crops such as cotton, rice, sugar, and oilseeds, both for export and for domestic agro-industries (SDR 1981).

The expansion of the fisheries industry, especially deep-sea trawling, was also thought likely to lead to greater earnings in foreign exchange through increases in exports of both processed and unprocessed marine products. The resettlement of nomads was therefore considered necessary to provide manpower to achieve the objectives of greater foreign currency earnings, import substitution, and self-sufficiency in food.

### Provision of social services

After the revolution of 1969, the Supreme Revolutionary Council expressed in its first charter its concern that social services were not being equitably distributed to Somalia's largely rural and nomadic population. Nomads had in the past received little benefit from such social services as health care and education. As a first step toward delivering social services to this dispersed and mobile population, the government created a more finely meshed administrative structure by dividing Somalia's eight regions into 16 and increasing the number of administrative districts from 48 to 84.

While some progress has been made, the difficulty and cost of providing social services and economic benefits to a dispersed and mobile population remain formidable. Because of this, one of the foremost national goals continues to be the resettling of a large proportion of the nomadic population into fishing and agricultural communities in order to achieve greater cost-effectiveness.

### Restructuring of tribal society

While colonial and post-independence administrations have produced profound changes in the organization of Somali society, its traditional fabric is still intact.

The Somali's traditional world was understood fundamentally in terms of kinship. As each clan regarded itself as more or less a state within a state, competition over scarce resources frequently led to armed conflict. This conflict often spilled over into the urban centers, and inter-tribal feuding formed the background for the revolution of October 1969.

From the beginning, the present Somali government has made it a major policy objective to eliminate tribalism, and to do this effectively it has considered it necessary to remove the economic and social conditions that give rise to such political manipulation and overt rivalry. While one strategy has been regulation of grazing through land management schemes and the creation of pastoral cooperatives, another has been agricultural and maritime development. This culminated in 1975 in the creation of the six nomad resettlement schemes and in an ongoing policy of resettling a large proportion of the nomadic population.

## Dismantling the war refugee camps

In June 1983 the Somali government announced its decision to rehabilitate through resettlement projects some 700,000 ethnic Somalis in
refugee camps as a result of the Ethiopian–Somali war. This was a hu-
manitarian decision, apart from its inevitable social and economic consequences for Somalia. The experience gained from the 1975 resettlement
program should go a long way toward the successful attainment of this
most recent objective.

## THE NOMAD RESETTLEMENT SCHEMES

Of the six nomad settlements, only one fishing settlement, Eil, is in
northern Somalia (900 kilometers from Mogadishu), where the majority
of the 1974 famine victims were recruited from relief camps. A second
fishing settlement, Adale, is 250 kilometers north of Mogadishu and
accessible by dirt road only. The third fishing settlement, Brava, is next
to the ancient coastal town of Brava south of Mogadishu, only recently
linked to the capital by a 180-kilometer paved highway.

The three agricultural settlements, Dujuma, Kurtunwary, and Sablaale, are south of Mogadishu. Kurtunwary (140 kilometers) and Sablaale (220 kilometers) are next to the Shabeelle River (running north-
south), and are not far inland from the new Brava-Mogadishu highway.
Sablaale is in the close vicinity of Brava, while Kurtunwary is more
readily accessible from Mogadishu. Dujuma is in a relatively remote
area, 650 kilometers south of Mogadishu, on the Juba River not far from
the Kenyan border.

The agricultural settlements are much larger than the fishing settlements. The former contain 17,000 to 25,000 settlers, while the latter
usually have between 3000 and 5000 settlers.

The agricultural settlement of Dujuma, once the largest nomadic settlement, has by and large been relocated by the SDA to two areas near
Jelib, south of the Juba River. Relocation was necessary because in the
emergency context of resettlement in 1975, no soil survey of the Dujuma
area was undertaken; in 1977, however, it was determined that the land
at Dujuma, because of its high salinity, was not suitable for irrigated
agriculture and only marginally suited to rain-fed cultivation.

## Organization and sociopolitical structure

The organization of the settlements was established at three levels:
the SDA and CDP headquarters at Mogadishu; the resettlement scheme
management organization; and a sociopolitical structure within the overall framework of the provincial administration.

## SDA and CDP headquarters

The SDA and CDP were established in 1975 on the recommendation of a World Bank mission. A chairman responsible for the drought rehabilitation programs heads the SDA/CDP and provides a direct link with the president's office.

Until 1982 the SDA was completely separate from the Ministry of Agriculture, and it is still semiautonomous. It is staffed by a general manager, a deputy, and seven directors representing the various departments. These are supported by a number of junior staff members. In general, the SDA has suffered from shortages of qualified staff, which have affected both continuity and program implementation.

The CDP is a semiautonomous body under the direction of the Ministry of Fisheries; it is staffed in a manner similar to the SDA. The CDP and the SDA are responsible for the direction and coordination of their respective settlement programs, though the SDA has generally had greater responsiblity for liaison, both with other ministries and with donor and aid agencies.

## Settlement scheme organization

Each of the settlement schemes has its own management structure, headed by a manager who is responsible for the day-to-day operations. He is supported by a team of professional officers heading the four departments: agriculture, livestock production, forestry, and farm administration in the SDA settlements; the marina, processing plant, transportation, and construction in CDP settlements.

Because of the nomadic background of the settlers, a high level of supervision was thought to be essential; this was reflected in the large numbers of junior staff supporting the senior management structure. The SDA staff in 1980 numbered 272, while the CDP, with a much smaller settler population, had as many as 500 people on its payroll, 400 of them in the settlements (World Food Program 1980a).

## Sociopolitical structure

The policy of the government has been to establish an administrative district for each settlement scheme, and as there is no area other than the settlement involved, the chairman of the settlement is the *de facto* chairman or commissioner of the district. In addition to the usual staff associated with an administrative district, the settlement chairmen at the SDA schemes direct an agricultural project coordinator whose status is equivalent to that of a district administrative officer. The settlement chairmen also head important committees established at different levels within the settlements to represent the views of the settlers. Committees

have been used extensively by the settlement management to dissemi-
nate information and organize production.

## Settlers' background

### Origins of the settlers

Table 7.1 indicates the place of origin of the agricultural and fishing
settlement populations at the time of resettlement. The six northern
regions of Togdheer, Nugal, Mudug, Sanaag, Galgadud, and Bari account for more than 95 percent of the population of former nomads. As
indicated earlier, these regions were the ones most affected by the 1974
drought. These same six regions account for only 28 percent of Somalia's
population (SDR 1979c: 273; based on 1975 figures). The three southern
regions (Gedo, Bakool, and Shabeellaha Dhexe) contributed 4.4 percent
of the ex-nomad settlers, all of whom went to the fishing settlements.

### Settler's demographic and social characteristics

Table 7.2 compares the age and sex distribution of the population in
the six agricultural or fishing settlement schemes with that in the urban,
rural, and nomadic sectors of Somalia as a whole in 1980–81. Because
different sources have used different age categories, it is not possible to
make a direct comparison, except for the age groups 0-14 and 15 + years.
While the percentages of Somalia's urban, rural, and nomadic populations in the 0-14 age group are high, they are not as high as those for
the same age group in the resettlement schemes. The reverse is true for
the age group 15 + years.

The data also indicate that settlers over the age of 50 years comprise
nearly 4 percent of the population of the fishing settlements, while
settlers aged 46 and over make up 5.8 percent of the agricultural settlement population (Table 7.3). Comparable figures for the urban, rural,
and nomadic sectors of Somalia as a whole are between 9 and 10 percent
(Afzal 1982). In other words, the data show that the settlement population is relatively younger than that of Somalia as a whole.

If we look more carefully at the individual settlement schemes (Table
7.3), we see that they have a disproportionate number of school-age
children (6–14 years). At Dujuma, for instance, this group makes up
nearly half of the 25,000 settlers. Dujuma was the largest and most
ambitious of the resettlement projects, with the most extensive educational infrastructure, in terms of school buildings and staff. When it
became apparent that the land around Dujuma was unsuitable for agriculture and most of the settlers were removed southward along the
Juba River to Marerey and Faanoole, the original settlement remained
an educational center, particularly for technical education.

While males aged 15 to 30 almost equal females of that age group in Dujuma, and outnumber them in Sablaale, they are considerably fewer in Kurtunwary. Further, there are a third to a half fewer men aged 31 to 45 than women of the same age in all three agricultural settlements. Comparable figures for Somalia as a whole (for the age gorup 30–44) indicate that men and women are about equal in number, their proportion of the total population varying between 7 and 10 percent (Afzal 1982).

It is probable that a large number of working-age males left the Dujuma scheme during the dislocation that occurred when the majority of the population was shifted to development projects near Jelib, not only because of discouragement arising from the move itself but also because of the accumulation of frustration from months and years of unemployment.

### Settlers' employment characteristics

Because in 1975 resettlement meant a change in occupation for the drought-affected nomads, a considerable training effort on the part of the agencies administering the resettlement schemes was required. The SDA, while awaiting the arrival of mechanized equipment (which did not reach the settlements until the spring of 1979), undertook an extensive training program that lasted from 1977 to the beginning of 1980. At the CDP settlements, modern boats were in use as early as 1976, so that the training of some 692 fishermen, 131 engine operators and mechanics, 404 net menders, 244 processing workers, and 58 auxiliary and administrative workers was imparted more or less on the job (Haakonsen 1980).

At the SDA, training was provided at first through an adult literacy program for those who had not previously attended formal schools, and then through skills training in agriculture, construction, handicrafts, clerical work, transport and communications, and health care. While Table 7.4 gives some indication of the number of settlers trained, it does not indicate the total size or structure of the work force.

According to SDA figures, the overall population of the three agricultural settlements in April 1981 was 61,336, and the potential work force (15–60 years) 25,443; of the latter, only about 11 percent had received technical skills training. This accords with Rajagopalan's findings in a 1981 labor availability survey at Sablaale and Kurtunwary that only 12 percent of working adults at the former and 6 percent at the latter reported having undergone in-service training (Rajagopalan 1981).

Table 7.5 (based on Rajagopalan's survey and national data available for 1975) compares the crude activity rates for Sablaale and Kurtunwary and for the fishing settlements with those for the urban and rural areas of Somalia as a whole. In the fishing settlements the rates are uniformly lower than for Somalia as a whole. In the agricultural settlements, the crude activity rate for women is slightly higher than that for men (Table 7.5). Their rate is also 7 to 10 percent higher than that for women in Somalia as a whole. This is largely because of the greater reliance on women in agricultural activities (Table 7.6).

## Income and work incentives

The settlement agencies at first ran the settlements as state enterprises, providing all services and facilities, including food, clothing (mostly for schoolchildren), and housing, as well as production requisites. Most settlers in agricultural settlements received their rations and their 2 Somali shillings cash incentive per day whether they worked or not, though in theory the cash incentive, at least, was tied to the work done. Those given skills training received up to 10 shillings per day according to the level of skill acquired and their occupation.

Fishermen received a cash incentive based on a standard 0.80 shillings per kilogram of fish caught, regardless of species. In addition, the captain ("master fisherman") and engine operator both received 15 percent of the money earned from the daily catch, while each of six fishermen received 10 percent and two apprentice seamen received 5 percent (Haakonsen 1980; SDR 1977). In 1979, a boat's captain and engine operator could both have received a monthly average of 112 shilings at Adale, 331 shillings at Brava, and as much as 565 shillings at Eil. A fisherman's wage varied from 75 shillings at Adale to 221 shillings at Brava, and to as much as 438 shillings at Eil.

The work attitudes of the settlers had serious implications for the planned self-sufficiency of the settlements. Throughout the settlements, absenteeism was reported to be high and productivity low. The inadequate participation of the settlers in production activities became a matter of increasing concern, and various alternative ways of providing incentives for productive work were considered. One possibility was to increase incentive payments, but it was doubtful whether the government could afford an increase. Another alternative was to create a more genuine cooperative structure for the settlements and effectively turn them over entirely to the settlers. The major question here was whether former nomads could handle this responsibility with any hope of success.

The possibility that seemed the most promising was to provide input, extensions, and marketing services, while the household was to be responsible for generating its own income and bearing the cost of the services provided by the agency.

Both the SDA and the CDP set up pilot projects to test the feasibility of this seemingly attractive alternative. Though at first productivity at the fishing projects remained low, it was encouraging that for the three settlements the average catch per day showed a marked improvement from 53.5 kilograms in 1978 to 130.9 kilograms for the first six months of 1980.

The SDA's pilot program began in April 1980, with the aim of transforming a highly subsidized state farm into a family-operated tenant-farming system. In the pilot project a cost-accounting system was to be established by a management committee consisting of tenant representatives, the farm manager, and other technical personnel.

The SDA was to continue the management of the settlements, but each household was expected eventually to bear full operational costs: machinery operations, inputs, irrigation, infrastructure maintenance, extension and marketing services, and so on. It was estimated that these operational costs would generally account for about half the yield, though they were calculated differently for different crops. At first the settlers were to be subsidized and expected to pay only the costs of inputs such as seeds, fertilizers, and insecticides.

The SDA estimated that rice production would yield 18–20 quintals per hectare, which, at a selling price of about 320 Somali shillings per quintal, would bring an average family a gross income of 5760 shillings. Maize was expected to yield 16 quintals per hectare, and, at 180 shillings per quintal, to provide 2880 shillings. Including income earned for sesame, cowpeas, bananas, and vegetables such as onions and tomatoes, the total gross income for one family was expected to be around 12,921 shillings, of which about 47 percent was to be returned in kind or cash to the SDA for operational costs, leaving each family with about 6848 shillings net income.

The family net money income was therefore expected to be about 570 shillings a month, excluding income obtained from poultry, livestock rearing, and handicrafts. This was to be compared with an estimated average national family income of only 292 shillings a month in 1976.

Obviously the settlers had high expectations that their income would rise substantially once the program was implemented. Despite enthusiasm and hard work on the part of the settlers through this period, however, overall yields were considerably lower than those estimated by the SDA. At Kurtunwary, the settlers who initially received the distributed land wished to grow only maize, but the yield was only 7–8 quintals per hectare for some 537 hectares. At Sablaale, where rice was grown as well as maize, a yield of about 12 quintals per hectare for maize was achieved on 290 hectares, but this was still considerably below the 16 quintals expected. The average yield was only about 6 quintals per hectare in Kurtunwary and 10 at Sablaale.

The difference in the yields of the two settlements may be due to the fact that at Kurtunwary the pilot project included the presettlement indigenous farmers who (at least initially) adhered to the traditional methods of agriculture, which are known to produce low yields. The ex-nomad farmers who participated in Sablaale's tenant pilot program were more willing, because of their inexperience, to follow expert advice.

A very rough calculation of net annual income (after paying the SDA for production costs) indicates that, on average, settler households received less than 2000 shillings, an income considerably below the projected net annual family income of 6848 shillings.

### Settlers' access to social services

In 1975, the first mandate given to the SDA and CDP settlement agencies was to attend to the immediate needs of the settlers such as food, housing, health, education, and other social services.

The provision of adequate social services for the settlements has been a controversial issue, however. Housing programs have perhaps received the most criticism (Haakonsen 1980; Scudder 1981). It has been suggested that the provision of housing, which uses a large component of imported materials, has been too expensive.

In 1978 the Netherlands and United States governments took over the sponsorship of the housing schemes at Sablaale and Kurtunwary, respectively. They favored a phased approach, each agreeing to undertake an 800-house satellite village pilot project. Because of a much slower implementation of land development than expected, and the chronic shortage of labor, these pilot projects were scaled down to 400 houses at each settlement. Average cost per housing unit was estimated at about U.S. $3650—ranging from just under U.S. $3000 for the USAID-designed houses at Kurtunwary to U.S. $4300 for the Netherlands government-assisted project at Sablaale. With infrastructure (roads, water, schools, and dispensaries) and consultants' fees included, unit costs at Sablaale were expected to run to about U.S. $6000. The projects were to be completed in about 18 months, with 400 completed units at Sablaale by May 1981 and at Kurtunwary by October of the same year.

The projects experienced a number of difficulties. The design of the foundations of the houses at Kurtunwary was ill suited to the settlement's soft black cotton soils. By the time scheduled for project completion, the Netherlands project had only 50 units completed, most without doors or windows, and the USAID project an estimated 150 units out of the projected 400. Neither had basic infrastructure or roads.

The second serious problem was cost. By the end of 1980, the Netherlands project manager calculated the unit cost (including infrastructure and consultants' fees) at about U.S. $10,000, mostly in foreign exchange, and the U.S. unit cost was calculated at U.S. $9,000, with expected cost overruns of as much as 50 percent, bringing unit costs at Kurtunwary to U.S. $15,000.

A new management team appointed in April 1981 introduced various improvements in design at Sablaale. By August 1982, 250 of the newly designed houses at Sablaale were completed, as well as much of the settlement infrastructure; the two Netherlands managers, already looking beyond the revised pilot project completion date of May 1983, were examining other possible ways of reducing unit costs for completing the target of 400 family houses for Sablaale. At Kurtunwary, on the other hand, progress appeared to be as slow as ever.

*Education*

The establishment of the settlement schemes in 1975 coincided with efforts by the government to increase greatly the intake of primary school-age children into the nation's schools and ultimately to achieve universal primary schooling.

The new wave of children entering schools at the settlement schemes was of quite monumental proportions, relative to education generally in Somalia (SDR 1982a).

In 1977, the first Director of Planning for the SDA published education goals for the SDA settlements to be achieved by the end of six years (Omar 1977). Table 7.7 presents figures for targets and achievements in 1980–81.

One can see that the SDA's goal for classrooms was very close to being achieved by 1980–81, but there were 23 *more* schools than were anticipated and 360 *fewer* teachers.

*Health*

In 1975, the provision of health care was one of the foremost immediate goals of the resettlement schemes. The settlers arrived at their new homes thin and malnourished, prey to pneumonia, diarrhea, and a host of other diseases. At the camps they had to adjust to poor sanitation, mud, and initially, overcrowding.

The first six-year budget for the SDA bears out the emphasis placed on health care (Table 7.8). Health expenditure accounted for 16 percent of the proposed budget of the SDA, and was second only to agricultural expenditure.

Settlement agency records indicate treatment of over 44,000 cases at SDA clinics and nearly 8000 at the CDP settlements during 1975. The 1975–80 goals at the SDA for physical health-care infrastructure were: Dujuma, 230 hospital beds and 9 dispensaries; Sablaale, 140 and 5; and Kurtunwary, 130 and 5, respectively—a total of 500 beds and 19 dispensaries (Omar 1977). This seemed to be, relative to the rest of Somalia, a substantial investment in health-care infrastructure. In 1977, for example, Togdheer, the region that supplied the great majority of settlers, had for its estimated population of 258,000 only ten dispensaries and two hospitals with 257 beds, while Nugaal, with 85,000 people, had only seven dispensaries and 122 hospital beds (SDR 1979c: 290).

While health-care facilities at the settlements might appear more than adequate, data concerning actual use of the facilities is scant and un-reliable. A mere increase in the provision of health-care facilities does not necessarily imply an improvement in the health of the settlement populations since resettlement. The figures in Table 7.9 indicate a high incidence of malaria and bilharzia at most settlements.

## ASSESSMENT

### Infrastructure and social services: Availability and use within the settlement areas

The progress achieved to date in providing facilities and social services in the three agricultural settlements is impressive. A significant number of public buildings requiring central locations have been built in the main village sites using permanent materials. Provision of infrastructure in the fishing settlements is even more advanced.

The housing pilot projects at the agricultural settlements remain a point of controversy, however. By 1981, as has already been seen, the targeted 400 houses at Sablaale and Kurtunwary were still far from completion.

Many observers have argued that housing would be better provided by the settlers themselves, and that the first settlement agency priority should be to make the new settlements economically viable. For those sharing this opinion, social services were a second priority, and housing a third. The line of argument was that when incomes in the settlement rose, the settlers themselves would build permanent housing to their own specifications. The argument went on to say that while the housing projects were certainly an attraction that might serve, as the government had hoped, to keep the former nomads at the settlements, only the promise of a higher income could ensure the settlers' commitment to the schemes.

Provision of education and health care at the settlements appears to be well above the national norm. The elementary school program at the SDA/CDP settlements ranked behind only five of the 16 administrative regions in size of enrollment. The intermediate grades (5–8) had more students than all of Somalia's regions except the Banaadir (Mogadishu) and Shabeellaha Hoose (of which the settlements themselves contributed about half the enrollment). At the secondary level, the settlement en-rollment was less than only three regions (and again Shabeellaha Hoose was one of these).

Health facilities also appear to be more than adequate. Kurtunwary and Sablaale each have a central hospital with about 130 and 140 beds respectively, while Dujuma has two central hospitals of about 115 beds each. Each settlement has a lower ratio of persons per dispensary than the national average (and much lower than that of the home regions). SDA records indicated that in 1980 about 250 patients were treated daily at Kurtunwary; at Sablaale an average of 110 were seen; and at Dujuma the two doctors and health staff saw between 180 and 220 patients per day. The fishing settlements have access to the medical facilities at their nearby towns. Despite the availability of health facilities at the SDA settlements, however, it is not clear that the health of the former nomads is actually better. In particular, the spread of bilharzia among the settlers appears to have increased, while the incidence of malaria seems quite a bit higher than that prevalent in northern Somalia.

Rations supplied by the Somali government, the European Economic Community, and the World Food Program of 3000 calories and 70 grams of protein greatly exceeded the 1770 calories and 56.9 grams of protein per person day average for Somalia. Unlike the situation under nomadic conditions, food was available throughout the dry seasons. There was speculation that the short-term effects of providing free rations, as well as housing and fishing/farming equipment, would be "a lack of incentive for the resettled people to work hard" (Haakonsen 1980: 6), and that the long-term effect might be too great a dependency on state assistance. By the end of 1984, however, the rations were planned to be phased out.

## Retention of former nomad settlers

Table 7.10 shows the total number of settlers in agricultural and fishing settlements over six-month periods from June 1976 to April 1980, and the net change in population during this period. Since their beginning in August 1975, the SDA agricultural settlements have experienced a precipitous drop in population of as much as 40 percent, whereas the CDP fishing settlements appear to have leveled off in size relatively earlier without the same degree of population decline.[2]

The years 1976–78 saw the greatest loss of population, with the departure of over 28,000 SDA/CDP settlers. Indeed, these were years of profound readjustment for the former nomads, who had barely survived one of the worst droughts in the history of Somalia. The settlers, in addition, faced new problems: inadequate sanitation, mud, overcrowding, a high incidence of malaria, and, as the nomads had not learned to be wary of river water, bilharzia.

At the SDA settlements the late start in production activities (farm machinery did not arrive until spring 1979) and the delays in providing housing and other infrastructural factilities caused much discouragement, while the milieu at the CDP settlements was described by a Ministry of Fisheries publication as one of "devastating worry, instability, and confusion, with many settlers becoming frustrated and drifting back to their herds and the pasture lands" (SDR 1977: 8).

While difficulties of adjustment and organizational consolidation during the transitional years were probably unavoidable, given the emergency conditions, there may well have been other reasons for the population loss. First, many of the settlers who had acquired skills working on modern, large-scale irrigation projects and mechanized fishing operations may have migrated to the Gulf States, where such skills were commanding much higher remuneration. Second, many of the nomads may simply have abandoned the settlements during the early years because their perception of the settlements was based on social and cultural norms that were not taken into account by the resettlement agencies. The highly individualistic nature of the nomads may well have been in conflict with the collective basis on which the settlements were at first run, and many nomads who left may have intended from the beginning to remain in the settlements only so long as it was useful for them in their effort to return to a pastoral life.

### Resettlement objectives

The earlier analysis shows that the government was successful, to some extent, in achieving the resettlement objectives of providing Somalia's nomadic population with social services. With regard to self-sufficiency in food production and improving the foreign trade balance, evidence suggests that Somalia may have been further from attaining these goals by the end of the Three-Year Development Plan, 1979–81 (TYDP), than before the resettlement program began in 1975. The data show that there was an overall increase in Somalia's crop production of 11.1 percent for maize, 24.1 percent for sorghum, and 50 percent for rice between 1978 and 1981. However, the TYDP evaluation report conceded that the total rainfall as well as its distribution was better in 1981 than in a normal year and better than in 1978, the date used as a baseline, so that the increases were "mainly due to favourable rainfall conditions and only a small proportion due to the impact of the TYDP" (SDR 1982b: 117).

During the TYDP, importation of cereals and edible oil increased sharply—rice and wheat flour by as much as 77 percent and edible oil by 19 percent. The TYDP evaluation report attributed this in part to "a normal increase in population," but more especially to the large numbers of refugees who entered Somalia during 1980 (SDR 1982b: 116–18).

A sharp decline in banana exports during the TYDP period led to an increasingly unfavorable balance of agricultural trade and a mounting burden of debt. The TYDP program evaluation report noted that the only comfort that could be taken from this rather bleak picture was that things would have been worse if agricultural production had not increased during the TYDP period.

From the standpoint of the SDA settlements' contribution to import substitution, it is noteworthy that among food commodities alone, sugar imports actually decreased from 90,818 tons in 1978 to none by 1981 (SDR 1982b: 117–18). Dujuma's newly transferred former nomads, contributing their labor to the new Juba Sugar Estate, were in large part responsible for this success in sugar import substitution.

Several Rangelands Development Projects were set in motion to stabilize the pastoral population and halt the deterioration of Somalia's pasturelands. Their general objectives were "to improve the income of pastoralists, make way for the adoption of modern ranching practices and a more settled way of life" (SDR 1979c: 69–70).

Unfortunately, by the end of the TYDP, capital investment was only 39 percent and physical implementation only about 20 percent of that planned (SDR 1979c: 104–5). Accelerating inflation, communications problems, and insufficient numbers of qualified and experienced personnel were some of the problems encountered. As for the plans for involving pastoralists in range management through informal education, the TYDP evaluation report concluded that "it was not yet clear to what extent pastoralists in the north understood and supported the objectives of the [rangelands management] project" (SDR 1979c: 101–2).

The TYDP program evaluation report's conclusions regarding organizational defects in range management projects would be equally true for the SDA and CDP administration; in fact, they would apply to most projects in Somalia:

Project implementation and evaluation, and particularly annual budgeting, were adversely affected by the lack of documents (except in the case of most externally-assisted working projects) and of disciplined recording, reporting and monitoring procedures. *Indeed, in many instances project staff appeared to be quite unaware of the programme of development and the targets to which they were, in theory, committed* [emphasis added]. . . . Subsectoral programmes appear to lack underlying definition of long range objectives and strategies and of the interrelated roles of their projects. It is recommended that "master" or "perspective" plans should be prepared on a subsectoral basis which would define development stages and strategies through to ultimate objectives for, say, the year 2000. (SDR 1979c: 106–7)

Worst of all were events the Somali government had no control over: a drought in 1979–80 and the arrival of war refugees from the Ogaden with their livestock. Somalia had had several years of good rainfall following the 1974 drought, when the 1979–80 drought hit.

Although [the 1979–80 drought] was less severe than the previous drought *its effects were almost as serious, which is indicative of increasing pressure on a deteriorating resource* [emphasis added]. Firstly, 5.9 million animals were estimated to have died, approximately the same as in the 1973–75 drought, with losses particularly high in the North-west, Togdheer and Gedo regions. Secondly, there was greatly increased prevalence of disease, especially trypanosomiasis. Thirdly, milk production was estimated by the Food Security Project to fall from 1.3 million tonnes in 1978 to just under 0.8 million tonnes in 1980 and 1981, thereby creating greatly increased demand for alternative foods for the bulk of the population. (SDR 1982b: 80)

By the end of 1981, therefore, the condition of the rangelands had deteriorated even further, thus heightening the sense of emergency underlying Somalia's resettlement policy.

## SDA/CDP program implementation

### Achievement of financial targets

Although their expenditures were mostly incurred during the last two years of the Five-Year Development Plan (FYDP) of 1974–78, the SDA and CDP had high financial implementation rates compared with the agricultural and fisheries sectors as a whole. The SDA spent nearly U.S. $11,851,000, which was 63.3 percent of planned expenditure. For the agricultural sector as a whole, actual expenditure was only 55.1 percent of planned expenditure (Table 7.11). The CDP spent almost U.S. $10.9 million, which was 68.6 percent of its planned budget, compared with 50.9 for the fisheries sector as a whole.

During the next development plan (the Three-Year Development Plan of 1979–81), however, the implementation rate for the SDA (41.5 percent) fell *below* that of the agricultural sector as a whole (47.7 percent), which was itself lower than that in the previous planning period. CDP expenditure was 53 percent of all fisheries sector expenditures during the FYDP, but during the TYDP it was no longer disaggregated from the overall fisheries sector budget figures. The fisheries sector financial implementation rate, however, went up from 50.9 percent during the FYDP to 90.2 percent during the TYDP period.

### Achievement of physical targets

As already discussed, social services including education and medical facilities were given adequate attention in SDA/CDP settlements. Achievement of production targets was, however, less satisfactory. The SDA's original target for developing irrigated and nonirrigated agricultural land in 1974–78 was 56,000 hectares for its three settlements (SDR 1979a: 36).[3] This target was subsequently scaled down to 30,000 hectares.

By the end of 1978, only 2438 hectares of rain-fed land had been re-claimed and improved (SDR 1979a: 92). No new irrigated land was under cultivation by the end of the FYDP in 1978, and agricultural equipment did not arrive at the settlements until spring 1979 (SDR 1979a: 29, 31).

The SDA's TYDP (1979–81) objective was to develop 22,000 hectares of land, half of it irrigated. However, since 10,000 hectares of this was to be at Dujuma, the overall target was again reduced to 12,000 hectares when Dujuma was abandoned at the end of 1980. Soon after, even this modest goal was further scaled down to a mere 3050 hectares (SDR 1982b: 135–37).

Table 7.12 provides some indication of overall physical implementation at the SDA agricultural settlements during the period 1979–81. The figure of only 954 hectares developed was low, even bearing in mind the sharp reduction in the target set initially for this item in the TYDP, and yield levels attained on both irrigated and rain-fed land were reported to be "low for most crops." Even though the rate of acquisition for machinery and equipment almost met planned targets, shortages of fuel and spare parts for agricultural machinery, and lack of financial resources were cited as reasons for the slow progress in land preparation.

The development of 954 hectares was, however, no small achievement considering that this was the first irrigated land to be developed by the SDA. It was distributed to the settler families for cultivation through a pilot project in April 1982. Land preparation and supply of inputs continued to be the responsibility of the SDA (only a small proportion of the cost of these services was recovered at harvest time), and all labor was to be supplied by the families themselves. This pilot project seems to have had a favorable impact on farm production: "a number of male adults who had left the settlements were reported to have returned and the problem of labour shortage during the peak seasons was solved to a large extent" (SDR 1982b: 136).

However much scarcities of fuel and spare parts slowed the SDA's progress in land development, the same was true for all agricultural projects in Somalia. Moreover, the "manpower constraints [were] one of the major reasons for the relatively low growth rate of agricultural output and productivity" (SDR 1982b: 33).

The fishing catch for Somalia had remained around 4000 tons during the TYDP period 1979–81, despite the distribution of some 685 small motorized boats to the four CDP settlements (including the small El Ahmed settlement) and to the Ministry's 19 fishing cooperatives. By 1981, only 308 of these motorized vessels were still in operation, primarily because of a high incidence of mechanical failure and hull damage (SDR 1982b: 154–61).

To reverse this situation the Ministry of Fisheries began to emphasize the importance of profit-making in early 1981, and the motorized boats were sold to their crews. These sales were first introduced in the Lower Juba region and were later extended to Mogadishu and other coopera- tives, though not as yet to the CDP settlements. By the end of 1981, around 110 modern fishing boats had been transferred to private own- ership. The responsibility of ownership was accompanied by "a re- markable decrease in mechanical failures. Vessels [were] now operated more effectively and individual catches [rose]. . . . In like manner, private merchants were encouraged to participate in marketing the fisheries' produce, and this resulted in better prices and a more efficient collection and distribution of the catch" (SDR 1982b: 157–58).

Despite these encouraging signs, settlement production levels, par- ticularly those of the SDA settlements, appeared to be far below those necessary to achieve any population redistribution on a scale large enough to stabilize Somalia's pastoral population.

### Implementation of the CDP/SDA resettlement program in the national context

While the smallholdings sector prduces most of Somalia's food grains, the TYDP continued the government's earlier policy of heavy investment in irrigation development, which is considered necessary for "food se- curity" because of the uncertainties of dry farming, given Somalia's low and erratic rainfall. Of the planned outlay of U.S. $133 million for 31 projects, approximately half was for irrigation. Somalia's 11 major irri- gation and crop production projects were expected to contribute sub- stantially toward an increase in production of both food and nonfood crops during the TYDP. However, only 50 percent of the target increase for maize, 16.9 percent for rice, and 20 percent for cotton and groundnuts were achieved for the country as a whole during the plan.

The TYDP target was to implement seven irrigation projects, bringing 16.985 hectares of land under irrigation, but by the end of the period only 7000 hectares (41.2 percent of the target) had been added to the total irrigated area. It is interesting to note that the Juba Sugar Estate at Marerey, where the bulk of Dujuma's population was transferred to work as farm laborers, was responsible for 4000 hectares of this, which would probably not have been feasible without the former nomad (ex- Dujuma) settlers' labor input (SDR 1982b: 119).

The two other major agricultural development programs in the TYDP's crop production subsector did little better than the SDA, in terms of either financial implementation or program achievement. The Agricul- tural Cooperatives Program, for instance, spent U.S. $1,071,000, a fi- nancial implementation rate of only 27.1 percent, much lower than the SDA's 41.5 percent rate. Rating the program's achievements, the TYDP program evaluation report concluded that "rapid progress in quantita- tive terms [of increased membership] was achieved at the cost of quality of services provided to members. Except for channeling government grants and bank loans, the agricultural cooperatives had little to offer member farmers because extension, input supply, tractor hiring and marketing services were weak" (SDR 1982b: 137).

Though the agricultural crash program spent U.S. $3.4 million during the TYDP, with a relatively high implementation rate of 53.2 percent, it, too, fell far short of its physical targets, reclaiming only some 4700 hectares of land for cultivation, about 31.3 percent of the target (the same percentage as the SDA during this period).

## Population redistribution goals

The 1980 World Bank *Agricultural Sector Review* for Somalia argues that if the rangelands are to continue to carry only their current population, between 1.5 million and 1.7 million additional persons will have to be absorbed in the nonpastoral sectors between 1980 and the year 2000, or about 75,000 to 85,000 per year (Scudder 1981: 1–3). The World Bank further estimates that if an additional 85,000 hectares of irrigated land were developed (and Somalia's current 50,000 hectares of irrigated land were rehabilitated and production intensified), and another 750,000 hectares of land were added to the current 540,000 hectares of rain-fed agricultural land, the agricultural sector could absorb all but 350,000 to 550,000 of Somalia's population increment during the 20 years from 1980 to the year 2000.[4]

If appropriate surveys were to be completed, appropriate organizational structures created and staff trained, the formation of new settlements based on rain-fed and irrigated agriculture would necessarily occur relatively slowly during the initial years (Scudder 1981: 7–8). The resettlement schedule set forth in Table 7.13 would be a realistic one for this sort of phased approach.

It is the agricultural sector that must bear the brunt of any major population redistribution in Somalia. By the beginning of the TYDP, the government was placing greater emphasis on standard large-scale irrigation schemes, run as state farms, rather than replicating the SDA schemes, which in terms of production incentives appeared to be moving away from the state farm model.

If the agricultural projects already under way are completed by 1990, Somalia could well meet and even go beyond the gradual World Bank target for absorbing its population increment into the agricultural sector by the year 2000.

Where the SDA resettlement schemes can contribute is through the lessons learned in the process of implementing them. One very important question remains to be answered, however: If the birth rate for nomads who have been settled goes up, because of access to health care and a less perilous existence, how will this affect the feasibility of a policy of settling Somalia's population increment to take the pressure off its deteriorating rangelands? A second question may be equally important: Will the first generation of educated former nomads in the SDA/CDP settlements choose to stay in the rural sector, or will they, by virtue of their education, be attracted to urban centers, thus undermining one of the goals of the resettlement program, that of slowing urban growth? These two questions have very serious implications for future resettlement schemes in Somalia.

## CONCLUSIONS AND POLICY IMPLICATIONS

While Somalia undoubtedly has untapped fishing and agricultural resources, its rangelands are rapidly becoming overpopulated; this surplus population must be absorbed into other sectors of the economy. While the 1974 drought dramatically highlighted the overstocking and mismanagement of the rangelands, unfortunately the subsequent range management and nomad resettlement programs have been less than successful in halting the deterioration of Somalia's rangelands.

The range management programs were hampered by the 1979–80 drought, by the arrival in Somalia of war refugees with considerable additional livestock for the rangelands to support, and by various internal organizational inadequacies within the programs themselves.

The ambitious SDA and CDP resettlement programs begun in 1975 also fell far short of the goal recommended by the ILO in 1977 of resettling 216,000 persons within the agricultural sector by 1981. By 1981 only 75,000 of the original 120,000 former nomads (62 percent) remained in the SDA/CDP schemes, and it remains to be seen how plausible is the World Bank goal of absorbing into agriculture by the year 2000 an expected rural population increase of between 1.5 and 1.7 mllion.[5]

Whatever the success of these programs, the urgency of relieving the pressure on Somalia's rangelands is greater than ever, and the SDA/CDP resettlement programs are the only experience the Somali government has in attempting to redistribute the nation's population to achieve a better match of resources and manpower.

There is certainly no reason to suppose that such a match of resources and manpower could not be made. From Somalia's history, it seems that, given a clearly workable resettlement program that offered a greater measure of security to Somalia's pastoralists, many would opt for agriculture.

Unfortunately, the SDA/CDP schemes, at least in the early 1980s, do not appear to have been sufficiently successful in economic terms to make them worth emulating in future resettlement programs. The value of their produce, whether in fish or grain, has generally been quite modest, while the costs of developing and running the schemes have been high.[6]

The SDA/CDP schemes have not been economically effective for a number of reasons: there was little comprehensive planning when they were first established; there has been inadequate management; the provision of social services, especially housing, has been expensive and not cost-effective; and settlers have been left out of settlement planning and given little incentive to produce.

Because they were conceived during a period of national emergency, the settlements were physically created long before any social or economic planning could be carried out. Because it was an emotional time, and things were done quickly, very ambitious and unrealistic goals were set, to be achieved in far too short a time. Local host populations were not taken into account, and the settlements were not conceived of in terms of their regional context. Along the Shabeelle River, for instance, local reactions were hostile because the new settlements competed with other irrigation projects for limited water. Retrospective and more realistic planning eventually led to greatly reduced land development goals at Kurtunwary and Sablaale. The largest of the resettlement schemes at Dujuma had to be abandoned five years after it was established because of the salinity of the soil.

The general lack of policy and planning still remains one of the foremost obstacles. As with the range management projects, and generally with Somalia's development efforts, project implementation and evaluation (and particularly annual budgeting) have continued to be "adversely affected by the lack of working documents . . . and of disciplined recording, reporting and monitoring procedures" (SDR 1982b: 107). This difficulty has made it virtually impossible to define development stages and strategies for long-range planning to meet ultimate objectives.

A major factor in the inadequate management of the settlement schemes is a scarcity of qualified manpower. Low government salaries force many staff, at all levels, to take part-time employment in addition to their settlement jobs. A number of qualified persons have left Somalia altogether, for more lucrative employment in the Gulf States. Other development projects with newer sources of foreign aid compete for the few qualified Somalis still in government service.

From a social rather than a narrow economic view, the overall performance of the settlements might not be unreasonable. This is particularly true if the nonquantifiable benefits of the schemes are also taken into account: the resettlement and creation of employment opportunities for some 15,000 families, and the creation of a social infrastructure that has improved hygiene, nutrition and educational opportunities for these families, as well as helping them to acquire agricultural and fishing skills they did not previously possess.

Whatever the merits of this argument, there are attendant problems associated with the provision of social services. While health facilities are generally at a higher level than the national norm, the former nomads face unprecedented health hazards in bilharzia and in the year-round incidence of malaria. Housing, which was expected to be low-cost, has turned out to be expensive, involving a large component of imported goods and services. The educational program at the settlements ranks among the very best in the country in quantitative terms, and certainly far above that in the northern regions, where the settlers came from. But there is some question as to whether aspirations resulting from this education may in the long run make the SDA/CDP settlements only a halfway station for migration from the countryside to urban centers.

Somalia's resettlement policy was from the beginning intended to establish a devolved system of management, with small-scale coopera- tives managing their own production within an overall framework pro- viding services, advice, and coordination. The initial management structure, however, was that of a state-run enterprise, where decisions were made at the top and passed down to the settlers, whose status was analogous to that of paid laborers. This was thought to be a more efficient way of using scarce managerial talent. Transition to cooperative management was delayed because failure to achieve development tar- gets, as a result of inadequate detailed planning and implementation, seemed (according to a kind of circular reasoning) to confirm the need for a rigid, top-down managerial structure.

Work incentives and family income were not given adequate weight because the agencies provided the settlers with all their basic needs. With the benefit of hindsight, however, it can be seen that maintaining the settlements as relief camps produced a large measure of apathy and dependency among the settlers, which had a counterproductive effect on the economic performance of the settlements. A shortage of labor for agricultural production continued to be a problem through the early years, as working-age men left the settlements for presumably more profitable endeavors elsewhere.

By the end of 1982, experiments were under way involving the dis- tribution of plots among settler families in the SDA schemes and the selling of motorized boats to fishing cooperative members in CDP set- tlements. Early results seemed to indicate a rise in production and, at the SDA schemes, an inflow of agricultural manpower. Though it is too early to be sure how these experimental measures will affect the long- term self-sufficiency of the resettlement schemes, the prognosis for their economic rehabilitation does seem much improved.

In general, the analysis in this study suggests that planning is crucial to the success of future resettlement programs. While this is true for both fishing and agricultural settlements, it is more critical for the latter, which involves larger populations and where the resources to be exploited, through irrigated and rain-fed farming, are, for Somalia, more problematic.

With the recent decision to settle 750,000 war refugees, there is considerable doubt whether Somalia can meet long-range goals for redistribution of its own population, unless future resettlement programs are more carefully planned and executed than in the past and projects can reach self-sufficiency reasonably quickly. In the case of government-supplied housing, which has not proved cost-effective, better housing may have to be phased in later as settlers become able to afford to upgrade traditional structures; the same could apply to other social services provision. Settlers will have to be involved in production decisions and given more incentive to produce. A policy of encouraging voluntary, spontaneous settlement of nomads in regions where agricultural potential is greatest may be a more efficient alternative to planned resettlement schemes.

## NOTES

1. The data have been extracted from official files at both the SDA, which administers the agricultural schemes, and the CDP, which administers the fishing settlements. Some of the secondary data are from technical studies, reports, and earlier surveys by Somali officials and foreign consultants, while much contextual information had to be derived from an extensive survey of anthropological and historical literature on Somalia.

2. Perhaps the CDP population remained relatively stable because thousands of nomads who initially chose to join the fishing settlements changed their minds at the very outset and either returned to their homeland or joined the SDA settlements (Kaplan 1977a: 271).

3. Dujuma alone was to have 30,000 hectares, Kurtunwary 18,000 hectares, and Sablaale 8000 hectares.

4. This estimate did not take into account the 700,000 refugees in Somali war refugee camps from 1980 onward.

5. And, in the process, lowering the nomadic pastoralist proportion of the national population from two-thirds to one-third.

6. Very rough estimates of gross income from fishing and agriculture, for instance, range under the most favorable conditions from U.S. $30,000 for the CDP settlements to about U.S. $900,000 for the SDA settlements, a far cry from the millions spent annually to maintain them. In fact, however, it is hard to quantify in any meaningful terms the economic achievements of the settlements, as production costs have not been adequately assessed, nor have separate accounts been kept for the settlements apart from the agencies that administer them.

## BIBLIOGRAPHY

Afzal, M. 1982. *Assistance to Demographic Analysis and Studies: Technical Progress Reports*. Mogadishu: Central Statistical Department, Ministry of National Planning.

Cassanelli, Lee V. 1975. *The Sahelian Drought and Its Demographic Implications*. Washington, D.C.: Overseas Liaison Committee, American Council on Education.

————. 1982. *The Shaping of Somali Society: Reconstructing the History of a Pastoral People, 1600–1900*. Philadelphia, PA: University of Pennsylvania Press.

Haakonsen, J. M. 1980. *The Fishing Cooperatives for Resettled Nomads Revisited*. Report presented to the Ministry of Fisheries, Somali Democratic Republic, and the FAO, Rome and Mogadishu. Montreal: Labour Studies Group, Centre for Developing Area Studies, McGill University.

International Labour Office/Jobs and Skills Programme for Africa. 1977. *Economic Transformation in a Socialist Framework: An Employment and Basic Needs Oriented Development Strategy for Somalia*. Addis Ababa: JASPA.

Kamrany, S., and M. Nake. 1977. "The Sahel Drought: Major Development Issues." *Ekistics* (Athens), no. 258: 314–19.

Kaplan, I. 1977a. *Area Handbook for Somalia*. Washington, D.C.: U.S. Government Printing Office.

————. 1977b. *Area Handbook for Ethiopia*. Washington, D.C.: U.S. Government Printing Office.

Omar, J. Mohamed. 1977. "The Drought in the Semi-Desert of Somalia." In *Conference on Alternative Strategies for Desert Development*, Sacramento, May 31-June 10, 1977, vol. 4, pp. 8–12. Davis, CA: University of California.

Rajagopalan, V. K. 1981. "In-Depth Labour Availability Survey in the Two Nomad Settlements of Somalia (Kurtunwary and Sablaale). Assignment report. Mogadishu: ILO.

Scudder, T. 1981. *From Relief to Development: Some Comments on Refugee and Other Settlements in Somalia*. Pasadena, CA: Institute for Development Anthropology.

Settlement Development Agency and International Development Research Centre (SDA/IDRC). 1983. "Report on the Socioeconomic Research on Nomad Resettlement in Somalia." Mogadishu.

Somali Democratic Republic (SDR). Ministry of Fisheries. 1977. *New Life at Brava. The Instant Fishermen of Somalia Series*. Mogadishu.

SDR. State Planning Commission. 1979a. *Performance of the Five-Year Development Programme, 1974–1978*. Mogadishu.

————. 1979b. *Special Statistical Issue for the Tenth Anniversary of the 21st October Revolution*. Mogadishu.

————. 1979c. *Three-Year Plan, 1979–1981*. Mogadishu.

SDR. Central Statistical Department. Ministry of National Planning. 1981. *The Five-Year Development Plan, 1982–1986*. Draft. Mogadishu.

SDR. Ministry of Education. Planning Department. 1982a. *Statistics of Education, 1980–1981*. Mogadishu.

SDR. Ministry of National Planning. 1982b. *Evaluation of the Three-Year Development Programme, 1979–1980*. Mogadishu.

World Bank. 1983. *Somalia: Agricultural Sector Review*, 3 vols. Washington, D.C.

World Food Program. 1980a. *Project Summary. WFP-Assisted Project Somalia 2294: Resettlement of Nomads and Assistance to Refugees*. Rome: Food and Agriculture Organization of the United Nations.

————. 1980b. *Report on Interim Evaluation of WFP-Assisted Project Somalia 2294: Resettlement of Nomads as Farmers and Fishermen*. Rome: Food and Agriculture Organization of the United Nations.

Table 7.1
Percentage distribution of settlers by place of origin, 1981

| Place of origin | SDA agricultural settlements | | | | CDP fishing settlements* | | | | All |
|---|---|---|---|---|---|---|---|---|---|
| | Kurtunwary | Sablaale | Dujuma | Total | Brava | Adale | Eil | Total | |
| Bakool | 2.5 | -- | -- | 2.0 | 20.0 | -- | -- | 7.0 | 1.9 |
| Bari | 6.9 | 1.6 | 14.9 | 8.5 | -- | -- | 7.0 | 2.0 | 7.0 |
| Galgadud | 2.9 | 4.1 | -- | 0.7 | -- | 15.0 | -- | 6.0 | 2.7 |
| Gedo | -- | -- | -- | -- | 30.0 | -- | -- | 11.0 | 2.1 |
| Mudug | 4.9 | 16.3 | 5.9 | 8.9 | 40.0 | 50.0 | 34.0 | 42.0 | 15.1 |
| Nugal | 14.6 | 11.5 | 17.8 | 15.0 | 10.0 | 30.0 | 26.0 | 22.0 | 16.2 |
| Sanaag | 17.7 | 17.0 | 19.8 | 18.4 | -- | -- | 20.0 | 5.0 | 16.2 |
| Shabeellaha Dhexe | -- | -- | -- | -- | -- | 5.0 | -- | 2.0 | 0.4 |
| Togdheer | 50.5 | 49.5 | 41.6 | 46.5 | -- | -- | 13.0 | 3.0 | 38.4 |
| Total | 100.0 | 100.0 | 100.0 | 100.0 | 100.0 | 100.0 | 100.0 | 100.0 | 100.0 |
| n | 16,542 | 18,917 | 25,278 | 60,737 | 5,236 | 5,300 | 3,444 | 13,980 | 76,717 |

Source: SDA and CDP Administrative Records, 1981.
*Percentages for fishing settlements are estimates.

Table 7.2
Percentage distribution of resettlement, urban, rural, and nomadic
populations, by age and sex, 1980-81

|  | 0-14 years | | | 15+ years | | | |
|  | Male | Female | Both sexes | Male | Female | Both sexes | Total |
|---|---|---|---|---|---|---|---|
| **Settlements** | | | | | | | |
| Agricultural | 31.5 | 24.9 | 56.4 | 17.9 | 25.7 | 43.6 | 100.0 |
| Fishing | 30.3 | 23.3 | 53.6 | 22.5 | 23.9 | 46.4 | 100.0 |
| Total | 31.3 | 24.6 | 55.9 | 18.8 | 25.3 | 44.1 | 100.0 |
| **Somalia** | | | | | | | |
| Urban | 22.4 | 21.1 | 43.5 | 28.9 | 27.6 | 56.5 | 100.0 |
| Rural | 24.0 | 22.0 | 46.0 | 25.6 | 28.4 | 54.0 | 100.0 |
| Nomadic | 26.0 | 22.1 | 48.1 | 27.8 | 24.1 | 51.9 | 100.0 |

Sources: SDA and CDP Administrative Records, Mogadishu, 1981;
Central Statistical Department, Ministry of National Planning,
1980 Sample Survey, Mogadishu.

Table 7.3
Percentage distribution of settlers by age and sex, 1980

| Age | Male | Female | Both sexes | Male | Female | Both sexes | Male | Female | Both sexes |
|---|---|---|---|---|---|---|---|---|---|
|  | **Dujuma** | | | **Kurtunwary** | | | **Sablaale** | | |
| 0-5 | 5.6 | 5.7 | 11.3 | 6.9 | 6.5 | 13.5 | 7.1 | 7.4 | 14.4 |
| 6-14 | 28.5 | 19.8 | 48.3 | 20.0 | 16.4 | 36.4 | 25.3 | 18.9 | 44.6 |
| 15-30 | 9.7 | 10.5 | 20.3 | 12.2 | 17.9 | 30.1 | 12.0 | 10.9 | 22.9 |
| 31-45 | 3.4 | 10.4 | 13.7 | 4.4 | 10.3 | 14.7 | 4.3 | 8.5 | 12.8 |
| 46-60 | 2.1 | 1.9 | 4.1 | 2.1 | 2.4 | 4.5 | 1.7 | 1.8 | 3.6 |
| 60+ | 1.2 | 1.2 | 2.3 | 0.4 | 0.4 | 0.8 | 0.9 | 0.8 | 1.7 |
| Total | 50.5 | 49.5 | 100.0 | 46.0 | 53.9 | 100.0 | 51.3 | 48.3 | 100.0 |
| n | 12,640 | 12,391 | 25,031 | 8,528 | 10,009 | 18,537 | 8,579 | 8,043 | 16,622 |
|  | **Brava** | | | **Adale** | | | **Eil** | | |
| 0-5 | 6.0 | 5.4 | 11.4 | 5.8 | 5.6 | 11.4 | 6.1 | 5.1 | 11.2 |
| 6-14 | 24.1 | 17.3 | 41.4 | 20.5 | 15.4 | 35.9 | 30.8 | 22.4 | 53.2 |
| 15-50 | 18.1 | 22.4 | 41.5 | 27.7 | 23.8 | 51.6 | 13.3 | 17.3 | 30.7 |
| 51+ | 2.6 | 3.0 | 5.7 | 0.6 | 0.5 | 1.1 | 2.8 | 2.1 | 4.9 |
| Total | 50.8 | 48.1 | 100.0 | 54.6 | 45.3 | 100.0 | 53.0 | 46.9 | 100.0 |
| n | 2,651 | 2,566 | 5,217 | 2,902 | 2,404 | 5,306 | 1,818 | 1,609 | 3,427 |

Sources: SDA and CDP administrative records, Mogadishu, 1981.

Table 7.4
Distribution of settlers who received training at
agricultural resettlement schemes during 1977-80,
by major occupational categories

| Occupation | No. | Percentage |
|---|---|---|
| Farming | 1,180 | 41.95 |
| Construction/trades | 1,142 | 40.59 |
| Health (professional/technical) | 286 | 10.17 |
| Transport/communications | 140 | 4.98 |
| Clerical and related | 65 | 2.31 |
| Total | 2,813 | 100.00 |

Source: SDA and CDP administrative records,
Mogadishu, 1981.

Table 7.5
Crude work activity rates (per 100) for Somalia, 1975, and
for fishing and agricultural settlements, 1980-81

| | Male | Female | Both sexes |
|---|---|---|---|
| Somalia | | | |
| Urban | 44.4 | 21.4 | 33.5 |
| Rural | 48.1 | 28.5 | 38.8 |
| Settlements | | | |
| Fishing | 37.6 | 13.8 | 26.4 |
| Agricultural | 36.4 | 38.4 | 37.4 |

Sources: SDR (1981) p. 31, Mogadishu; CDP administrative
records, 1980-81, for fishing settlements, Mogadishu;
Rajagopalan (1981 survey) for agricultural settlements,
Mogadishu.

Table 7.6
Percentage distribution of working male and female population at
CDP/SDA settlements, by occupational groups, 1980-81

| Occupation | Fishing settlements | | | Agricultural settlements | | |
|---|---|---|---|---|---|---|
| | Male | Female | Total | Male | Female | Total |
| Farming/fishing | 90.77 | 81.39 | 88.45 | 71.54 | 89.48 | 81.00 |
| Construction/trades | 5.05 | 10.79 | 6.47 | 7.40 | 5.33 | 6.31 |
| Professional/technical | 1.15 | 4.07 | 1.88 | 2.58 | 1.30 | 1.91 |
| Transport/ communications | -- | -- | -- | 6.27 | -- | 2.96 |
| Administrative | -- | -- | -- | 4.18 | 0.43 | 2.20 |
| Clerical and related | 3.03 | 3.75 | 3.20 | 4.18 | 0.14 | 2.05 |
| Services | -- | -- | -- | 0.48 | 1.01 | 0.76 |
| Sales | -- | -- | -- | 0.64 | -- | 0.30 |
| Other | -- | -- | -- | 2.70 | 2.32 | 2.51 |
| Total | 100.00 | 100.00 | 100.00 | 100.00 | 100.00 | 100.00 |
| n | 2,772 | 908 | | 622 | 694 | |

Sources: CDP administrative records, 1980-81, for fishing
settlements; Rajagopalan (1981 survey) for agricultural settlements,
Mogadishu.


Table 7.7
SDA settlements: Target and actual number of schools, teachers, and
classrooms, 1980-81

| Settlement | Schools | | Teachers | | Classrooms | |
|---|---|---|---|---|---|---|
| | Target | Actual | Target | Actual | Target | Actual |
| Dujuma | 9 | 18 | 324 | 145 | 216 | 177 |
| Kurtunwary | 5 | 9 | 278 | 192 | 185 | 186 |
| Sablaale | 5 | 15 | 278 | 183 | 18 | 175 |
| Total | 19 | 42 | 880 | 520 | 419 | 538 |

Source: SDA administrative records, Mogadishu.

Table 7.8
SDA proposed budget, 1975-80

|              | Amount (U.S.$) | Percentage |
|--------------|----------------|------------|
| Agriculture  | 121,921,900    | 68.2       |
| Health       | 28,521,590     | 16.0       |
| Housing      | 16,682,860     | 9.3        |
| Education    | 4,289,048      | 2.4        |
| Utilities    | 3,905,873      | 2.1        |
| Poultry      | 2,581,270      | 1.4        |
| Food storage | 1,071,905      | 0.6        |
| Total        | 178,974,446    | 100.0      |

Source:  Omar (1977).

Table 7.9
Percentage of heads of households at SDA settlements reporting specified diseases, 1981

| Disease      | Kurtunwary (737) | Sablaale (668) | Dujuma (903) | All settlements (2308) |
|--------------|------------------|----------------|--------------|------------------------|
| Malaria      | 93.2             | 97.6           | 70.2         | 85.5                   |
| Bilharzia    | 83.4             | 94.2           | 20.3         | 61.8                   |
| Helmintions  | 13.4             | 35.5           | 22.4         | 23.3                   |
| Tuberculosis | 1.8              | 16.8           | 1.7          | 6.1                    |
| Other        | 3.8              | --             | 6.6          | 3.8                    |

Source:  SDA/IDRC (1983: 30).
Figures in parentheses are number of settlements reporting.

Table 7.10
Total number of settlers at the three SDA agricultural and three
CDP fishing settlements, 1976-80

| Year | Month | Agricultural settlements | Net population change | Fishing settlements | Net population change |
|------|-------|------------|------------|------------|------------|
| 1976 | June | 102,608 | | 15,000 | |
| | December | 95,145 | (-7,463) | 15,000 | (0) |
| 1977 | June | 87,658 | (-7,487) | 15,000 | (0) |
| | December | 81,447 | (-6,211) | 14,000 | (-1,000) |
| 1978 | June | 78,596 | (-2,851) | 13,996 | (-4) |
| | December | 74,983 | (-3,613) | 14,048 | (+52) |
| 1979 | June | 60,391 | (-14,592) | 14,349 | (+301) |
| | December | 60,077 | (-314) | 14,379 | (+30) |
| 1980 | April | 60,190 | (+113) | 14,408 | (+29) |

Sources: SDA and CDP administrative records, Mogadishu; World
Food Program (1980b: 18).

Table 7.11
Expenditures on selected projects in the agricultural and fisheries
sectors in the Five-Year Development Plan, 1974-78, and the Three-
Year Development Plan, 1979-81 (thousands of U.S.$)

| | FYDP 1974-78[a] | Percentage of planned | TYDP 1979-82[b] | Percentage of planned |
|------|------------|------------|------------|------------|
| Total agricultural sector | 102,693 | 55.1 | 54,119 | 47.7 |
| Service/institutional | 16,956 | 124.5 | 18,142 | 55.3 |
| Crop production | 28,121 | 62.1 | 10,083 | 47.1 |
| SDA program | 11,851 | 63.3 | 2,053 | 41.5 |
| Irrigation | 57,616 | 45.9 | 25,894 | 43.7 |
| Fisheries sector | 20,659 | 50.9 | 19,285 | 90.2 |
| CDP program | 10,922 | 68.6 | -- | -- |

Sources: SDR (1979a: 44-47, 67; 1982b: 150-51).
[a] At 6.19 Somali shillings per U.S.$.
[b] At 12.46 Somali shillings per U.S.$.

Table 7.12
SDA agricultural settlements: Targets and achievements, 1979-81

| Land and infrastructure development | Target | Achievement | Implementation rate (%) |
|---|---|---|---|
| Land reclamation/ improvement (ha) | 3050 | 954 | 31.3 |
| Canals constructed (km) | 70 | 20* | 28.9 |
| Machinery/equipment (no.) | 43 | 42 | 97.7 |
| Transport vehicles (no.) | -- | 30 | -- |
| Farm roads (km) | 70 | 28* | 40.6 |
| Dams/barrages (no.) | 1 | (under construction) | -- |

Source: SDR (1982b: 135).
*Figures from original table are rounded.

Table 7.13
Proposed resettlement program for Somalia's agricultural sector, 1980-2000

| Year | New rain-fed land (hectares) | New irrigated land (hectares) | Settled population |
|---|---|---|---|
| 1980 | 37,500 | 4,250 | 57,500 |
| 1981-90 | 187,500 | 21,250 | 287,500 |
| 1991-95 | 225,000 | 25,500 | 345,000 |
| 1996-2000 | 300,000 | 34,000 | 460,000 |
| Total | 750,000 | 85,000 | 1,150,000 |

Source: Scudder (1981).

P. S. Maro

8

# Land Settlements and Population Redistribution in the United Republic of Tanzania

## INTRODUCTION

Many countries in Africa have adopted land settlement schemes as part of their national planning strategy for socioeconomic development with the common objectives of increasing agricultural production, redistributing population by relocating landless and displaced persons or moving people from heavily populated regions to those with low population densities, and facilitating the provision of essential social services such as health care, education, and clean water. Between 1961 and 1966 the United Republic of Tanzania attempted to transform agriculture through the establishment of capital-intensive settlement schemes; these were limited in scope and affected only 100,000 people. After the Arusha Declaration (1967), which ushered in the philosophy of socialism and self-reliance, Tanzania embarked on the collectivization of the entire rural population into nucleated settlements (*ujamaa* villages) as a precondition for rural development. Both the policy objectives and the strategies of implementation envisaged a future society based on nucleated settlements in which land and labor were to be mobilized for cooperative

Professor, Department of Geography, University of Dar es Salaam and communal production, and where there was to be equitable income distribution. The villagization program was also expected to make it easier and cheaper to provide social services.

This study analyzes the United Republic of Tanzania's experience with land settlement schemes and population redistribution; it is organized into six major sections. Following the introduction, section 1 discusses the pre–Arusha Declaration settlement schemes as a historical background to villagization; it analyzes the policy objectives, the implementation process, the reasons for the failure of the earlier settlement schemes, and their influence on ujamaa policy. Section 2 discusses the objectives behind the establishment of ujamaa villages and the strategies adopted for establishing them. Section 3 describes the process and progress of establishing the villages, and their impact on population redistribution. Section 4 analyzes the effects of the ujamaa program on employment, agricultural production, and the reduction of poverty. Some of these effects are contrasted with those of the earlier settlement schemes. Section 5 assesses the effectiveness of the ujamaa experience in terms of provision of social services and infrastructure, retention of settlers, and future employment opportunities. Section 6 examines the costs and benefits of the land settlement program. The concluding section highlights the problems and prospects for settlements and puts forward some suggestions for settlement policy.

## HISTORICAL BACKGROUND: PRE–ARUSHA DECLARATION SETTLEMENTS

### Colonial settlement schemes

By the time of independence in 1961, the United Republic of Tanzania had had some experience of land settlements under British colonial rule. In the 1930s and 1940s, force was used to concentrate peasants into compact settlements; this was a method both of checking the spread of tstetse fly infestation and of increasing agricultural production. Up to 1945, 64 land settlements involving 195,037 people had been formed (McHenry 1979). In the 1950s the colonial government encouraged capitalist cash crop farming settlements, especially on some of the land abandoned by the failed Groundnut Scheme in Urambo, Kongwa, and Nachingwea. The most famous of these settlements was the Sukumal Development Scheme, which resulted in the migration of 30,000 people between 1948 and 1957 into Geita District (McCall 1983).

The objective of colonial agricultural policy was to increase production, particularly of cash crops, and the land settlements were established with this single objective in mind. The changes envisaged were improvements in traditional agricultural practices through soil conservation, terracing, and land use planning. There was no emphasis on the introduction of new techniques or innovations, nor any concern for the welfare of the peasant producers or the provision of social services. One consequence of colonial agricultural policies was anticolonial resistance on the part of the peasants, which was mobilized into a mass nationalist movement demanding self-government (Hyden 1980: 65).

## Postcolonial settlement schemes

In 1962 the independent United Republic of Tanzania, advised by the World Bank, embarked on the establishment of land settlements on formerly unused land by persuading people from areas of land shortage to move to selected sites. By removing people from their traditional social environment and establishing them on new land, the government believed that they would be more open to change and therefore more likely to adopt new ways of farming. A Village Settlement Agency (VSA) was set up to supervise the schemes and advise the government on their implementation. Pilot planned settlement schemes were established in various parts of the country as centers of modern farming; at their peak period they numbered about 20, with a population of 20,000 people. Each settlement village was to have 250 families, a government-paid manager, and some agricultural and other experts. The government supplied machinery for opening up new land for cultivation.

After only five years most of the pilot settlement schemes were abandoned or converted to ujamaa villages; the VSA was dissolved in 1966. The transformation of agriculture through the establishment of settlements had failed for several reasons. First, there was overcapitalization in many of the schemes. There was more machinery than necessary in relation to land and available labor. At Upper Kilete in Arusha Region, for example, 100 settler families began to farm about 650 hectares of maize with ten tractors. Kabuku settlement in Tanga Region imitated neighboring Amboni Sisal Estates by introducing bulldozers and tractors, with the result that the settlers started off with a debt of 2.5 million Tanzania shillings (Hyden 1980: 72–73). Consequently, both labor and heavy equipment were underutilized. Second, production tended to take place on scattered individual farms that could not be easily supervised; production thus remained low. Only Upper Kitete had a viable communal farm producing major crops, but even here, as in other schemes, the government had to pay settlers an income unrelated to their labor contribution or output. In 1963 the VSA had promised the Upper Kitete settlers an annual income of U.S. $429 per settler, but it paid only U.S. $286 and in 1964–65 only U.S. $194, most of which came not from the sale of crops but directly from the government, with the objective of retaining the settlers in the scheme. The estimated cost of each village settlement was U.S. $428,571; by the time they were discontinued the schemes were absorbing over 75 percent of the national agricultural budget. Third, the village settlement schemes were managed by inexperienced officials, with no settler participation in management.

In addition to the pilot settlement schemes, there were other settlements established on former Groundnut Scheme land and supervised by the Tanganyika Agricultural Corporation (TAC). The aim of these schemes was the production of cash crops, including tobacco; in Urambo ten settlements involving over 1000 settlers were supervised by the British-American Tobacco Company (BAT). In Kongwa, cattle ranches were established, while in Nachingwea mixed farming schemes were encouraged. The Agricultural Development Company International of Israel (Agridev) was invited to finance three settlements where modern irrigated farming was established under expert Israeli management. Finally, the Ministry of Agriculture initiated mechanized block production of cotton under the Victoria Federation Co-operative Union, which involved 5000 settlers. Both these and the Agridev settlements were closed down after only a few years.

### Spontaneous settlements

In addition to the various supervised settlements, there were voluntary spontaneous settlements that were run on a cooperative basis and received some assistance from or through the government. Motivated by the party ideology of self-reliance and equality, the TANU Youth League (TYL) recruited youths from the urban areas and established their own "nation-building" settlements in various parts of the country. Simultaneously, National Service youths established several farms. It is estimated that more than 500 small settlements were established by politically motivated youths. The TYL settlements were less capital-intensive than the VSA settlements and involved politically dedicated young people who could devote all their time to productive efforts on their farms. An evaluation of 12 settlements carried out in 1967–68 placed one of the youth settlements (Mbambara in Tanga Region) at the top in terms of hard work, self-reliance, and cooperation (Kates et al. 1969). The causes of the eventual failure of most of the TYL settlements, however, were mismanagement and misuse of funds.

One successful spontaneous settlement was the Ruvuma Development Association (RDA). In 1963 about 400 families from very poor scattered habitations voluntarily moved into 17 new settlements. The guiding principles were communal farming and self-reliance; each settlement elected its own manager and a management committee from among the peasants. Among their communal activities, the RDA settlers cultivated a wide range of crops, raised cattle, and established weaving and spinning, brick making, flour milling, and timber production, and reinvested their savings in social services and transport. In 1968, after the Arusha Declaration, the RDA was banned, allegedly for representing an elite. One of the settlements, Matetemeka Village, remains as a monument of what can be achieved through hard work, commitment, and self-reliance.

A final group of 400 voluntary cooperative settlements was established. These sisal and "coconut and cattle" settlements were started in various parts of the country. However, the settlers retained individual farms and had only a token commitment to cooperative activities. These settlements did not fare as well as the TYL and RDA settlements and were also abandoned.

Two lessons, however, were learned by the government from the settlement experience. First, they came to accept that nucleated settlements and a broad extension of social services were the prerequisites for rural development and for checking the rural–urban drift of youths. This idea influenced the formulation of the ujamaa policy. The second lesson was that capital was scarce and could not therefore form the basis for rural development; rather, land and labor, which were plentiful, should be mobilized as the basis for socioeconomic development. The failure of the post-independence land settlements set the stage for nationwide planned settlements with wider objectives than merely increasing the production of cash crops.

## THE UJAMAA POLICY AND ITS OBJECTIVES

### Definition of ujamaa

While the Arusha Declaration in 1967 spelled out the general policies for building socialism in the United Republic of Tanzania, the document *Socialism and Rural Development* (Nyerere 1967b) provided guidance as to how the socialist goals of the Arusha Declaration could be achieved in relation to rural development. The concept of ujamaa, broadly translated to mean "familyhood," was based on traditional African socialism; the underlying principles included respect for the rights and place of each member of the community, acceptance of the sharing of the resources and property of the community by all members, and the obligation of each member to contribute to the development of the community by working hard. Hence ujamaa means living and working together in communities for the good of all. In order to work together the people had to be brought together to live in ujamaa villages. The document did not specify clearly how people were to be brought together, nor what size the settlements should be. This left some room for different interpretations by government officials and party members, which led in turn to gradual modifications of the policy during the subsequent period.

## Objectives of ujamaa

The goals behind the establishment of ujamaa settlements have been stated in the Arusha Declaration, in *Socialism and Rural Development*, in village constituencies, and in the 1975 Villages and Ujamaa Villages Act, which specified the following three objectives of ujamaa villages:

i. to build a society in which all members have equal rights and opportunities and in which all members have a gradually increasing basic level of material welfare;

ii. to develop new socialist relations of production based on communal land utilization, communal ownership of the means of production, socialist organization of labor, and the principle of trying income to efficiency, so as to eliminate every form of exploitation in collective production and to allow residents of ujamaa villages to develop their activity and create initiative to the full; and

iii. to promote a spirit of self-reliance in social and economic activities such as building schools, dispensaries and the like (Government Notice No. 168, 1975: 8).

To these must be added earlier objectives of the ujamaa village policy, namely mobilizing people for national defence by using the villages as paramilitary organizations; establishing villages as self-governing communities; facilitating national planning that would take advantage of economies of scale in production and marketing, and giving villagers an opportunity to obtain education, medical care, and other necessities of life.

The objectives of ujamaa villages lent themselves to different interpretations by the peasants and by the government. The great majority of the peasants assumed that the ujamaa policy would enhance their autonomy, and they expected the promised good life to start immediately after they moved into villages. The officials, on the other hand, interpreted the revolutionary objectives as inviting the state to play a major role in transforming the rural areas; most of them therefore applied the bureaucratic and managerial strategy of force in the formation of ujamaa villages, and in so doing sometimes discouraged peasants' voluntary initiative and compliance.

## Strategies for implementing ujamaa

*Socialism and Rural Development* also spelled out the strategy to be used in the formation of ujamaa villages: "An ujamaa village is a voluntary association of people who decide of their own free will to live together and work together" (Nyerere 1967b: 67). Hence ujamaa villages were to be formed through education and persuasion and not by force. But following the issuance of Presidential Circular No. 1, 1969, incentives became important in trying to make people move to ujamaa villages. Because the formation of villages was slow, from 1973 force was widely used in order to achieve the party objective of moving all the rural population into ujamaa villages by 1976. It should be noted that in applying compulsion, the party separated the objective of living together from that of working together, force applying only to the former. The villages formed, therefore, were not based on the earlier objectives of working together on communal land, and this fact has had lasting repercussions on production in ujamaa villages. Living together, previously seen as an important step toward working together, thus tended to become an end in itself.

From the beginning it was envisaged that the ujamaa policy would be implemented in stages. In *Socialism and Rural Development*, the president proposed three stages: the initial stage, when people moved so as to live together, but continued to engage in individual or private production until they attained economic viability; the second stage, when the village community had gained some experience of living together and participating in communal activities; and a third stage, when the villagers could be persuaded to become communal farmers with small individual plots and other communal productive activities. This policy of forming ujamaa villages by stages was logical, given the socioeconomic, cultural, and political conditions of the United Republic of Tanzania, and was considered to be "revolution by evolution" (Mushi 1971). The problem with the policy was that once villagers were settled and used to the idea of individual farm production, stage three tended to be resisted.

## Institutional structure of ujamaa villages

Because of the way the objectives and strategies have evolved, the concept of government-recognized ujamaa villages has also changed. Villages formed voluntarily before 1973 were loosely referred to as ujamaa villages, although they did not have any communal activities. With the "operation villages" campaign to move people forcibly to villages, the new villages were referred to as "permanent" or "development" villages to distinguish them from earlier villages. Some regions therefore recognized three types of village: the normal "village," which had no cooperative or communal (ujamaa) activities; the "cooperative village," which had been registered as a cooperative; and the "ujamaa village," which carried out all its activities on a communal basis. The 1975 Villages and Ujamaa Villages Act recognized only two types of village: "villages" and "ujamaa villages," the latter being a village with more communal activities and a greater degree of self-reliance. The ujamaa village had to have a constitution; contain a minimum of 250 families in a defined area; have a village assembly consisting of all residents aged 18 and over; have a village council of 25 members elected by the assembly, which could set up committees to deal with finance and planning, production and marketing, education, culture and social welfare, works and transport, security and defence; have a village chairman and secretary, who were also the chairman and secretary of the party branch; and have all land under the control of the village council and all major machinery and buildings collectively controlled. When all these criteria had been met, the village could apply for registration, and where "a substantial portion of the economic activities of the village were being undertaken and carried out on a communal basis," the village could apply to become an ujamaa village (Villages and Ujamaa Villages Act 1975). The act stressed communal production as the precondition for recognition as an ujamaa village, and provided a nationwide meaning for "living and working together." According to these criteria, however, there are at present very few ujamaa villages in the United Republic of Tanzania.

Although the villages are supposed to be self-governing socioeconomic units, they operate within the wider context of a national political and economic system. Through the village party branch the villagers participate indirectly in the selection of subnational and national leaders and are represented on the district and regional party organs. The village is also linked to the central government's administrative system at the district level through the election of a representative to the District (Development) Council and through the election of a district member of parliament. In spite of the common institutional framework of the villages there has emerged a great diversity in size, economic activities, and degree of cooperation in the process of establishing ujamaa villages in the United Republic of Tanzania.

The selection of settlement sites was usually arbitrary; the only discernible criteria often seemed to be the desire to locate villages along all-weather roads. The poor selection of sites for villages has had undesirable repercussions concerning the availability of fertile land for the villagers, the distances to fields, and the proximity of sources of water and fuel.

## FORMATION OF UJAMAA VILLAGES AND POPULATION REDISTRIBUTION

### Persuasion

When the ujamaa village policy was initiated in 1967, about 5 percent of the rural population lived in traditional villages. Few of the traditional villages were nucleated, and the majority of the rural population lived in individual scattered homesteads. To implement the ujamaa policy, therefore, most people had to move from where they lived to new homes. From 1967 to 1969 persuasion was used as a technique for making people move to villages. Seminars and meetings, tours and campaigns were organized in different parts of the country to persuade leaders and peasants to implement the ujamaa policy.

By 1969 there was a total of 800 ujamaa villages in the United Republic of Tanzania; 400 were in Lindi, Mtwara, and Ruvuma regions, and the rest scattered in regions with little agricultural potential and no perennial crops. These villages accounted for only 300,000 people, representing 2.5 percent of the rural population. The leadership was becoming impatient with this disappointingly slow progress, and the promise that ujamaa villages would transform the rural areas was losing credibility.

Between 1970 and 1972 the party began to take a more active role in the formation of ujamaa villages, while the government increased the incentives for people to move to villages. In 1970, in the chronically famine-stricken region of Dodoma, the president took the personal initiative of living there and participating in the "operation" of persuading and helping people to move into villages where they would undertake communal production. As a result of this operation, the number of villages in Dodoma Region increased from 75 in 1970 to 246 in 1971. Some regional commissioners emulated the president's example in Dodoma, and campaigned energetically to make pople move into villages. In the intensified campaigns for ujamaa villages between 1970 and 1972, most capitalist farmers left the country, espcially in Arusha and Kilimanjaro regions, the majority of the sisal plantations were nationalized, and many large-scale grain farms were converted into state farms or divided up into ujamaa villages. The number of villages in the country rose to 4864, and by 1973 about 2 million people, representing 15.7 percent of the rural population, were living in ujamaa villages (Tables 8.1 and 8.2).

## Incentives

Along with the intensified campaign to discourage capitalist farming, the government launched an equally intensive campaign to encourage villagers and help them succeed in their efforts once they had decided to live together. The collective incentives to villagers included the provision of clean water, access to land, building materials, and preferential prices. Millions of shillings were spent on bringing piped water to ujamaa villages in regions such as Dodoma, Tabora, Coast, Morogoro, Mtwara, Lindi, and Mbeya.

A variety of agricultural inputs to facilitate production were supplied to various ujamaa villages; these included better seeds, fertilizers, insecticides, tractors, storage sheds, flour milling machines, cattle, trees, fishing equipment, and ploughs (McHenry 1979: 128–29). Many small-scale industries were established in ujamaa villages as part of the government's effort to provide nonfarm employment opportunities and thus attract other people to live in villages. Early small-scale village industries included masonry, carpentry, pottery, blacksmithing, shoemaking, and tailoring.

Agricultural inputs and small-scale industries initially required large sums of money. The government established the Tanzania Rural Development Bank (TRDB) in 1971 to provide loans to villages for their development. In 1971–72 TRDB loans to individuals constituted only 6.5 percent of total loans, while loans to ujamaa villages constituted 13.7 percent of the total. In the following financial year, the percentage loaned to individuals fell to 0.1 and that to ujamaa villages rose to 19 percent. Loans to ujamaa villages were used for village projects.

Among the most effective incentives used to attract people were the promises of a primary school and a dispensary or clinic once the people had formed an ujamaa village. Both primary schools and dispensaries were built on the principle of self-help, whereby the villagers supplied the labor and the government supplied some of the building materials. The government also provided drugs and equipment, as well as staff for dispensaries and primary schools. The lure of education and health care was a powerful factor in encouraging reluctant peasants to join ujamaa villages.

## Compulsion

In spite of the use of persuasion and incentives, only 15.7 percent of the rural population had responded positively by 1973. The villages formed so far did not conform to the model envisaged by the president, as most of those registered did not have any communal activities. In some cases people simply moved to the nearest existing village or trading center, and efforts were then made to create an ujamaa village out of that unit.

The use of compulsion from 1973 went on alongside the continued use of persuasion and incentives. Each region and district drew up a timetable for moving people to new sites. There was no uniformity in planning and executing the operations, however, and each region and district was left to find its own strategy for moving people. The military, the police, and the militia were all used, with or without lorries, to make people pack up their belongings and move to selected sites (McHenry 1979: 140–45). In some areas people tried to avoid forced villagization by hiding or fleeing, while in others peasants put pressure on officials whom they had elected (for example, the member of parliament) to help them resist. In several parts of the country rich farmers, rather than resisting the operations, tried to help in the selection of new sites in order to take advantage of the situation and minimize losses of land and property.

During the operations little attention was paid to the production potential of the villages. In 1976 the president had to launch "re-operations" to relocate villages that had been located by the roadside without consideration of soil fertility, or the availability of water and pasture. In Mwanza and Shinyanga regions, some people were moved three times in an attempt to correct mistakes made in choosing sites (McCall 1983: 4).

The immediate aftermath of the operations left a trail of undesirable effects. First, the operations had been very expensive, estimated at 430 Tanzanian shillings per family moved in Dodoma, 2513 shillings per family moved in Kigoma, 341 shillings per family moved in Kibondo, 1437 shillings per family moved in Iringa, and 275 shillings per family moved in Mpanda (cited by McHenry 1979: 146–47). The average cost of moving a family was therefore probably not less than 800 shillings (U.S. $112). Given that a total of about 5 million people are estimated to have moved during the operations, the total cost could be estimated at not less than 800 million shillings (U.S. $112 million), assuming an average family size of five. Most of the money was drawn from the Five-Year Plan allocation for the regions, and represented expenditure that had not been planned for.

Second, because the operations were hurriedly planned and executed, the food production cycle was often badly disrupted. Crops were not harvested because people had been moved away, and in some cases they were not allowed to return to the old farms for harvesting. The new sites could not produce enough food immediately. This caused an initial shortfall in food production, which was made worse by the 1973–75 drought. Third, little attention was paid to communal production because the peasants were preoccupied with survival in a new environment. Neither did the government insist that the operations should result in communal ownership of land and communal production.

## Population redistribution

The impact of villagization on population redistribution has not been adequately assessed, but some picture can be formed from the numbers of people who changed residence during the villagization period. In the persuasion and incentives stages, between 1967 and 1973, it is estimated that only 1.5 million people were involved in physical movement to new settlements. But between 1973 and 1976 not less than 5 million people moved to new sites. The degree of population redistribution differed from one region to another, however, and to a lesser extent among the different districts in each region. Regions with sparse and scattered populations and a large amount of uninhabited land had more of their population redistributed than regions with high population densities and permanent cash crops. In 1976, at the one extreme, redistribution involved 60 percent of the population in Dodoma Region, 55 percent in Mtwara and Lindi, and 30 percent in Iringa. At the other extreme, the least redistribution occurred in Kilimanjaro, Kagera, Morogoro, and parts of Mbeya, where no more than 10 percent of the population was resettled (Maro and Mlay 1982).

There has also been some doubt whether all the 5 million people moved in the operations experienced physical movement of any significance. In many villages there was already a nucleus or "traditional" settlement to which people living in scattered homesteads nearby moved to set up new permanent settlements; there was also a tendency to create villages near roads or existing trading centers. Hence, the population movements involved were only short-distance relocations, except in a few cases where the government encouraged people to move longer distances from areas of population pressure such as Kilimanjaro to the western parts of the country, and from the overcrowded Mbeya highlands to Chunya District. A study conducted in nine districts in 1976 revealed that movement to villages generally involved distances of less than 10 kilometers from the original locations (Table 8.3), although in the case of six districts some movements of over 10 kilometers to new settlements were also recorded.

Inter-regional migration during the villagization period was not significant, and probably retained its historical character involving population exchanges around Lake Victoria (Mwanza, Shinyanga, Tabora, and Kagera) and in the northeast and coastal areas (Morogoro, Tanga, Arusha, Kilimanjaro, and Dar es Salaam). Although at the national level villagization involved massive changes in population distribution, at the local level redistribution generally took place within each administrative region. By 1977, however, the rural population had been collectivized into nucleated land settlements. This was a considerable achievement, and one that laid the foundation for rural transformation.

## IMPACT OF PLANNED SETTLEMENTS

The ujamaa village had been envisaged as the basic institution for providing an effective organization of production and ensuring more efficient use of labor and other productive resources. This was to be achieved through cooperative and communal endeavor in production, distribution, and marketing. The incomes of the peasants were expected to rise, thus narrowing the urban–rural income gap. This section analyzes the extent to which employment and agricultural production have increased, and the degree to which income distribution has improved. The social effects of villagization are discussed briefly in the last part of this section.

## Agricultural production in land settlements

Villagization ensured that there was land available for every peasant. Each village has a defined area with "enough" land to meet all agricultural and other needs. Each family is allocated an equitable plot of land. On this piece of land each peasant family is expected to produce subsistence crops and, in most cases, cash crops as well. In this way, villagization has eliminated landlessness among the rural population; coupled with restrictions in the hiring of labor, it has also resulted in the elimination of large individual landholdings and land speculation. There is also the government requirement that all able-bodied persons must work. Organization of production on both individual and communal farms has increased work discipline among the peasants.

The size of new farms, both individual and communal, varies considerably from one area to another, largely as a result of differences in the physical environment, the degree of communal farming, and the kinds of agricultural inputs available to peasants. Generally, farm size per household remains as small in the new settlements as it was in the traditional settlements, mainly because of labor constraints, but individual holdings vary greatly; 1.2 hectares is average, but they can be as large as 5 hectares or more in livestock grazing areas. A survey carried out in six villages in Arusha, Dodoma, and Kilimanjaro in 1979 showed that personal plots varied between 1 and 4 hectares (Ghai et al. 1979: 64).

The size of communal farms per household is even smaller. Although officials had hoped that villagization would enable each peasant to operate 1.2 hectares in a communal farm, labor constraints have kept the communal farm very small in most villages. Even where the government ploughed the communal farm land for the villagers, the area eventually planted and weeded was smaller than that ploughed, because the village labor force could not cope with all the land ploughed with the aid of a tractor (Hyden 1980: 109). In 1980 the prime minister recommended that each village should have at least 40 hectares farmed communally, which averages 0.4 hectares per household (Prime Minister's Office 1980: 16). Although there is plenty of cultivable land, both individual and communal farms in the villages thus remain small, largely because of labor constraints and the use of primitive technology.

In the years following villagization, agricultural production did not increase significantly. In fact, there is some evidence that production of

export crops actually declined (Table 8.4). The share of agricultural production in GDP also declined during the period 1965–81. Calculated at
1966 prices, agriculture contributed 46.7 percent of the GDP in 1964,
42.0 percent in 1969, 36.7 percent in 1974, 37.0 percent in 1976, and 36.1
percent in 1981 (Table 8.5).

Several factors account for the lack of growth of agricultural production. First, there has been a low level of investment in agriculture. In
the 1961–62 to 1963–64 period, for example, 24 percent of national development resources went to agriculture, but this had declined to 15
percent in the 1976–77 to 1980–81 period. Despite the emphasis on modern farming techniques under ujamaa, agriculture remains backward
because of the lack of adequate credit facilities to farmers, the low level
of mechanization, and the shortage of effective agricultural extension
officers. Marketing institutions and the transport system are largely inefficient. Crops are usually not collected in time, and up to 40 percent
of the grain harvested is destroyed by pests. Farmers have often received
less than the costs of production. The decline in production for export
has also been accompanied by unfavorable terms of international trade.
Finally, there has been minimal peasant commitment to communal farming because of the low level of politicization.

There are signs, however, that village communal farms may do something to improve agricultural output. The communal farm has received
official support and therefore enjoys an array of modern inputs. It can
borrow money for agricultural inputs; it can buy or hire tractors and
other machinery; it can get fertilizers on credit. It is a channel for introducing new techniques and forms the basis of a social security system
for the village. The communal farm is being used to demonstrate the
advantages of using tractors, high-yielding varieties of seeds, fertilizers,
and appropriate spacing in planting. In Iringa and Mbeya regions, the
application of these techniques has shown that considerable increases
in yields per hectare can be obtained: 30 bags of wheat, 60 bags of beans,
and 24 bags of coffee per hectare from a communal farm. Through
demonstration private smallholders have been encouraged to use modern methods and tools and have been able to improve yields in Iringa
and Mbeya regions from less than 12 bags of maize per hectare to 36
bags, from 7 bags of beans to 12 bags, and from 2 bags of coffee to 25
bags (Schultheis et al. 1982). The only problem is that the communal
farms are generally less than 10 percent of all cultivated village land and
average less than 1 hectare per household.

## Utilization of labor and employment opportunities

Data on rural employment are scarce, except for the 1966 labor force
survey and the 1967 and 1978 population censuses, which contain some

information on rural employment. The question of labor utilization and rural employment can be analyzed at the national level, and more important at the village level. At the national level agriculture is the main source of employment for the rural population. Rural wage employment suffered a 31.6 percent drop between 1963 and 1969 from 76,363 to 52,232, mainly due to deterioration in the sisal industry. This in turn was largely due to the decline in the price per ton from U.S. $364 in 1963 to U.S. $146 in 1970. In 1967 the economically active population totaled 5.7 million, of which 5.4 million were in the agricultural sector. Rural unemployment was then recorded at 1 percent and urban unemployment at 4 percent. The 1978 census recorded 8 million people in the labor force. Wage employment accounted for only 6 percent of the available labor force.

The problem in rural areas is not lack of work but fluctuations in the demand for labor, which peaks in the ploughing, weeding, and harvesting seasons. It was hoped that as a result of the ujamaa village policy every Tanzanian would be gainfully employed throughout the year. There is some evidence that many villages have been able to reduce unemployment during the slack periods through generating cooperative nonagricultural activities.

Most villages have a similar but limited range of nonfarm activities, but they vary slightly from district to district. The most common nonagricultural activity in all villages is construction of village houses, schools, dispensaries, and water projects, to which the villages contribute labor and the government contributes materials, equipment, and supervisory staff. This sort of self-help cooperative endeavor has not only reduced the costs of development but has also provided villagers with some training in working together for their common good. The best illustration of the utilization of labor in a cooperative manner for the benefit of all villagers is the village shops. After the dissolution of primary cooperative societies in 1975 and secondary cooperative unions in 1976, the government launched "operation maduka" (operation shops), according to which every village that had a constitution and could register as a cooperative society under the 1975 Villages and Ujamaa Villages Act was required to establish a village cooperative shop or shops that would eventually replace individual shops. The villagers responded by contributing money, materials, and labor to establish cooperative shops, the number of which increased from 300 in 1976 to 3284 in 1977 and 6114 in 1979 (Prime Minister's Office, various years). In some regions, such as Dodoma, private retailers have completely disappeared.

An illustration of the importance of collective labor can be provided by the village of Singe in Arusha Region. In 1979 the village had 307 families (1330 total population) and a very small communal farm. In 1976 villagers contributed a capital sum of 6000 shillings and built a cooperative shop, on a self-help basis. By 1979 the shop had assets worth 110,000 shillings and villagers had started to construct a canteen, to be financed from profits from the shop (ILO/JASPA 1978: 79). Although not every village shop has enjoyed financial success, they have generally provided employment to not less than four or five villagers, as well as distributing essential commodities to villagers.

Besides building a social and economic infrastructure, village labor has also been used to establish a variety of income-generating small-scale industries and crafts throughout rural areas. The government established the Small Industries Development Organization (SIDO) in 1973 in an effort to provide employment to the rural population. In 1975 there were 1742 SIDO industries, increasing to 3946 in 1977–78, but they were unevenly spread throughout mainland Tanzania. The total number of people employed in small industries increased from 12,583 in 1975 to 51,042 in 1977–78 (SIDO 1980: 17). It should be pointed out, however, that most of the SIDO efforts are concentrated in Dar es Salaam and the regional centers, where "industrial estates" are being established; little financial or managerial assistance from SIDO has so far filtered through to the village level.

Small-scale industries and crafts are nevertheless important in providing nonfarm employment in all villages. Most villages have established cooperative full-time or part-time flour-milling machines, furniture workshops, soap factories, motor/machine and bicycle repair services, blacksmithing, food processing, weaving and tailoring, beekeeping, and fishing. The effects of these nonfarm activities, in terms of providing employment and generating income, have not been fully studied, but they certainly represent an area of great potential for employment in villages.

In connection with rural employment it is perhaps worth observing that through the 1972 decentralization of government and the setting up of planning and managerial machinery, the villagers now have an opportunity to initiate, plan, and implement their own development programs. Some of the village programs include employment-generating projects. In 1978, to help them in the planning and implementation of development projects, the government posted managers and technicians in the villages and started a village training program in skills such as bookkeeping and shop management, agriculture and animal husbandry, and elementary project planning. In addition, in 1974 the government instituted rural integrated development programs (RIDEPS), and in 1982 reinstated cooperative societies and rural district councils (1982), all in an effort to stimulate meaningful rural development. Although these administrative reforms and training programs do not directly provide employment, they do help the villages to expand their employment-generating capacity and to keep their labor force gainfully employed throughout the year.

## Rural income distribution and reduction of poverty

There is ample evidence to show that the government is committed to an equitable distribution of the benefits of development among the population as well as among the regions. The Second Five-Year Development Plan (1969–74) had as its first objective "social equity," spreading of the benefits of growth to the entire society, while the Third Five-Year Development Plan (1976–81) mentioned explicitly the need to provide infrastructure throughout the country and to reduce the income gap between rural and urban areas. As far as land settlements are concerned, the government has made efforts to promote rural incomes. The nationalization of land in 1962 gave every Tanzanian equal rights to the use of land, while it also put an end to feudal land tenure systems and preempted the growth of a landlord class. Since villagization, land allocation throughout the country has been controlled by the village authorities. This assures every peasant of at least subsistence farming and thus eliminates the basis for landlessness and extreme poverty as found in some Third World countries, where less than 20 percent of the population controls over 80 percent of the land.

The Arusha Declaration, on which the ujamaa policy is based, emphasized equitable distribution of income and access to basic social services. The village has become the basic center for the provision of free primary education, free primary health care, and clean water, and for sociopolitical interaction. This more equitable distribution of social services obviously helps to reduce ignorance, disease, and poverty in the rural areas. In an effort to increase farm incomes, the government has introduced farm import subsidies and has eliminated export tax. At the same time producer prices, especially for food crops, have increased steadily. The government also controls prices and has established a Wages, Income and Price Policy aimed at achieving some equity in income distribution in both rural and urban areas. Urban minimum wages were increased from 150 shillings per month in 1969 to 240 shillings in 1973, 380 shillings in 1975, and 600 shillings in 1981. Minimum wages and peasant incomes are not taxed. As a result of these policies income disparities have declined considerably; in 1960 the highest paid earned 50 times more than the lowest paid, but this had dropped to 20 times in 1967 and only nine times in 1976.

Of more importance are the real improvements in family incomes in the rural areas. Although growth in rural incomes has been slow compared with that of urban incomes, there was a lessening of inequality in the rural areas between 1969 and 1976–77, as shown by the decline in the Gini coefficient (Table 8.6). The top rural (farm and nonfarm) incomes were "reduced," while the bottom incomes increased. One of the factors that accounts for this trend is the redistribution of land and the introduction of income-generating communal activities through the villagization program. The relative lessening of income disparities in rural areas can also be observed from changes in the distribution of household incomes (Table 8.7).

In spite of these improvements, which meant that fewer people lived below the poverty line in 1976–77 than in 1969, there are significant variations in the incomes of households within rural Tanzania. According to the World Bank, the income gap among smallholder farmers widened between 1969 and 1975, varying from a low of 557 shillings per annum and a high of 1351 shillings in 1969 to a low of 575 shillings and a high of 2675 shillings in 1975 (World Bank 1977: 7). Furthermore, farmers in the Central Zone, with less than 500 millimeters of rain per annum, have always had lower incomes than those in other regions.

Rural–urban income disparities have been similarly reduced, but a wide gap remains. In 1964 the absolute income gap between an average smallholder and an average urban wage earner was 1484 shillings, which had widened to 3243 shillings in 1974–77 (ILO/JASPA 1978). But the World Bank found that the average rural income in 1969 was 982 shillings, whereas the average urban income was 6036 shillings, giving an urban–rural income ratio of 6 to 1. In 1975 the ratio was 4 to 1 (World Bank 1977). It has been estimated that 70.5 precent of rural households received less than the rural mean income of 2169 shillings, while urban households received, on average, 7302 shillings. This means that rural mean cash income was less than one-third of urban mean cash income, and that more than two-thirds of rural households received less than the rural mean cash income (Maeda and Msambichaka 1983).

Not so many studies have been carried out in the United Republic of Tanzania to establish the actual income per village and per villager, but there are indications that through communal farming and communal nonfarm activities the income per household can be greatly increased. In the years before villagization most peasants were reluctant to join in communal farming because it competed with subsistence production. Hence income from the small communal farms was generally low, except in regions such as Iringa, where ujamaa villages were established with a strong communal farm basis.

A study by McHenry in 1975 in villages in Dodoma, Iringa, Kigoma, and Kilimanjaro regions revealed low income per member from communal farms (McHenry 1979: 156, 164). But by the late 1970s and as a consequence of villagization, village communal farms had been greatly expanded. The village of Mlowa-Barabarani in Dodoma, for example, had only a 12-hectare communal farm in 1970, but this had been increased to 120 hectares by 1978. This farm produced a revenue of 300,000 shillings in 1978, and the village authorities collected an additional 36,000 shillings as a levy on private crop sales. Of the total revenue of 336,000 shillings, 150,000 shillings was distributed as cash payments to all those who participated in work on the communal farm, 60,000 shillings was allocated to the village shop, 40,000 shillings went to service the village lorry, and 86,000 shillings was deposited in the bank (ILO/JASPA 1978: 78). Although this success story is not universal, the communal sector is becoming more important in generating income throughout the United Republic of Tanzania. With diversification of the village economy, proper accounting and reinvestment policies, rural incomes, particularly from communal undertakings, are bound to increase, thus narrowing the gap between urban and rural incomes.

## Social and cultural impact

Given the magnitude of the exercise and the short period in which it was accomplished, some degree of social dislocation was inevitable. There were problems associated with the actual movement of people and the siting of villages, as well as the human relations problems of the people living together in the new communities. Villages were often poorly sited in relation to available land, so that there was overcrowding; land disputes were common in many areas, including Mwanza, Mbeya, and Singida. In Singida fighting broke out between the Wanyaturu agriculturalists and the pastoral Barabaig tribes over land rights in the new villages. Ordinary prejudices and suspicion led to diminished respect for customary laws and rights of property where people had not adapted to cultural heterogeneity.

Once the villagers had settled down to agricultural and other activities the social tensions and uncertainties eventually lessened, and people started to experience the advantages of living together and cooperating in various economic activities. Social interaction has also occurred in the access to schools, health facilities, and clean water, and through adult literacy and adult education classes. The establishment of nursery schools and day-care centers has released mothers to engage in productive activities. Most peasants have now realized the advantages of living together and are gradually learning the importance of cooperative economic undertakings.

One important social consequence of villagization has been the improved position of women in society. Women are entitled to village membership in their own right and play an active role in communal agriculture. In most villages women are represented on the village councils. The provision of clean water in most villages has released rural women from the arduous task of fetching water from great distances away from the village. But the problem of firewood has not yet been solved. The concentration of population in villages has put heavy pressure on the surrounding woodland, and women sometimes have to travel long distances, of up to 30 kilometers in the worst cases, to collect firewood. The government has now started a massive Village Woodlot Campaign, which has been successful in mobilizing people to plant trees for firewood. The ultimate success of this campaign will depend on the care and management of the young trees and their rational use when they mature.

## THE VILLAGIZATION PROGRAM AND PROVISION OF BASIC SERVICES

After the Arusha Declaration, the government decided that apart from giving everyone access to productive opportunities, there was a need to provide free basic services in the form of primary education, health facilities, and clean water, both for the sake of social justice and as a necessary input for socioeconomic development. The collectivization of the rural population into nucleated settlements enabled the government to provide these basic services to the maximum number of people at the minimum cost. The provision of basic services in the United Republic of Tanzania has been extremely successful, and has been very effective in improving the quality of life of the majority of Tanzanians. Because it is not possible to quantify the benefits of such social services in terms of their impact on productivity, success is assessed in terms of achievement of stated objectives and targets.

It should be emphasized that in spite of very limited resources, the United Republic of Tanzania has recorded considerable achievements in building up an egalitarian and effective social infrastructure for meeting the basic needs of society. The establishment of this infrastructure was made possible by villagization. The United Republic of Tanzania can boast a successful system of free universal primary education, with over 70 percent of school-age children (7–13 years) attending school. There has been an equally vigorous and even more successful adult education program and drive to eradicate illiteracy, which has resulted in the decline of illiteracy rates from 69 percent in 1967 to 27 percent in 1975 and 15 percent in 1983. A shift of policy in the early 1970s away from urban-based, high-technology hospitals toward a free universal health-care system, with the emphasis on rural health centers and dispensaries, has brought health services within an easy access of 5 kilometers for over 50 percent of the rural population. One of the consequences of this has been a relative decline in illness and an absolute improvement in life expectancy from 37 years in 1967 to 50 years in 1981. A universal rural water supply policy has made it possible for 35 to 45 percent of the rural population to have access to an adequate supply of clean, drinkable water within a distance of 4 kilometers. The siting of the villages near or along good roads has also meant that accessibility has generally improved.

In spite of these achievements, there is a need for a more detailed analysis of the costs and problems involved in providing education, health facilities, and a clean water supply.

## Primary education

Every village in the United Republic of Tanzania has at least one primary school. This is a result of the government's commitment, after the Arusha Declaration, to provide education to every child of primary-school age. At the launching of the Second Five-Year Plan (1969), it was envisaged that universal primary education (UPE) would be achieved by 1989. But after making villagization compulsory, the government brought the target for attainment of UPE forward to 1977. In accordance with *Education for Self-Reliance* (Nyerere 1967a), the primary school curriculum was changed to make primary education a complete preparation for rural living, and to include income-generating self-reliance activities. The school was also to be integrated with the village community, with villagers involved in teaching and other activities of the school.

On the basis of enrollment figures, UPE appears to have been rather successful. Enrollment rose from 0.47 million in 1961 to 2.2 million in 1976 and 3.54 million in 1981, 71 percent of whom were in the 7 to 13 year age group. Standard enrollment in the peak year 1976–77 was 848,293 children, but by 1981 this had dropped to half a million, of whom 25 percent were 7-year-olds. This means that a significant proportion of 7-year-olds are not admitted to primary school until they are older. But there are inter-regional variations based on occupational and cultural characteristics; in pastoralist economies, for example, children are expected to look after livestock, while in other regions enrollment is 100 percent. The total capital expenditure on UPE during the Third Five-Year Plan period (1976–81) was estimated at 2068 million shillings.

There are nevertheless certain problems that cause actual achievements to fall short of expectations. Because building and other materials were not easily available and their prices have increased rapidly, the projected number of classrooms has not been realized. Together with the shortage of teachers and textbooks, this has affected the quality of education offered. Second, the socioeconomic impact of UPE on society in terms of stated goals is unlikely to be attained if present trends and practices continue. Primary education was supposed to be complete in itself, and its content was supposed to equip children with the attitudes, skills, and knowledge they need for a productive village life. But primary-school teaching is still oriented toward examinations and paper qualifications. In principle, there is still a requirement that primary education should include activities that generate some income for the school. From this income schools are supposed to meet 25 percent of their recurrent costs. But income from such activities accounted for only 3 percent of recurrent costs in 1977 and 5 percent in 1980. It is also true that the primary school has not been "genuinely integrated" into the local community, mainly because the whole system is centralized and controlled by the Ministry of National Education through national examinations and national supply of teachers and materials. Concepts of community education have been tried, but generally the local community has not found a proper role to play in the heavily academically oriented curriculum.

## Health facilities

It was envisaged that by 1980, 300 rural health centers (one per 50,000 rural population) and 2300 dispensaries (one per 6500 rural population) would be established. Personnel training, mass media educational campaigns, and active community participation were to be an integral part of the successful implementation of this policy.

The government accordingly shifted funds away from hospital services to health centers and dispensaries and the training of new paramedical staff. The proportion of the health development budget allocated to hospital services was scaled down from 52 percent in 1971–72 to 27 percent in 1973–74 and 12 percent in 1974–75. Funds for training paramedical staff for rural service were increased from 13 percent of total health development expenditure to 55 percent by 1974–75.

By 1978–79 an efficient rural health service network had been established and the initial objectives had been fulfilled. The number of rural health centers in mainland Tanzania with up to 20 beds and staffed by about 20 paramedical personnel had increased from 50 in 1969–70 to 194 in 1978–79. In the same period the number of dispensaries had increased from 1444 to 2512 (United Republic of Tanzania 1979: 73). The population per health center declined from 234,000 to 56,000, while the population per rural dispensary declined from 8100 to 6600 in the same period. Thus the population per health facility goal has nearly been achieved.

The effectiveness of health services must be inferred from their accessibility and availability. In 1972 only one in eight people lived within 5 kilometers of the nearest hospital, and only one in four people lived within 10 kilometers of a hospital. The villagization program made it possible for the government to implement its policy of spreading health facilities equitably throughout the country. By 1980, 35 percent of villages had at least a dispensary (Prime Minister's Office 1980: 13). Sixty percent of villages either had a health facility in the village or were within 5 kilometers of a village with one, and 90 percent either had a health facility or were within 10 kilometers of a village or town with one. Villagization and the self-help drive by peasants have thus complemented government efforts to make health facilities available within a reasonable walking distance to the majority of the rural population.

In addition to rural health centers and dispensaries, a maternal and child health (MCH) program was started during the villagization drive; by 1979 47 percent of the health institutions were providing MCH services at least once a week (United Republic of Tanzania 1979). A related program in the rural health package is that of family planning, which emphasizes the importance of education and child-spacing as means of slowing population growth. Family planning services are available throughout the Ministry of Health MCH program and in hospitals, largely free of charge.

Although the United Republic of Tanzania has made very impressive progress in providing health services to the majority of the people, the quality of services is low, due to the shortage of drugs and medicines, and the unavailability or malfunctioning of essential medical equipment.

In spite of these problems, one can conclude that the rural health program has been effective, in conjunction with education, water supply, agriculture, and other programs, in reducing mortality rates and in raising life expectancy throughout the country. There has also been considerable success in controlling disease and improving the quality of life, although the incidence of some diseases such as intestinal worms and malaria seems to have increased.

### Rural water supply

With villagization the question of providing a clean and dependable water supply in the new village communities became an urgent one. In 1975 the government had therefore to change its earlier target of supplying clean water within 400 meters by 1991 to a target of providing a universal rural water supply system within 4 kilometers by 1980. The provision of water at a reasonable walking distance is supposed to have an indirect effect on productivity, as easy access to water saves time and energy that can be spent on other productive work.

By 1979 over 3000 villages (38 percent of all villages) had a clean water supply system (Prime Minister's Office 1980: 13), but the actual number of people served is not known; some estimates suggest that the percentage of people benefiting from the facilities varies from 22 percent to 75 percent in different regions. However, because of the lack of fuel for the pumps, the lack of spare parts, and the lack of trained artisans, rural water supply systems have not become universal. The improved water supply systems currently installed have the potential of serving only 35 to 45 percent of the rural population (ILO/JASPA 1982).

Most of the water is piped from shallow wells, springs, and rivers. The quality of water is therefore not as high as expected because of high mineral content (fluoride).

The rural water supply program has also been expensive, in spite of the shallow well technology adopted. It still costs about 50 shillings per capita. The Third Five-Year Plan allocated only 1.45 million shillings to water development, whereas 75 million shillings was required. The recurrent expenditure allocated to maintenance of the existing system was only 18 million shillings, compared with the 40 million shillings required. The Third Five-Year Plan therefore emphasized the need for villagers to participate in planning, construction, and maintenance of the water supply systems. In addition to cutting down costs considerably, the idea of this strategy was to make the villagers view the project as their own rather than as a government project run by experts. The plan also emphasized the need for water pumps and spare parts to be produced locally.

### Retention of settlers in villages

It is widely believed that peasants have been returning to their former homes illegally, though on a very small scale, but no studies have been carried out to document this trend. Given the compulsory nature of villagization and the ten-year settling down period, the number of peasants returning to their former homes is now probably insignificant. In areas where there is great population pressure on land or where the number of families far exceeded the official figures (minimum of 250 and maximum of 600 families), there is a need to establish satellite settlements in order to bring farmers closer to their fields. Satellite villages were initially officially resisted by high-level authorities, who considered the move as "anti-villagization." But in some regions such as Mwanza and Mbeya, peasants initiated the move and, on the recommendation of the official land planning units, land evaluation officials allowed satellite villages to be established. Satellite villages increased both the effective working time, by reducing travel time to the fields, and the average size of farm holdings. The central village also benefited from reduced population pressure, and in some cases cash crop (cotton) production increased significantly (McCall 1983).

## COSTS AND BENEFITS OF LAND SETTLEMENTS

There are two kinds of financial costs involved in land settlement: the costs of moving people to villages, and the costs of providing them with their basic needs. The cost of moving 5 million people has been estimated at 800 million shillings, which is a very large sum of money, especially since it was not initially planned or budgeted for. The opportunity cost of spending this sum of money on moving people to villages must have been great, but has never been assessed.

Of more importance has been the cost of providing people with their basic needs once they had moved into the villages. "In 1973–74 education, health, water, extension, credit, seed, fertiliser, public works, and related goods and services supplied to ujamaa villages probably totalled 300 million shillings" (Green 1979: 27). This does not include the costs of social services and infrastructure that were borne by voluntary agencies or private companies.

The ujamaa village provides the most suitable institutional framework for political and economic organization and mobilization of physical and human resources for self-reliant development. Equitable distribution of land has been achieved throughout the country, although individual farm holdings differ both within villages and from one village to another, and communal farm sizes differ among the villages. Compared with the preceding period, significant expansion in the area under cultivation has taken place in the ten years since villagization. The government has insisted that each village must have a communal farm, and after the initial years of hesitant experimentation, peasants have come to value these farms as a source of extra income. The trend has been to increase their size, partly to meet minimum hectarage requirements and partly to increase agricultural production. Assuming the modest average of 40 hectares communally farmed per village suggested by the prime minister in 1980, there should be a minimum of 320,000 hectares communally farmed land throughout the country, excluding livestock grazing areas. Most of the land that is communally farmed is additional to the individual household farms on which the bulk of the subsistence crops are grown. And most of this land would probably not have been cultivated if villagization had not taken place.

The communal farm is important in two other respects. First, because it has privileged access to credit and technical assistance, it is being used for the introduction of modern agricultural inputs such as fertilizers, high-yielding seeds, and mechanization; and, second, because communal labor is compulsory for all villagers, the communal farm is contributing to the rational use of labor and to work discipline. If present trends continue and the size of the communal farm is increased to allow meaningful large-scale mechanization, the communal farm will indeed form the basis of the agricultural revolution in the United Republic of Tanzania.

Conventional food crops and traditional export crops that were being grown before villagization have continued to receive official encouragement, and in general no new crops or new agricultural products have been developed as a consequence of villagization. Where there are no dominant export crops such as cotton, coffee, or cashew, there have been localized shifts in the types of crops grown, mainly from unimportant cash crops such as castor seed to food crops such as maize, beans, groundnuts, and rice, which can be sold for cash and produce a higher income (Maro 1983b). This trend is more common in the regions with low agricultural potential in the center of the country, which also depend on livestock production. Villagization has, however, made it possible for the government to initiate livestock rearing in the tsetse-prone southern regions such as Mtwara and Lindi.

The greatest benefit of villagization has been the provision of basic services. The availability of education, clean water, and health services has led to a reduction in mortality and an increase in life expectancy, a reduction in the incidence of some diseases, and the ability on the part of a more literate society to comprehend and implement technical and scientific innovations. All this has enabled the peasants to engage effectively in productive activities and to improve the quality of their lives. Whatever the costs of providing these basic services, their effect on society has been positive and seems to justify such costs.

## CONCLUSION AND SUGGESTIONS FOR RESETTLEMENT

Unlike the pre–Arusha Declaration settlement schemes that failed and were abandoned because they were narrowly conceived and overcapitalized and relied on foreign funding, the villagization program "amounts to a veritable agrarian revolution and it is hardly possible to exaggerate its importance in shaping the economic, social, and political future of Tanzania" (ILO/JASPA 1978: 49). There are over 15 million people living and working together in over 8000 villages in rural Tanzania. In 1981, agriculture contributed 75 to 80 percent of foreign exchange earnings and 40 percent of the GDP. This underlines the importance of the village as the core of development and well-being for the entire population. The village, with its full array of sociopolitical institutions, is firmly established and moving toward full achievement of the goals for which it was set up. Under their village governments, the villagers are engaged in the cultivation of individual plots and communal farms and in various cooperative productive activities. They are involved in the formulation and preparation of projects relevant to the development of the village; these are scrutinized at ward and district levels—and are then incorporated into the regional plans. Villages are therefore firmly and permanently established in the United Republic of

Tanzania and are making a significant contribution to socioeconomic development.

The process of development initiated by the villagization program now faces several problems, however. The most pressing problem in all villages is that of low yields and low productivity in agriculture. Smallholder agriculture depends on weather and on family labor. Most peasant households are constrained by a shortage of labor; hence the effective area they can cultivate, weed, and harvest without labor-saving machinery is not more than 2 hectares. And because they need to ensure sufficient production for subsistence, they devote most of their labor to the individual plots. Modern inputs such as fertilizers, machinery, improved seeds, and credit can easily be obtained for the communal farms, and the use of such inputs has resulted in significant increases in the output of both cash and food crops. But the problem remains of how to persuade peasants to invest more labor in the communal farms, which should be expanded and operated on a profit maximization basis. In most villages small-scale local irrigation, carried out communally, could enable peasants to harvest several crops per year instead of relying on the vagaries of rainfall alone. There is an encouraging use of ox ploughs in most areas, but the use of tractors should receive more emphasis. There is also the problem of timely delivery of agricultural inputs, caused mainly by poor distribution systems, dependent on the availability of foreign exchange. Finally, a system of incentives to encourage peasants to produce both food and cash crops will need to be devised if the current trend, whereby peasants prefer to grow food crops rather than traditional export crops because the former can fetch higher prices, is to be arrested.

Most of the villages suffer from the related problems of lack of competent leadership, management, and technical skills, all of which call for village-based training in government administration and management, artisan skills, and skills in bookkeeping, shop management, modern agriculture, and animal husbandry. Villagers would be much more likely to understand and accept fellow villagers trained in matters of local development than government-supplied change agents who might not be sympathetic to village development problems. The government has started training programs for villagers, but the fruits of such efforts have yet to be realized.

Other problems experienced by the villages arise from the fact that there has not been significant transformation in other sectors of the national economy, especially industry. This has created serious bottlenecks in the supply of inputs, the collection and marketing of agricultural produce, and the provision of infrastructure. Most local industries have failed to produce the essential consumer goods needed in the villages as part of the incentive package to enable peasants to produce more efficiently.

Nevertheless, the results of this study in general suggest that the villagization policy has been successful in getting people to live and work together in communal farms and nonfarm activities. Because of low productivity, however, the policy on communal farming needs to be modified in order to strengthen this sector. More land should be made available in the villages for expansion of the communal farms. Two recommendations should therefore be considered.

A large number of villages, especially in Shinyanga, Kigoma, Mwanza, and Mara regions, started off with populations in excess of the 600 families maximum set by the government, and it is believed that by 1980 the majority of villages throughout the country had over 800 families in a nucleated central area within a well-defined village area. This has implications for the availability of sufficient land for communal and individual plots within reasonable walking distance, and for the deterioration in land quality in the vicinity of the settled area. It is therefore recommended that evaluation studies on land availability and distribution be carried out with the objective of moving "excess" human and livestock population to new areas within the village boundaries (satellite villages) or to new settlements. It is important that this population redistribution is carried out now in regions where output is declining, and wood and fuel resources are obtained at increasing distances because of "overpopulation" in some villages.

Second, the government should have a more "emphatic" policy on how to establish and maintain communal farms in the villages. The average of 40 hectares suggested in 1980 is too small on a per capita basis, and most villages do not have communal farms half as large as this. Depending on local conditions, there should be some form of inducement or pressure from the government to make villages expand the communal farms to an economic size so as to allow the introduction of some form of appropriate mechanization and large-scale use of modern inputs. Expansion of communal farms has to be accompanied by labor-saving mechanization in order to remove the current labor constraint on cultivation, weeding, and harvesting. Communal farming should not depend solely on the hand-hoe.

## BIBLIOGRAPHY

Boesen, J. 1979. "From Ujamaa to Villagization in Tanzania." In *Towards Socialism in Tanzania*, edited by B. Mwansasu and C. Pratt, pp. 125–44. Toronto: University of Toronto.

Bukuku, E. S. 1981. *Income Distribution in Tanzania*. University of Dar es Salaam, Economic Department. Mimeo.

Cliffe, L., and G. Cunningham. 1973. "Ideology, Organization, and the Settlement Experience in Tanzania." *Socialism in Tanzania*, vol. 2, edited by L. Cliffe and J. Saul, pp. 131–40. Dar es Salaam: TPH.

Dumont, R. 1969. *Tanzanian Agriculture after the Arusha Declaration*. Dar es Salaam: Government Printers.

Ellman, A. 1970. "Progress, Problems and Prospects in Ujamaa Development in Tanzania." Economic Research Bureau Paper 70.18. University of Dar es Salaam. Mimeo.

Food and Agriculture Organization of the United Nations. *Production Yearbook*, vol. 31, 1977; vol. 33, 1979; vol. 35, 1981.

Ghai, D., E. Lee, J. Maeda, and S. Radwan, eds. 1979. *Overcoming Underdevelopment*. Proceedings of a Workshop on Alternative Agrarian Systems and Rural Development, Arusha, Tanzania, April 4–14, 1979. Geneva: ILO.

Government Notice No. 168. 1975. Dar es Salaam.

Green, R. H. 1979. "Tanzania Political Economy Goals, Strategies, and Results, 1967–74: Notes Towards an Interim Report." In *Towards Socialism in Tanzania*, edited by B. Mwansasu and C. Pratt, pp. 19–45. Toronto: University of Toronto.

Hyden, G. 1980. *Beyond Ujamaa in Tanzania: Underdevelopment and an Uncaptured Peasantry*. London: Heinemann.

International Labour Office/Jobs and Skills Programme for Africa. 1978. *Towards Self-Reliance: Development, Employment and Equity Issues in Tanzania*. Addis Ababa: JASPA.

———. 1982. *Basic Needs in Danger: A Basic Needs Oriented Development Strategy for Tanzania*. Addis Ababa: JASPA.

Jamhuri ya Muungano wa Tanzania. 1980. *Hotuba ya Waziri Mkuu, Nd. Edward Sokoine (MB), Kuhusu Makadirio ya Fedha Mwaka, 1980–81*. Dar es Salaam: Government Printers.

Kates, R. W., J. McKay, and L. Berry. 1969. *Twelve New Settlements in Tanzania: A Comparative Study of Success*. University of Dar es Salaam, BRALUP. Mimeo.

Kweba, E. B., and A. R. Swai. 1983. "Agrarian Transformation Policies, Institutions and Programmes for Integrated Rural Development in Africa: The Case of Tanzania." Paper for the Workshop on Transformation of Agrarian Systems in Centrally Planned Economies in Africa, Arusha, Tanzania, October 17–23, 1983.

Maeda, J. H., and L. A. Msambichaka. 1983. "Agrarian Transformation and Rural Development in Tanzania." Paper for the Workshop on Transformation of Agrarian Systems in Centrally Planned Economies in Africa, Arusha, Tanzania, October 17–23, 1983.

Maro, P. S. 1983a. "Population Distribution and Density." *Census Publications, Vol. 8: The Population of Tanzania, 1978*, edited by M. Rafia, pp. 91–109. Dar es Salaam: Bureau of Statistics.

———. 1983b. "Settlement Policy and Development in Tanzania." In *Wiss Mit No. 10, The National Settlement Systems, V*. Papers at the 7th Meeting of the International Geographical Union Commission on National Settlement Systems, Leipzig, German Democratic Republic, June, pp. 77–90.

Maro, P. S., and W. F. I. Mlay. 1982. "Population Redistribution in Tanzania," in *Redistribution of Population in Africa*, edited by J. I. Clarke and L. A. Kosinski. London: Heinemann.

McCall, M. 1985. "Environmental and Agricultural Impacts of Tanzania's Villagization Programme." In *Population and Development Projects in Africa*, edited by J. I. Clarke and L. A. Kosinski. Cambridge, England: The University Press.

McHenry, D. E. 1979. *Tanzania's Ujamaa Villages: The Implementation of a Rural Development Strategy*. Berkeley, CA: University of California, Institute of International Studies.

Mushi, S. S. 1971. "Ujamaa: Modernization by Traditionalization." *Taamuli* (Dar es Salaam) 1, no. 2: 13–29.

Nyerere, J. K. 1967a. *Education for Self-Reliance*. Dar es Salaam: Government Printers.

———. 1967b. *Socialism and Rural Development*. Dar es Salaam: Government Printers.

———. 1969. *Presidential Circular No. 1 of 1969: The Development of Ujamaa Villages*. Dar es Salaam. Mimeo.

———. 1972. *Decentralization*. Dar es Salaam: Government Printers.

———. 1977. *The Arusha Declaration Ten Years After*. Dar es Salaam: Government Printers.

Odegaard, K. 1982. *On the Output Growth Rate in Tanzanian Agriculture*. University of Dar es Salaam, Economic Research Bureau Seminar Paper. Mimeo.

Prime Minister's Office. Planning and Research Division. *Maendeleo ya Vijiji vya Ujamaa*. Dar es Salaam (various years).

Schultheis, M. J., et al. 1982. *Rural Development and Incentives: A Comparative Study of Village Development in the Southern Highland Regions of Tanzania*. University of Dar es Salaam, Economic Research Bureau Report. Mimeo.

Semboia, L. 1983. *Income Distribution in Tanzania*. Ph.D. diss., University of Illinois.

Small Industries Development Organization. 1980. *Small Scale Industry Census in Tanzania*. Dar es Salaam.

Tanzania African National Union. 1967. *The Arusha Declaration and TANU's Policy on Socialism and Self-Reliance*. Dar es Salaam: Government Printers.

Tanzania, United Republic of. *Survey of Employment and Earnings* (for the years 1962, 1964, 1973–74, 1975–76, 1977–78). Dar es Salaam.

———. *Economic Survey* (for the years 1970–71, 1975–76, and 1981). Dar es Salaam.

———. 1970. *Tanzania Second Five-Year Plan for Economic and Social Development, 1st July, 1969–30th June, 1974*. Dar es Salaam: Government Printers.

———. 1975. *The Villages and Ujamaa Villages (Registration, Designation and Administration) Act*. Government Notice No. 162, August 22.

———. 1976. *Third Five-Year Plan for Economic and Social Development, 1st July, 1976–30th June, 1981*. Dar es Salaam: Government Printers.

———. 1979. *Inventory of Health Facitilies, 1978*. Dar es Salaam: Ministry of Health.

———. 1980. *Evaluation of the Health Sector, 1979*. Dar es Salaam: Ministry of Health.

World Bank. 1977. *Tanzania Basic Economic Report, Labour Market Allocation and Income Distribution, Annex II*. Washington, D.C.: International Bank for Reconstruction and Development.

Table 8.1
Number of ujamaa villages and population by region, 1970-74

| Region | By 1970 | | By 1971 | | By 1972 | | By 1973 | | By 1974 | |
|---|---|---|---|---|---|---|---|---|---|---|
| | No. of villages | Total population | No. of villages | Total population | No. of villages | Total population | No. of villages | Total population | No. of villages | Total population |
| Arusha | 25 | 5,200 | 59 | 14,018 | 92 | 19,818 | 95 | 20,112 | 110 | 25,356 |
| Coast | 56 | 48,300 | 121 | 93,503 | 185 | 119,636 | 188 | 115,382 | 236 | 167,073 |
| Dar es Salaam* | -- | -- | -- | -- | -- | -- | -- | -- | 25 | 4,713 |
| Dodoma | 75 | 26,400 | 246 | 239,366 | 299 | 400,330 | 336 | 378,915 | 354 | 504,952 |
| Iringa | 350 | 11,600 | 631 | 216,200 | 630 | 207,502 | 659 | 243,527 | 619 | 244,709 |
| Kagera | 22 | 5,600 | 46 | 9,491 | 83 | 16,747 | 85 | 13,280 | 77 | 15,968 |
| Kigoma | 34 | 6,700 | 132 | 27,200 | 129 | 114,391 | 132 | 115,672 | 123 | 111,477 |
| Kilimanjaro | 9 | 2,700 | 11 | 2,616 | 24 | 5,009 | 24 | 4,934 | 14 | 3,176 |
| Lindi | 283 | 70,673 | 592 | 203,128 | 626 | 175,082 | 589 | 169,073 | 339 | 218,888 |
| Mara | 174 | 84,700 | 376 | 127,371 | 376 | 127,370 | 271 | 108,068 | 111 | 233,632 |
| Mbeya | 91 | 32,900 | 493 | 64,390 | 713 | 98,571 | 715 | 103,677 | 524 | 86,051 |
| Morogoro | 19 | 6,000 | 113 | 10,513 | 116 | 23,951 | 118 | 19,732 | 96 | 25,509 |
| Mtwara | 465 | 173,027 | 748 | 371,560 | 1,088 | 441,241 | 1,103 | 466,098 | 1,052 | 534,126 |
| Mwanza | 28 | 46,000 | 127 | 18,641 | 211 | 32,099 | 284 | 49,846 | 153 | 40,864 |
| Rukwa* | -- | -- | -- | -- | -- | -- | -- | -- | 121 | 24,988 |
| Ruvuma | 120 | 9,000 | 205 | 29,433 | 205 | 29,430 | 242 | 42,385 | 184 | 62,736 |
| Shinyanga | 98 | 12,600 | 150 | 12,265 | 123 | 15,292 | 108 | 12,052 | 134 | 18,425 |
| Singida | 16 | 6,800 | 201 | 51,230 | 263 | 59,420 | 263 | 59,420 | 317 | 141,542 |
| Tabora | 52 | 16,700 | 81 | 18,408 | 148 | 25,115 | 174 | 29,295 | 156 | 28,730 |
| Tanga | 37 | 7,700 | 132 | 35,907 | 245 | 77,858 | 245 | 77,857 | 255 | 67,557 |
| Total | 1,954 | 572,600 | 4,464 | 1,545,240 | 5,556 | 1,988,862 | 5,631 | 2,029,325 | 5,000 | 2,560,472 |

Source: Prime Minister's Office.
*Dar es Salaam was created out of Coast Region, and Rukwa out of Mbeya and Tabora regions.

Table 8.2
Summary of the process of villagization, 1967-79

| Year | Number of villages | Total population in villages | Village population as percentage of total population |
|---|---|---|---|
| February 1967 | 48 | 5,000 | 0.04 |
| December 1968 | 180 | 58,000 | 0.5 |
| December 1969 | 809 | 300,000 | 2.5 |
| 1970 | 1,954 | 572,600 | 4.3 |
| 1971 | 4,464 | 1,545,240 | 12.3 |
| 1972 | 5,556 | 1,988,862 | 15.3 |
| 1973 | 5,631 | 2,029,325 | 15.7 |
| 1974 | 5,000[a] | 2,560,472 | 17.6 |
| May 1975 | 6,944 | 9,140,229 | 61.6 |
| 1976 | 7,684 | 13,061,000 | 85.0 |
| December 1977 | 7,373[b] | 13,506,044 | 85.0 |
| July 1978 | 7,631[b] | 13,775,532 | 87.0 |
| June 1979 | 8,299 | 14,874,522 | 87.0 |

Source: United Republic of Tanzania, Economic survey, 1970-71. Dar es Salaam, Prime Minister's Office, Maendeleo ya Vijiji vya Ujamaa (various years).
   [a] The decrease in the number of villages during this year was caused by the merger of several villages into larger ones.
   [b] Only villages registered under the 1975 Villages and Ujamaa Villages Act.


Table 8.3
Percentage distribution of settlers by distance moved

| District | Distance in km. from original settlement | | | | | |
|---|---|---|---|---|---|---|
|  | 1 | 1-5 | 6-10 | 11-15 | 16+ | Not known |
| Arusha | 29.4 | 35.2 | 0.0 | 0.0 | 5.8 | 29.6 |
| Dodoma | 10.0 | 30.0 | 40.0 | 10.0 | 10.0 | 0.0 |
| Kibondo | 10.0 | 45.0 | 15.0 | 5.0 | 25.0 | 0.0 |
| Kilosa | 5.8 | 74.2 | 17.1 | 0.0 | 0.0 | 2.9 |
| Magu | 8.4 | 49.8 | 25.0 | 8.4 | 8.4 | 0.0 |
| Mtwara | 3.0 | 69.6 | 18.2 | 0.0 | 0.0 | 9.2 |
| Nzega | 0.0 | 24.7 | 36.9 | 16.8 | 21.3 | 0.0 |
| Songea | 44.8 | 16.8 | 0.0 | 0.0 | 32.8 | 5.6 |
| Tukuyu | 13.5 | 86.5 | 0.0 | 0.0 | 0.0 | 0.0 |

Source: Maro and Mlay (1982: 178).

Table 8.4
Production of major agricultural commodities, 1970-80 (in
thousands of metric tons)

| Crops | Production | | | | | | | | | |
|---|---|---|---|---|---|---|---|---|---|---|
| | 1971 | 1972 | 1973 | 1974 | 1975 | 1976 | 1977 | 1978 | 1979 | 1980 |
| Coffee | 51 | 48 | 55 | 45 | 58 | 48 | 50 | 51 | 43 | 55 |
| Cotton | 65 | 65 | 65 | 66 | 45 | 69 | 59 | 56 | 64 | 50 |
| Sisal | 181 | 157 | 155 | 135 | 123 | 119 | 105 | 92 | 85 | 80 |
| Tea | 11 | 13 | 13 | 13 | 14 | 14 | 17 | 17 | 18 | 19 |
| Tobacco | 12 | 14 | 13 | 18 | 14 | 19 | 19 | 22 | 23 | 23 |
| Cashew | 126 | 126 | 146 | 143 | 117 | 97 | 86 | 58 | 70 | 65 |
| Cloves | 10 | 15 | 12 | 5 | 8 | 6 | 3 | 3 | 4 | 4 |
| Sunflower | 15 | 15 | 12 | 10 | 9 | 7 | 6 | 7 | 12 | 7 |
| Sugar | 90 | 92 | 106 | 110 | 96 | 102 | 101 | 136 | 130 | 130 |
| Paddy | 193 | 171 | 204 | 310 | 150 | 175 | 195 | 260 | 200 | 195 |
| Wheat | 84 | 99 | 78 | 46 | 56 | 58 | 35 | 38 | 37 | 33 |

Source: ILO/JASPA (1982: 176).

Table 8.5
Share of agricultural production in GDP, 1965-81 (1966 prices)

| Year | GDP (million shillings) | Agricultural production as percentage of GDP | Agricultural production per capita |
|---|---|---|---|
| 1965 | 5,773 | 44.6 | 222 |
| 1966 | 6,514 | 45.3 | 247 |
| 1967 | 6,777 | 43.6 | 241 |
| 1969 | 7,259 | 42.6 | 239 |
| 1970 | 7,680 | 41.7 | 241 |
| 1971 | 8,001 | 39.6 | 233 |
| 1972 | 8,539 | 40.1 | 246 |
| 1973 | 8,800 | 39.3 | 241 |
| 1975 | 9,553 | 37.7 | 234 |
| 1976 | 10,188 | 37.0 | 249 |
| 1977 | 10,980 | 37.3 | 259 |
| 1978 | 10,925 | 39.4 | 267 |
| 1979 | 11,291 | 37.8 | 252 |
| 1980 | 11,261 | 37.6 | 243 |
| 1981 | 11,149 | 36.1 | 241 |

Sources: Jamhuri ya Muungano wa Tanzania, Hali ya Uchumi
wa Taifa (various years); United Republic of Tanzania, Economic
survey, 1981; FAO, Production yearbooks, vol. 31, 1977; vol. 35,
1981.

Table 8.6
Rural household income distribution trends,
1969 and 1976-77

| Income distribution measures | 1969 | 1976-77 |
|---|---|---|
| Gini coefficient | 0.57 | 0.49 |
| Top 10 percent | 46.4 | 38.2 |
| Top 20 percent | 62.4 | 55.2 |
| Bottom half | 14.5 | 18.2 |
| Bottom third | 8.1 | 9.2 |

Source:  ILO/JASPA (1982: 380).

Table 8.7
Percentage distribution of households by level of income,
1969 and 1976-77

| Income | | Percentage of households | |
|---|---|---|---|
| | | 1969 | 1976-77 |
| Less than 1,000 shillings per annum | Rural | 69.0 | 46.8 |
| | Urban | 7.2 | 10.6 |
| | Total | 66.0 | 41.4 |
| Less than 2,000 shillings per annum | Rural | 87.9 | 70.2 |
| | Urban | 20.4 | 20.2 |
| | Total | 84.6 | 62.7 |
| Less than minimum wage* | Rural | 87.2 | 84.2 |
| | Urban | 20.4 | 32.2 |
| | Total | 84.6 | 76.4 |

Source:  Bukuku (1981).
 *Minimum wage was 170 shillings per month in 1969 and 380
shillings in 1976-77 for urban areas.

Sally E. Findley                                                      9

# Colonist Constraints, Strategies, and Mobility: Recent Trends in Latin American Frontier Zones

## INTRODUCTION

Internal colonization is part of the current development strategy of many Latin American nations, especially those with large tropical, relatively unpopulated frontier areas. Indeed, colonization of frontier areas seems an ideal solution to many pressing problems. It serves to redistribute population from densely populated, resource-scarce areas to sparsely populated, resource-rich areas. It also provides land and income to the landless and generally promotes development of the frontier areas.

While this somewhat oversimplifies the justification for colonization, it does summarize the ideology of settlement programs in most Latin American countries. This chapter examines the available evidence to determine whether colonization programs have lived up to their promise. Do settlers actually obtain land? Do they stay in the colonization zones? Do they produce for the market?

One measure of success in the current analysis will be the attainment of population redistribution goals. Individual colonists will be considered successful if they stay on in the colonization zone, preferably on

From the Population Studies and Training Center, Brown University, USA the original plot of land. Another measure of success will be staying on in the colonization zone without having to rely on repeated migration of household members to obtain wage earnings outside the zone. Basically, colonists will be considered successful if the majority of their household cash or subsistence needs are met by work within the colonization zone. Other indicators of success will include the settler's own estimation that life is better since resettlement, obtaining a net income that exceeds what is attainable at the place of origin, and partial or full commercialization of production. Settlements will be considered successful if they have a high rate of retention of settlers or if the number of households remains fairly stable over time, despite some turnover.

The study is divided into five sections. Section 1 contrasts integrated rural development programs with frontier colonization programs. Section 2 presents an overview of recent Latin American colonization activities. Section 3 describes different phases of the colonization process, outlines the problems and constraints encountered in each phase, and discusses possible structural changes or state interventions that could facilitate transition from one phase to another. Section 4 provides some examples of successful and unsuccessful colonization programs. Section 5 summarizes the major findings of the study and highlights their policy implications.

## COLONIZATION AND INTEGRATED RURAL DEVELOPMENT AS ALTERNATIVE STRATEGIES FOR RURAL DEVELOPMENT

Colonization programs and integrated rural development programs address a common set of problems: impoverishment of rural small farmers and the landless, lack of rural employment opportunities and low rural incomes, heavy rural out-migration to cities, inefficient use of rural resources, and insufficient capacity to satisfy basic human needs.

But although colonization and integrated rural development programs share a common concern with rural poverty, their proposed strategies to counter it differ in one crucial aspect. Integrated rural development programs assume the population distribution to be given and seek to stabilize that distribution, albeit with some minor shifts within the region. Colonization programs, on the other hand, have as their primary objective the redistribution of population, with stabilization of the population only after redistribution. Essentially, the integrated rural development programs are built on the premise that people will stay if there is development, while the colonization programs assume that if people move then development will follow.

While the two programs differ in their assumptions about the sequence of development and population stabilization, their approaches to development are fairly similar.

Although the exact mix and emphasis on each element may differ from project to project, integrated rural development programs include the following elements: supported land reform, credit for small farmers, improved varieties, labor-intensive agricultural innovations, complementary and coordinated provision of physical infrastructure, development of a marketing network for inputs and produce, rural vocational training for education for self-help, expansion of off-farm employment opportunities, and creation of rural market towns to serve as links between farm and nonfarm sectors.

With so many project components, project planning and coordination are obviously of considerable importance. In practice, few integrated rural development programs are able to achieve their stated objectives. But if they are fully implemented, integrated rural development programs are expected to foster commercialization of the small-scale farm sector and therefore to enhance the ability of the rural area to retain its population.

Colonization differs from such plans in that supported land reform is not part of the program. Instead, colonization programs substitute title or secure tenure rights to project participants. In other respects, however, program inputs are similar. A convenient summary of colonization program elements is given by Takes (1975: 25): water supplies; roads, both within the settlement area and to link up with the outside world; means of transport, for both people and goods; agricultural material and equipment; workshops for the maintenance and repair of mechanical equipment; credit facilities; processing plants for agricultural produce; marketing facilities; shops; communications and electrification networks, where feasible; and social services, including schools, medical aid, meeting halls, and sports fields.

Takes' list does not include development of market towns in colonization areas, though elsewhere he does consider this aspect. In fact, development of rural market towns has been a part of several recent Latin American colonization programs, including Brazil's Trans-Amazon colonization projects and Bolivia's semidirected projects in the Chapare. The more significant omission from Takes' list is rural employment. There is no mention of labor-intensive agricultural innovations, nor of creating off-farm employment. As we shall see, the absence of concern for employment is a major factor influencing the population retention capacity of the colonization areas.

Colonization programs, regardless of their scale, face several added constraints. These are:

1. *Problems stemming from the population relocation.* Whereas integrated rural development programs start by selecting an area and then making

program inputs available to farmers or the whole population of the area, the colonization programs start by selecting the people to move to a designated area. Selection of the "right" settlers has been problematic in many of the directed colonization programs.

2. *Problems associated with the establishment of a new community.* Integrated rural development programs are implemented in existing communities with a given social and physical structure. Colonization programs, on the other hand, often put people in the middle of the forest. Not only are they faced with the daunting job of carving out their own homes and farms, but they must also build up a community where one did not previously exist. And the community needs themselves are not insignificant. To name just a few, new settlers must organize themselves to maintain roads, build and staff schools, lobby for clinics and health care, establish cooperatives or syndicates, and defend their claims to land. All this they must do with relatively little initial internal organization. In addition, community efforts may be constantly hampered by the poor road and communication links with cities or other regions.

3. *Problems related to the transition to life in the tropics.* Not only must the settlers cope with relocation and loss or previous community resources, but they are often thrust into a completely new environment. Many prime colonization zones are located in the humid tropics, whereas the principal sending areas tend to be climatically dissimilar highland or plain regions. A completely different agricultural strategy is called for, as well as adaptations to housing and lifestyle. Further, settlers are often expected to accomplish these changes at the same time as attempting to shift from subsistence to commercial farming. To add to their problems, the settlers are often exposed to a host of unfamiliar tropical insects and diseases that weaken them and destroy their crops.

4. *Problems stemming from government attitudes to colonization.* The settlers are expected not only to repay the government for the cost of their land and housing, but also to contribute to the costs of providing roads and services to the area. This results in extremely large debts, compared with those of the integrated rural development project participants, who often pay only for specific crop inputs, or are asked to cover a smaller proportion of total program costs.

All these constraints work against the success of a colonization scheme. Why, then, do governments pursue colonization programs, either directly or indirectly by fostering spontaneous colonization?

Perhaps the most important reason for pursuing colonization rather than integrated rural development programs is that the latter include supported land reform, which for whatever reasons politicians feel cannot be achieved. Yet a strong demand for land may exist among the landless and *minifundistas* in the more densely populated areas. In this situation, colonization is offered as a substitute for land reform.

A second reason for pursuing colonization is the mentality inherited from earlier days. Modern colonization continues the historical pattern of exploitation of the frontier, but with internal colonists replacing external colonists. The focus is not on population redistribution, or even on relieving pressure on the land, but on retrieving the wealth from the frontier, mining the "empty lands" for their mineral and natural resources (Shoemaker 1981; Kleinpenning 1975: 13–39). Some observers have even argued that the real goal of colonization programs is to open frontiers for capitalist expansion. According to this view colonization is basically a justification for the huge government outlays used to open up the frontier (Moran 1981: 69–84; Wood and Schmink 1979). The large capitalist enterprises establishing cattle ranches or other agribusiness ventures benefit not only from the massive infrastructure investments but also from the inexpensive clearing accomplished by the colonists before they sell out their land (sometimes under substantial legal or illegal pressure) to the big buisiness interests.

A third justification for encouraging colonization is the attitude that "land is enough." According to this line of reasoning, the major obstacle to rural development is lack of access to sufficient land of high quality. If the colonists are provided with land, therefore, they can transform themselves from impoverished peasants into modern, commercialized farmers. Obviously, these assumptions are diametrically opposed to those underlying integrated rural development, where land alone is not considered sufficient for development. Yet they are implicit in the reasoning behind suggestions that spontaneous settlements should be encouraged, and government investment limited to the roads, land titles and transport necessary to open up the land to eager colonists. Seen in this light, colonization is a relatively inexpensive way of creating employment for the rural work force. In Bolivia, for example, the government investment for colonization was estimated at U.S. $1082 per worker as against U.S. $200,000 per mining job or U.S. $50,000 per industrial job (ILO/PREALC 1979: 59).

## AGGREGATE POPULATION MOBILITY AND RETENTION IN COLONIZATION ZONES

A recent study of rural migration patterns in Peru indicates that only one in five rural emigrants from the Sierra go to the Selva, Peru's colonization frontier (Aramburú 1982: 20). Similar statistics hold for rural migration from one zone of the Sierra of Ecuador to the Ecuadorian Oriente. But the fact that only a minority of rural migrants choose to go to colonization zones does not imply that migration to colonization zones is unimportant. Even if only 20 percent choose the frontier, thousands are involved, simply because they are drawn from such a large pool of migrants.

Colonization activities are not limited to a few nations. On the contrary, there is evidence of colonization throughout most of Latin America, extending from Mexico all the way to Argentina. Literally tens of thousands of people are participating. In some nations, such as Peru and Colombia, the share of the total population in the colonization areas is increasing rapidly. In the humid tropics east of the Andes and in the Amazon basin, colonization occurs with and without government direction on vast tracts of relatively unsettled public or unoccupied private lands. The pattern is somewhat different in Central America, where colonists locate themselves on lands previously expropriated or purchased by the government and specifically designated for colonization.

The range of programs is wide. In Brazil, thousands have flocked to the Amazon to participate in the multi-million-dollar Trans-Amazon colonization program launched in 1970. In Bolivia, many colonists have been attracted spontaneously by the lure of frontier land. Most of them do not have the benefit of government support or substantial assistance. Depending on the nature of the program, government investment ranges from several hundred to several thousand dollars per settler. The more expensive are the directed programs where the government chooses the settlers and the colonization area, develops the infrastructure and services, and provides a range of agricultural credit, inputs, and services. At the other end of the cost continuum are the spontaneous programs, where government activity is limited to constructing major roads and sometimes providing other services, such as staffing schools established in settlements. In between are the semidirected or oriented programs, which seek to rationalize spontaneous settlement patterns by constructing feeder roads, establishing rural service centers in colonization zones, expediting land surveying and titles, and generally helping to maintain the roads and structures built by the earlier settlers. Because the semidirected programs function as an adjunct to a process of spontaneous colonization, they are grouped with spontaneous activities in this study. Where statistics are available, there is every indication that the spontaneous colonists outnumber the directed colonists by at least two to one.

Since most of the colonists come spontaneously without government assistance, they are usually involved in raising food crops, particularly during the initial period. The longer the settlement has been in existence, the more likely it is to have a proportion of colonists who produce either food or nonfood items for the market.

While it seems that many of the colonists dream of becoming prosperous cattle ranchers or coffee plantation owners, the realities for most bear little resemblance to the dream. In the face of the harsh realities of life in a colonization zone, we must ask why colonists come. In numerous cases the choice of colonization is dicated by the lack of alternatives. Those who have other options, such as migration to cities or cultivation of an adequate plot of land, are much less likely to consider the strenuous life of a colonist. It is the landless and the near-landless who are most likely to opt for colonization, as shown in Table 9.1. The data show that at least half of the colonists surveyed in several countries were previously landless.

The common image of settlement is that the colonists are drawn from faraway regions, attracted by the lure of land in the frontier area. While this may be true for at least half of the settlers (Table 9.2), a significant proportion of colonists move relatively short distances within the frontier zone. In the Brazilian states more distant from the Trans-Amazon Highway, such as Amapa and Roraima, more colonists appear to have come from within the northern frontier region than from outside it. Accessibility is obviously a factor in determining whether colonists come from nearby or from more distant places, and for certain types of settlement this may be a more influential factor than the quality of land. Blanes and Flora (1982: 8) conducted a study among colonists in Bolivia's Chapare region. They found that the majority of them had come from the nearby Cochabamba region. Their analysis also showed that many of the colonists had first come to the Chapare as seasonal laborers, and had only subsequently decided to stay. Similar patterns have been observed among colonists in Ecuador's Oriente (Preston 1978; Bromley 1972: 238). While there may be differences in the relative attractiveness of a particular colonization zone to short- versus long-distance migrants, it is clear that not all the landless obtaining land in colonization zones are new to the zones.

The sequence of events by which individuals acquire land and become colonists varies widely. It is only the minority who arrive in the colonization zone and immediately acquire land of their own. Particularly among the spontaneous colonists, the more common pattern is to work as a hired laborer in the zone for a few years, often without any initial plan to become a colonist. The initial visit to the zone may follow a request to help out friends or relatives already there. This may lead to several years of traveling between the home and the colonization zone until the individual decides to acquire his own land.

Once the individual has acquired a plot of land in the colonization zone, he still may not intend to settle there permanently. In fact, the colonization may be undertaken solely to earn sufficient capital to buy additional land in the home community. Alternatively, colonists may intend permanent settlement but not until after the land is cleared and production well established. By retaining some land in the place of origin, the settler retains a fallback option in the event of poor harvests or outright failure in the colonization zone.

Considering that many migrants to a colonization zone have no initial intention of residing there permanently, it is a mistake to see their departure as an indication of failure. If we are interested in the permanence of settlers we should only look at those who have at least acquired land. Ideally, the evaluation period should extend over several years, since colonists take time to develop commitment to the settlement.

The figures presented in Table 9.3 are an attempt to summarize the evidence regarding the proportions of settlers staying on after the initial critical year or so. Most of the cases deal with directed settlement, where we have to assume that most settlers originally intended to stay, and acquired land at the beginning of the period. The proportions staying range from a low of 17 percent after eight years (Cotoca, Bolivia) to a high of 88 percent after five years (Ouro Preto, Trans-Amazon,Brazil). While this is a limited sample from which to generalize, it seems that directed settlements are unlikely to retain much more than 50 to 75 percent of their original settlers.

Comparative assessment of the retention capability of spontaneous settlement areas is extremely difficult, since there are few, if any, records of when the colonists first began clearing and cultivating the land, let alone of when and if they have left the area. Spontaneous settlers arrive at different times and often delay applying for a title for several years; some never apply at all. The few statistics for spontaneous settlements were obtained either from intensive anthropological fieldwork investigating the history of a particular settlement(Pérez Godoy, Peru), or from surveys of current residents regarding their intentions as to staying on in the settlement. They suggest a higher retention rate among spontaneous settlers (Shoemaker 1981).

The fact that between one-half and one-third of all colonists leave their original plots does not mean that they have necessarily abandoned the colonization area. On the contrary, there is considerable evidence that many colonists quit one plot only to start clearing and cultivating another. A recent survey of colonists in the San Julián settlement area of Bolivia shows that 17 percent of the settlers had changed plots at least once since arriving in the area (Blanes et al. 1980: 30). Others may abandon agriculture in favor of wage labor or petty commercial activities within the colonization zone. Evidence relating to settler abandonment of plots cannot therefore be taken as the sole or even the most reliable indicator of a zone's capacity to retain its population.

While figures for abandoned plots may underestimate the population retention capacity of a colonization zone because of their lack of adjustment for turnover or migration within the zone, they may overestimate the long-term population retention capacity if they ignore the out-migration of the colonists' children. The few surveys that have questioned colonists about their aspirations for their children indicate that majority of them do not expect or even want their children to inherit their plot. In the Yapacani and San Julián setlement areas of Bolivia, only 44 percent of the surveyed settlers wanted their children to be colonists. In the Chapare the proportion was only 24 percent (Blanes et al. 1980: 71a). The better-off want their children to leave early to attend the superior urban schools and prepare for an urban career, while the poor send their children out to look for wage employment. Only the small, less impoverished group in the middle seems to be able to contemplate passing their land on to an heir, and even this may not be possible if the land's productive capacity has been depleted or if there is no surplus land within the settlement for parents to pass on to their children.

When factors such as inter-zonal turnover, retention of children, and net in-migration are taken into account, it seems that the best measure of population retention of a zone is net population growth. The best source of such estimates is comparison of census population figures. Unfortunately, not all zones fit neatly into existing census subdivisions. The population growth rate figures for colonization zones in Brazil, Colombia, Paraguay and Peru show that the population of these zones is growing, and often at a rate well above the national average. In both Brazil and Colombia, recent intercensal growth was extremely high at 39 percent (Cardoso and Muller 1977: 53; Giraldo and Ladrón 1981: 108). The rural Peruvian Selva Alta grew ten times faster than the national rural growth rate between 1972 and 1981 (Aramburú 1981: 13).

## COLONIST STRATEGIES IN EACH PHASE OF COLONIZATION

Like other migrants to new areas, it takes time for the new migrants to a colonization zone to establish themselves and begin realizing the goals that originally prompted their migration. Except for the wealthy few who arrive with sufficient capital to buy cleared land and immediately establish an agricultural enterprise, even under favorable circumstances most colonists require several years to become established commercial farmers. The transition is marked by three distinct phases: selection, pioneer, and consolidation. In the first or selection phase, the potential colonist "selects" himself or is selected as a colonist, and then proceeds to select a plot. During the second or pioneer phase, the colonist clears his land and begins cultivating crops, usually subsistence food crops. After a few years the colonist begins the third phase, which consists of consolidation or commercialization. During this time he begins planting and harvesting cash crops or shifts to cattle ranching, depending on the predominant commercial pattern of the zone. By the end of the consolidation phase, the colonist is expected to be fully commericalized and earning a decent living from his agricultural activities.

## Selection phase

Although most discussions of colonization start after the colonist has acquired a plot of land, the various case studies clearly suggest that the process often begins not with the acquisition of land, but with the first few visits to the colonization area. Particularly for spontaneous colonists, these visits serve to introduce the potential colonist to the zone's problems and prospects. After one or several visits the individual may decide to look for his own land. For directed colonists, the selection phase is slightly different. First, the government agency must select the colonists as well as the colonization site. Only then do the colonists select their land, if that is possible within the structure of the program.

Most government colonization agencies seek out married men in good health, preferably with agricultural experience and perhaps some education or skills. Some governments impose additional requirements, such as place of residence (75 percent of the colonists to Trans-Amazon projects were to be northeasterners, according to Moran [1981: 77]), landlessness, or payment of a cash entrance or commitment fee. Generally, it has been found that these selection criteria impose a considerable strain on the settlement agency, and do not correlate strongly with the subsequent success of the colonist. In his review of Bolivian settler incomes, Zeballos-Hurtado (1975) found little relation between the standard selection criteria, especially education, and colonist farm income level. Moran's analysis is consistent with these findings and suggests that at least for Trans-Amazon colonists, the agricultural experience did not have much effect on subsequent farm incomes (Moran 1981: 150).

On the other hand, government agencies often tend to gloss over some fairly important group selection issues. Having carefully selected individual colonists for a project, some agencies put together persons of dissimilar ethnic or regional origins. The resulting antagonisms within such groups have more deleterious results for their success as colonists than any bad individual selection criteria. In addition, settlers are sometimes misled by unfulfilled promises and have little prior understanding of the harsh realities of colonization.

Another problem with the selection process in government-organized programs is the necessity to deal with the excess demand for lots. In the Brazilian planned settlement of Ouro Preto, for example, by mid–1977 there were about 30,000 families who had come but had been unable to obtain a lot. Many of them re-migrated to try elsewhere. Their searches and struggles appear only to have added to the process of minifundization and to the number of land disputes (Martine 1982: 159–61).

These problems are generally avoided by the self-selection process of spontaneous colonization. First of all, in spontaneous settlements the colonists form their own groups, often 10 to 20 men from the same community or place of origin. Together they seek out land, petition for title, and begin the work of clearing and road building. This results in homogeneous colonization groups that are able to develop a communal spirit and the mutual help patterns that are considered essential to timely clearing and planting of plots. Second, the colonists have a chance to discover what frontier life demands before committing themselves to owning and clearing their own land. During the initial visits, the potential colonists essentially serve as apprentices, learning the techniques of slash-and-burn agriculture and acquiring some familiarity with life in the tropics. Presumably those who think that they would not be able to cope with the life would not subsequently seek out their own lands. As a result of both these factors, the spontaneous settlers are more likely to remain in the settlement.

Once the migrant worker has deciced to become a colonist, the next task is to select and acquire a piece of land. Needless to say, his choices are not entirely free, despite the vast frontier expanse. Ideally the colonist should have a plot with the folowing characteristics: alluvial soils with good drainage and agricultural potential; access to a year-round water supply; freedom from flooding; level or rolling terrain, free from cliffs or steep slopes; direct access to a year-round road on which transport is readily available; proximity to friends and kin as well as to a rural market center or frontier town for essential services; "free and clear" land title; a plot of adequate size (20–50) hectares) to permit subsequent commercialization and longer fallow periods; and proximity to sources of seasonal or temporary labor.[1] With so many conflicting demands, it is rare that a colonist is able to find the ideal location.

In most cases, the colonist's choices are constrained by the existing pattern of landholdings, lack of information about soil quality, and lack of income to purchase adequate land. Studies of spontaneous settlement zones in Bolivia, Guatemala, Brazil, Colombia, and Peru indicate that the best land is located along roads, where either early colonists or the rich have bought all the prime sites. What remains for the later arrivals are marginal plots, several kilometers from roads or waterways, with poor soil, on hilly or broken terrain, far from towns or transport services. Thus, even before the colonist begins clearing his plot, the odds may be stacked against him due to the inferior quality and location of his land.

Why do migrants go ahead with clearing and buying what appears to be poor-quality land? An answer to this question is essential to an understanding of the dynamics of spontaneous settlement. First, usually migrants are not familiar with the local environment and what constitutes a desirable plot. Particularly when the colonists arrive in a group to establish a settlement (for example, foreign colonists or delegates from one region), they may have little prior information to guide their selection and little time in which to make the choice. Second, the settlers' choice may be limited to a few designated "reform" areas, all of which may have poor land and location. Third, migrants generally seek out land near that of neighbors or friends who are already established in the zone. There may simply be no more "good" land left in the area, so they have to make do with what they find. And finally, those who choose to colonize may have few other options. Even if they are aware that their plot of land is poor, it may still be preferable to not colonizing, particularly if they are unemployed or underemployed, as is usually the case in the highlands or other densely populated rural areas.

*Selection phase program recommendations*

What, if any, structural changes or government interventions might enable the migrant to select a better plot? According to several observers, the most pressing need is extension of roads, especially feeders. This would open up more land with a favorable roadside location, but the road building could also be used to rationalize the pattern of development, channeling it into areas with more suitable soil and water resources.

Reforming the land titling system would also expedite the acquisition of land. It should be feasible to select larger plots and to legalize occupancy soon after the colonists' arrival. A major problem encountered by spontaneous colonists in Brazil, Bolivia, and probably elsewhere is that colonists may purchase "rights" to land that later turn out to be owned by someone else, usually a large firm or wealthy family. The settlers often discover this too late, and have little recourse when they are forced to quit the land (Bunker, forthcoming: Chap. 11, p. 12). A host of complications may induce the colonists to delay applying for land title, the net result being that many may simply occupy their chosen plot and hope they will not be evicted by private interests or government agencies. In Bolivia's Chapare, Yapacani, and San Julián zones, it was found that only 25 percent of the surveyed settlers possessed titles to their land, although most of them had been in the settlement for several years (Blanes et al. 1980: 14–16a).

What can be done about this? Thome (1971) has suggested the use of mobile land titling teams such as those established in parts of Bolivia's colonization zones. These teams move with colonists as new areas are opened up. Potential areas can be surveyed and lots demarcated in an orderly fashion before colonists commit themselves to a particular lot. This enables colonists to find out if there are any title conflicts before they invest their time and money in clearing and cultivating land. In addition, it is suggested that reduced title costs, both direct and indirect (e.g., taxation based on titled area), would encourage more spontaneous colonists to apply for land titles.

None of these reforms, however, addresses the basic issue, which is that the prime sites are often acquired legitimately or illegitimately by large corporate interests. One solution is for the government to designate some areas for individual colonists or cooperative groups, while other areas are reserved for agricultural enterprises. Individual colonists are then safe from eviction in the colonist areas, as documented by Wood and Schmink (1979) in Brazil's Trans-Amazon. But these measures will be effective only if some advance planning is done, and if the land titling agency is relatively free from corruption, so that false titles are not upheld and land meant for colonists is actually allocated to them.

A final recommendation is that the layout of the settlement be planned in advance to facilitate the growth and expansion of the community. The various suggestions include designation of specific sites to be set aside for subsequent construction of community facilities such as schools, churches, and meeting halls; allocation of nearby lands to be made available to children of the colonists; adoption of plot layouts that facilitate interaction among groups of colonists; distribution of large enough plots to make commercialization feasible; assignment of plots so as to guarantee road and water access to all colonists. Clearly, this would necessitate some form of government planning to direct settlement patterns, or at the very least the assignment of field workers to be on location to advise on settlement layout in the earliest stages.

Admittedly, these proposed measures are tantamount to adopting a policy of orienting spontaneous settlers. But the costs per settler should still not be as large as in the directed settlement. Several of the interventions could be made by using mobile field teams, which do not require expensive administrative and other overheads. Other activities, such as road building and maintenance, can be accomplished with the help of the colonists, who often organize road building and maintenance activities communally. With the help of an agency-provided bulldozer or land-clearing equipment, their work could be much more productive, while still remaining a relatively low cost to the government.

## Pioneer phase

The second phase of colonization is the pioneer phase, in which the colonists clear their plot and begin cultivation. Some colonists establish a permanent residence on their plot when they start clearing the land,

while others do not establish their home there until clearing and cultivation are well under way, a period that may last up to five years.

During the pioneer phase the principal task of the colonist is to clear
the land and establish a subsistence farm. In most frontier areas, the
land is cleared using slash-and-burn techniques, but in areas without a
dry season the slash-and-burn system is modified to a "slash-and-
mulch" system. For both the first step is to clear undergrowth and fell
larger trees. All this is left to dry for a month or so, after which the field
is burned. The process requires some knowledge of how to fell the trees
and clear undergrowth so that it is all burned as completely as possible.
If no burning is planned, the brush is left to act as mulch, and crops
are planted among the trunks and remaining vegetation. (For a discussion of the slash-and-burn process, see Moran 1981.) After the area has
been cleared, crops are planted. Usually the first to go in are food crops,
such as rice, yucca, or corn. After a couple of cycles of slash-and-burn,
the colonists may have a sufficient area cleared to enable them to start
planting tree crops such as coffee or other cash crops. Because cash
crops seldom yield any output in the first year of cultivation, these cannot
be planted until the colonists have cleared enough for both subsistence
and cash crops, or they have an alternative source of income to fulfill
subsistence needs (e.g., income from other landholdings, off-farm jobs,
or capital available on credit).

The situation of directed colonists is somewhat different. If the land
they occupy has been pre-cleared, the colonists can plant crops immediately. It if is available, the colonists may aply for credit to facilitate
immediate cultivation of cash crops or forage crops for livestock. But
not all directed colonists do so, for reasons that will be outlined below.

The major problem faced by the colonists at this stage is lack of capital.
If the colonists had plenty of money, they could hire labor or equipment
to clear as much land as they needed to support their family. For most
colonists, however, credit is either not available or the terms under which
it is available make it difficult for them to make use of it.

Credit may not be available for several reasons. First, banks and colonization agencies restrict credit to cultivation of commercial crops. It
is rarely made available for food crops. Second, even if credit is available,
loans are granted only if the colonists provide collateral security, such
as the title to their land. But most colonists do not have titles to their
land, and they are even less likely to have them at the time they need
cash for clearing land. Even if credit is available and the colonists do
have title to their land, it may not be practicable for the colonists to
obtain a loan. In many cases, the direct and indirect costs of obtaining
a loan from a bank or lending agency are prohibitive. One recent estimate
of the transport and opportunity costs of obtaining a loan places the
cost of obtaining the loan at about 50 percent of the total loan value

(Bunker, forthcoming). The time required to travel to agency head-quarters and complete the application also delays the work of clearing and planting, and colonists are reluctant to jeopardize their year's pro-duction. In addition, the amount that is loaned may be insufficient to cover the clearing and cultivation costs, even without deducting the costs of obtaining the loan. Finally, loans made through government agencies often restrict a farmer to seeds or other inputs supplied by the government agency and to selling agricultural products to a state agency. The seeds may not arrive in time, the extension agent may give poor advice or none at all, and sales to produce to the state agency may require the crop to be transported to the government warehouse.[2] For all these reasons, many colonists do not feel that they can afford the risks associated with obtaining loans from institutional sources. Small farmers obtaining loans from INCRA (National Institute of Colonization and Land Reform) in the Amazon were found to be seven times more likely to lose money than to make a profit in any given year, due to the high level of production and credit costs relative to final sales prices (Bunker, forthcoming).

Labor is another essential resource for the colonists. It is ironic that colonization zones are also sometimes labor-shortage zones. Colonists need to hire labor to assist with land clearing and harvesting. In Ecua-dor's coastal Esmeralda region, it is estimated that a 15-hectare plot requires on average a daily labor input of 3.5 workdays, which exceeds the number of family workers for all but a few of the largest families (Barsky et al. 1982: 135).

Large families are an obvious asset in the pioneer phase, especially if children are in their teens. Various studies show that colonists with adolescent children at home do better than those without, because they do not need to hire as much labor. In the relatively successful settlement of Vitoria, Brazil, the average number of children over the age of 14 was 2.6 per household, compared with 1.6 for six other Brazilian settlements (Darnel 1972: 377–78). Few studies have explicitly examined the hiring of labor in the settlement areas, but the available figures indicate that between a third and a half of all colonists hire labor at some time during the year. Even when they are still clearing land and establishing food crops, colonists need to hire labor.

Not all are able to hire as much labor as they need, however. Settle-ment zones are usually not linked to the wider labor markets. Since the process of recruiting labor is both time-consuming and costly, many of the colonists simply do not do it. Some recruit only informally, asking friends or neighbors to come and help when they return for a home visit. Others do not recruit from outside the region at all. In the Satipo area of the Peruvian Selva, for example, colonists lament the recent agrarian reforms, because they find that a sufficient number of day laborers no longer come to the region (Shoemaker 1981: 123). This places the colonists at the mercy of the wage laborers, who may or may not appear when they are needed, with ensuing potential losses in output or productivity. In Guyana, for example, the government-sponsored settlement schemes have a substantially lower yield per hectare than the national average, in part because the isolated settlers are forced to harvest early (or late) when they have access to labor (Vining 1975: 13–15).

Another important requirement in the pioneer phase is the knowledge of appropriate clearing and cultivation techniques. Even when colonists have had prior agricultural experience, they may be totally unfamiliar with the techniques of tropical agriculture. Traditional varieties of corn and beans may be planted that are unable to thrive in the humid environment and are much more susceptible to molds and infections.

Of course, colonists could learn about more appropriate crops and technologies from extension agents, but for numerous reasons agents have not been effective in conveying this sort of information. Agents may only visit farmers who have taken out institutional loans, and even these visits may be perfunctory or uninformative. Where agents are routinely assigned to cover farms in an area, regardless of their loan status, the farmers still may not benefit from such visits. In Peru, for example, agents are not provided with transport so that field visits are possible only rarely, and then only to farmers near the administrative centers (Martínez 1976).

During the pioneer phase, colonists generally have relatively small amounts of marketable surplus, but this does not mean that they do not need access to roads and reliable transport. Where colonists are located 2 to 3 kilometers from the nearest road, as they are in some fringe settlement areas of coastal Ecuador and the Colombian Amazon, any produce taken to market must be carried on foot. The additional time and energy required to go to town is thus added to the already hard, sunrise-to-sunset schedule of the pioneer. In addition, the fact that the plot is located off the road forces the colonists to burn valuable timber, because they have no way of sending it to a lumber mill.

A final requirement in the pioneer phase is community services. In the absence of hired labor or the ability to pay hired labor, the colonists rely on each other for help in clearing the land. Yet their communities often lack any real nucleus, and colonists are isolated from each other because their plots are so widely dispersed. Just at the time when they need to establish strong supportive, mutual-exchange relationships, they find themselves too far from neighbors to build these links properly. As a result, not only does the colonist suffer from having less help than he needs, but the community fails to develop the communal spirit needed to accomplish collective goals such as road maintenance, school construction, and so on. These problems are particularly acute in directed settlements, where the colonists are usually told that all services will be provided and the roads maintained, only to discover upon arrival that little exists of the promised social and economic infrastructure. In both directed and spontaneous settlements, settlers complain about the lack of basic health services, and the poor or nonexistent schools. The absence of health care has serious consequences, because the combination of poor sanitation and exposure to an unfamiliar tropical environment results in increased morbidity and mortality rates. Several surveys also report that colonists have experienced much higher incidence of parasitic and respiratory infections (Martínez 1976: 200–209; Blanes and Flora 1982; Ziche 1979; Millet 1974: 44–48). A poor state of health obviously has a negative effect on labor productivity.

How do the colonists cope with these resource constraints during the pioneer phase? The natural response to the shortage of labor is to develop patterns of mutual exchange. In Colombia, for example, colonists in the Amazonia develop reciprocal labor exchange relationships with friends, relations, and neighbors. Each takes turns helping the others at times when labor requirements exceed family labor supply, such as for clearing and harvesting.

For colonists who own land in their home communities, however, bringing their wife and children to the colonization zone has certain disadvantages. If the wife and children come to the colonization zone, the family must forgo the output from their original landholdings. Given the risks of the pioneer phase, those who own land in the areas of origin usually retain their land, and many of them leave their wives and young children behind to continue cultivating it. This strategy enables the family to maintain their original farm as their main source of income until the colonization plot starts generating income. If the venture proves unsuccessful, they have not lost their original land. Some observers also suggest that some colonists actually do not intend to sell their original lands. The pioneer activity is then undertaken not to create a new land base for the family, but to enable the family to survive on its traditional land and to earn enough additional cash to purchase more land in the home community. As Martínez (1976) comments, this hampers development of the new plots, since the colonists are not committed to the colonization zone.

Although mutual labor exchanges fulfill some of the labor demands in the pioneer phase, other strategies are required to cope with the capital shortages. Few colonists bring any significant savings with them. In his survey of Bolivian colonists, Zeballos-Hurtado (1975: 81) found that most settlers had brought less than U.S. $42 with them. Those without savings turn to family and friends for help. Another Bolivian survey showed that 30 percent of the colonists had utilized this form of help (Blanes et al. 1980).

To fulfill their cash requirements, many settlers seek off-farm wage employment. Surveys in several colonization zones show that about two-thirds of all colonists work off their plots for some portion of the year. Table 9.4 summarizes the available statistics regarding participation in off-farm wage employment.

Most commonly, the colonist who takes up off-farm employment works within the local colonization area as an agricultural laborer. In San Julián, Bolivia, 66 percent of the colonists work on others' plots in the colonization zone (Blanes et al. 1980: 123–24). Colonists may obtain work on banana plantations, sugar cane plantations, or coffee estates, or clearing land for large landowners. If the settlement is near a town or commercial center, colonists may find nonagricultural work. Children are sometimes encouraged to find jobs in nearby towns, or older sons open stores or restaurants nearby or buy trucks in order to diversify family income sources. Women also sometimes take up off-farm work, such as running a small rural store, raising chickens for sale, or processing food for others. Colonists with some education and/or appropriate skills may find employment in government agencies serving the settlements. In such cases, the colonists usually work full time at their jobs and hire labor for their farms. Colonists with nonagricultural off-farm jobs may well have off-farm incomes exceeding those from their farms. Off-farm work is most common during the first few years of colonization.

But off-farm employment often has negative consequences for the development of the colonists' own farms. In the settlements, especially during the initial period, the work of clearing, land preparation, and planting can occupy a large part of the year. In Yapacani, for example, the colonists are free from major farm tasks only in January, April, September, and October. Unless they can find off-farm work in these slack periods, their own production suffers. One solution to the conflict between off-farm work and on-farm demands is to circulate between the colonization zone and area of origin, where the agricultural calendar may differ. This strategy has its drawbacks, however, namely competition with many others seeking work in the traditional settled zone and the costs of transport between zones. Circulation is only practical for colonists located not too far from their area of origin.

But there is a limit to the amount of labor a family can sell; for many colonists their cash and in-kind income may not cover their expenses. In many settlements surveyed in the Eje Norte of Paraguay, for example, it was found that on average colonists spend more than they earn in any given year. In 1978, the average debt was about 20 percent of annual income, and for most (72 percent) debt was an annual event. Since it is usually difficult to obtain institutional credit, those whose incomes cannot cover their costs must turn to private credit sources. Like peasants elsewhere, they thus become indebted to the private shopkeepers and moneylenders.

Detailed investigation of credit relations in the Colombian Amazon reveals that the colonists adopt a number of alternative credit relations, depending on their needs (Roberts 1975). The most common, of course, is an informal one between a local shopkeeper and the colonists. The colonists obtain credit from the shopkeeper, who in turn benefits in a number of ways. First, the colonists may be obliged to work for the shopkeeper, who may in turn pay less than the market wage rate. Second, the colonists may pay more for goods from the local merchant than they would pay at a cooperative. Alternatively, the local entrepreneur puts a lien on the colonists' crops. In return for a cash advance sufficient to cover farm and household expenses until harvest, the colonists agree to turn their produce over to the entrepreneur in payment of the debt. The colonists must usually accept a lower price than they could get in the open market.

There are other credit relationships that colonists enter into, depending on their resources. Those who have cleared enough land for subsistence food crops but lack enough land or capital to raise livestock may establish an arrangement of *al partir*, whereby the creditor provides the animals while the colonists provide the labor and land. The colonists then share the proceeds from sale of the animals or their offspring with the person who provided the animals. Sharecropping is another credit arrangement whereby the owner lends land in return for a share of the profits. Some colonists become sharecroppers or tenants when the soil fertility on their own plots declines so much that it is more economical to cultivate someone else's land. Those who are forced to sell their land to pay off debts may also enter into sharecropping or tenancy agreements. Contrary to the conventional image of the colonist as an independent landowner, in some areas many of the colonists do not own their land and must share their meager returns with a landowner. In a sample of Eje Este settlements in Paraguay, between 54 and 67 percent of the colonists were not landowners (Alegre 1977: 145).

Although by combining farm and nonfarm work some colonists are able to move from the pioneer to the consolidation phase, many of them stay perpetually within the pioneer phase. Others, as we have seen, fail completely and are forced to abandon or sell their plots.

*Pioneer phase program recommendations*

What could be done to facilitate the successful transition from pioneer to consolidation phase? Probably the most important change concerns expectations regarding the colonization process. While the rural peasants in a traditional zone already have a subsistence farm established and are in a position to respond to state programs designed to foster commercialization, the colonists must first establish a subsistence farm. They cannot be expected to arrive and immediately commercialize. Assistance in this phase should therefore focus on the establishment of viable subsistence farms.

The first set of recommendations involves enhancing the security and viability of the colonists' land ownership. The most critical reform, related to the land title system, has already been discussed in the recommendations regarding the selection phase. Improvements in the system would also help the pioneering colonists. If more colonists had title during this phase, more could apply for institutional credit, assuming that the requirements for obtaining credit were acceptable to the colonists and fulfilled their needs. More important, colonists with title are less susceptible to intimidation and eviction, and there would be fewer violent confrontations between squatters and large landowners. Recommendations regarding the qualities of the land have also been discussed above ("Selection Phase"). The larger lots recommended there (25–50 hectares) would enable colonists to have a longer fallow period between rotations, which would slow down the process of soil depletion, thereby giving colonists a better chance of attaining sustained yields for at least 10 to 15 years. Likewise, road maintenance and construction of feeder roads would reduce transport costs for settlers and facilitate their access to town or community resources.

A second group of recommendations addresses the pioneer's need for capital, especially during the clearing phase. One possibility is obviously to make credit available. The whole credit system should be reoriented to take account of the colonists' need to establish subsistence farms as their first priority. Institutional credit should not be limited to cash crops or livestock.

But offering credit for subsistence agriculture is not sufficient to induce greater use of institutional credit sources, since there are other constraints such as accessibility and flexibility of terms which restrict such use. One possible change would be to have mobile field offices that could process loan applications at the time a settlement is established, similar to the mobile land titling teams employed in Bolivia. Alternatively, credit could be extended through the colonists' *sindicatos* or cooperatives, as has been suggested in Bolivia. The requirements for obtaining credit could also be eased, for example, by not requiring legal evidence of land ownership. Kleinpenning (1975: 129) suggests that the need for a loan should be assessed on the basis of production costs so that the amount loaned actually covers those costs. Finally, repayment of the loan could be made more flexible, specifically by not requiring loan applicants to sell their produce to government agencies alone.

A third set of program recommendations relates to development of human capital in settlement areas. Nonformal education, farmer-oriented training programs, and area-specific technical assistance, which are recommended in integrated rural development programs, would help the colonists avoid mistakes and inefficient practices. Extension agents should provide information on mixed cropping systems, which would enable the colonists to meet their subsistence needs and gradually expand their cash crop production. And such assistance should be made available to all colonists, not just those who obtain institutional credit.

The final set of recommendations relates to community development in the frontier zones. As noted above, the lack of communal spirit and community structure hampers the pioneer colonists' efforts to organize mutual labor exchanges; the lack of community spirit also exacerbates the sense of isolation in the frontier areas. Establishment of colonists' cooperatives can lead to the development of mutual exchange networks and communal spirit. Such cooperatives may not be a solution to all the pioneer colonists' problems, but they could be a start toward delivering services truly needed by colonists and toward obtaining fairer prices for their produce.

None of these program interventions would change the basic character of the pioneer stage, namely the need to clear land and establish a subsistence farm. But they might ease the burdens somewhat and shift the odds a little more in favor of the colonists.

## Consolidation phase

The third phase of colonization is the consolidation phase. During this phase the colonists move from subsistence to commercial cultivation. The transition may be complete (with the colonists growing no crops for their own consumption) or partial. The transition to this phase is largely dependent on external market conditions and community-level services, although the colonists' own efforts, and the location of their plots are also important.

The first condition for successful consolidation is that the plot should be of sufficient size and quality to permit commercialization. Though land would seem plentiful in frontier areas, average lot sizes in some settlements are too small to allow either profitable mechanization of agriculture or a shift to livestock. The problem is exacerbated by the lot layout, which does not allow subsequent acquisition of additional nearby land. Most observers estimate that about 50 hectares is required to commercialize. Land requirements for conversion to cattle raising are particularly large (Kirby 1978: 16).

But sufficient land is not the only requirement. The soil must also be fertile and able to withstand the stresses associated with monoculture or livestock raising. Varese (1974: 24) estimates that only 3 percent of the land in the Peruvian Selva is suitable for intensive agriculture. If the colonists attempt to commercialize without sufficient land or on poor soil, they are not likely to succeed.

A second and essential condition for consolidation is capital; conversion to cash crops requires long-term investment in livestock and forage crops, in tree crops, or in seeds, fertilizer, and other necessary inputs. Commonly this capital is available to colonists from banks, colonization agencies, or cooperatives. But not all who wish to commercialize have access to these loans. In some instances, for example in Colombia, government loans were available only to those with a certain minimum area cleared (Roberts 1975). And, as mentioned earlier, there are significant costs associated with obtaining an institutional loan. As a result, colonists may turn to private lenders who are willing to fund a smaller-scale operation, but at higher interest rates. When colonists do obtain credit, the capital may still not be enough. In Peru, for example, coffee growers do not obtain sufficient funds to permit proper fertilization and pest control. As a result they experience a rapid decline in productivity.

Availability of sufficient labor is the third condition for consolidation. Fortunately for many colonists, the consolidation phase occurs when their children reach working age, but even then most of them depend on hired labor, particularly if they are raising crops with heavy seasonal labor demands. Mutual labor exchange is not usually sufficient for commercialization.

An often overlooked condition for successful commercialization is selection of an appropriate crop or activity. In parts of Colombia and Guatemala, for example, cattle raising is unsuitable because the soils cannot support the right kind of pasture and suffer from compaction and loss of protective tree cover.

Raising livestock may also be inconsistent with the colonists' way of life. In the Jenaro Herrera project in Peru's Selva Baja, the colonists were expected to take up cattle raising, but this conflicted with their hunting and fishing way of life and few were persuaded to change their lifestyle (CENCIRA 1975).

Demand is another critical consideration in selecting a cash crop. Although farmers in traditional settlement areas are also susceptible to changes in demand for their commodities, the colonists are more affected by price variations. Due to their isolated location, they must pay dearly both for necessary crop inputs and for transport of their produce to market. The distance between the colonists and final consumers also adds costs associated with the additional middlemen involved in getting the crops to market.

In most settlements transport costs dictate the pattern of commercialization. Transport costs alone dictate the viability of sugar cane cultivation along the Chane-Piray highway in Bolivia. More than 14 kilometers away from Chane, sugar cane cannot be grown economically, despite its high yield. Several areas in Paraguay and Guatemala have been unable to commercialize at all, for lack of adequate transport facilities (Ziche 1979; Millet 1974).

A successful transition to commercial agriculture entails development of community services such as credit, technical assistance, marketing, and transport. Alternative allocations of the family labor force between farm and off-farm work are generally insufficient for accumulation of the necessary capital; nor can individual families develop the required marketing structure. Initial capital from family, corporate, or institutional sources enables successful colonists to buy cleared land, land located near market centers, and/or good quality land.

Initial capital also permits colonists to hire labor to clear their land or, if it is already cleared, to purchase implements and hire labor to begin immediate cultivation of cash crops. Colonists with enough capital may skip the pioneer-subsistence phase entirely.

But initial capital is not the only prerequisite for a settler's success. In his study of Brazilian colonists in Itaguai settlement, Santa Cruz, Galjart (1968) specifically investigated the characteristics distinguishing innovators, or commericalized farmers, from noninnovators. He concluded that a major distinction was that the innovators were committed to staying in the colony and making the frontier their life. They therefore treat their farm as a commercial venture, invest their savings in the farm, and develop a wider network of political and social contacts that may be tapped for help or advice as needed.

Even with such a commitment to the frontier zone, not all who attempt commercialization succeed. Not infrequently, hard work and commitment fail to overcome the initial handicaps, such as too little capital and poor location. Evaluations of colonists' returns in coastal northeastern Brazil and Costa Rica show that most colonists earn less than the minimum wage. In the Satipo region of Peru and the Eje Norte of Paraguay, the average colonist spends more than he earns.

The latecomers to colonization zones find it increasingly difficult to commercialize successfully. They are often forced to take plots that are further out, on poorer soils, and without access to transport, which is vital to commercialization. They are therefore at a greater risk of failure and complete proletarianization than the earlier settlers.

Not surprisingly, settlements moving into the consolidation phase exhibit a high incidence of the twin phenomena, sales of improved land

and differentiation into *minifundia–latifundia*. The newer arrivals with smaller plots obtain land, clear it, work it for a few years, and then sell the "improvements." The consolidators buy the improved land, thus adding to their existing holdings. The result is the emergence of the minifundia–latifundia pattern so evident throughout settled, traditional areas of Latin America. This sequence of colonization has been observed in virtually all of Latin America's frontier zones.

Some who sell their land, however, are not compelled to do so by debts or lack of capital. With the rise in land values, colonists sometimes find it more profitable to sell their land with its improvements after only two or three years of occupation. In Colombia's Llanos Abriertos and Departamento del Meta, for example, professional colonists can earn up to U.S. $30,000 per hectare of improved land sold (Giraldo and Ladrón 1981: 110, 139). Some of them hope to amass enough capital eventually to establish their own cattle ranches, but for many clearing and selling becomes a way of life.

A significant consequence of this process is the emergence of increasing inequality among the colonists, despite relatively equal plot sizes at the start of colonization. In Bolivia's Santa Cruz zone, the majority of the settlers no longer possess their original 20 hectares. After 10 to 15 years, over one-third of the land (38 percent) is possessed by one-sixth (13 percent) of the colonists (Maxwell 1980).

The process of land concentration is well documented by Martine (1982) in his study of colonization in Brazil's Rondônia. Concentration also results from the sale of land by "failed" colonists. By 1976, the small farmer colonists (those with less than 50 hectares) made up 31 percent of the farms but owned only 1 percent of the land. Almost 60 percent of the land was controlled by a minority of 1.2 percent of the landowners, each with 5000 hectares or more.

Shifts in cropping patterns and labor force demand accompany the land concentration process. Like large landholders in traditional settled zones, the large landholders in frontier zones concentrate on livestock or commerical crops that do not require large or year-round labor inputs. In Colombia's colonization zones, traditional production dropped from 28 to 16 percent in the short four-year interval of 1972–75. During this period, agro-industry increased substantially, as in the rest of Colombia. By 1975, 20 percent of all agro-industrial crops were produced in the colonization zones. While the attendant shifts in labor demand have not been explicitly examined for the Colombian example, experience elsewhere indicates a drop in permanent labor demand with these types of crops (Kay 1982: 47–50; Matos Mar and Mejía 1982: 84–86). This can only have an adverse impact on the population retention potential of the colonization zones, where many colonists depend on off-farm agricultural wage labor.

If the process of land concentration continues, turnover and re-migration will become characteristic of settlement zones in the consolidation phase. After consolidation, labor force requirements will be less than those in the pioneer stage, so net population retention will fall below the level of the pioneer phase, unless alternative employment is generated.

### Consolidation phase program recommendations

To reverse the trend toward increased concentration of land will require significant changes. Instead of explicitly or implicitly aiding concentration and large-scale commercialization of agriculture, programs would have to be redirected toward commercialization among colonists with smaller landholdings. Essentially, this implies adoption of integrated rural development programs especially tailored to the conditions of colonization areas and to the situation of colonists in the pioneer phase, with some subsistence crops already established.

Several program and policy shifts are needed in order to make commercial agriculture profitable for the colonist with 10 to 50 hectares. First and foremost, the internal terms of trade must be changed so that colonists may earn reasonable profits from the sale of their produce. But colonists in frontier zones need more than favorable prices if they are to commercialize their production and settle permanently. Attempts must be made to reduce producer costs. Colonists' locational disadvantage compared with farmers in traditional zones must be minimized through improvements in transport services. In addition, frontier agriculture could be made more profitable if the colonist could process his produce to reduce perishability as well as volume *before* shipping it out of the zone. Finally, credit costs in frontier areas should be reduced. If institutional credit is to serve the needs of the average colonist, it must be much more accessible and less costly. At the same time, private usury could be regulated or restricted to guard colonists against exploitation.

The process of sell-out and concentration could be abated by improvements to the land-titling system, as were suggested to help colonists in earlier phases. Particularly in the spontaneous colonization zones, title security would lessen the chance of a surprise eviction by another land claimant. The larger lots recommended earlier would also facilitate commericalization among colonists.

Productivity increases would also facilitate long-term, sustained commercialization. It has been suggested that the crops recommended are usually inimical to the long-term viability of the frontier soils. Crops should be carefully selected to mesh with frontier soil and climatic conditions. If the goal of the colonization program is to retain the settlers fully within the colonization zone, then attention must also be paid to the full utilization of the family labor force. In particular, off-farm employment or family enterprise opportunities are a necessary complement to a family's agricultural activities. The availability of regular off-farm employment opportunities would be ensured by the introduction of processing and other rural industries, as well as by the adoption of labor-intensive technologies in frontier agriculture. In short, population retention in colonization zones requires development of both agricultural and nonagricultural sectors.

Population retention would also be facilitated by improved health, education, and social services in the colonization zones. Like their compatriots in other relatively isolated rural zones, colonists and their children would be more committed to staying in the colonization zones if the level of services and quality of life were not so abysmal.

These program suggestions are quite similar to those outlined for integrated rural development. The two significant exceptions are the explicit recommendations to rectify the internal terms of trade in favor of the frontier agriculturalists and to tailor the commercialization process to the ecology of the frontier areas. Although implementing all the recommended changes would serve the goal of retaining a frontier population, it is these last two interventions that would probably provide the most powerful and lasting impetus to population stability in the frontier zones.

## SETTLERS' SUCCESS AND FAILURE

In the frontier zones, success and failure are not always easy to distinguish. When does the colonist struggling to cope with the difficulties of frontier agriculture pass the threshold of success? Or of failure? By our definition, he fails if he gives up and leaves the zone entirely. But there are gradations of success and failure, and the colonist who has managed to commercialize his production, is free from unmanageable debts, and plans to continue farming his plot is clearly more successful than the colonist who is barely making a subsistence living and only sees his prospects worsening. For this struggling colonist, failure seems a more likely prospect than success. We shall briefly discuss some examples of success and failure to give a better view of the overall dynamics of the process.

An interesting contrast between successful and less successful families in one settlement is given in Vessuri's (1973) account of a well-established settlement in Tucumán, Argentina. The settlement is a privately sponsored project with funding from the Banco Hiptocecario Nacional. Each colonist purchased a 100-hectare lot at the outset. The settlement was 30 years old at the time of the survey. Successful families had not only managed to retain their original plot, but many had purchased additional land. Production was fully commercialized and many owned both a tractor and a truck. Less successful families had also commercialized production, but incomes from their holdings were much lower and most of them had to rely on earnings from off-farm labor. Few of the less successful farmers had retained their original holdings, some having given them up on a rent or sharecropping basis.

What are some of the features distinguishing these two sets of colonists?

1. The successful colonists had not subdivided their holdings, whereas the less successful had split their land among their heirs. As a result, the latter no longer had enough land to cultivate on a commercial scale.

2. The more successful colonists had arrived earlier than the less successful.

3. Most of the successful colonists were decendants of Spanish lineage, while the less successful were of Argentine origin. The author of the study does not give reasons for the success of the former group of settlers, but it is possible that they had more capital at the time of arrival. In Paraguay, for example, Brazilian colonists do better than the Paraguayans because they start with more capital (Alegre 1977).

Another set of examples of individual success and failure can be drawn from Robin Shoemaker's account of migrants to a settlement in Satipo, Peru (1981: 172–202). Located in Peru's Ceja de Selva or high jungle, the settlement has a long history of colonization. In 1928 the area was opened to spontaneous colonization by the Peruvian government. The settlement has alternately thrived and languished through boom–bust cycles of the coffee and *barbasco* (a natural insecticide) trade. At the time of the study (1975–76), most of the colonists were engaged in both subsistence and cash crop production. Many had settled along steep canyons where the soil is poor and subject to severe erosion, since the better soils in the valleys had already been occupied by earlier settlers. The following vignettes illustrate the contrast between the more and less successful settlers.

Compared with other colonists, Juan Paredes is successful, at least at the time of the study. Juan is the son of a peasant sharecropper who came to Satipo in 1955 to visit a sister. He liked what he saw and decided to stay. At first he worked for others, until he had enough savings to purchase land. In 1962 he acquired 50 hectares. Although the coffee bust had already started, he had no choice but to plant coffee, since no other crop could be marketed without great risk of loss if trucking were delayed. With the fall in coffee prices he turned to alternative crops for additional cash income. Currently, he is selling valuable timber on his land, which he can do since his land is located on a road. Although his future prospects are cloudy, for the present he is doing well with the combination of coffee and lumber production. A major strategy that has worked to his advantage is that Juan Paredes never obtained a loan for his coffee grove from the state bank, so he has no large outstanding debts or high interest payments to drain off his working capital.

Another relatively successful colonist in Satipo is Teodoro Acuna. He heard about the region from friends and decided to give it a try. He arrived in 1960 and started out as a sharecropper. When the landowner died, Teodoro assumed the land (30 hectares, including 8 hectares of coffee), along with the loan debt to the state bank. He has been unable to pay off the loan and continues to be burdened by the 12 percent interest payments. Like Juan Paredes, Teodoro Acuna continues to cultivate coffee, but he, too, has diversified his production. He now earns most of his cash income from commercial production of bananas, papayas, and oranges. He is constantly trying new products and techniques, and is very proud of his farm. Teodoro also benefits from a good location near a main road, and soils that are suitable for fruit growing. The combination of innovation and good location has served him well in overcoming the handicap of the coffee loan debt.

In contrast to these two, Jacinta de Samaniego appears to have had little success. Jacinta came to Satipo with her husband in 1956. They were young and had visions of obtaining virgin land; however, they soon discovered that all the accessible land had been claimed. Her husband found a job on a coffee estate and they eked out a meager existence there for several years. In 1963 they joined a group of 28 families who, like them, had no hope of purchasing land. They squatted on an abandoned estate. In this manner the family obtained 30 hectares, and they obtained loans to plant 6 hectares of coffee. When prices plummeted, they could neither pay off the debts nor maintain the coffee groves. Jacinta's husband died three years ago from tuberculosis, leaving her with nine children. They are very poor and able to earn only half of what they need to live decently. The children are malnourished, and the youngest has just died. If Jacinta had still had the original 30 hectares, they might have had a chance to develop a farm that could support her family, but the government granted title to only 16 hectares, and this is too small a plot for the long fallow periods required to sustain soil fertility and prevent erosion. And then there are the bank debts that drain off a major part of her income. The outlook for this family is certainly not good.

The last example of a relatively unsuccessful colonist is someone who could have been like Teodoro, were it not for bad luck and poor advice. Guillermo Vega and his family came from the highlands in 1958 in search of cheap land and well-paid work. Due to heavy demand for land for establishing coffee estates, they were unable to obtain any land, so the family went to work on a coffee farm. When his father died, Guillermo went to work on a smaller coffee grove as a permanent hired worker. In 1963 the landowner abandoned the grove and gave Guillermo the land (5 hectares) in lieu of unpaid wages. Since this was at the time of the coffee bust, Guillermo knew that he would have a hard time, but he decided to stay anyway. At least in Satipo he could raise subsistence crops and be assured of food for his family, which was better than his prospects back in his home community. The bank advised him to plant bananas, which he did. Production was much lower than anticipated, and he was unable to repay his loan. He says that the bank gave him bad advice on how to plant the bananas, but the bank disowns any responsibility. To make matters worse, Guillermo lost the first year's crop when a mudslide washed out the road to his plot. The bank did not renew his credit, and he was stuck with the unproductive banana plants.

These vignettes are too brief to convey fully why some settlers have been successful and others not, but there are some features that appear to be common among the more successful: a large enough plot to permit commercialization, diversified production, and good road access. A willingness to adopt innovations, initial capital, and early arrival in the settlement area also seem to enhance the chances of success.

Now let us turn to some examples of community success. Here, success is indicated by a high population retention rate in the community, relatively low turnover rates, and expectations that some, if not all children will stay in the community when they are older. In addition, the more successful communities also have higher farm incomes and productivity levels than the less successful communities.

One specific factor associated with a greater chance of success appears to be foreign origin. Colonists arriving from other nations such as Germany, Italy, and Japan generally have much more capital upon arrival, either from personal savings or from government sources. This means that the foreign colonists are likely to start with a large lot and sufficient capital to finance clearing and planting. They may also bring with them agricultural expertise and managment skills that facilitate commercialization. Consequently, they may be better able to choose appropriate crops and develop sustained yields early in the colonization period. In his account of Japanese settlers, Stewart (1967: 164) notes that the directed colonists of La Colmena, eastern Paraguay, were preselected for their agricultural experience and were required to adopt predetermined cropping patterns, which included a mix of annual and perennial crops. The crops had been carefully selected to meet existing market demand. While not all colonists proved as successful in the Paraguayan environment as the Japanese sponsors had hoped, most were able to capitalize on the commercial possibilities afforded by these crops.

In Costa Rica, the success of the Quaker spontaneous colonists at Monteverde was due to a similar set of circumstances: exploration and selection of a site with adequate, though not superior, agricultural potential; selection of a product (cheese) that capitalized on the prior farm experience of some of the colonists and which had the advantages of being high value, low bulk, and relatively nonperishable; and access to a pool of private savings and loans to establish the cheese factory. In addition, the cheese factory provided some off-farm employment. Ironically, it could not exist without milk supplied from Costa Rican colonists in the area, who supplied well over half of all the milk processed between 1958 and 1962. In this case, the foreign colonists did not compete with their native neighbors, as they did in Paraguay. Rather, their efforts to build a cheese industry enabled neighboring Costa Rican colonists to commercialize their dairy farms successfully.

These successful foreign settlements serve to illustrate that it is possible for a whole group to consolidate its frontier farms, but that this cannot be done without considerable planning, training, and capital. Translating these requirements to internal colonization, the implication is to lean toward fully directed settlements. Yet, as we have already seen, these efforts have proved extremely costly and have failed to achieve the planned consolidation. Direct application of the experiences of foreign colonists is unrealistic, given limited administrative and managerial resources. Instead, the successful features of the foreign settlements need to be incorporated into a form compatible with existing internal organizational and capital resources.

Let us now turn to a few other examples of settlements or areas that seem *on the whole* to have been relatively successful in commercializing. It should be borne in mind that these were considered successful at the time they were evaluated; subsequent changes in market prices or demand can reverse consolidation. For each of these selected cases, we will review briefly the outstanding structural features that contributed to widespread consolidation.

The first case is that of Pindorama, in coastal northeast Brazil. This directed settlement was established with substantial German and Swiss financial and technical asistance. These foreign inputs have undoubtedly facilitated the organization and strengthening of the settlement's cooperative. The settlement has focused on production of passion fruit jam and juice for the Brazilian market, but it also produces tapioca from casava and manioc flour. The success of the settlement has been due to a number of factors: selection of a crop, passion fruit, for which there was large potential demand; foreign advice on running the cooperative; and a location close to Recife, a major demand center. The cooperative obtains healthy gross returns. Due to its high administrative expenses, however, it is not as profitable as it appears. In 1969, despite gross returns of over U.S.$100,000, the cooperative netted only U.S. $20,705, which was shared among its over 400 members. Darnel (1972) suggests that the cooperative could provide its members with greater returns if there were less foreign participation and reduced overheads. Nonetheless, compared with many other settlements, Pindorama must be considered relatively successful.

A success story that does not involve heavy foreign participation is that of Treze, also located in coastal northeastern Brazil. Treze was established in 1961 by private interests. Settlers have to undergo an initial probationary period before they are accepted in the settlement. Like Pindorama, Treze also has a cooperative, but it is not a production cooperative. The cooperative provides equipment, seeds, seedlings, and fertilizer to its members, who repay the cooperative at the time of harvest. If necessary, the cooperative provides subsistence loans to tide a family over until the harvest. It also provides technical assistance. The cash crops grown in Treze are tobacco and citrus fruits. Within three years, most colonists are able to pay off their initial debts, build a permanent home, and plant cash crops. Despite the poor soils, unreliable rainfall, and distance to the market, the settlement has been fairly successful. Returns on labor exceed the minimum wage, and 82 percent of the settlers reported that they have a better living standard than they had before coming to the settlement (Darnel 1972: 325–37).

What are some of the structural conditions that contributed to Treze's success?

1. Appropriate crops were selected, for which demand and marketing facilities existed.
2. The cooperative provided an effective organization to facilitate commercialization. In particular, it provided inputs in a timely fashion and bought settlers' produce at reasonable prices.
3. Credits to settlers were based on potential yields, which enabled settlers to shift from low-return food crops to high-return cash crops.
4. Settlers were a fairly homogeneous group, drawn predominantly from nearby areas. This resulted in less dislocation and more continuity and cooperation between settlers.
5. The project stressed colonist leadership and did not demonstrate paternalism.

Turning now to some examples of relative failure, let us return to the Satipo region of Peru, again drawing the information provided by Shoemaker (1981: 108–37). The community of Pérez Godoy, 5 kilometers from Satipo, was formed spontaneously when 18 families encroached on abandoned land. They claimed the land under the Jungle Lands Law, which provides that owners receiving land from the state must bring at least 30 percent of the land into cultivation within five years of purchase. The government authorities did not oppose the encroachment, and after eight years of waiting the community received titles. Each family claimed 30 hectares, while 100 hectares was set aside for communal use. Each family agreed to contribute one day a week for communal work. Three years after the community was established, the government decided that it wanted to distribute some of the land to new settlers. Each family's plot was cut in half, leaving them with only the land they were currently working and none for fallow periods during rotations. As a result, the families were no longer able to practice traditional agriculture. This led to rapid soil erosion and depletion. Productivity declined rapidly, and many families could no longer survive on their farm income alone. By 1974 two-thirds of the original 64 families (28 plus 36 newcomers) had left. The rate of turnover continues to be high. In one year another four of the 64 families had left, and others were planning to leave.

There are several structural constraints that have hampered this community's attempts at success: (i) after the government assigned the additional families to the community, the lots were too small to permit soil conservation practices; (ii) the dependence on coffee alone made the colonists very susceptible to fluctuations in its price; at the time of the survey the price of coffee was not keeping pace with the prices of inputs; (iii) credit from public or private sources was insufficient to allow the families to increase coffee yields; (iv) attempts to supplement incomes through off-farm work had led to a significant decline in output; and (v) lack of community organization had crippled the potential of the settlement to respond collectively to its problems.

Another example of a less successful settlement is that of El Eje Norte, in Paraguay. This area was opened to spontaneous settlers 12 years ago, but in recent years the government has been attempting to develop the area's agricultural potential. Over a period of 10 years the colonists have made few gains in their standard of living, and the settlement has failed to fulfill its residents' expectations.

Perhaps the most salient indication of the settlement's failure is the emergent differentiation between colonists, in terms of both land ownership and income. Although all the residents started with equal plots of 20 hectares, few have retained the original plot. In 1978, 19 percent had fewer than 10 hectares, while 12 percent had more than 20 hectares. Those with smaller plots had subdivided their land among their children. The result of this fragmentation has been unequal distribution of farm income. Although the average annual farm income is U.S. $1,600, 52 percent less than half this amount, and 20 percent earn less than U.S. $400. Not surprisingly, most of the colonists have been forced to supplement their farm earnings with off-farm work. In 1978, 62 percent reported working off the farm.

What are some of the specific problems that have led to this situation?

First, almost two-thirds of the colonists sell their produce to private merchants, and most of them complain of exploitation. Second, transport costs are very high, so that colonists cannot afford to ship their produce to Asunción where they could obtain better prices. Third, they are obliged to buy goods at higher prices in the settlement areas. These sometimes cost 20 to 60 percent more than in Asunción. Fourth, although there is a cooperative, its loans are too small and arrive too late to be of much help to the settlers.

Again, the cumulative impact of these factors has led to a high rate of desertion. In the 12 years since the settlement was established, 37 percent of the settlers have left. A survey carried out in 1978 showed that 14 percent were planning to leave. Not surprisingly, it was the poor who were planning to leave.

It appears, then, that there are two patterns of settlement failure. The first, typified by El Eje Norte, is accompanied by increasing differentiation between large and small landowners, with population loss and turnover concentrated among the colonists with the smaller plots. The second, typified by Pérez Godoy, exhibits widespread failures and desertions. Those who leave sell their land to new arrivals, not to landowners amassing large estates. The differences between the two patterns of failure seem to arise out of the differences in location, accessibility, and agricultural potential.

## CONCLUSIONS AND POLICY IMPLICATIONS

Present colonization patterns in Latin America are diverse and changing. A large number of families are involved in clearing and farming frontier lands in the Amazon and other major tropical colonization zones. If recent trends continue, we can expect many more to be involved in colonization, assuming that lands with settlement potential are opened to settlement.

Colonization is by no account an easy route to prosperity. The work is arduous and risky and rarely profitable. Given these prospects, why do people continue to be attracted to the frontier life? Although they are certainly aware of the difficulties, some come convinced that they are "smarter" and stand a better chance of making a go of it (Shoemaker 1981: 187). More commonly, colonists come from extremely impoverished circumstances, with insufficient land to support their families. Colonization seems to offer better prospects if the household head or his children can work as casual laborers in the colonization zones. Life is hard in the colonies, but the colonists at least have their subsistence crops to fall back on.

Whether the colonist is convinced that he has a better chance than other colonists or has no choice except colonization, the would-be pioneers are distinguished from other migrant workers by their commitment to owning and cultivating a piece of land. Before settling in the zone, most of them have either owned small amounts of land (a few hectares) or worked as farm laborers. They choose to continue the agrarian life by settling in a frontier zone. In fact, the colonists often possess better farm management skills than those who remain to farm in traditional areas.

Compared with their lives before moving to the colonization zones, the evidence presented in Table 9.5 indicates that the majority of settlers feel that their standard of living is better, or at least no worse than it was before moving. This does not mean that there are no dissatisfied colonists; indeed, many are saddled with debts just as they were prior to coming to the frontier. Many of the unsuccessful colonists may also have left.

The review of various studies has also shown that there is considerable labor migration between colonization and settled zones, as well as within the colonization zones. Because the colonists' subsistence agriculture may fail to meet the family's cash requirements, family members often seek off-farm work to supplement farm earnings. Further, casual workers move about within the frontier zones to meet the seasonal labor demands associated with commercial agriculture. In each of these patterns, migration *within* the colonization zone enables the family to stay in the settlement. Like their rural compatriots in nonfrontier zones, the colonists are increasingly involved in circulation and migration within the region.

The colonists, however, have fewer labor migration and circulation opportunities than residents in settled rural areas. The frontier location isolates them from the broader national labor markets, while the limited urbanization of frontier areas restricts off-farm employment opportunities within the zone. As a result, colonists often seek employment opportunities on neighboring farms. The more enterprising send their wives and children to nearby towns, where the wives can establish independent businesses such as small stores. A strategy unique to colonization areas is that of the "perpetual pioneer," who repeatedly clears land for resale to others or under contract to the owner.

While the earnings from off-farm work may enable the family to meet subsistence needs, most frontier jobs pay poorly and only rarely do they provide enough to invest in commercialization. For many, off-farm earnings simply cannot fill the gap between net farm income and consumption expenses. So they have to obtain credit from local merchants to tide their families over until the next harvest. When they cannot clear their debt, they have to sell their land. The debtors either start anew, or become tenants or sharecroppers on a large landowner's farm, or become casual workers in the frontier zone. The net result is that land is increasingly held by a smaller and more select group of rich individuals, while the poorer colonists find themselves on successively smaller plots after each forced sale.

The emergent differentiation has certainly not been an explicit goal of the colonization programs; nonetheless, the evidence presented here suggests that in many instances the chances of success have been biased in favor of colonists with more land or capital. As in the traditional settled areas, those who are able to take best advantage of government assistance and agricultural credit are the commercial farmers, not the subsistence farmers for whom the programs were seemingly designated.

How is it that government programs aimed at assisting all colonists end up reaching a select group? First, most of the government credit and assistance programs are based on the premise that the colonists have titles to their land. But the evidence contradicts this premise. At least half of all colonists are spontaneous settlers, of whom only a minority obtain title upon arrival. A majority of colonists are thus barred from seeking institutional credit. Second, even if the colonists can meet the loan eligibility requirements, the conditions for proper use of the credit may be wanting. The loan may be restricted to cash crops; the costs of obtaining the loan may be high; the loan may not arrive in time to ensure a good "burn" or timely planting; and the loan may require use of government inputs. For some or all of these reasons, the colonists engaged in establishing a subsistence farm may feel that otaining institutional credit would be too risky. Third, the government programs aimed at assisting colonists focus on the consolidation phase. Yet immediate commercialization of production is neither desirable nor practical for most colonists. Their first priority is to establish a subsistence farm and only then to cultivate commercial crops. Furthermore, commercialization requires well-developed storage, transport, and marketing networks, but these seldom exist until after a few years. Only settlements that start with adequate market and transport linkages can entertain early commercialization as a viable option, and even then the typical pioneer will first establish his subsistence crops. In the Trans-Amazon directed colonization areas, which started with an adquate provision of services, most of the assistance and credits have gone to individuals or firms who have amassed very large landholdings. Similar patterns are evident in Colombia, where 90 percent of the Agrarian Bank's funds go to cash crops and 25 percent of the loan applicants are agro-industries.

Clearly, if a larger proportion of colonists are to be retained in the colonization zones as small farmers, government programs need to be reoriented to meet their needs at each phase of colonization. This review has highlighted the tasks, resources, and constraints confronting the typical colonist in the selection, pioneer, and consolidation phases. Alternative government measures that could facilitate accomplishment of the colonist's goals in each phase have also been reviewed. Among the recommendations included for the selection phase are (i) extension and maintenance of feeder roads, (ii) reforms of the land titling system, and (iii) advance planning of settlement layout. For the pioneer phase the recommendations include (i) larger lot allocations; (ii) credit oriented to needs of subsistence farmers, without exploitation by middlemen; (iii) training in tropical subsistence agriculture; and (iv) development of settler communities and cooperatives.

Recommendations specific to the consolidation phase include:

i.   improvements in the internal terms of trade;

ii.  improvements in transport services;

iii. producer-oriented credit;

iv.  adoption of mixed cropping systems;

v.   generation of off-farm employment; and

vi.  expanded health and education services.

Improved access to transportation and credit have been identified repeatedly as critical to the colonists, but, as in the traditional settled rural areas, neither these two nor any other single intervention can be viewed as a complete panacea for success. Not surprisingly, the mix of measures suggested here resembles that of integrated rural development programs. Colonists are no different from small farmers elsewhere in their need for a diverse set of programs fostering economic and social development.

Though there is certainly a strong case for adapting and expanding integrated rural development programs into frontier areas, widespread implementation of such programs has not been possible, nor is it likely to become so, given the current financial constraints of governments throughout the region. But this constraint need not prevent governments from implementing some of the recommended changes. The success stories described above suggest that colonists are strongly motivated and, given the right conditions, can commercialize production. The most critical conditions are higher prices for colonists' produce, reliable roads and transport services, and reformed land titling and distribution systems.

However, stabilization of the frontier population cannot occur without important structural changes, such as:

i.  restructuring the terms of trade in favor of frontier agriculturists;

ii. infrastructure development to foster linkages within frontier zones and between frontier and settled zones;

iii. development of more off-farm employment opportunities in frontier areas; and

iv. a reorientation of colonization attitudes and approaches toward sustained development.

In Latin America today there are literally thousands of people who go to the frontier to make their fortune, however large or small. As we have seen, many do stay there, but only a small fraction realize their dreams. The twin processes of soil depletion and indebtedness foster population turnover, income differentiation, and mobility, rather than stability and success. Colonization programs in their present forms will not counter these trends. A fundamental reorientation is needed if population redistribution with stability is to be attained.

## NOTES

1. For a discussion of the preferred soil and site characteristics, see Moran (1981). Shoemaker (1981) also discusses these criteria; others mention the proximity to labor market criterion only in passing, although this is an important desideratum.

2. Shoemaker (1981: 201–9) provides an excellent discussion of the pitfalls of using institutional credit sources.

## BIBLIOGRAPHY

Albo, J. 1980. "La colonización espontanea de Caranavi: Discusión preliminar." Paper presented at the Seminario de la probemática agraria en Bolivia y expansión del capitalismo. Centro de Investigación y Promoción Campesína (CIPCA), La Paz, January 5–10.

Alegre, H. 1977. "La colonización en el Paraguay: El Eje Este." *Revista Paraguaya de Sociología* (Asunción) 14, no. 38: 135–55.

Aramburú, C. E. 1981. "Expansión de la frontera agraria y demográfica en la Selva Alta Peruviana." In *Colonización en la Amazonía*, edited by C. E. Aramburú et al., pp. 1–39. Lima: Ediciones CIPA.

———. 1982. *Las migraciones en la sociedad campesina: El caso de Puno.* Serre Publicación no. 21. Lima: Publicaciones CISEPA.

———. 1982. *Colonización en la Amazonía.* Lima: Ediciones CIPA.

Barsky, D., E. O. Bonilla, C. Furche, and R. Magrani 1982. *Políticas agrarias, colonización y desarollo rural en Ecuador: Reflexiones sobre el proyecto de desarollo rural integral Quininde, Malimpia, Nueva Jerusalem.* Quito: Organización de los Estados Americanos, Ediciones Ceplaes.

Blanes, J., and C. Gonzalo Flora 1982. *Campesino, migrante y "colonizador": Reproducción de la economía familiar en el Chapare tropical.* La Paz: Centro de Estudios de la Realidad Económica y Social.

Blanes, J., F. C. Gutierrez, J. H. Dandler, J. P. Bohrt, and L. L. Garcia. 1980. *Migración rural-rural en Bolivia: El caso de las colonias.* Serie Estudios Poblacionales no. 2. La Paz: Centro de Estudios de la Realidad Económica y Social.

Bromley, R. J. 1972. "Agricultural Colonization in the Upper Amazon Basin: The Impact of Oil Discoveries." *Tijdschrift voor Economische en Sociale Geografie* (Rotterdam), 63 (July–August): 278–294.

Bunker, S. G. (forthcoming). *Underdeveloping the Amazon: Extraction, Unequal Exchange and the Failure of State Planning*. Urbana-Champaign, IL: University of Illinois Press.

Cardoso, F. H., and G. Muller. 1977. *Amazonia: Expansão do capitalismo*. São Paulo: Paz e Terra.

Centro Nacional de Capacitación e Investigación para la Reforma Agraria (CENCIRA). 1975. *Informe de los aspectos socio-económicos de la colonización Jenaro Herrera*. Lima.

Clausner, M. D. 1973. *Rural Santo Domingo: Settled, Unsettled and Resettled*. Philadelphia, PA: Temple University Press.

Collin-Delavaud, A. 1973. "Migrations, colonisations et structures agraires sur la côte équatorianne." *Cahiers des Ameriques Latines* (Paris) 7 (September): 65–95.

Crist, R. E., and C. Nissly. 1973. *East from the Andes*. Gainesville, FL: University of Florida Press.

Darnel, B. W. 1972. "Land settlement in northeast Brazil: A study of seven projects. Ph.D. diss., McMaster University, Hamilton, Ont., Canada.

Delaine, B. L. 1980. "Coca Farming in the Chapare-Bolivia: A Form of Collective Innovation." Ph.D. diss., Saint Louis University, Missouri.

Dorner, P., ed. 1971. "Land Reform in Latin America: Issues and Cases." Madison: University of Wisconsin, Land Economics Monographs no. 3.

Fogel, R. 1979. "Colonización agraria y distribución espacial de la población: Características del proceso." *Revista Paraguaya de Sociologia* 44 (January–April): 109–64.

Galjart, B. 1968. *Itaguai: Old Habits and New Practices in a Brazilian Land Settlement*. Wageningen, Netherlands: Centre for Agricultural Publishing and Documentation.

Giraldo Samper, D., and L. Ladrón de Guevara. 1981. *Desarollo y colonización: El caso Colombiano*. Bogotá: Universidad de Santo Tomás.

Gladhart, P. M. 1972. "Capital Formation on the Ecuadorian Frontier: A Study of Human Investment and Modernization in the Rio Bambenos Cooperative. Agriculture Economics Research Report 72–5. Ithaca, New York: Cornell University, Department of Agricultural Economics.

Hiraoka, M., and S. Yamamoto. 1980. "A Agricultural Development in the Upper Amazon of Ecuador." *Geographical Review* (New York) 70, no. 4 (October): 423–45.

Ianni, O. 1979. *Colonização e contrareforma agraria na Amazonia*. Coleçao Sociologia Brasileira, vol. 11. Petrópolis, Brazil: Vozes.

Instituto Colombiano de la Reforma Agraria. 1974. *La colonización en Colombia: Una evaluación del proceso*. Bogotá.

International Labour Organisation/Regional Employment Programme for Latin America and the Caribbean. 1979. "Distribución del ingreso, migraciones y colonización: Una alternativa para el campesinado Boliviano." Docu-mento de Trabajo 176. Santiago: PREALC (July).

James, W. E. 1983. "Settler Selection and Land Settlement Alternatives: New Evidence from the Philippines." *Economic Development and Cultural Change* 31, no. 3 (April): pp. 571–86.

Kay, C. 1982. "Agrarian Change and Migration in Chile." In *State Policies and Migration: Studies in Latin America and the Caribbean*, edited by P. Peck and G. Standing. London: Croom Helm.

Kirby, J. 1976. "Agricultural Land-Use and the Settlement of Amazonia." *Pacific Viewpoint* (Wellington) 17, no. 1 (May): 105–32.

———. 1978. "Colombian Land Use Change and the Settlement of the Oriente." *Pacific Viewpoint* 19, no. 1 (May): 1–25.

Kleinpenning, J. M. G. 1975. *The Integration and Colonization of the Brazilian Portion of the Amazon Basin*. Nijmegen, Netherlands: Katholreke Universiteit, Geo-grafische en Planologisch Instituut.

Martine, G. 1982. "Colonisation in Rondônia: Continuities and Perspectives." In Peek and Standing, *State Policies and Migration*.

Martínez, H. 1976. *Las colonizaciones selváticas dirigidas en el Perú: Antecedentes, actualidad y perspectivas* (preliminary version). Estudios de Población y Desarollo. Lima: Centro de Población y Desarollo.

Matos Mar, J., and J. M. Mejía. 1982. "Casual Work, Seasonal Migration and Agrarian Reform in Peru." In Peek and Standing, *State Policies and Migration*.

Maxwell, S. 1980. "La differenciación en las colonias de Santa Cruz: Causas y efectos." Working Paper 13. Santa Cruz: Centro de Investigación Agrícola Tropical (CIAT).

Millet, A. 1974. "The Agricultural Colonization of the West Central Peten, Gua-temala: A Case Study of Frontier Settlement by Coopoeratives." Ph.D. diss., University of Oregon, Department of Geography.

Molion, M. A. C. 1975. "Colonization projects in the Amazon region of Brazil." Ph.D. diss., University of Wisconsin.

Moran, E. F. 1981. *Developing the Amazon*. Bloomington, IN: University Press.

Muller, K. D. 1974. *Pioneer Settlement in South Brazil: The Case of Toledo, Panama*. Publications of the Research Group for European Migration Problems, no. 19. The Hague: Martinus Nijhooff.

Partridge, W. L., and D. R. Kohler. 1982. "The Papaloapan Dam and Resettle-ment Project: Human Ecology and Health Impacts." In *Involuntary Mi-gration and Resettlement*, edited by A. Hansen and A. Oliver-Smith. Boulder, CO: Westview Press.

Partridge, W. L., and D. R. Kohler. 1982. "Cultural Transmission among Re-settled Mazatec: Incorporation of the Second Generation." Paper pre-sented at the American Anthropological Association Meeting, December.

Peek, P., and G. Standing. 1982. *State Policies and Migration: Studies in Latin America and the Caribbean*. London: Croom Helm.

Preston, D. A. 1978. *Rural Migration to the Ecuadorian Oriente*. Working Paper 223. Leeds: University of Leeds, School of Geography.

Recharte Bullard, J. 1982. "Prosperidad y pobreza en la agricultura de la Ceja de Selva." In Aramburú et al., *Colonización en la Amazonía*, pp. 105–61.

Roberts, R. L. 1975. "Migration and Colonization in the Colombian Amazonia: Agrarian Reform or Neo-latifundismo." Ph.D. diss., Syracuse University, Department of Anthropology.

Royden, T. C. 1973. "The Impact of Access Roads on Spontaneous Colonization, Chane-Piray Area, Department of Santa Cruz, Bolivia." M.S. thesis, Utah State University.

Ruche, A. 1978. "Situación del empleo y de los recursos humanos en las regiones de colonización del Instituto de Tierras y Colonización (ITCO) de Costa Rica." Documento de Trabajo 125. Santiago: PREALC.

Shoemaker, R. 1981. *The Peasants of El Dorado: Conflicts and Contradiction in a Peruvian Frontier Settlement*. Ithaca, NY: Cornell University Press.

Stewart, N. R. 1967. *Japanese Colonization in Eastern Paraguay*. Publicaion 1490. Washington, D.C.: National Academy of Sciences, National Research Council.

Takes, A. P. 1975. "Land Settlement and Resettlement Projects: Some Guidelines for their Planning and Implementation." Bulletin 14. Wageningen, Netherlands: International Institute for Land Reclamation and Improvement.

Thiesenhusen, W. C. 1965. "Agrarian Reform and Economic Development in Chile: Some Cases of Colonization." Land Tenure Center Paper no. 6 (November).

———. 1971. "Colonization: Alternative or Supplement to Agrarian Reform in Latin America." In Dorner, *Land Reform in Latin America*, pp. 209–25.

———. 1977. "A Venezuelan Agrarian Reform Settlement: Problems and Prospects." In *Tradition and Dynamics in Small-Farm Agriculture: Economic Studies in Asia, Africa and Latin America*, edited by R. D. Stephens, pp. 177–210. Ames, IA: Iowa State University Press.

Thome, J. R. 1971. "Improving Land Tenure Security." In Dorner, *Land Reform in Latin America*, pp. 229–40.

Vallejo, J. 1975. *La fuerza de trabajo en el proceso de desarollo de la agricultura capitalista*. Bogotá: Corporación Centro Regional de Población (CCRP) (January; unpublished).

Varese, S. 1974. "La Selva: Viejas fronteras, nuevas alternativas." *Participación* (Lima) 3, no. 5: 18–31.

Vessuri, H. M. C. 1973. *Colonización y diversificación agrícola en Tucuman*. Tucuman, Argentina: Universidad Naciónal de Tucuman, Departamento socioeconomico, Facultad de Agronomía y Zootécnica.

Vining, J. W. 1975. "The Rice Economy of Government Settlement Schemes in Guyana." *Interamerican Economic Affairs* (Washington, D.C.) 29, no. 1: 3–20.

Wiggins, S. L. 1979. "Tropical Land Settlement in Bolivia and Paraguay: A Comparative Study of Agrarian Policy." Bulletin 172. Manchester: University of Manchester, Department of Agricultural Economics.

Wood, C. H., and M. Schmink. 1979. "Blaming the Victim: Small Farmer Production in an Amazon Colonization Project." Quoted in G. Martine, "Recent Colonization Experiences in Brazil," in *Why People Move*, edited by J. Balan. Paris: UNESCO.

Zeballos-Hurtado, H. 1975. "From the Uplands to the Lowlands: An Economic

Analysis of Bolivian Rural-Rural Migration." Ph.D. diss., University of Wisconsin.

Ziche, J. 1979. "El desarollo de la situación socioeconómica de los colonos en el Eje Norte de colonización, Paraguay." *Revista Paraguaya de Sociología* 16, no. 45: 37–56.

Table 9.1
Proportions of colonists previously landless

| Country | Area | Landless (percentage) |
|---------|------|----------------------|
| Bolivia | Chapare zone[a] | 48 |
|  | Chapare[b] | 61 |
|  | Several zones[c] | 54 |
| Brazil | Coastal northeast colonies[d] | 62 |
| Colombia | Several zones[e] | 65 |
|  | Caqueta zone[f] | 93 |
|  | Lower Putumayo area[g] | 72 |
| Costa Rica | Rio Frio area[h] | 70 |
| Venezuela | Leonardo Ruiz Pinada settlement[i] | 50 |

Sources:
[a] Delaine (1980: 188).
[b] Blanes and Flora (1982: 30).
[c] Zeballos-Hurtado (1975: appendix).
[d] Darnel (1972: 340).
[e] INCORA (1974: 79).
[f] Roberts (1975: 265).
[g] Vallejo (1975: 44).
[h] Ruche (1978: 65).
[i] Thiesenhusen (1977: 182).

Table 9.2
Percentage of colonists coming from within frontier zones

| Country | Area | Moved within frontier zone |
|---------|------|---------------------------|
| Bolivia | Several zones[a] | 1 |
| Brazil | Toledo, Paraná[b] | 7 |
| | Trans-Amazon, 1970-74[c] | 36 |
| | Altamira[c] | 12 |
| | Maraba[d] | 56 |
| | Altamira-Maraba-Itaituba[d] | 41 |
| | North region, 1970[e] | 69 |
| | Rondônia[e] | 77 |
| | Acre[e] | 48 |
| | Amazonas[e] | 79 |
| | Roraima[e] | 93 |
| | Para[e] | 67 |
| | Aruapa[e] | 94 |
| | Treze, northeast coast[f] | 85 |
| Colombia | Caquetá zone colony[g] | 28 |
| | Caquetá zone[h] | 23 |
| Costa Rica | Rio Frio[i] | 48 |
| Ecuador | Coastal zone, 1962[j] | 56 |
| Peru | Tingo Maria-Tocache-Campanilla[k] | 30 |
| | Genaro Herrera and Marichin[k] | 100 |

Sources:
[a] Zeballos-Hurtado (1975: 76-82).
[b] Muller (1974: 17).
[c] Moran (1981: 81-82).
[d] Ianni (1979: 23).
[e] Cardoso and Muller (1977: 63).
[f] Darnel (1972: 325-330).
[g] Roberts (1975: 265).
[h] Giraldo and Ladrón (1981: 144).
[i] Ruche (1978: 64).
[j] Collin-Delavaud (1973: 72).
[k] Martínez (1976: 185).

Table 9.3
Percentage of colonists remaining in settlement (specified durations)

| Country | Area | Duration (years) | Percentage remaining |
|---------|------|------------------|----------------------|
| Bolivia | Cotoca[a] | 8 | 17 |
| | Alto Beni-Chimore-Yapacani[b] | 16 | 57 |
| | Several zones[c] | "plan to stay" | 90 |
| Brazil | CRC projects, coastal northeast[d] | 5-9 | 63 |
| | Trans-Amazon, to 1973[e] | 2-3 | 85-90 |
| | Ouro Preto[f] | 5 | 88 |
| Colombia | Caquetá colony[g] | "plan to stay" | 63 |
| | Four zones[h] | n.a. | 72 |
| Ecuador | Shushufindi[i] | 4-5 | 26 |
| | Las Esmeraldas, coast[j] | "plan to stay" | 86 |
| Guatemala | Manos Unidos, Peten[k] | 1 | 24 |
| Mexico | Las Margaritas, Papaloapan region[l] | 24 | 22 |
| Paraguay | Pirareta[m] | 21 | 50 |
| Peru | Genaro Herrera[n] | 2 | 48 |
| | Pichari[n] | n.a. | 52 |
| | Tingo Maria-Tochache-Campanilla[n] | n.a. | 70 |
| | Perez Godoy, Satipo region[o] | 2 | 66 |
| | | 8 | 33 |
| Venezuela | Leonardo Ruiz Pineda settlement[p] | 5 | 83 |

Sources:
[a] Crist and Nissly (1973: 136).
[b] Royden (1973: 7).
[c] Zeballos-Hurtado (1975: 84).
[d] Darnel (1972: 120).
[e] Kleinpenning (1975: 128).
[f] Molion (1975: 68).
[g] Roberts (1975).
[h] Giraldo and Ladrón (1981: 110).
[i] Haraoka and Yamamoto (1980).
[j] Barsky et al. (1982: 71).
[k] Millet (1974: 123).
[l] Partridge and Kohler (1982: 251).
[m] Fogel (1979: 43).
[n] Martínez (1976: 206).
[o] Shoemaker (1981: 118, 126).
[p] Thiesenhusen (1977: 180).
n.a., Not available.

Table 9.4
Colonist households with off-farm incomes

| Country | Area | Households with off-farm income (%) |
|---------|------|-------------------------------------|
| Argentina | Tucuman[a] | 50* |
| Bolivia | Chapare[b] | 35 |
| | Chane-Piray[c] | 12-85 |
| | Abanico, Santa Cruz | 50 |
| Brazil | Altamira PIC[e] | 75-100* |
| Colombia | San Andreas, Caquetá[f] | 45 |
| Ecuador | Rio Bambeno[g] | 55 |
| | Upper Amazon[h] | 65-70 |
| Mexico | Zacatal, Papaloapan region[i] | 50 |
| | Las Margaritas, Papaloapan[i] | 32 |
| Paraguay | El Eje Norte[j] | 62 |
| Peru | Jenaro Herrera, Selva Baja[k] | 100 |
| Venezuela | Luiz Pineda Reform settlement[l] | 75-100* |

Sources:
[a] Vessuri (1973).
[b] Blanes and Flora (1982: 124).
[c] Royden (1973: 57).
[d] Maxwell (1980: 18).
[e] Moran (1981: 94-95, 152-54).
[f] Roberts (1975: 227, 239, 265).
[g] Gladhart (1972: 32).
[h] Hiraoka and Yamamoto (1980: 436).
[i] Partridge et al. (1982: 251, 256).
[j] Ziche (1979: 48).
[k] Martínez (1976: 206).
[l] Thiesenhusen (1977).
*Estimated from statements like "half", or "most."

Table 9.5
Colonist evaluation of improvements

| Country | Area | Percentage saying life is: | | |
|---------|------|--------|------|-------|
| | | Better | Same | Worse |
| Bolivia[a] | | 74 | 20 | 6 |
| Brazil | Coastal NE[b] | 52 | 25 | 23 |
| Colombia | Caquetá[c] | 34 | 63 | 3 |
| Costa Rica | Rio Frío[d] | n.a. | n.a. | 25 |
| Ecuador | Rio Bambeno[e] | 96 | -- | 4 |
| Guatemala | Peten[f] | n.a. | n.a. | 33 |
| Paraguay | Seven zones[g] | 90 | n.a. | n.a. |
| Venezuela | Reform area[h] | 43 | n.a. | n.a. |

Sources:
[a] Zeballos-Hurtado (1975: 236).
[b] Darnel (1972: 338).
[c] Roberts (1975: 238).
[d] Ruche (1978: 71).
[e] Gladhart (1972: 38-39).
[f] Millet (1974: 52).
[g] Alegre (1977: 154).
[h] Thiesenhusen (1971).
n.a., Not available.

María Helena F. T. Henriques **10**

# The Colonization Experience in Brazil

## INTRODUCTION

Colonization in Brazil has followed many different models, varying from completely private schemes, through a combination of private interests with government support, to more recent examples where settlements have been organized and financed totally by the government. The objective of this study is to evaluate the latter, first as an investment directed toward the creation of more productive uses of land and human resources, and second, with respect to its demographic consequences. To accomplish the first objective, an attempt is made to put the directed colonization policy into historical perspective. This facilitates an assessment of its achievements and failures. The demographic consequences are examined by looking at the indicators of the basic demographic components (fertility, mortality, and migration) and the socioeconomic profile of the settled population.

The study is divided into three main sections. Section 1 gives a description and evaluation of colonization policy in Brazil, with emphasis on the Amazon experiment. Section 2 provides an analysis of the de-

From the Brazilian Institute of Geography and Statistics, Rio de Janeiro.

mographic and economic changes in the Rondônia settlement region during the last decade. The concluding section examines information on the settlers' families in order to evaluate their well-being as an indicator of the success of the policy.

## BRAZILIAN COLONIZATION POLICY: AIMS AND ACCOMPLISHMENTS

### Theoretical and institutional considerations

The colonization program in Brazil has encompassed a wide variety of activities, preceded by either government or private initiative. When initiated by private interests, profit has been the main motive. The aims of official colonization, on the other hand, are to provide land to the landless, to control illegal migration, and to strengthen national frontiers.

The role of the state in the supervision of colonization attempts started during the nineteenth century with the aim of directing European migration. Various incentives were offered by the government to encourage the creation of agricultural colonies, mainly in the southern states. Of those who came to Brazil during the nineteenth century, Germans formed a large majority in the first 50 years, while the Italians dominated during the second half of the period.

The 1930s were a landmark in Brazilian colonization policy, as it moved away from a concern with foreign migration and settlement to the relocation of Brazilians within the national territory. In 1938 the Divisão de Terras e Colonização (Department of Land and Colonization) was created in the Ministry of Agriculture to receive and settle poor Brazilian workers already engaged in agricultural activities. Its main objective was to reduce social tension in already occupied rural areas and to extend the area of land under cultivation. In 1954 this department was transformed into the Instituto Nacional de Imigração e Colonização (Institute of Immigration and Colonization), and in 1962 this was in turn put under the Ministry of Agriculture.

By this time it had become clear to government officials that directed colonization was not a simple matter, and that infrastructural facilities had to be provided if settlers were to be retained. Rather than proceeding in this direction, efforts were made to introduce land reform. A land statute was written and the question became a topic of national debate.

After the military takeover in 1964, the Instituto Brasileiro de Reforma Agrária (IBRA; Brazilian Institute of Land Reform) was created to study the question of land reform and to specify the conditions under which it could be promoted. However, no initiative was taken in that direction. In 1970 the Instituto Nacional de Colonização e Reforma Agrária (INCRA;

National Institute of Colonization and Land Reform) replaced IBRA, and at the same time it was decided to promote large-scale colonization along the national highways in the Amazon region.

The emphasis was put on provision of credit, minimum prices for output, and technical assistance in order to modernize agriculture and increase productivity. The land tenure system was left untouched. As Pacheco pointed out, "The government intervention in the agricultural sector took the form of granting privileges to private enterprise, not only through the creation of the physical infrastructure required for its expansion, and the establishment of credit and fiscal incentives, but also through the supply of agricultural labor" (Pacheco 1979: 26).

The First National Development Plan (1972–74) had a "Programa de Integração Nacional" (PIN: National Integration Program) as its main objective. This meant a reunion of abundant resources: land in the north and central west, unskilled labor in the northeast, and capital and skilled labor in the south and southeast. PIN and the construction of the northern highways were the main instruments of this plan. These objectives were reinforced in the Second National Development Plan, which placed its emphasis on the modernization of agriculture and the occupation of the frontier zones by private, national, or foreign enterprises. Colonization was given less weight, while mineral extraction and cattle raising were assigned a higher priority.

The fiscal incentives proved successful in attracting private investment. A large number of enterprises were established in the Amazon. These projects have done very little to create employment in the region, however, and have merely had the effect of driving small-scale peasant farmers out of the area. The peasants, expropriated and forced off the land, have moved to new areas. Unless stricter measures to protect their land rights are put into effect, this outward migration seems likely to continue. The new directed colonization policy is aimed at solving these problems. Seven of the ten projects designed under this new framework are located in Rondônia.

## Past and present experiences

In the past there have been four distinct frontier movements in Brazil: The Paulista plantation movement, the new coffee frontier movement in Paraná, the westward frontier movement, and the directed colonization policy in the Amazon (Merrick and Graham 1979: 126–28).

The Paulista plantation movement, from 1885 to 1930, developed out of the coffee expansion in São Paulo, which generated considerable foreign immigration, particularly to the southeastern part of the country. Coffee planters had a mixed background; among them were both landowners and merchants. This movement stimulated modernization in

Brazil. The increasing exports also provided favorable conditions for the rise of urban centers and the growth of financial institutions. As Redwood puts it, "[T]he coffee exports helped to provide both the capital and the financial system which later spurred the industrialisation of São Paulo, while the system of railways and highways connecting the coffee growing regions with the city of São Paulo and the port of Santos provided an important transportation infrastructure" (Redwood 1970: 160).

As exports of coffee declined, many of the coffee estate workers migrated to other rural and urban centers, where they played an important part in promoting industrial development.

The new coffee frontier movement lasted from 1940 to 1960, and was mainly located in Paraná. The settlement in the area was the initiative of a British company that bought 12,643 square kilometers in northern Paraná and subdivided the land into smaller plots. This well-established enterprise, which was sold to Brazilian entrepreneurs in 1944, is fairly described in Nicholls' words:

In general, rural lots were delineated according to a plan in which each farm was to be an independent unit with mixed activities. From the ridges—which the main transportation lines followed—the less frost-prone upper slopes were reserved for coffee while the lower-lying land was left for subsistence crops and pasture, with access to a spring-fed water supply. Widespread propaganda was used to attract settlers, the first of whom were offered free transportation, with the promise of full ownership of the land within four years and even some financial and technical assistance. Since it was first necessary to clear the forests, the initial economic activity was the exploitation of timber, followed by the planting of coffee, sugar cane, cereals and other crops. Livestock production also developed rapidly, particularly swine production on the smaller farms and cattle raising on the excellent planted pastures of the larger farms, many of which were established on lands less suited for coffee production. (Nicholls 1970: 75).

The population and economic growth that occurred in the area was without precedent in Brazilian history. Paraná became the destination for migratory flows. The type of land tenure system that was introduced accommodated many rural workers for many years to come, and it was only in the 1970s, because of changes in land use, that many of these workers had to leave Paraná. Table 10.1 indicates the direction of movement in Brazil from 1940 to 1980. Rondônia, Acre, Roraima, Amapá, and Fernando de Noronha may be excluded from the analysis because of their small populations and Federal Territory status, which was recently modified for the firtst two territories. Among other areas, the data show that in the 1940s Paraná experienced the highest rates of both urban and rural growth. The data also show that the rural growth in Paraná was its most distinctive feature, since it was almost double that in any other state. The 1950s showed an increase in urbanization in all areas, although it was highest in Paraná. It shared, therefore, the double frontier characteristic, a rural upsurge in the 1940s, followed by an urban breakthrough in the 1950s (Waibel 1955).

In the 1950s, however, there was also some movement toward the rural areas of northern states. It was a spontaneous movement of short duration, and its immediate consequence was the introduction of commercial agriculture in the area. Rice, formerly produced on a subsistence basis, became a commercial crop. This did not benefit the large majority of the agricultural labor force, however. As a result there was an increase in out-migration from rural areas stimulated by the pattern of income and land concentration.

During the 1960s there was an increase in government control over development activities in Brazil. Work began on the foundation of the new capital, Brasília, in the interior and on the construction of highways connecting several regions of the country. Given this impulse, the agricultural frontier expanded and began to incorporate millions of hectares of new land, potentially exploitable to serve big business interests.

This was the westward frontier movement. Forestry and subsistence agriculture dominated initially as poor peasants entered the area looking for land. The construction of a highway gave an impetus to commercialization by providing a means of transporting frontier-grown staples to the southeastern urban markets.

The Goías and Mato Grosso settlements had both an urban and a rural component. The first was directly connected to the building of the new capital, Brasília, and to the growth of intermediate cities, such as Goiânia and Anápolis. The rural growth in Mato Grosso de Goías was due to a flourishing system of agriculture based on rice, corn, beans, and coffee.

The westward frontier movement differs from the Paulista plantation movement and the new coffee frontier movement in Paraná in at least two ways. First, the government played a key role in the settlement process rather than private capital, and second, urban growth was more significant than rural growth. The expansion of agriculture was made possible by bringing new land under cultivation and creating enclosures for cattle raising. In addition, the majority of the migrants in this case came from different states. On the Paulista frontier, foreign immigrants had played a major role. On the Paraná frontier, more than three-fifths of the migrants came from the richer areas to the south of São Paulo. Of the westward migrants, on the other hand, approximately four-fifths were small peasants coming from the poor north and northeastern areas of the country (Redwood 1970: 179).

The Amazon frontier started in the 1970s. Here public investment was the rule. The construction of the Trans-Amazon Highway and the colonization policy were both part of the PIN. The highway network had three parts: The Transamazón, the Cuiabá-Porto Velho, and the Belém-Brasília highways. The idea behind this network was to transform the Amazon land into fertile land and to ease population pressure in the most densely populated rural areas of the northeast. As for the development policy embodied in the PIN, the main objective was to create new growth centers and to reduce regional imbalances. Other objectives were to:

a. extend the economic frontiers to the banks of the Amazon river;

b. create the conditions to integrate the region into the market economy;

c. establish conditions for the effective agricultural transformation of the semi-arid region of the northeast;

d. redirect the northeast labor migration to the humid valleys of this region and to the new agricultural frontiers, thus avoiding their migration to the urban areas of the central-south; and

e. assure the northeast of federal government support and stimulate a process of industrialization (Chaloult, 1979, p. 2).

The government not only put forward these objectives, but initiated a series of decrees to achieve them.

It defined a priority area along the Transamazon Highway for the implementation of agrarian reform; created the Regional Department of INCRA (National Institute for Settlement and Land Reform); determined that the agrarian reform projects should include 100,000 family units; called for the organisation of 100 cooperatives and for studies on the socio-economic conditions of the area; called for the granting of rural landholding titles in favour of those squatters actually occupying the land and, finally, stated that the resources for the whole enterprise should be provided by the INCRA and the PIN (Chaloult, 1979, p. 4).

The application of this policy in the area freed 6.5 million hectares in the priority zone and 2.2 million square kilometers situated in a 100-kilometer-wide strip on either side of the Amazon highways, thus enabling the government to distribute the land better.

These structural changes were expected to operate within the framework of what was called "rural urbanism." This involved three elements called *agrovilas, agrópolis, rurópolis.* The agrovila was the basic unit, a residential area with about 50 families containing an administrative center, a soccer field, an elementary school, a health unit, and a small commercial center. For each 20 agrovilas, there was an agrópolis, which was expected to have a cooperative, and elementary and a secondary school, a bank, and a post office. The rurópolis was the largest unit, and was to serve as a major service center, with an airport, a hospital, and technical offices, as well as the processing plants for agricultural products such as cotton, rice, and sugar.

Basic services were to be provided to the incoming settlers by several federal agencies. INCRA was made responsible for the demarcation and provision of the lots, for construction of modest houses, and initially for provision of education and health-care facilities. The ACAR (Associação de Crédito e Assistência Rural) was to give assistance in technical matters. The Bank of Brazil was to provide credit at low interest rates, while the CIBRAZEM (Companhia Brasileira de Armazenamento) was expected to guarantee minimum prices and provide storage for the produce. COBAL (Companhia Brasileira de Alimentos) was given the responsibility of distributing food to the settlers at low cost. The production units were to be 100-hectare plots for growing both subsistence and commercial crops (Wood and Schmink 1978: 7–8).

Unfortunately, however, the whole operation was a failure. The scheme, prepared by a group of technocrats in Brasília, proved to be too sophisticated for the Amazon area. The peasants were not used to centralized planning. The implementation costs were also very high, giving a low rate of return on the project, and it was in fact impossible to put all the ideas into practice.

The INCRA settlement target for the 1971–74 period was 100,000 families; by 1974 it had succeeded in settling only 5717, in the Marabá, Altamira, and Itaituba projects (Wood and Schmink 1978: 8). Inadequate provision of seed and other inputs, loss of production, settlers' indebtedness, and lack of transportation, credit, and storage facilities were largely responsible for the failure of the scheme. In analyzing the history of the Trans-Amazon project, it is clear that "to a large extent, low agriculture productivity in the first years of the colonization project was attributable not to a failure on the part of the colonists to produce, but to the inadequate functioning of the systems designed to support production and commercialisation" (Wood and Schmink 1978: 17–18).

By that time, however, government priorities had changed. Emphasis on social goals had given way to concerns of a purely economic nature. The new policy guidelines advocated the division of the area into 500- to 3000-hectare plots, supposedly to attract large agricultural and livestock enterprises, foreign and national, to occupy the Amazon. In consequence, land prices rose and became an object of speculation. Most of the small peasants left their lots (in 1980, 60 percent of the project lots did not belong to their original owners) or sold them, which was illegal according to the project rules. The ones who stayed became sharecroppers or were involved in leasing or piecework contracts.

Colonization in Brazil has thus involved large inter-regional (or intercontinental) transfers of labor (the exception being the recent Amazon experience), but no significant agrarian reforms, though the Paulista and

Paraná settlements did make important tenancy changes. All four frontier expansions appear to have followed the classic Brazilian pattern of raising agricultural output by increasing the area cultivated rather than increasing productivity. Abundant land resources and improved transport made this a logical strategy, at least until the rise in fuel costs. In more recent years, the pattern of increased output has become associated with larger units of operation and more capital-intensive and mechanized forms of production. More public-sector involvement is emerging, with the emphasis on extensive use of fiscal subsidies and the provision of infrastructure such as highways and marketing facilities. However, public policy on colonization has been confused and hesitant. Recent public-sector initiatives have not been largely successful, except in Rondônia; here some of the earlier mistakes have been corrected, but new problems have emerged (Merrick and Graham 1979: 128).

## Rondônia: The last frontier

### The plan

In the second half of the 1960s, the federal government started advertising the availability of land in Rondônia. The campaign was massive in rural areas with high population densities, and attracted a much greater response than originally expected. The major concentration of the new migrants was along the BR–364 highway. As the areas close to it became occupied, the movement spread to the hinterland, immediately causing conflicts with the Indians who were either in their original settlements or in the reserved areas. Private enterprises, calling themselves settlement companies, started to demarcate and illegally sell land to migrants. Conflicts over the land started in the area and by the late 1960s the situation in Rondônia was chaotic. At that point INCRA started to play a decisive role in the area, coordinating the land distribution and establishing a directed colonization scheme.

INCRA's activities in Rondônia concentrated on two major areas: the legalization of land occupancy and the settlement of newcomers. These activities were to be carried out through 12 program components which included land distribution, territorial organization, administrative organization, settlement, organization of agricultural units, promotion and execution of basic public works, and provision of infrastructure. All these were entirely INCRA's responsibility to develop. The remaining programs concerned health, housing, education, credit, cooperatives, and commercialization of production, and were to be coordinated by INCRA but implemented by other organizations (INCRA 1971).

The territorial organization program was the most successful, despite the difficulties in coping with the rising demand for land. It basically aimed at land demarcation and distribution and the establishment of sites for the public services to operate. The major difficulty with the program, however, was its rigidity, particularly with regard to the size of farms, which was 100 hectares in the Amazon.

The other programs were beset with difficulties. No evaluation of the area chosen for settlement was made. The administrative staff had little interaction with local people. Settlers took almost no part in planning, and were called upon only to build their shacks and clean the dirty roads near the plots.

The program relating to the implementation of a physical infrastructure was one of the worst failures. The BR–364, the only connecting road, has been badly maintained. Schools and qualified teachers are in short supply. Public health service units are few, and most of the time the settlers and their families have to go to private doctors, whose services are usually poor and expensive. Storage facilities are inadequate and have been a source of corruption.

Credit concessions have not worked as originally expected. First, the settler has to own land to qualify for credit. Second, the applicant must give details about the project, specify the nature of the operation, and indicate time limits for the release of funds. Moreover, after the first payment, release of the remaining funds is dependent on an evaluation of how the first funds were spent. These stringent conditions have been difficult to apply in practice. None of the Rondônia settlers have a clear title to their land. Most of them are illiterate or do not know how to create a credit project. And, finally, there are not enough officials to check the spending of money, which means a major delay in the release of further funds.

Thus, in spite of improvements in the settlement policy that was first attempted in the Amazon, the Rondônia model has some basic weaknesses. In the word of Pacheco (1979: 26):

The absence of adequate criteria and flexibility throughout the various programs indicates not only the lack of knowledge but also the distance between the institution responsible for the colonization and the reality and interests of the target population. Therefore, though there is recognition of the need to have a structure that can be adapted to several regions, these programs are in fact rigid and authoritarian models. There is also a gap between the detailed planning and the implementation of activities. The large majority of the programs, when implemented, especially the ones relating to the basic social and physical infrastructure, fall far below the planned targets.

Today there are seven colonization projects operating in Rondônia. They are mainly located along the BR–364 highway, encompassing between 225,000 and 500,000 hectares.

Not only is the settlement operation behind schedule in all respects, but it has underestimated demand for land. In 1977 there were already 30,000 persons waiting for plots. The plan was to have 23,000 families settled by 1980. In 1981, INCRA decided to reduce the size of the plot to 30 hectares to accommodate more people. The work of plot demarcation is proceeding at a slow pace, however, and the programs responsible for providing a physical infrastructure, credit, technical assistance, and storage have made little progress.

Why then does the government insist on this type of intervention? Direct colonization is a type of social investment through which the government pursues two objectives: to secure its own position and to provide the basis for capital accumulation in remote areas.

In order to promote capital accumulation in the region, the government has to create a labor reserve to be used by large-scale private enterprises. The redirection of surplus rural population to frontier areas through settlement schemes provides labor at a lower cost as the workers obtain their subsistence from their own plots. "In the directed colonisation projects, based on family units, a trend was observed that within 2 or 3 generations the process of small farming starts enabling the formation of a rural reserve army. . . . The plot provides for the workers' subsistence through the periods of seasonal unemployment, and at the peak of labour demand they are hired as paid workers by the enterprises" (Pacheco 1979: 106–7).

### The reality

The first government-directed colonization project created in Rondônia was Ouro Preto. It aimed at settling 300 families. However, news quickly spread that the government was giving away good quality land in the area, and people with different interests immediately moved in. The original intended capacity of Ouro Preto was increased to accommodate 500 families.

As the migratory movement into the area strengthened, INCRA set up new projects in an effort to cope with the quickly rising demand for land. During this early stage, the difficulties were enormous. The demarcation of plots and the construction of access roads proceeded slowly, due to the need to clear the jungle; resources were insufficient to put the whole scheme into operation as planned, and there were already squatters, previous landlords, and other people claiming rights over the land.

These difficulties did not discourage newcomers, however. According to Martine, migration into the area began to be significant in the years 1970–74, and further increased in 1974 as a consequence of the change in government priorities in the Amazon. In 1975 a receiving center for migrants was opened in Vilhena, a southern city near the territorial boundaries with the state of Mato Grosso. The stream of migration peaked sharply in 1976 and then declined, due to government counter-propaganda in the sending areas. The movement was at its most intense during the dry months of June, July, and August, when the whole BR–364 was passable. According to the available data, 5587 migrants entered during the second half of 1978 through Vilhena. From January to October 1979, the number increased to 36,164. The composition of the migration flows was also different. Mato Grosso, which had earlier provided one-third of the migrants, reduced its share to about 20 percent, while Paraná increased its share to almost 50 percent (Martine 1979: 8–9).

In spite of the difficulties, INCRA appears to have done much better in Rondônia than in other settlements. As data in Table 10.2 reflect, the area brought under colonization was quite significant, as was the number of settled families. INCRA also claims that Rondônia is now self-suffi-cient in food and is even exporting food to other regions of Brazil and to foreign countries.

These gains did not go unnoticed by the federal government. The territory was upgraded to the status of a state, and, just before the political-administrative change, General Figueiredo, then president of Brazil, went to the area and raised the final settlement objective to 25,000 families and distributed several land titles, especially in Ouro Preto.

INCRA's achievement needs to be examined from the point of view of two other objectives, however: whether it has improved the settlers' quality of life, and whether it has reduced regional inequalities.

With regard to the first objective, evaluations conducted in the Ouro Preto (Pacheco 1979) and Gy-Paraná (Gonçalves 1981) projects have iden-tified several problems experienced by the settlers. In particular, the services provided by INCRA such as credit, transport, warehousing, and social infrastructure were poor.

The intensity of the colonization scheme has also attracted to Rondônia many spontaneous migrants, with hopes of receiving some land. Their expectations have not been fulfilled, however. If they decide to stay in the area, there are three alternatives open to them to earn a living: squatting on unoccupied land, full- or part-time employment on some-one else's plot, or migration to the local urban areas in search of em-ployment in commerce or in a service sector.

The paving of the main road, the BR–364 highway, which is currently under way with the assistance of the World Bank, is expected to lead to an increase in land values and greater viability for agricultural pro-duction and distribution in Rondônia.

James O'Connor argues that directed colonization has fulfilled two roles. On one hand it has given poor landless peasants access to land, thus easing their desire for redistribution of private land in other regions of Brazil; on the other hand, it has opened up new areas for capital investment by bringing manpower to formerly unutilized land (O'Connor 1977).

Fears have often been expressed that small-scale family agriculture may provoke rather than absorb migratory flows in the Amazon. There is also the question of its economic viability. However, there is no evidence that people who become settlers are by nature a group with a high propensity to migrate, or that settlement policies per se enhance population movements rather than stabilize them. The economic viability of small family farms in frontier areas obviously depends partly on the level of technology employed and the consequent levels of productivity. However, it is not the use of traditional technology that keeps family agriculture at a subsistence level, so much as market conditions that prevent the producers from making a decent living from the sale of their output. The economic forces that perpetuate this situation therefore need to be investigated. These issues apart, there are other relevant considerations, such as providing access to land and means of employment to landless peasants.

## SOCIO-ECONOMIC AND DEMOGRAPHIC CHANGES IN THE RONDÔNIA AREA

Rondônia, which is a new state of the union, has an area of 243,044 square kilometers and is located at the junction of the north and central-west regions of Brazil. Despite the heavy immigration during the 1970s, it still has one of the smallest population densities in the country, 2.5 inhabitants per square kilometer.

Porto Velho, the capital city, is the major urban center. In 1970 its population represented 49.7 percent of the total population of the state, but it has decreased in importance as other urban centers directly related to the colonization projects have emerged.

Population growth in the area has been uneven. Between 1950 and 1960 the population increased by nearly 90 percent, but in the following decade the increase was only 58 percent; during the 1970–80 period, however, the population grew by more than 400 percent.

### Family and Household Characteristics

Changes in family composition in Rondônia have been directly related to the requirements for becoming a settler. The percentage of spouses and children has increased in both urban and rural areas. The fact that only 2.7 percent of the rural population consists of relatives other than spouses and children indicates that the extended family system is not common in the area.

The quality of life seems to have improved in the last 20 years, as measured by the access of the population to basic services and the possession of household durables, though the changes in urban areas have been more significant than those in rural areas (Table 10.3). In rural areas the only noteworthy change is in the ownership of radio sets, which has increased substantially, thus easing communication with the rest of society.

## Demographic Characteristics

The sex ratio (i.e., the ratio of men to women) was already high in Rondônia by 1970. For the total population, it was 113.2 men to 100 women, and it remained at that level in 1980. The urban sex ratio was close to 100 during the period, an unfamiliar pattern for Brazil, where women usually predominate in urban areas.

Persons aged less than 20 years represented 53 percent of males and 60 percent of females in 1970. By 1980 the proportion of males under 20 had increased to 55 percent. In 1970 the 20–49 age group represented only 33 percent of the urban population for both sexes, about the same for rural females, and 43 percent for rural males. In 1980, the percentage of persons aged 20–49 had increased to 36 percent for the urban population, but had decreased to 36 percent for rural males.

Rondônia is also distinguished from other Brazilian states in that it is the only one where the urban population decreased in relative terms during the 1970s. This was largely due to the colonization schemes. According to the 1970 census, urban males represented 50.6 percent of the total male population; in 1980 this figure had dropped to 44.8 percent. The corresponding figures for females were 57.1 and 48.3 percent, respectively. The ratio of nonmarried to "in a marital situation" dropped from 0.88 in 1970 to 0.65 in 1980 in urban areas. In the rural areas the change was even more dramatic: it dropped from 0.79 to 0.49.

The data on the number of years of schooling show that the educational profile of the population is very low. In 1970, the urban males had had on average 2.9 years and urban females 2.7 years of schooling. The figures for the rural population were even lower, as expected: both males and females had had on average 1.2 years of schooling. The figures for 1980 reflect the profile of the migrants to the settlement schemes during the period 1970–80. In 1980 the urban males had had on average 3.4 years and the urban females 3.2 years of schooling. A similar change was observed in the rural population, where the average number of years of schooling had increased to 1.7 years.

The data on the place of birth show that Rondônia is quite heavily weighted toward migrants. The percentage of native-born population dropped in the 1970–80 period from 50.5 to 32 percent for males and from 58 to 35 percent for females. In 1970, people from the north and northeast represented 50 percent of the migrant population; in 1980 the inflow of migrants was mostly from the central-south (Minas Gerais, Paraná, and Mato Grosso). While Minas Gerais is traditionally an emigration state, the exit from Paraná and Mato Grosso is directly related to the end of frontier colonization in these states, and to declining employment opportunities.

Changes in the age structure of the migrant population were noticeable over the period. The mean age of the migrants was 30.6 years in 1970, and it was the same for both rural and urban migrants. By 1980 this had dropped to 26.4 for urban migrants and 24.1 for rural migrants.

The sudden increase in migration made Rondônia the Brazilian state with the largest proportion of migrants relative to its resident population. In 1980 two-thirds of Rondônia's residents were not living in the municipality where they were born. The distribution of migrants was not even among the seven Rondônia municipalities. The older areas, Guajará–Mirim (30.98 percent) and Porto Velho (43.75 percent), had a smaller share of migrants, in spite of the latter being the capital city. In all the other municipalities (Ariquemes, Cacoal, Gy-Paraná, Pimenta Bueno, and Vilhena) more than 80 percent of the population were migrants. As all of these are the sites of colonization projects, this demonstrates the effectiveness of the projects in attracting people to Rondônia.

### The natural growth of the population

The analysis in the previous section shows that the contribution of migration to the new population profile for Rondônia during the 1970–80 decade was substantial. Natural growth was also remarkable, however.

Brazil experienced a fertility decline during the 1970s. The results of the 1980 census show that:

a. overall fertility dropped by 28 percent during the period 1970–80, although the decline was uneven in different states as well as in rural and urban areas;

b. the decline in urban areas in the southern and southeastern states started as early as 1965;

c. following them in this decline were the rural areas of these same regions and the urban areas of the less developed regions;

d. finally, around 1975, the decline spread into the rural areas of the north, northeast, and central-west regions.

Rondônia did not escape from this general trend. The 1970 census showed very high fertility levels, even higher than those appearing in the previous census. But, despite the drop in 1980, both urban and rural fertility levels were higher than the averges for Brazil as a whole, as reflected in Table 10.4. The data also show that in spite of the considerable drop, fertility in the area remained high.[1] Urban fertility in Rondônia in 1980 was higher by almost two children than in urban Brazil as a whole.

Mortality estimates were also derived from the census data.[2] As in the case of fertility, the Rondônia levels are higher than for Brazil as a whole. The differences in mortality account for nearly 10 years of life expectancy. Because mortality levels in urban and rural areas of Rondônia are very similar, estimates were made for the total population of the area, only differentiating by sex. Table 10.5 provides the estimates of life expectancy at birth as a summary indicator of mortality.

While there is a high natural growth rate, the rural areas in Rondônia are also experiencing a high rate of population growth due to migration. It is urgent, therefore, for local authorities to consider the need to create jobs, not only for migrants but also for the next generation.

The population growth of 400 percent experienced in Rondônia in the decade 1970–80 was unprecedented in Brazilian history, even in frontier areas. It was largely due to immigration, but there is little likelihood that it will be followed by a substantial out-migration. This is because there are not many other places to go. Rural frontiers are closed and the government, now confronting a serious economic crisis, is unlikely to develop new agricultural areas. Nor is large-scale migration to the urban areas of more developed regions likely to occur, because of the absence of job opportunities and the low levels of education among the population of Rondônia.

## Economic Characteristics of the Population

In 1970, 65 percent of the female labor force was in the services sector. In 1980 this had decreased to 59 percent, but the services sector and commerce together accounted for 75 percent. Employment in rural areas, though rising tenfold during the period, was still quite limited. There was, however, a major change in its composition. In 1970, 53 percent of the rural female labor force was in the services sector. By 1980 this had dropped to 23 percent. The proportion of the female labor force in the farming sector had, however, increased to 66 percent. This change was largely due to the colonization policy, and most of these women were unpaid family workers.

Between 1970 and 1980 the male labor force increased fourfold, and rapid changes in the labor market were needed to absorb this. Employment in agriculture and manufacturing grew at 4.5 percent per annum, in commerce and construction the annual rate was around 2 percent, and the percentage of the male labor force in the services sector doubled during the period. Again, the changes in the rural labor force were most significant. Male employment in rural areas grew more than fivefold during the decade, and more than 80 percent of males were directly employed in agriculture. Male employment in the services sector was almost negligible.

These changes in agricultural employment are a reflection of the changes in the land tenure system. The availability of data from the agricultural censuses carried out every five years has made it possible to examine this issue. From 1970 to 1975, there was a substantial reduction in the overall mean size of plots as well as in the mean size of the larger holdings (Table 10.6). There was, however, some increase in the mean size of the 10 to 100 hectare class. Although this may be regarded as an improvement in land distribution, it led to another problem in the region, that of mini-farms. The number of plots of less than 10 hectares grew tenfold between 1970 and 1975, although the area occupied by them increased only sixfold. By 1980, however, there had been a reversal of this trend. The overall mean size of plot had still declined slightly, partly as a consequence of the decline in the mean size of the 200 to 500 hectare class, which had the highest share in the total area. All other classes of holdings increased in mean size, albeit marginally. The increase that deserves to be singled out as an indication of the process of concentration, however, is that experienced by the very large farms. The mean size for this group increased by almost 75 percent, which represented a clear change with respect to the previous trend.

Table 10.7 describes changes throughout the decade according to landholding status. From 1970 to 1975, a large increase in the proportion of plots held by landowners can be observed. The number of plots occupied by tenants and sharecroppers decreased in absolute terms, both in number and area. Even though squatting almost doubled in absolute terms, it decreased relatively. In 1975 squatters occupied almost a third of all holdings in Rondônia, and a fifth of the area under colonization. The next five years saw a reversal of these trends. The number and area of plots directly used by their owners decreased in relative importance. There was an increase in tenancy and sharecropping arrangements, though their importance in relative terms remained low. Squatting, however, multiplied several times, and at the time of the 1980 agricultural census, accounted for more than 50 percent of the number and area of holdings.

Tables 10.6 and 10.7 provide a clear indication that government efforts to effect a distribution and use of land consistent with its land settlement policy lasted only for the first five years following the implementation of the settlement projects. After that, the process took its own course and land distribution became more skewed, with increases both in very large farms and in squatting.

While the total population grew by about 400 percent, employment in agriculture increased by more than 850 percent. The area under cultivation also increased tremendously, 13 times in the case of permanent crops and six times for seasonal crops. The number of tractors multiplied almost tenfold, as did the number of head of cattle and poultry. There is thus no doubt that the structure and organization of the economy changed considerably. The colonization projects and the migratory stream they attracted brought a new dynamism to the area.

Table 10.8 indicates the distribution of income among the various population percentiles in 1980, from the richest to the poorest. The richest are identified with a plus sign and the poorest with a minus sign. The income distribution was quite concentrated, as might be expected. Differences between urban and rural males were not important, nor were differences by sex in the urban population. For rural women, however, income distribution was more unequal. The data show that the richest 10 percent of urban males earned about 46 percent of the total male income, while for urban females and rural males the figure was about 43 percent. In the case of rural females, however, the richest 10 percent received 52 percent of all the income.

The data also show that while the poorest 75 percent of urban females earned a third of the total urban female income; in the case of rural females the poorest 75 percent received only 17 percent.

It appears, therefore, that the process of development in Rondônia has preserved the inequalities commonly found in other regions. In spite of the social goals behind the land redistribution policy, the uneven income distribution pattern has persisted.

## THE RONDÔNIA SETTLERS: ACHIEVEMENTS AND FRUSTRATIONS

This section briefly describes the socioeconomic and living conditions of settlers in Rondônia. It also attempts to analyze their future intentions. The analysis is based on data collected in the socioeconomic survey conducted by INCRA in most colonization projects in 1977 and in a sociodemographic survey carried out in the area in June and July of 1980.

For purposes of comparison, two projects were selected, Ouro Preto and Gy-Paraná. The former is the oldest; it has good quality soil and is considered well structured by INCRA. The latter is one of the newest, lacking basic services and with a high turnover of INCRA administrators.

### Living conditions and health of settlers

Table 10.9 provides information on housing materials, water, and sewage facilities. The data show that a large majority of families have wooden houses, often constructed with material obtained while clearing the land. In Ouro Preto, more than half, regardless of their landholding status, had wooden-frame houses. In Gy-Paraná, the situation was more precarious. Here the majority of the settlers and a much higher proportion of the *agregados* live in log cabins.[3] As a general rule, these are small houses, with one family room and only one or two bedrooms where all family members sleep and the food is stored. The houses have cracks between the logs and are so poorly built that it is difficult to prevent the entry of disease-transmitting mosquitoes.

Piped water is almost nonexistent. Again, Ouro Preto seems to be doing better than Gy-Paraná, and within each area settlers are doing better than agregados. However, there is ample scope for improvement in the provision of water facilities in both projects.

The percentage of agricultural workers who have no sewage facilities is large in both projects, and it is higher for agregados.

With these living conditions, the health of the settlers is naturally poor. Since the output from the plot depends mainly on the family members' labor, their health is of considerable importance. Disease in the settler's family might not only make it impossible for them to obtain their subsistence from the plot, but might also force them to sell it to pay for medical treatment.

Indeed, it is a common belief in the project areas that the abandonment and/or sale of the plots by their first owners is often due to sickness. Analysis of data (on whether or not settlers and agregados had interrupted work because of sickness during the month before the survey, and the type of medical care received) gives some idea of the health of the population in the area (Table 10.10). The data show that about 65 percent of settlers and 57 percent of agregados had to interrupt their work at least once for health reasons. The smaller figure for agregados does not necessarily mean that they are healthier. It may simply mean that, though sick, they could not stop working, as they depended on the landowner for their survival. As for the type of illness, the survey reported that malaria (11.1 percent in Ouro Preto and 6.5 percent in Gy-Paraná) and influenza (21 percent in Ouro Preto and 23.9 percent in Gy-Paraná) were the most common illnesses. The former often resulted in interruption of work for periods of between one and three months. It should be mentioned that a large majority of the settlers could not tell the name of the disease, but indicated symptoms such as weakness, exhaustion, and lack of energy, and have therefore been grouped under the category of "other" diseases. About half of them were not seen by any doctor. In Gy-Paraná, approximately 28 percent of the agregados were seen at pharmacies.

Data were also obtained for the health of settlers' and agregados' family members. The total number of persons considered to have been sick during the month prior to the survey was approximately 10 percent in each project. Influenza and malaria were again the two most frequent diseases. The incidence of malaria was higher in Ouro Preto than in Gy-Paraná. Malaria, together with chronic malnutrition and poor food habits, slowly exhausts resistance to new diseases. In both projects, 70 percent of the sick persons had to interrupt their work or other normal activity.

The health situation was therefore as bad as it could be and appears to have adversely affected the quality of the family labor force.

## Migration patterns

More than 99 percent of settlers in both projects were born in states other than Rondônia. The data in Table 10.11 show that a relatively large share of migrants came from Minas Gerais, followed by the whole group of northeastern states.

The distribution of migrants by state of previous residence leads to even higher concentration than that by state of birth. The data show that 90 percent of the migrants came from Minas Gerais, Espírito Santo, Paraná, and Mato Grosso. The major difference between the projects is the relative position of Mato Grosso and Paraná as previous state of residence. The former had a higher share in Ouro Preto, the latter in Gy-Paraná, in each case accounting for nearly one-third of the migrants.

Migrants from Rio de Janeiro and São Paulo appear to have come to Rondônia mainly through Mato Grosso and Paraná, as did their northeastern counterparts. Roughly a quarter of the migrants born in Minas Gerais had come directly to Rondônia, but a sizable proportion had come through Mato Grosso. A very large proportion of migrants from Espírito Santo had come direct. Finally, migrants from other states had mostly come through Paraná.

Table 10.12 provides information on year of arrival in Rondônia. The survey data indicate that 37 percent of the settlers in Gy-Paraná arrived in 1976 or later. Shorter lengths of residence in Rondônia are even more characteristic of the agregados: 59 percent in Ouro Preto and 74 percent in Gy-Paraná arrived after 1975.

## Land titles and infrastructural facilities

Receiving a plot does not mean ownership of it. Table 10.13 gives a breakdown of land titles at the time of the settlers' arrival. In 1980 there was a more marked trend toward land ownership in Ouro Preto. The percentage of settlers holding authorizations of occupation, the last step toward the final title of land ownership, was much higher in Ouro Preto than in Gy-Paraná. Following President Figueiredo's visit to the project area in 1981 this percentage further increased to 90 percent. However, the fact that a sizable proportion of the settlers had bought land shows that the practice of illegally buying and selling land did exist in the settlement areas.

Table 10.14 shows the extent to which settlers had access to credit. Differences between the projects are small. In 1977 more than one-third of the settlers in each project declared they had made use of credit. Data from 1980 suggest a reversal in this trend, though it is possible that the question, "Did you ever use credit?" was misinterpreted by some to mean, "Are you currently using credit?" or that the settlers represented a group different from the one that had answered the INCRA inquiry. Whatever the explanation, the fact remains that credit is not widely used, even though the importance of access to it is emphasized in the settlement policy.

For settlers who had ever used credit, the Banco do Brasil appears to have been the most important credit agency, accounting for approximately 20 percent of all transactions. For those who had never used credit, the fear of not being able to pay back the borrowed money and the feeling that the operation was more complicated than they could handle were the reasons most frequently cited.

Technical assistance is another institutional facility theoretically available to settlers. Table 10.15 shows the extent to which technical assistance had been received by settlers in 1977 and 1980.

No differences between projects are apparent from the data. The proportion of settlers who had received some form of technical assistance had increased to almost one-third in 1980. This was, however, very low for a project such as Ouro Preto, which had been operating for almost ten years.

At the time of their arrival, settlers had little experience of cooperatives or labor unions. In 1977 the INCRA survey found that only 7.8 percent had a cooperative affiliation. It should be mentioned, however, that these cooperatives had not come into existence through the settlers' own initiative, but were initiated by INCRA and were frequently criticized by the settlers themselves. By 1980 there was a sizable increase in the number of cooperatives, and in Gy-Paraná settlers had created a trade union that has been involved in many disputes to protect settlers' basic rights over their land.

Credit and technical assistance have also not been sufficiently widespread. On the contrary, they are heavily concentrated. Information from both surveys indicates that these services are biased in favor of permanent crops and large farms. For example, 100 percent of settlers with more than 30 hectares of temporary crops had received credit, as against 38 percent with less than 10 hectares. Similarly, 100 percent of smaller farms of 20 to 30 hectares, but with permanent crops, had received credit.

## Socioeconomic characteristics of the settlers

Education levels are extremely low in both project areas. The 1980 Socio-Demographic Survey data show that 48 percent of the settlers do not know how to read or write at all, 50 percent are functionally illiterate, and only 2 percent have some elementary education. They are usually helped by their wives, who play the role of record-keepers. Very often the latter were the most knowledgeable informants on basic aspects of production.

Past agricultural experience of selected settlers shows that they were far from being minifundia planters. One-third of them were familiar with cropping 25 hectares or more of land. The 1977 data (not presented here) show that agricultural production in Ouro Preto was more diversified than in Gy-Paraná, and productivity in the former project was higher than that in the latter. This may have been due to the relatively shorter period of operation of the Gy-Paraná project. However, wood extraction, which is a typical activity in the first few years of a project, also existed to a smaller extent in Gy-Paraná at the time of the survey.

By 1979–80, however, there had been a considerable increase in the area under cultivation, and production of the most important crops had increased in both projects. This is revealed by data from the Socio-Demographic Survey presented in Table 10.16. The advantage that Ouro Preto seems to have had in 1977 had apparently disappeared. By 1980 similar types of crops were being cultivated in both projects. The most important commercial crops such as coffee and cocoa, which started in Ouro Preto, were being grown in Gy-Paraná as efficiently as in the former, despite the lack of institutional help.

The lack of financial resources and the inadequate infrastructure provided by INCRA have led to the subdivision of plots and the emergence of the agregados. The latter are basically hired as sharecroppers, keeping only half or a third of what they produce.

The number of agregados grew in the second half of the 1970s, as the land assigned for settlement became more scarce. The Socio-Demographic Survey revealed that agregados constituted 30 percent of all settlers in Ouro Preto and 20 percent in Gy-Paraná.

If the agregados' search for a livelihood has led them to accept unfair conditions of work, the output of the settlers' plots is not sufficient to provide for the needs of their families. The Socio-Demographic Survey revealed, for instance, that in Gy-Paraná 33.5 percent of settlers and their family members worked as wage workers during the 1979–80 agricultural year (Pacheco 1982). The time spent away from their plots as wage earners was far from insignificant, as revealed by the data shown in Table 10.17.

During their periods as wage workers, the settlers left their own plots to the care of other family members, usually the eldest son. The perception of difficulties was higher in Ouro Preto than in Gy-Paraná. Lack of roads was mentioned as the major difficulty. It is surprising, however, that even under these conditions a large majority of the settlers and agregados in both projects said that their present situation was better than before (Table 10.18) and that they intended to stay (Table 10.19).

## CONCLUSIONS

The major objectives of the state in pursuing the settlement policy in Brazil were two: the provision of land and better living conditions for the rural worker, and the creation of a basis for capital accumulation in remote areas through the formation of a reserve army that would guarantee an adequate supply of cheap labor. One of the consequences of this type of strategy has been to stimulate population growth in the colonized area. Reliance on family labor for land development has also generated a demand for large families.

According to 1980 census results, natural growth was quite high in the area. The cumulative fertility was about six in urban and seven in rural areas. Mortality levels were also high. Life expectancy was almost ten years lower than the Brazilian average.

Changes in the land tenure system have been significant. Larger holdings experienced almost a doubling of their mean size between 1975 and 1980, a clear sign of a land concentration process. The proportion of landowners and squatters has also increased significantly in recent years. The latter represented more than 50 percent of the number and area of holdings in 1980, a sign that illegal land transactions are taking place in the colonization schemes.

The implementation of a colonization policy in Rondônia has not significantly enhanced people's well-being, as measured by the access of the population to basic services. The analysis of data from the field surveys shows that in 1980, 93 percent of the settlers' houses were made of unfinished wood. A similar percentage of houses had no source of water except a nearby river or an untreated well. Sewage facilities were also lacking; 73 percent of the settlers had none at all and 22 percent had only a rudimentary cesspool.

Health standards were found to be low among settlers and agregados. Disease was part of their lives. In 1980, 60 percent of the settlers reported that they had been sick during the month prior to the survey, and most of them had had to interrupt their normal activity as a result.

The lack of institutional support was also evident from field surveys. The only aspect that seemed to have improved through the years was land demarcation and allotment of plots. Credit and technical assistance did not reach more than one-third of the settlers, benefiting only the large farmers and those who grew commercial crops.

In spite of all these difficulties, the analysis shows that the settlers' economic performance is not bad, as measured by their agricultural output. The majority of settlers felt that they were doing better than before, and a large majority expressed the intention of remaining in the area.

However, population projections show that Rondônia will face a considerable increase in population during the 1980s. Only a policy of more equal distribution of wealth among the different regions can slow down the rhythm of population growth in the near future. An attempt should also be made to create a westward movement within Rondônia. In the older city of Guajará-Mirim, on the boundary between Brazil and Bolivia, trade activities could easily be developed, as well as basic industries which use local raw materials such as chestnuts and cocoa. Porto Velho, the northern capital city, could be developed as an administrative and cultural center for the area. This has perhaps already started, as many federal agencies have local headquarters there, and there are plans to create a university. In the rural areas, more demarcation of plots and legalization of land ownership is needed. The government still owns a vast proportion of the area available for development, and the number of settled families could easily be increased to 50,000. The size of new plots could be reduced, as most surveys conducted in the area have shown that not even one-third of the 100 hectares allotted is used. The model of settlement based on family units should be maintained to avoid out-migration from colonization areas. In order to accomplish this, settlers need to be assured as to their rights to their own plots and informed about channels for commercialization of their production.

## NOTES

1. The age-specific fertility rates for 1970 and 1980 were obtained through the use of the Brass P/F ratio method. The results should be interpreted with caution, since some of its basic assumptions are violated in the application of this method to the 1980 census data. In particular, fertility by age is unlikely to have remained constant. Moreover, it is difficult to accept that there is no difference in fertility between migrants and nonmigrants.

2. The estimates were obtained by using the Brass children surviving method.

3. Agregados are people who rent, sharecrop, or work for wages for the landowner and live on his plot.

## BIBLIOGRAPHY

Chaloult, N. B. 1979. "Settlement Along the Transamazon Highways: Planning and Reality." Paper presented at the Conference on the Development of Amazonia, Cambridge, MA, September.

Gonçalves, Maria da Graça O. 1981. "Reprodução da força de trabalho em uma área de fronteira agrígola: Rondônia." M.A. thesis, University of Brasília.

INCRA (National Institute for Settlement and Land Reform). 1971. *Metodologia para programação operacional dos projetos de asentamento de agricultores.* Brasília.

Martine, G. 1979. "Colonization in Rondônia and the Reproduction of Conditions Prevailing in Older Areas." Paper presented at the Informal Technical Workshop on Migration Policies, ILO, Geneva.

Merrick, T. W., and D. H. Graham. 1979. *Population and Economic Development in Brazil—1800 to the Present.* Baltimore, MD: John Hopkins University Press.

Nicholls, W. H. 1970. "The Agricultural Frontier in Modern Brazilian History: The State of Paraná, 1920–1965." *Revista Brasileira de Economia* (Rio de Janeiro) 24, no. 4 (October–December).

O'Connor, J. 1977. "A crise do estado capitalista." *Paz e Terra* (Rio de Janeiro), quoted in G. Martine, "Colonization in Rondônia."

Pacheco, L. M. T. 1979. *Colonização dirigida: Estratégia de acumulação e legitimação de um estado autoritário.* M.A. thesis, Department of Social Sciences, University of Brasília (August).

———. 1982. "Estratégia de sobrevivência da pequena produção na fronteira agrícola: Projetos de colonização Ouro Preto e Gy-Paraná." Paper presented at the Terceiro Encontro Nacional de Estudos Populacionais, Vitória.

Redwood, J. 1970. "Internal Migration, Urbanization and Frontier Region Development in Brazil since 1940." M.A. thesis, Urban and City Planning Department, University of California at Berkeley. Mimeo.

Waibel, L. 1955. "As zonas pioneiras do Brasil." *Revista Brasileira de Geografia* (Rio de Janeiro) 17, no. 4.

Wood, C., and M. Schmink. 1978. *Blaming the Victim: Small Farmer Production in an Amazon Colonization Project.* Interciencia Association Symposia series on "Nutrition and Agriculture: Strategies for Latin America." February. Mimeo.

Table 10.1
Annual rates of growth for the urban and rural populations by states, 1940-80

| States | 1940-50 | | 1950-60 | | 1960-70 | | 1970-80 | |
|---|---|---|---|---|---|---|---|---|
| | Urban | Rural | Urban | Rural | Urban | Rural | Urban | Rural |
| Acre | 4.17 | 3.64 | 4.80 | 3.05 | 5.94 | 2.24 | 8.41 | 0.84 |
| Alagoas | 2.26 | 1.11 | 4.10 | 0.44 | 4.14 | 1.35 | 4.48 | 0.54 |
| Amapá | 20.78 | -1.93 | 9.80 | 3.57 | 6.07 | 4.63 | 5.25 | 3.21 |
| Amazonas | 2.77 | 1.22 | 5.70 | 2.50 | 5.50 | 1.37 | 7.82 | 0.50 |
| Bahia | 2.92 | 1.86 | 5.24 | 0.87 | 4.19 | 1.29 | 4.21 | 0.87 |
| Brazil | 3.84 | 1.58 | 5.47 | 1.63 | 5.15 | 0.65 | 4.48 | -0.61 |
| Ceará | 3.65 | 2.24 | 5.17 | 0.94 | 4.88 | 1.93 | 4.74 | -0.40 |
| Distrito Federal | n.a. | n.a. | n.a. | n.a. | 19.31 | -8.46 | 8.31 | 5.88 |
| Espírito Santo | 2.35 | 1.83 | 7.31 | 2.96 | 6.18 | -0.47 | 6.07 | -1.82 |
| Fernando de Noronha | n.a. | n.a. | 9.11 | n.a. | 0.58 | n.a. | 0.23 | n.a. |
| Goiás | 5.63 | 3.54 | 9.32 | 3.41 | 7.79 | 2.46 | 6.88 | -1.50 |
| Maranhão | 3.98 | 2.23 | 5.04 | 4.56 | 5.58 | 1.03 | 5.32 | 2.14 |
| Mato Grosso | 2.90 | 0.21 | 6.61 | 3.47 | 6.99 | 5.99 | 10.88 | 2.81 |
| Mato Grosso do Sul | 3.51 | 2.16 | 7.86 | 5.59 | 6.63 | 5.01 | 7.40 | -1.90 |
| Minas Gerais | 3.21 | 0.74 | 5.49 | 0.94 | 4.52 | -1.10 | 4.06 | -2.07 |
| Pará | 3.09 | 1.11 | 4.95 | 2.28 | 5.10 | 2.34 | 5.08 | 4.52 |

| | | | | | | | | |
|---|---|---|---|---|---|---|---|---|
| Paraíba | 3.90 | 1.24 | 4.48 | 0.42 | 3.71 | 0.85 | 3.80 | -0.43 |
| Paraná | 5.74 | 5.44 | 9.66 | 1.38 | 6.73 | 4.13 | 6.01 | -3.32 |
| Pernambuco | 4.01 | 1.60 | 4.75 | 0.23 | 4.42 | 0.48 | 3.05 | -0.01 |
| Piauí | 3.22 | 2.35 | 5.74 | 0.98 | 6.53 | 1.98 | 5.20 | 0.83 |
| Rio Grande do Norte | 4.44 | 1.69 | 5.54 | 0.11 | 5.61 | 1.77 | 4.27 | -0.36 |
| Rio Grande do Sul | 3.23 | 1.84 | 5.57 | 0.91 | 4.00 | 0.43 | 4.05 | -2.07 |
| Rio de Janeiro | 4.37 | -0.89 | 4.56 | 0.96 | 4.22 | -2.48 | 2.78 | -1.63 |
| Rondônia | 10.61 | 9.71 | 8.36 | 5.62 | 6.98 | 3.45 | 14.74 | 16.74 |
| Roraima | 14.14 | 3.67 | 9.50 | 2.59 | 3.49 | 3.52 | 10.72 | 3.17 |
| São Paulo | 4.25 | 0.76 | 5.43 | 1.09 | 5.88 | -3.09 | 4.54 | -2.04 |
| Santa Catarina | 3.64 | 2.62 | 6.72 | 1.94 | 6.18 | 1.37 | 5.68 | -1.15 |
| Sergipe | 2.12 | 1.57 | 3.74 | 0.55 | 3.60 | 0.54 | 4.09 | 0.76 |

Source: Instituto Brasileiro de Geografias e Estadística (IBGE). Sinopse Preliminar do Censo Demográfico 1980, vol. 1, tomo 1, no. 1, table 6, pp. 10-11. Rio de Janeiro (1981).

n.a., Not available.

Table 10.2
Rondônia, 1979: Directed colonization projects

| Projects | Total area (hectares) | Number of settled families | | | Land titles distributed | |
|---|---|---|---|---|---|---|
| | | Until 1978 | Expected 1979 | Target | Until 1978 | Expected 1979 |
| Adolpho Rohl | 413,552 | 2,247 | 500 | 4,341 | 1,131 | 340 |
| Burareiro | 304,925 | 731 | 203 | 1,214 | 158 | 401 |
| Gy-Paraná | 486,137 | 3,922 | 834 | 4,756 | 1,294 | 1,000 |
| Marechal Dutra | 494,661 | 2,220 | 703 | 4,520 | 397 | 673 |
| Ouro Preto | 512,585 | 4,414 | 719 | 5,133 | 2,932 | 876 |
| Paulo de Assis Ribeiro | 294,580 | 2,463 | 511 | 2,974 | 712 | 1,568 |
| Sidney Girão | 60,000 | 485 | 15 | 500 | 383 | 90 |
| Total | 2,565,440 | 16,482 | 3,485 | 23,438 | 7,007 | 4,948 |

Source: Martine (1979: p. 11, Table 2).

Table 10.3
Percentage of households with access to basic services and
ownership of domestic appliances: Rondônia, 1960, 1970, and 1980

| Area and basic services and domestic appliances | 1960 | 1970 | 1980 |
|---|---|---|---|
| Urban | | | |
| Piped water supply | 7.58 | 15.77 | 17.10 |
| Piped sewage system | 1.40 | -- | 2.19 |
| Gas | 0.74 | 7.23 | 34.33 |
| Radio | 8.60 | 33.90 | 31.22 |
| Refrigerator | 2.94 | 12.85 | 22.07 |
| Television | -- | 0.65 | 22.86 |
| Rural | | | |
| Piped water supply | 0.26 | 0.99 | 1.20 |
| Piped sewage system | -- | -- | 0.13 |
| Gas | 0.09 | 2.41 | 4.32 |
| Radio | 2.14 | 16.18 | 27.23 |
| Refrigerator | 0.71 | 1.67 | 2.31 |
| Television | -- | 0.04 | 1.13 |

Source:  IBGE, Rio de Janerio, Censo Demográfico 1980,
Rondônia, Table A.2.1.

Table 10.4
Age-specific fertility rates and total fertility rate for urban
and rural women: Rondônia, 1970 and 1980

| Age groups | 1970 | | 1980 | |
|---|---|---|---|---|
| | Urban | Rural | Urban | Rural |
| 15-19 | 0.096 | 0.169 | 0.116 | 0.144 |
| 20-24 | 0.329 | 0.421 | 0.297 | 0.346 |
| 25-29 | 0.395 | 0.520 | 0.279 | 0.332 |
| 30-34 | 0.395 | 0.351 | 0.202 | 0.242 |
| 35-39 | 0.307 | 0.353 | 0.130 | 0.190 |
| 40-44 | 0.171 | 0.253 | 0.084 | 0.080 |
| 45-49 | 0.084 | 0.087 | 0.011 | 0.029 |
| TFR* (Rondônia) | 8.88 | 10.77 | 5.59 | 6.82 |
| TFR (Brazil) | 4.55 | 7.74 | 3.63 | 6.40 |

Source:  IBGE, Rio de Janeiro, Censos Demográficos 1970 and
1980, Rondônia.
*The total fertility rate (TFR) is the sum of age-specific
fertility rates; it is thus independent of age distribution.
When ages are grouped, as they are here, each age-specific rate
is multiplied by the number of years covered by the age bracket.

Table 10.5
Life expectancy at birth, 1970 and 1980

| Area | 1970 | | 1980 | |
|------|------|------|------|------|
| | Male | Female | Male | Female |
| Rondônia | 46.5 | 50.8 | 50.8 | 55.0 |
| Brazil | 56.8 | 61.0 | 60.2 | 65.1 |

Source: IBGE, Rio de Janeiro, Censos Demográficos 1970 and 1980.

Table 10.6
Mean size of plots by size of holding: Rondônia, 1960, 1970, 1975, and 1980 (hectares)

| Area | Mean size | | | |
|------|------|------|------|------|
| | 1960 | 1970 | 1975 | 1980 |
| <10 | 4.5 | 5.4 | 3.7 | 4.3 |
| 10-100 | 34.8 | 32.8 | 43.0 | 57.6 |
| 100-200 | 134.5 | 125.7 | 103.0 | 104.7 |
| 200-500 | 269.9 | 278.0 | 275.6 | 264.1 |
| >500 | 6,025.0 | 3,208.3 | 1,717.7 | 3,029.5 |
| Total | 299.7 | 230.4 | 120.9 | 114.9 |

Source: IBGE, Rio de Janeiro, Censos Agropecuários, Rondônia, 1970, 1975 and 1980.

Table 10.7
Percentage distribution of the number and area of holdings by
landholding status: Rondônia, 1970, 1975, and 1980

| Landholding status | 1970 | | 1975 | | 1980 | |
|---|---|---|---|---|---|---|
| | No. of holdings | Area | No. of holdings | Area | No. of holdings | Area |
| Landowner | 26.7 | 39.5 | 66.1 | 78.4 | 37.4 | 46.0 |
| Tenant | 10.8 | 9.1 | 1.7 | 0.2 | 3.9 | 1.0 |
| Sharecropper | 18.4 | 22.7 | 3.4 | 0.7 | 5.0 | 0.5 |
| Squatter | 44.1 | 28.7 | 28.8 | 20.8 | 53.2 | 52.1 |
| No information | -- | -- | -- | -- | 0.5 | 0.4 |
| Total (n = 100 percent) | 7,082 | 1,631,640 | 25,483 | 3,082,052 | 49,517 | 5,688,269 |

Source: IBGE, Rio de Janeiro, Censos Agropecuários, Rondônia,
1970, 1975 and 1980.


Table 10.8
Distribution of income, by area and sex: Rondônia, 1980
(percentages)

| Population percentiles | Urban | | Rural | |
|---|---|---|---|---|
| | Male | Female | Male | Female |
| 5+ | 33.77 | 29.70 | 30.89 | 35.81 |
| 10+ | 45.81 | 42.78 | 42.56 | 51.99 |
| 10 | 14.91 | 16.15 | 16.30 | 21.98 |
| 10 | 9.89 | 10.87 | 12.71 | 17.14 |
| 10 | 7.33 | 7.95 | 9.96 | 8.74 |
| 10 | 6.28 | 6.19 | 8.44 | 0.15 |
| 10 | 5.13 | 5.09 | 6.17 | 0.00 |
| 10 | 4.19 | 4.34 | 3.73 | 0.00 |
| 10 | 3.40 | 3.55 | 0.12 | 0.00 |
| 10 | 2.46 | 2.40 | 0.00 | 0.00 |
| 10- | 0.59 | 0.67 | 0.00 | 0.00 |
| 75- | 34.06 | 35.22 | 34.36 | 17.07 |
| 25+ | 65.94 | 64.78 | 65.64 | 82.93 |
| 15+ | 54.24 | 51.86 | 51.29 | 63.76 |

Source: IBGE, Rio de Janeiro, Censo Demográfico, Rondônia,
1980, Table A.21.

Table 10.9
Percentage distribution of settlers and agregados, by type of house, type of water provision, and type of sewage disposal facilities, Rondônia, 1980

| | Settlers | | Agregados | |
|---|---|---|---|---|
| Items | Ouro Preto | Gy-Paraná | Ouro Preto | Gy-Paraná |
| Type of house | | | | |
| Brick | 10.74 | 4.25 | 3.96 | 1.47 |
| Wooden frame | 58.39 | 40.12 | 51.49 | 29.41 |
| Adobe | 7.38 | 9.73 | 12.87 | 11.77 |
| Log cabin | 17.11 | 42.25 | 27.72 | 57.35 |
| Other | 6.04 | 1.52 | 1.98 | -- |
| No response | 0.34 | 2.13 | 1.98 | -- |
| Water provision | | | | |
| With pipes | 10.40 | 3.95 | 5.94 | 1.47 |
|   Well or river | 9.06 | 3.95 | 4.95 | 1.47 |
|   Other | 1.34 | -- | 0.99 | -- |
| Without pipes | 89.60 | 95.74 | 93.07 | 97.06 |
|   Well or river | 85.58 | 90.88 | 88.12 | 92.65 |
|   Other | 3.02 | 4.86 | 4.95 | 4.41 |
|   No response | -- | 0.31 | 0.99 | 1.47 |
| Sewage disposal facilities | | | | |
| Covered | | | | |
|   Cesspool | 5.37 | 1.52 | 0.99 | 1.47 |
| Open | | | | |
|   Cesspool | 22.82 | 20.68 | 15.84 | 5.88 |
|   Other | 1.68 | 0.91 | -- | -- |
|   Nothing | 69.12 | 76.90 | 80.20 | 92.65 |
|   No response | 1.01 | -- | 2.97 | -- |
| Number of settlers (n) | 298 | 329 | 101 | 68 |

Source:   INCRA, Brasília, Rondônia Socio-Demographic Survey, 1980.

Table 10.10
Percentage distribution of settlers and agregados, by the extent
to which illness led to an interruption of normal activity and
by type of care received, Rondônia, 1980

| Items | Settlers | | Agregados | |
|---|---|---|---|---|
| | Ouro Preto | Gy-Paraná | Ouro Preto | Gy-Paraná |
| Have interrupted work | | | | |
| Yes | 67.8 | 62.2 | 58.7 | 56.3 |
| No | 14.2 | 24.9 | 14.3 | 25.0 |
| No response | 17.1 | 12.9 | 27.0 | 18.8 |
| Type of care | | | | |
| Doctor | 55.2 | 49.2 | 47.6 | 46.9 |
| Pharmacy | 15.3 | 18.3 | 15.9 | 28.1 |
| Other | 3.0 | 1.3 | -- | -- |
| None | 12.3 | 25.0 | 14.3 | 12.6 |
| No response | 14.3 | 6.3 | 22.2 | 12.6 |
| Number of settlers (n) | 205 | 241 | 63 | 32 |

Source: INCRA, Brasília, Rondônia Socio-Demographic Survey, 1980.

Table 10.11

Percentage distribution of settlers by project, state of birth, and state of previous residence, Rondônia, 1980

| State of previous residence | State or region of birth | | | | | |
| --- | --- | --- | --- | --- | --- | --- |
| | Northeast | Minas Gerais | Espírito Santo | Rio de Janeiro and São Paulo | Other states | Number of settlers ($\underline{n}$) |
| Ouro Preto | | | | | | |
| Minas Gerais | -- | 25.6 | 6.7 | 6.1 | -- | 26 |
| Espírito Santo | 1.9 | 22.1 | 66.6 | 3.0 | -- | 41 |
| Paraná | 20.8 | 18.6 | 6.7 | 27.3 | 86.6 | 51 |
| Mato Grosso | 58.5 | 29.1 | 16.7 | 42.4 | 6.7 | 76 |
| Other states | 18.8 | 4.6 | 3.3 | 21.2 | 6.7 | 23 |
| Number of settlers ($\underline{n}$) | 53 | 86 | 30 | 33 | 15 | 217 |
| Gy-Paraná | | | | | | |
| Minas Gerais | -- | 16.9 | 2.2 | -- | -- | 11 |
| Espírito Santo | 5.5 | 6.8 | 80.0 | -- | -- | 43 |
| Paraná | 29.1 | 40.7 | 13.4 | 42.9 | 56.2 | 79 |
| Mato Grosso | 50.9 | 35.6 | 4.4 | 42.9 | 25.0 | 74 |
| Other states | 14.5 | -- | -- | 14.2 | 18.8 | 19 |
| Number of settlers ($\underline{n}$) | 55 | 59 | 45 | 35 | 32 | 226 |

Source: Rondônia Socio-Demographic Survey, 1980.

349

Table 10.12
Percentage distribution of settlers, by project and year of
arrival in Rondônia

| Year of arrival in Rondônia | Ouro Preto | Gy-Paraná |
|---|---|---|
| Up to 1972 | 44.7 | 24.9 |
| 1973 | 23.5 | 15.1 |
| 1974 | 7.7 | 11.0 |
| 1975 | 5.7 | 12.3 |
| 1976 | 10.7 | 15.4 |
| 1977 and after | 7.7 | 21.3 |
| Number of settlers (n) | 298 | 318 |

Source: INCRA, Brasília, Rondônia Socio-Demographic Survey,
1980.


Table 10.13
Percentage distribution of settlers by land titles,
Rondônia, 1980

| | Settlers | |
|---|---|---|
| Land title | Ouro Preto | Gy-Paraná |
| Authorization of occupation | 43.6 | 29.9 |
| License of occupation | 24.9 | 34.3 |
| None | 9.3 | 13.1 |
| Agregado | 3.5 | 5.1 |
| Bought the plot | 18.7 | 17.6 |
| Number of settlers (n) | 289 | 312 |

Source: INCRA, Brasília, Rondônia Socio-Demographic
Survey, 1980.

Table 10.14
Percentage distribution of settlers in Rondônia, according to
whether they had ever used rural credit

| Ever made use of credit | Socioeconomic survey | | Sociodemographic survey | |
|---|---|---|---|---|
| | Ouro Preto | Gy-Paraná | Ouro Preto | Gy-Paraná |
| Yes | 34.8 | 35.1 | 26.0 | 27.3 |
| No | 46.4 | 45.2 | 72.0 | 68.1 |
| No answer | 18.8 | 19.7 | 2.0 | 4.6 |
| Total number of settlers (n) | 701 | 228 | 398 | 396 |

Source: INCRA, Brasília, Socio-Economic Survey, 1977, and
Rondônia Socio-Demographic Survey, 1980.


Table 10.15
Percentage distribution of settlers, according to whether they
had received technical assistance

| Received technical assistance | Socioeconomic survey | | Sociodemographic survey | |
|---|---|---|---|---|
| | Ouro Preto | Gy-Paraná | Ouro Preto | Gy-Paraná |
| Yes | 27.4 | 29.8 | 34.0 | 30.2 |
| No | 62.3 | 58.3 | 54.0 | 58.6 |
| No response | 10.2 | 11.9 | 12.0 | 11.2 |
| Number of settlers (n) | 701 | 228 | 398 | 396 |

Source: INCRA, Brasília, Socio-Economic Survey, 1977, and
Rondônia Socio-Demographic Survey, 1980.

Table 10.16
Percentage distribution of settlers by type of crops, cultivated area, and volume of production, Rondônia, 1979-80

| Cultivated area and volume of production | Crops | | | | | |
|---|---|---|---|---|---|---|
| | Corn | Rice | Beans | Manioc | Coffee | Cocoa |
| **Cultivated area (hectares)** | | | Ouro Preto | | | |
| Up to 2 | 34.7 | 22.3 | 57.8 | 76.5 | 20.3 | 21.9 |
| 2-3 | 28.9 | 25.6 | 19.4 | 17.3 | 50.6 | 40.6 |
| 3-5 | 23.1 | 31.2 | 13.4 | 2.5 | 20.8 | 21.9 |
| 5-10 | 11.6 | 14.5 | 7.8 | 3.7 | 7.0 | 7.8 |
| 10 and over | 1.6 | 6.3 | 1.7 | -- | 1.3 | 7.8 |
| Number of settlers ($\underline{n}$) | 242 | 269 | 232 | 81 | 182 | 64 |
| **Cultivated area (hectares)** | | | Gy-Paraná | | | |
| Up to 2 | 40.1 | 20.0 | 47.8 | 85.4 | 20.1 | 50.4 |
| 2-3 | 28.7 | 28.5 | 25.0 | 8.7 | 16.8 | 8.3 |
| 3-5 | 19.0 | 27.8 | 18.5 | 4.8 | 20.1 | 4.2 |
| 5-10 | 11.0 | 19.6 | 7.3 | 1.0 | 29.1 | 20.2 |
| 10 and over | 1.3 | 4.1 | 1.3 | -- | 13.9 | 16.8 |
| Number of settlers ($\underline{n}$) | 237 | 270 | 232 | 103 | 244 | 24 |
| **Volume of production (sacks)** | | | Ouro Preto | | | |
| Up to 15 | 19.8 | 8.8 | 73.6 | 55.6 | 44.4 | 34.2 |
| 16-30 | 29.5 | 18.3 | 17.0 | 11.1 | 16.7 | 29.0 |
| 31-50 | 23.0 | 16.0 | 5.5 | 22.2 | 14.3 | 21.0 |
| 51-100 | 18.9 | 30.9 | 2.8 | 11.1 | 15.1 | 7.9 |
| 100 sacks and over | 8.8 | 26.0 | 1.1 | -- | 9.5 | 7.9 |
| Number of settlers ($\underline{n}$) | 217 | 261 | 182 | 9 | 126 | 38 |
| **Volume of production (sacks)** | | | Gy-Paraná | | | |
| Up to 15 | 25.0 | 11.6 | 68.9 | 50.0 | 48.3 | 53.9 |
| 16-30 | 31.9 | 15.9 | 15.8 | 50.0 | 10.2 | 15.4 |
| 31-50 | 22.0 | 19.5 | 10.8 | -- | 11.6 | 7.7 |
| 51-100 | 14.7 | 30.0 | 3.2 | -- | 20.4 | 23.1 |
| 100 sacks and over | 6.5 | 23.1 | 1.4 | -- | 9.5 | -- |
| Number of settlers ($\underline{n}$) | 234 | 277 | 222 | 4 | 147 | 13 |

Source: INCRA, Brasília, Rondônia Socio-Demographic Survey, 1980.

Table 10.17
Percentage distribution of settlers and agregados in the Gy-Paraná
project, by the duration of wage work in a year, Rondônia, 1980

| Duration of work | Settlers | Agregados |
|---|---|---|
| Less than 1 month | 8.0 | -- |
| 1-4 months | 54.7 | 38.9 |
| 4-8 months | 17.3 | 27.8 |
| 8-12 months | 14.7 | 11.1 |
| Did not know how to estimate | 5.3 | 22.2 |
| Number of respondents (n) | 75 | 18 |

Source: INCRA, Brasília, Rondônia Socio-Demographic Survey,
1980.


Table 10.18
Percentage distribution of settlers and agregados, by comparison
of their present and previous situations, Rondônia, 1980

| Comparison of present with previous situation | Settlers | | Agregados | |
|---|---|---|---|---|
| | Ouro Preto | Gy-Paraná | Ouro Preto | Gy-Paraná |
| Better now | 85.9 | 88.9 | 65.7 | 79.4 |
| The same | 7.7 | 7.7 | 24.2 | 17.7 |
| Worse now | 6.4 | 3.4 | 10.1 | 2.9 |
| Number of respondents (n) | 297 | 325 | 99 | 68 |

Source: INCRA, Brasília, Rondônia Socio-Demographic Survey,
1980.

Table 10.19
Percentage distribution of settlers and agregados, by their
preference whether to stay in or move out of Rondônia, 1980

| Preferences | Settlers | | Agregados | |
|---|---|---|---|---|
| | Ouro Preto | Gy-Paraná | Ouro Preto | Gy-Paraná |
| To stay in Rondônia | 90.0 | 91.1 | 82.0 | 76.1 |
| To move out | 10.0 | 8.9 | 18.0 | 23.9 |
| Number of respondents (n) | 297 | 325 | 100 | 69 |

Source: INCRA, Brasília, Rondônia Socio-Demographic Survey, 1980.

Jorge Carpio                                              **11**

# Settlement Policies in the Forest Highlands of Peru

## INTRODUCTION

The primary objective of this study is to analyze the process of colonization in the forest highlands of Peru, both from the point of view of
population distribution and as a means of creating more employment.
Between 1940 and 1981, the population of the forest regions grew from
414,452 to 1,813,887 inhabitants. While in 1940 the forest population
represented 6.7 percent of the total population of Peru, at the last census
in 1981 it accounted for 10.6 percent (Table 11.1). In 1940 it accounted
for 38.4 percent of the total population of the Peruvian Amazon region,
but by 1981 this figure had risen to 58 percent (Aramburú 1982).[1]

In the last decade, however, there has been a decline in the rate of
population growth in 15 of the 19 provinces of the forest highlands. This
trend is reflected in the growth rates for the region as a whole: 3.6 percent
per year between 1940 and 1961, 4.1 percent between 1961 and 1972,
and 3.4 percent between 1972 and 1981 (Table 11.1).

In an area where the fertility rate has not declined and where mortality
has fallen somewhat, the real cause of the decline in population growth

At the time of this study, the author was an ILO expert living in Peru.

is to be found in the reduction of immigration or the increase in emigration, or a combination of both (Lesevic 1983).

There is thus clearly a need for an in-depth analysis of the reasons behind the population movements in this region, and of the extent to which the forest highlands have constituted an alternative for migrants from the sierra. Several recent studies suggest that "less than 10 percent of the national population growth has been absorbed by these regions and less than 20 percent of the Andean migrants have chosen these areas as their destination in the last 40 years" (Aramburú 1982). This shows that this region has not constituted a real alternative to the coast as a settlement region.

The study is divided into seven sections. The remainder of the introduction discusses major factors that have influenced settlement patterns in the forest highlands. Section 1 provides a historical background to colonization policies in Peru. Section 2 discusses the primary objectives of planned settlement projects in the forest highlands and examines alternative resettlement strategies. Section 3 evaluates current colonization policies and their impact on the ecological balance. Section 4 gives a general description of the agricultural economy in the forest highlands and the structural changes that are taking place there due to large-scale migration from the sierra. Section 5 discusses land use and cropping patterns in the colonization areas and their impact on the material economy. Section 6 examines social and ideological conflicts between indigenous communities and agricultural settlers. Section 7 brings together the major findings of the study and highlights their policy implications.

Until 1940, the population of the Peruvian forest highlands remained relatively static. The type of activities pursued (such as forestry and animal raising) required little labor and did not lead to economic expansion or lasting urban growth. The "rubber boom" did in fact result in an increase in the population of Iquitos from 10,000 to 15,000, but once the boom was over the population of the city returned to its normal level (Werlich 1975).

It was only recently, from 1940 on, that a massive process of settlement occurred in various basins of the forest highlands following the construction of roads that penetrated the area and linked it with the coastal and Andean regions. Although the occupation of the land occurred as a result of the agricultural and cattle-raising activities of large landowners, the principal factor was the establishment of spontaneous settlements by Andean migrants.

What is of interest for the present study, however, is the fact that the old plantations or *haciendas* did not produce a sustained growth in rural employment. In the case of Saipai and many others, a process of transformation occurred whereby casual day-laborers became tenants on plots of land outside the limits of the existing farms. The wage earners of Saipai, given the wide availability of land in Alto Huallaga, naturally chose to acquire their own plots and become settlers, thereby jeopardizing the production plans of the large plantations.

The expansion of large landholdings in the forest highlands in fact occurred well before 1940. The haciendas of Cuzco, which is situated in the southern part of the forest highlands, date from the early colonial period; the coffee plantations of Chanchamayo were established at the beginning of the present century; the tea and coffee plantations of Alto Huallaga date from the 1940s. A number of factors worked against the consolidation of relatively large plantations or haciendas in the forest highlands, however: the shortage of manpower, underutilization of land, and sharp fluctuations in international prices, especially of coffee. The size of the labor force, which was fundamentally of a casual nature, depended on foreign exchange earnings. When international coffee prices rose, for example, the plantation managers contracted a large number of wage earners; when prices fell, the reverse occurred (Bedoya 1982b). Thus large landholdings in the forest highlands have always suffered from a shortage of manpower as a result of the extension of the peasant economy (Bedoya 1983).

According to the agricultural census of 1972, 46.3 percent of the agricultural units of the whole forest region were less than 5 hectares in area, and 53.3 percent between 5 and 500 hectares; 99.6 percent were thus what are commonly referred to as small or medium-sized farms (Table 11.2). Furthermore, a large number of medium-sized farms comprised between 5 and 30 hectares.

The settlement process in the forest highlands reached its apogee toward the end of the 1970s. The completion of a series of roads that penetrated inward from the coast, crossing the sierra and finally entering the forest region, resulted in a network of large populated river basins, each with one or more sub-basins. Of all these basins, that of Alto Marañon (the northern part of the forest highlands) is the oldest and one of the most populated, containing 29.2 percent of the total inhabitants of the forest highlands. This is followed by Huallaga Central, in the north-central forest highlands, with 24.4 percent of the total. Then comes Ucayali, which comprises various sub-basins totaling 31.6 percent of the population; some of these sub-basins are situated in the central forest area (Pichis Palcazu, Chanchamayo, and Pachitea), and others, such as Alto Urubamba, in the southern forest area. Finally, there is the Alto Madre de Dios region, which accounts for only 4.6 percent of the total inhabitants.

## HISTORICAL BACKGROUND OF COLONIZATION POLICIES

Settlement policies in the Amazon refer to the whole of the forest region,[2] without distinguishing between the lowlands and the highlands, and take the form of appropriate legislation promulgated by respective governments. Martínez (1983) has described the various stages:

a. Between 1832 and 1898 legislative provisions were made to bring foreigners in to occupy the Peruvian forest.

b. Between 1898 and 1964 two important basic Acts were formulated. The second of these, Act No. 1220 of 1909, encouraged investment through large landholdings. However, particularly during the second government of President Augusto Leguía, in the 1920s, emphasis continued to be placed on foreign migrations.

   During the 1930s and 1940s, emphasis was placed on the construction of roads as a means of penetration and connection with river transport and migration to the forest by national pioneers, in particular Andean peasants. The state also promoted new technologies and provided basic services such as health and education. Finally, during this period, massive spontaneous settlements began, particularly in the forest highlands, leading to a considerable growth of small-scale farms. Furthermore, in the 1950s, settlement was viewed as an alternative to agrarian reform.

c. During a third stage from 1964 to the mid–1970s, the state participated by directly encouraging new settlements or the resettlement of local former settlers. However, it is important to differentiate clearly between the first government of Fernando Belaúnde and the first phase of the military regime. By means of the Agrarian Reform Act No. 15037, the first government of Fernando Belaúnde carried out a series of expropriations of large estates situated in the forest highlands, including Saipai, which was reduced from 15,000 to 532 hectares in 1966. The regime also initiated a massive program of human settlements in the region of Alto Huallaga and the construction of roads for the opening up of La Marginal, not just for the purposes of penetration but as a means to promote economic and agricultural development. At the same time, the government encouraged the establishment of so-called agricultural cooperatives, although the main emphasis was on small and medium-sized tenant farmers. During the first phase of the military government, planned settlement projects were continued although they were explicitly adapted to the agrarian reform policy and urban food consumption needs. An important instrument was the establishment of agricultural service cooperatives and agricultural production cooperatives, which resulted in a certain neglect of tenant farmers, especially as regards credits, in comparison with the previous government.

d. A fourth and final stage that can be dated from 1978 witnessed the establishment of Special Development Projects. Although these projects were initiated by the military regime, they continue to be given prominence by the present government. They incorporate plans not only for road expansion but also for the increase of agricultural production.

In Peru, planned forest settlements have not been significant, especially in terms of number of persons settled. Settlement schemes in

Genaro Herrera, Marichín-Rio Yavarí, and Pichari in the 1960s and 1970s did not involve more than 900 families. The original project for the settlement of Tingo María-Campanilla and Tocache, also during the same period, involved the settlement of 4227 families. These included 179 families who were brought from other regions of the country, such as Arequipa, Ancash, and Lima. These settlers were organized into three agricultural production cooperatives, El Porvenir, Arequipa, and Nuevo Horizonte (Cencira 1974). In 1974, however, the dropout rate for members of these three cooperatives fluctuated between 81 and 92 percent, as against 15 and 26 percent in the case of production cooperatives established in spontaneous settlements (Cencira 1974). A similar process of abandonment occurred in the agricultural service cooperatives, although to a lesser extent, since they offered a much greater scope for alternative activities.

Both the agricultural production cooperatives and the service cooperatives that were set up in the 1980s in the Tingo María-Alto Huallaga basin region (with persons brought in by the state) suffered from a series of shortcomings, despite the homogeneous nature of the population (Cencira 1974). The members of these cooperatives depended entirely on the state for measures to promote agricultural production and improvements in their standard of living.

Unfortunately, the level of their expectations was so high that they soon became frustrated and abandoned the planned settlement schemes. The few migrants who did settle permanently were those who had established close links with the state officials, from whom they received assistance or special concessions. In general, this small group of tenant farmers was composed of the leaders of the management or supervisory committees of the cooperatives and those with previous experience in agriculture, either on the coast or in the sierra. Special mention should be made here of the fact that a large number of tenant farmers coming from other regions were unaware of the serious practical difficulties posed by working in the humid tropical forest.

The data show, however, that throughout the forest regions, both highlands and lowlands, planned settlements were relatively less important than spontaneous settlements. To take an example, the 4227 families who were originally to be settled in the forest highlands of Alto Huallaga represented less than 5 percent of the approximately 100,000 rural families living in the forest highlands in 1972.[3] But it would be erroneous to assume that spontaneous settlements have been completely independent of state action. Large-scale migrations occurred, for examle, as a result of the seasonal demand for labor in the coffee plantations of Chanchamayo and Tingo María, but the establishement and consolidation of these estates were largely the work of the state (Chirif 1972). Although many plantations or haciendas had their own internal communication network, it was the state that constructed the roads to the sierra regions where Andean peasants were hired. Moreover, the process of transformation by which wage earners became tenant farmers by taking advantage of the relative availability of land was, on numerous occasions, initiated or promoted by the state through credit assistance. Indeed, at the beginning of the 1970s, plantation managers frequently complained that the shortage of manpower they experienced was a result of this very policy (Bedoya 1981).

In short, there were different phases of "semi-spontaneous" migration, such as that produced by labor recruitment, in which the state, directly or indirectly, played some sort of role up to the moment at which the casual indebted laborer became an agricultural tenant farmer. Rather than distinguishing between planned and spontaneous settlements, it is thus preferable to take the causes of population movements and the various legislative means that directly or indirectly promote the settlement process as a basis for classification. Furthermore, settlement policies must be seen in the context of the prevailing agrarian and economic policies of each period.

During the period of world economic depression at the end of the 1920s and the beginning of the 1930s, Peru was confronted with a serious balance-of-payments position that led the government to encourage export-oriented activities in the forest region (Werlich 1975). The Astoria Importing Company of New York opened a sawmill in Iquitos in 1928, and within a few years large quantities of timber were being exported. In the same way, experts from Ceylon began experiments with new tea plantations in 1930 in the Valle de La Convención-Cuzco. Only in the 1970s, as a result of the increase in the urban demand for food, did emphasis once again start to be placed on crops for human consumption—rice, for example, or agro-industrial crops such as hard yellow maize (Gonzáles 1983). Even the international loans granted by the World Bank reflected this shift of emphasis by making special provisions for agriculture and cattle-raising activities in the forest highlands (Cencira 1974; Bedoya 1981).

The Special Development Projects being implemented in various zones of the forest highlands by the present government are designed to expand the economic and physical infrastructure by providing roads and technological and credit support to tenant farmers. Recently it has been claimed that there is a need to use land more intensively, through the introduction of appropriate technologies and changes in the agricultural system, as well as to bring more land under cultivation in the forest highlands. We shall return to this matter later in the present study.

In order to analyze the various state settlement policies, we must first of all place them within a context of agricultural and other economic policies. A settlement policy should not be viewed merely as the building of roads, the establishment of schools, or the promotion of large estates or cooperatives, but as a means of solving problems such as a balance-of-payments deficit, as in the 1950s, or of satisfying urban demand, as in the 1970s. All these policies will in turn have some effect on the degree to which the peasant economy is integrated into the national or foreign market. If, from the 1930s, it was necessary to increase exports to cover deficits in the balance of payments, it is easy to understand the reasons for the wide cultivation of coffee and tea in the valley of La Convención; if, in the 1970s, the urban demand for foodstuffs determined the guide-lines for agrarian policy, it is clear why there was a shift in the crops grown in numerous regions of the forest highlands such as Huallaga Central and Alto Mayo. The Special Development Projects should thus be seen within the context of agrarian and other economic policies that are designed to meet certain objectives.

## OBJECTIVES OF PLANNED SETTLEMENTS

There have been three major objectives behind state settlement projects in the Peruvian forest.

First, the aim was to increase agricultural production so as to meet the increase in urban demand for food and solve balance-of-payments problems. Such an objective could only be met either through the acquisition of new land or through the reorientation of the rural economy, transforming what was originally a subsistence economy into a market-oriented economy. The changes introduced in the cropping patterns in the Huallaga Central and Alto Mayo valleys are eloquent proof of this (Bedoya 1983).

The second objective was to help solve the problems of landlessness and rural poverty. The agrarian reform initiated by the military government in 1969 had benefited only 20 percent of Andean peasant families. In the Peruvian sierra, where most of the rural population lives, the problem of smallholdings and poverty remained.

The planned settlements promoted in the 1960s, such as Pichari, Marichín-Rio Yavarí, Genaro Herrera, Saispampa, and Tingo María-Campanilla, apart from being insignificant in terms of the number of families settled, were prevented by a series of bureaucratic and other problems from improving the income and living standards of the settlers (Martínez 1976).

In no case were these settlement projects preceded by serious in-depth economic and social feasibility studies. In the cases of Genaro Herrera, Pichari, and Marichín, for example, the physical and economic objectives were formulated only after the technical and credit assistance had been initiated; indeed, in the case of Pichari, the objectives were defined *five years after* the project was launched. In Saispampa and Tingo María, the

objectives were laid down almost simultaneously with the start of settlement activities. Such projects were largely justified in terms of very
general objectives: "to fully exploit natural resources" (Genaro Herrera,
Marichín, and Saispampa); "to tranform subsistence agriculture into a
market-oriented one" (Genaro Herrera, Pichari, and Tingo María); "to
provide employment and improve standards of living" (Pichari and
Tingo María); "to satisfy the regional and national demand for meat"
(Genaro Herrera, Marichín, and Pichari); "to combat underemployment
in the sierra" (Saispampa); "to substantially increase agricultural production in order to improve the balance-of-payments position" (Tingo
María); and, finally, "to consolidate frontier nationalism by the definitive
possession of the area" (Genaro Herrera and Marichín; Martínez 1976:
83).

Furthermore, in no cases were detailed soil studies undertaken which
could have served as a guide in recommending the most suitable crops.
The soil analyses carried out in both Tingo María and Pichari were of
very limited use, since the research was on too large a scale and proved
to be technically inadequate. The result of this was low productivity per
hectare.

Finally, no provision was made to extend proper technical or credit
assistance to the planned settlement projects. In the case of Marichín,
the lack of communication roads made transport extremely expensive,
which meant that agricultural activities had very low profitability, while
in Pichari the distance from the input supply centers caused similar
problems.

A third major objective of some settlement programs has been the
settlement of the population in regions close to the borders with other
countries, either because of the marked settlement and economic activity
occurring across the frontier (as in the case of Marichín and Genaro
Herrera, areas that are close to Brazil) or as a result of problems arising
out of military conflicts (as with the new settlements in the Cordillera
del Condor on the border with Ecuador). In both cases, the establishment
of settlement projects was governed by geopolitical considerations and
involved planned migrations. However, the most critical factor determining the success of these settlements was the cost of transport, given
the distance from the urban centers.

Several studies on settlements in the Andean countries have concluded that planned settlements are less likely to reach the consolidation
stage than spontaneous settlements (Nelson 1973). These studies also
point out that the aim of state policies should be to promote spontaneous
settlements, because planned settlements are extremely costly.

As discussed earlier, however, planned settlements projects very often
induce spontaneous migration flows. Failure to take account of this
potential effect of planned settlements excludes the possibility of con-

sidering small pilot settlement projects that "combine the two options with a time-related shift in the emphasis of the policy" (Helmsing 1983: 23).

A slightly different point of view is put forward by Eduardo Durand (1983). He points out that while planned settlement programs produce results relatively quickly and can be evaluated in terms of economic and social returns, spontaneous settlements in frontier zones can be evaluated only after several decades. The negative aspects of planned settlements are well known—high drop-out rate, low productivity and low profitability; but spontaneous settlements are usually considered successful because no account is taken of the fact that there may have been other settlers who failed and left after initial attempts at settlement. Such departures may also be explained to some extent by the practice of shifting cultivation, which induces populations to move to new and virgin lands, as a result of low yield after the third or fourth harvest. The dry-land clearing and burning technique used by tenant farmers in regions of low agricultural productivity, such as that of the humid tropical forest of the Amazon basin, is the only viable alternative for most of the migrants from the sierra, given their limited knowledge of other forms of cultivation. Permanent settlements are therefore likely to occur only when there is an increase in agricultural production through the introduction of new technologies or an increase in farm incomes due to greater demand for agricultural products (Bedoya 1983).

## CURRENT COLONIZATION POLICIES

The rapid economic growth that is currently taking place in the forest highlands is due basically to the migration of peasants from the sierra and the subsequent expansion of the agricultural frontier. The present government has shown considerable interest in development projects for the forest highlands, a region that it is thought can solve the current food and employment problems of the country. There are still wide income inequalities in this region, however, although most tenant farmers enjoy higher standards of living than the inhabitants of the sierra.

One aspect of settlement policies that is of vital importance is ecology. Several studies have pointed out the negative effects of deforestation by the sierra migrants in the Amazon basin (Martínez 1976). In the last 50 years approximately 4.5 million hectares of forest have been destroyed, at an average rate of almost 100,000 hectares a year; what is even more serious, however, is the fact that the rate of deforestation is expected to increase, thus bringing the estimated total number of hectares lost between 1980 and 1999 to approximately 18 million (Table 11.3).

This destruction of the ecological balance cannot be viewed as the exclusive responsibility of the migrant tenant farmers; account must also be taken of the negative effects of mechanical clearing with caterpillar tractors (Bedoya 1981), forestry extraction, the exploitation of rubber, and destruction of the fauna. Nonetheless, it is the peasants from the sierra who have done most to destroy the humid tropical forest.

The Andean tenant farmers, on deciding to establish a farm in the Amazon basin, believe that they are starting a new stage in their life. In most cases, they bring along all members of their families to have the necessary manpower on hand.[4] A study of the Tingo María-Tochache Campanilla settlement noted that nearly 66 percent of migrants had come with all members of their families. The migrants initially begin to raise food crops such as maize, yucca, bananas, and so on, with the double objective of providing for their own needs and selling the rest. In the case of Huallaga, 89 percent of the tenant farmers stated that their principal activity was agriculture. However, unlike the indigenous forest communities, who attempted to achieve some degree of crop diversification in their plots, the Andean migrants specialized in single-cropping. Their use of the clearing and burning system also resulted in massive destruction of the vegetation, which would normally prevent the heavy rains from falling directly onto the soil.

The system of shifting cultivation involves not only excessive deforestation by migrant tenant farmers, but also the misuse of land. In Jaén and San Ignacio, for example, while there are approximately 32,700 hectares of land suitable for cultivation, in 1980 47,404 hectares were in fact planted with coffee, which meant that 14,704 hectares had been sown in areas that had been recommended exclusively for forestry use. This misuse of forest land undoubtedly has a negative effect on the fragile ecological balance.

Although an awareness of this problem has recently emerged through the Special Development Projects, due emphasis has to be given to educational and training programs concerning the protection of the environment. The problem can also be tackled in several other ways. First, technological developments should be accompanied by environmental protection; indeed, it is essential to make the future installments of bank loans dependent on strict adherence to ecological rules. Second, the farmers must be made responsible for preventing the misuse of land and protecting forests. Although the way in which tenant farmers occupy the land (along the paths and roads over an extremely dispersed area) does not encourage the formation of farmers' organizations, it would be useful to establish producer or service cooperatives, which could help make settlers aware of environmental problems.

The role of the Special Development Projects should also be extended to urban zones. Given the rapid process of urbanization in the valleys of the forest highlands and its negative environmental effects (through the disposal of waste products in the rivers) corrective measures must be taken.

Another undesirble feature of state settlement policies is the undue emphasis placed by the Special Development Projects and the departmental development corporations[5] on the building of roads at the expense of agriculture. In the final report of the military government of 1980, there appears: "an allocation of credits for investment in the Department of San Martín during the year 1979 totaling 3079.7 million *soles* for the building of roads, whereas only 826.4 million *soles* were earmarked for agricultural development" (Gonzáles 1983).

In the region of Alto Mayo, however, a more integrated concept of development has recently emerged. Here the establishment of basic services for the migrant populations is considered an essential part of each new development plan (Gonzáles 1983).

While the forest region does not constitute the main destination for the Andean peasants (less than 20 percent of migrants from the sierra go to the Amazon basin), those who do migrate there believe that this will satisfy their hunger for land. An interesting study by Robin Shoemaker (1981: 96) on the Satipo settlement area summarizes concisely the attitude of the migrant farmers from the sierra:

What the peasant migrant sees in the mountain is, in a word, land. They come from areas in the sierra where they might have possessed a few plots of land which together would not make more than 1 or 2 hectares. The opportunity to acquire 20 hectares, the average size of a tenant farmer's land holding in the forest, is a strong incentive to move. Looking back, they always say that the rich people in their original communities owned 5 hectares and that, therefore, 20 hectares would appear to be practically a state.

## THE PEASANT ECONOMY IN THE FOREST HIGHLANDS

The peasant economy in the forest region is undergoing a rapid process of transformation. Settlers are becoming commercial farmers and some of the Andean migrants are now partially employed as wage earners. This section briefly outlines the structural characteristics of the peasant economy, which need to be given greater attention in the Special Development Projects. One of the major errors in the various settlement programs was the initial assumption that agriculture in settlement areas would be largely based on capitalist farming, and that production would be organized in terms of profit maximization. Several studies indicate that during the early stages of settlement most tenant farmers are unable to organize their production in this manner. In the early years, the poor pioneer settlers, who are obliged to make a completely new start in the frontier region, lack resources and must therefore grow crops for their own consumption; in many cases, they combine their work in the sierra with their activities in the forest. This period is a phase of primary accumulation in which circular movement between the sierra and the high forest makes it possible for them to eventually move their families.

The Alto Mayo settlement, however, has been an exception where movement has not been from the sierra, but rather from another densely populated settlement in the forest highland basin of Alto Marañon (González 1983: 26). The low cost of land in Alto Mayo, compared with Jaén and San Ignacio, encouraged settlers to leave the Alto Marañon basin. The farmers sold their land and migrated to Rioja and Moyobamba with a certain amount of capital in cash. A significant proportion of the tenant farmers of this valley therefore do not appear to have had to go through the accumulation phase and were even able to buy "improved" land on arrival. The work relating to clearing forests and cultivating virgin land was therefore completed over a much shorter period than in other settlements, where the consolidation of the production unit took much longer and proved to be more expensive.

The average monthly family income varies substantially among settlements in the forest highlands. In the Alto Huallaga, for example, in 1980 the average monthly family income was U.S. $150, compared with U.S. $50 in the Tambopata Valley in 1979 (Aramburú 1982).[6] There are perhaps two main reasons for this income difference. First, farmers in the Alto Huallaga have more land—an average of 26.9 hectares, while those in the Tambopata Valley have only 2 hectares (Bedoya 1983). Second, growing coca provides farmers with a much higher level of income than other crops. Although not all farmers in Alto Huallaga grow coca, a large proportion of them do. The average earnings in this region are thus naturally higher than in other regions where hard yellow maize, rice, or coffee are the predominant crops.

In general, farmers in the forest highlands enjoy a higher standard of living than in their regions of origin. Take, for example, the area of Tambopata, which has been described in a recent study as one of the most depressed areas in terms of economic development and availability of basic services such as housing (Table 11.4); in 1979, 47 percent of families had real incomes below the legally established minimum rural wage. Nevertheless, this situation was still better than in the Puno region, from which most of the Tambopata farmers had migrated, where 56.3 percent of families earned less than the minimum wage (Aramburú 1982). Although it is difficult to conclude without further evidence that farmers in all the basins of the forest highlands enjoy higher standards of living than those of peasants in their areas of origin, this does seem to be the case in the Tambopata Valley, with its relatively low level of development. In a survey carried out in Alto Huallaga in 1973, two-thirds of the respondents indicated that their situation had improved after moving or simply that they were satisfied (Cencira 1974).

It should be borne in mind, however, that the improvement in farmers' incomes usually occurs over several years, as can be seen from a survey of 136 farmers carried out in 1967 in the Tingo María-Tochache area by the Food and Agriculture Organization of the United Nations (FAO) and the National Office for Agrarian Reform (ONRA). The study area was divided into four subzones: Naranjillo, Pueblo Nuevo, Aucayacu, and La Morada. The first of these covered farmers who had been living there for approximately 18 years on average; the second, for approximately seven years; the last two, for six years. The results of the survey indicated that the highest average monthly family income was in Naranjillo, the oldest settlement (U.S. $508); in Pueblo Nuevo the average was U.S. $92.5; and in Aucayacu and La Morada, U.S. $62.5 and U.S. $77.5, respectively (Nelson 1973). The Naranjillo settlement was a prosperous coffee-producing region. The first plantations were established there at the beginning of the 1950s, with the first crops harvested between 1954 and 1955, when there was a boom in international coffee prices. In the 1960s and 1970s, a large number of farmers also earned income from nonagricultural activities such as transport and commerce. The relatively higher incomes in this settlement were therefore partly due to greater occupational diversification. In the subzone of Pueblo Nuevo there were also coffee plantations, but these had been established more recently and international coffee prices during this period were not as favorable as in the previous decade. Aucayacu and La Morada were settlements established in 1961 and most of the crops sown were still for self-consumption: starchy maize, yucca, kidney beans, bananas, and a few coffee or cocoa plants in each plot. Although the evidence suggests that the move from subsistence to commercial farming is an important step toward increasing income, it seems that significant profits can be expected only after a number of years and when prices are favorable.

Several studies carried out in various agricultural regions with different levels of capitalist development show that the greater the capitalist development in a zone, the greater the inequalities in the distribution of incomes. In other words, the process of capitalist development generates social differentiation. In a comparative study of agricultural households in Cañete (which has a relatively high level of capitalist development), Bajo Piura (the coast), and Puno (the sierra, which has a relatively low level of such development), it was found that the former zones had a higher coefficient of variation of household income than the latter (Table 11.5). In the forest region of Puno, household income largely depends on the location of the plot of land (the closer the plot to the Sandia and San Juan del Oro road, the greater the income) and the amount of land planted with coffee (the greater the area, the higher the income). In the case of Alto Huallaga, the cultivation of coca is the main determinant of household income—the greater the area cultivated, the higher the income. Profits from coca can be up to ten times greater than those from other crops such as coffee and cocoa.

In Alto Mayo, a region that has the highest rank by socioeconomic development (Table 11.4),[7] the differences in household incomes are due partly to the differences in the area of land under cultivation and partly to the techniques (dry culture or irrigation) used in the cultivation of rice, a crop grown by 63.6 percent of the farmers in the valley (Peri 1983). In 1979, rice produced under irrigation generated, on average, gross incomes equal to 212,000 *soles* per hectare, compared with 95,000 *soles* produced under the dry culture system; in the same way, average profits were 102,000 and 39,000 *soles*, respectively. In 1982, the difference in gross income reflected a similar proportion: 990,000 *soles* in the first case, and 440,000 *soles* in the second, although net profits per hectare were negative because of an increase in direct production costs (Table 11.6; ILO-DGE 1984). These results show that the kind of technology used is an important factor in determining income—the difference between an average productivity of 4497 kilograms per hectare of rice cultivated under irrigation and 2000 kilograms per hectare under the dry farming system is the major source of income inequality (Gonzáles 1983).

Despite the rapid transformation of subsistence farming into commercial farming in many regions of the forest highlands, however, several characteristics of the former still remain.

A number of surveys recently carried out in Alto May (ILO-DGE 1984), Alto Huallaga (Aramburú 1981), and Huallaga Central-Bajo Mayo and Puno Selva (Aramburú and Ponce 1980) show that between 95 and 99 percent of farming households make use of unpaid labor for some of their agricultural activities. In Alto Mayo, for example, daily wage earners account for 73 percent of the labor used in the plots where rice is grown under irrigation and 50 percent in the more numerous units using the dry culture system, but the rest of the labor is still provided by family workers or obtained on an exchange basis (ILO/DGE 1984). In other words, unpaid work, especially that carried out by members of the family (24 percent of daily work in the plots operating under the dry culture system), continues to make a significant contribution to production activities. This explains why irrigated plots that showed losses of up to 276,687 *soles* per hectare in 1982 (Table 11.6) were nevertheless able to continue operating in 1983. One policy implication of these findings is that the training activities being carried out as part of the Special Development Projects should cover all members of the family and not just the head of the household.

Whereas farms in the forest highlands are able to make use of family labor, those in the sierra offer few employment opportunities to family members, thus forcing many to migrate out of the area. The greater availability of land in the forest highlands (plots with an average size of between 10 and 30 hectares),[8] the adoption of commercial crops (such as coffee, coca, rice, tea, and yellow maize), and relatively easy access to credit are important factors that help keep family labor on the farm in settlement areas (Bedoya 1983). The extent to which these family farms will be able to continue offering employment to future generations will very much depend on a series of measures which include:

a. the proper maintenance of the ecological balance of the tropical humid forest;
b. the greater utilization of uncultivated land and the replacement of the dry culture systems and their low labor demand with other technologies such as irrigated cultivation, which require more labor;
c. the regulation (through restriction of credits) of the land market to reduce the tendency toward fragmentation of landholdings, particularly in the regions with older settlements, such as the basin of Alto Maranón (Peri 1983).

For the consolidation of family farms, however, it is not sufficient simply to change production techniques to suit the environment or to avoid the fragmentation of landholdings through the strict regulation of credits. It is also essential to change the present producers' price structure, which is extremely unfavorable to farmers. In the short term, reliance on unpaid family labor may well reduce production costs. Eventually, however, production costs will rise as the children of the settlers leave the farm and become independent.

The situation will be different where prices become more favorable and where, despite the changes in market conditions, farms are able to maintain profitability.

Although a majority of farms in Alto Mayo and other basins in the forest highlands produce for the market, crop diversification for self-consumption needs, a characteristic feature of subsistence farming, is still common.

In Alto Mayo, rice cultivated under irrigation is the sole principal crop grown in only 19.4 percent of the farms, according to a recent survey carried out in the region (ILO/DGE 1984), whereas in 55.7 percent of the farms two principal crops and more than one secondary crop are grown (major diversified farming), and in 21.4 percent of cases there is one principal and one secondary crop (minor diversified farming). In the Alto Huallaga, Huallaga Central, and Puno forest too, most of the farmers practice crop diversification (Bedoya 1983). They do this not only to protect themselves against price fluctuations, but also to meet their own consumption needs. It is cheaper for farmers to produce some crops for their own consumption than to buy them in the market.

Another element that emerges from the analysis of the surveys carried out in the forest region of Puno, Alto Huallaga, Huallaga Central, and Alto May is the lack of occupational diversification among settlers. Only in the Alto Huallaga basin, and in the cattle-raising region of La Morada, which includes several planned settlements, is there a greater occupational diversification. Here, 51.6 percent of farmers carry on two activities (agriculture and cattle raising), although both are on-farm activities.

The differences in the occupational structure of the labor force among the provinces of the forest highlands are due not only to the different numbers of planned settlements in them, but also to the age of the settlements. As a result of massive agricultural development in Alto Mayo, the structure of the labor force in this region has undergone some significant changes. In 1972, the percentage of the labor force in the primary sector (agriculture, hunting, fishing) in Moyobamba and Rioja was 60 percent and 58 percent, respectively; in 1981, the figures had risen to 66.8 and 72.5 percent, with a corresponding percentage reduction in the secondary (manufacturing and building) and tertiary (services) sectors (Martínez 1983). These figures suggest that the settlement process has enlarged the agricultural sector in this region—migrants to this region are almost all agricultural workers (Lesevic 1983). The 1972 and 1981 census figures for other provinces of the forest highlands also show the increasing importance of the primary sector. In most cases, between 50 and 80 percent of the labor force is in this sector. In the older settlements, on the other hand (such as, for example, those in the provinces of Huallaga and Jaén), the secondary and tertiary sectors have increased their share in the labor force, and there has been a corresponding decline in the share of the primary sector, although a major proportion of the labor force is still engaged in the latter.

Occupational diversification could be of great benefit to farmers during the pioneering stage, when there is a great need for capital to reduce the time required for transforming virgin land into cultivated land; this period is usually long because of the difficult working conditions in the humid tropical forest (Helmsing 1983). A primary activity that can generate a significant level of cash income during this period is timber extraction. But the technique often practiced by the farmers to clear land for cultivation (cutting, clearing, and burning timber) is excessively wasteful. Moreover, wood is used only in the construction of houses and as a fuel for cooking. The marketing of this raw material could provide cash resources to the farmers precisely when they have the greatest need for them. However, their limited knowledge of such an alternative, and the small importance attached to this resource in successive development projects, explain why timber has not been marketed on a large scale. Despite the fact that the timber of the Amazon basin has less chance of finding a market than that of the tropical forests of

Africa (Nelson 1973: 183), such forestry resources are potentially very profitable for farmers and should not be undervalued.

A final aspect that is typical of all peasant economies is the exploitation of the farmers by the intermediaries who, as owners of capital, lend them money at the start of the agricultural season. To repay the loans, farmers are obliged to sell their produce to the intermediaries at prices usually well below the prevailing market prices. Such intermediaries are in a virtually monopsonistic position and take advantage of the lack of organization among the peasant population, which is widely scattered throughout the region. Their control of the means of transport, such as rafts and lorries, further exacerbates the dependence of the small farmers.

Many of the marketing and other related problems in a frontier region are due both to distance and to low physical yields in comparison with other more fertile zones that are closer to urban centers. The production of rice in Alto Mayo, for example, averages 4500 kilograms per hectare under irrigation, compared with 8000 kilograms per hectare in areas such as Arequipa (ILO/DGE 1984). On top of this, the intermediaries will try to reduce the prices paid to the farmers in order to recover transport costs and thus maintain the level of their own profits.

In most cases, the farmers for their part try to resolve the difficulties resulting from low prices and low yield by a more extensive use of land (which, in turn, implies greater use of paid labor or an increase in the work effort of family members) or by increasing productivity through the adoption of new technologies. However, since the latter course does not appear to be feasible in most cases, it is essential for the price structure to be changed so as to guarantee the farmers a minimum level of profit.

Small farmers in the most distant settlement areas have the greatest difficulties in planning their production activities (Helmsing 1983). On one hand they must cope with competition from the large plantations, and on the other they can grow only a limited number of crops because of their distance from the main market centers.

All these factors suggest the need for greater participation by the state, particularly in the area of marketing. There is an urgent need to guarantee minimum prices to producers, regulate the activities of the intermediaries, and encourage the diversification of occupational activities.

## PRESENT USE OF LAND IN THE FOREST HIGHLANDS

The total cultivated area in the forest highlands in 1979 was 527,000 hectares, 22 percent of the total cultivated area of the country. A recent study on the use of natural resources in the forest highlands provides a breakdown for that year of the total cultivated area by type of crop: 189,000 hectares of seasonal crops, 202,400 hectares of permanent crops, and 135,900 hectares of fodder crops (Table 11.7).

The data in Table 11.7 show that, in 1979, production in the forest highlands was largely oriented toward permanent crops, 90 percent of which were coffee and cocoa. The Jaén and San Ignacio, Alto Huallaga and Satipo-Chanchamayo basins appear to have developed their agricultural frontier essentially on the basis of coffee plantations.

Among annual crops, maize, rice, yucca, and bananas account for 70 percent of the total. In the Central Huallaga basin,[9] a relatively greater area is devoted to annual crops such as hard yellow maize, rice, and bananas. Although there are no precise studies on the increase in agricultural land under cultivation due to population growth in the forest highlands, approximate figures do exist. Between 1961 and 1979, the cultivated area in this region increased by 57 percent; this represents an increase from 7 to 22 percent of the total cultivated area in the country (Periaherrera 1983).

The most important aspect of the increase in the cultivated area in the forest highlands, however, is the clearing and burning technique, which was initially used to open up the Amazon forest. A study carried out in Central Huallaga points out that to develop 81,300 hectares of annual crops (equivalent to five times the area cultivated in 1979), 410,000 hectares of forest were destroyed. At the same time, the practice of shifting cultivation has led to underutilization of land so that often between 30 and 40 percent of the area is uncultivated (Bedoya 1983). A more rational use of the land in the forest highlands is therefore needed.

## EFFECTS OF RESETTLEMENT PROGRAMS ON INDIGENOUS COMMUNITIES IN PERU

According to the 1972 census, the Peruvian Amazon is inhabited by approximately 250,000 indigenous persons distributed among approximately 1000 communities, belonging to 12 different linguistic families and comprising 53 ethno-linguistic groups. These communities are completely isolated from the power structures of the country.

Generally considered as tribes, the ethno-linguistic groups of the Amazon are composed of large families, and are traditionally semi-nomadic. The organization of the production process in most cases revolves around the nucleus of the family; technology is of a paleolithic kind; productivity differences depend exclusively on differences in age and sex; private ownership of land does not exist, and it is the clans or family groups who decide its use; finally, the dry land clearing and burning technique is practiced—a characteristic of regions with a low population density.

Most production is for self-consumption. However, there is some evidence that the mercantile level of these ethnic minorities is increasing and resulting, in some cases, in a shift away from subsistence farming. There has also been an increase in the monetarization of their economies.[10] In other words, the subsistence strategies of the indigenous communities are changing, as a result of capitalist development, in some cases slowly, in others more rapidly.

The growth of the market economy has not occurred only in recent years, however. The rubber boom at the end of the last century is a clear example of this. Between the years 1870 and 1915, the Peruvian forest was transformed into one of the principal world suppliers of rubber, which was collected almost exclusively by the indigenous populations of the regions of the Amazon rivers of Marañón and Madre de Dios.

The expansion of the tea or coffee hacienda system, from the beginning of the present century up to approximately the middle of the 1970s, in lands that were historically held by indigenous communities (for example, by the Peruvian Corporation in El-Perené, Tournavista in River Pachitea, Huiro in El Urumamba, and Saipai in Alto Huallaga), has also had serious economic implications for these communities. In such cases, the state companies took various measures to appropriate native lands and, if possible, manpower by means of detribalization. In all the forest areas in which the hacienda systems were consolidated (the central and western forest area of Cuzco, and the Huallaga valley), the indigenous groups were absorbed as laborers or moved elsewhere after their lands had been taken over by the state companies (Varese 1974).

Likewise, timber extraction and the spontaneous migration of peasants from the sierra to colonize the forest highlands were very important factors in stimulating the growth of the economy in the frontier zone. Where pockets of indigenous people remained within the region occupied largely by migrant settlers from the sierra, the plots that were left to them were so small that all their economic and social systems had to be restructured on the basis of their new dependence on the Andean tenant farmers (Varese 1974).

## Social and ideological conflicts between indigenous communities and agricultural settlers

As the Andean settlements in the forest highlands have grown, land areas that were traditionally recognized as always having been held by indigenous forest communities have been taken over. Thus, the Aguarunas and Jíbaros of the northern forest, the Cashibos, Shipibos, Amueshas and Campas of the central and northern forest, and the Machiguengas and Yaminaguas of the southern forest have been slowly driven to areas in the forest lowlands as a result of the population pressure exercised by the migrant farmers from the sierra. The competition for land and labor has led to serious inter-ethnic conflicts. The priority recently given to road network development plans in the Amazon has aggravated these conflicts (Aramburú 1982),the most serious of which have been caused by the settlers' occupation of farms held by the indigenous communities. In his study on settlements in Satipo, Shoemaker points out that whereas the Campas have, on average, 3.4 hectares per family, the figure for migrant settlers is 20 hectares per family (Table 11.8).

The pressure from the migrant settlers has, in many cases, forced indigenous families to organize themselves into communities as a means of defense against the usurpation of their lands, resources, goods, and cultural identity. Further, in those regions where the settlement process has been most marked, hunting, fishing, and gathering are practiced relatively less frequently, and "in most cases, the quality of the products obtained is poor since, for the communities, settlement has meant the despoilment of their lands and resources. The opening up of roads and the resulting population pressure due to in-migration have led to the extinction of many animal and plant species and the significant reduction of others" (Shoemaker 1981: 297).

Finally, the settlement farmers frequently employ indigenous manpower, essentially for agricultural activities (Shoemaker 1981: 299). This dependence on the indigenous population also takes other forms. For example, farmers would not have been able to settle in the Satipo region without the assistance of the Campas, who taught them to hunt, fish, and grow crops in the forest. Moreover, many agricultural activities were originally assigned to the Campas by the Andean pioneers because of the speed with which they carried them out (Shoemaker 1981: 83).

Shoemaker points out in his study that, in the Satipo zone, the farmers from the sierra view the Campas as barbarian, backward, and uncivilized. Three factors should be borne in mind, however, in discussing this important aspect of inter-ethnic relations:

1. The concept of civilization was introduced by the Franciscan missionaries, who were the first to establish contact with the indigenous inhabitants and who subsequently brought in the first farmers from the sierra. The Campa religion was rejected as incomprehensible, both by the missionaries and by the Andean farmers for whom civilization was identified with Christianity.

2. The Campas, like many other indigenous communities, are seminomadic. They practice hunting, fishing, gathering, and long-term fallow farming, which implies continuous migratory movement. These practices were viewed as barbarian and backward by the sierra farmers,

who identified permanent residence or sedentariness with progress and civilization.

3. An important element in the "civilizing" ideology of the settlers was their view that, over the years, the inter-tribal bellicosity of the indigenous communities would gradually disappear.

The consequences of the colonizing process for indigenous communities, both in the forest highlands and in the lowlands, should therefore be evaluated within the context of this historical development. The arrival of peasants from the sierra inevitably leads to a break-up of native territorial integrity, which makes it impossible for such communities to reproduce themselves in the future as ethnically differentiated societies. Furthermore, the reduction in size of the indigenous areas leads to a slow but almost irreversible sapping of cultural identity.

The problem of the loss of land by the idigenous communities does not arise solely as a result of the Andean peasant migrations or the establishment of large estates in the various basins; the forestry concessions granted by the state are another factor. In certain areas of the forest lowlands (Bajo Huallaga and the Pastaza basin, for example), forestry concessions were granted to timber firms or to individual persons in areas occupied by the Cocamillas, Jíbaros, Achuales, and Candoshi ethnic groups. As a result the indigenous communities have been deprived of their legal rights of ownership of the land. A recent report points out:

Eight years after the coming into force of Legislative Decrees Nos. 20653 and 22175, land ownership has been granted to only 372 communities out of the existing 1000, involving an area of 1,314,142 hectares, which repreents only 1.8 percent of the total area. This means that the indigenous population, which accounts for 13 percent of the total population in the Amazon and 26 percent of the rural sector of the region, owns only 1.8 percent of the land in this region. (Mora 1982).

As far as the Special Development Projects are concerned, the attitude of the state has been somewhat ambivalent. In some cases, as in the Pichis-Palcazú project, measures were introduced to grant land titles to the resident communities. Others, such as those of Jaén and San Ignacio, include no such measures. This often leads to friction or serious conflict between settlers and indigenous communities. To make matters worse, the state bureaucracy in no way helps resolve the difficulties of the indigenous groups.

The real solution, however, is not the granting of land titles to the indigenous population, but the formulation of educational programs to make settlers and native inhabitants aware of the importance of mutual respect and coexistence. Recently, a number of technical studies on the most appropriate agricultural techniques for the forest highlands have recommended the use of the so-called mosaic of crops technology, which has been used by indigenous inhabitants for generations. Attention should be drawn, in introducing this technique to settlement farmers, to the fact that it forms part of the daily life of the indigenous communities. This would, in turn, foster respect and admiration for the indigenous communities.

## CONCLUSIONS AND POLICY IMPLICATIONS

Planned settlements in the Peruvian forest have from the beginning suffered from a series of structural failures. In no case has a project been preceded by a serious in-depth study of its economic and social feasibility. Even the objectives to be pursued have often been laid down after the technical and credit assistance programs were already under way. For these reasons, most of the projects have had limited success.

Given the availability of large areas of unexploited land, however, especially in the Peruvian forest lowlands, small pilot planned settlement projects could be drawn up, obviously on the basis of economic and social feasibility studies carried out prior to the initiation of settlement activity. These pilot projects would serve as a model to subsequent spontaneous settlements, provided that a series of strict technological and ecological requirements were observed.

The practice of shifting cultivation by settlers and excessive deforestation are the major reasons for the serious ecological deterioration that is occurring in the different basins of the forest highlands. The cultivation of crops that are not suitable for the area has also contributed to the environmental problems. In view of this, there is an urgent and immediate need for educational programs for the settlers covering the various aspects of environmental protection. Bank loans should also be made conditional on the strict compliance with specific ecological guidelines.

It is essential to recognize that while there is an urgent need for roads in a frontier zone, development must fully transcend this need. The establishment of basic services as well as technical and agricultural extension programs are essential aspects to be considered in each new development plan.

Insofar as the migration of poor settlers from the sierra is determined by push factors such as landlessness, unemployment, and low productivity, resources must be redirected to this region to generate the work and income earning opportunities that would discourage migration.

The results of the surveys carried out in the Puno forest, Alto Huallaga, and Alto Mayo show that there is an increase in income with the introduction of specific commercial crops. These become profitable only after a number of years, however, particularly when prices are favorable. The analysis nevertheless suggests that any shift from a pioneering self-consumption form of agriculture to one that is commercially oriented is a significant step toward increasing income.

In a number of valleys of the forest highlands, a rapid process of transformation in the mode of production is occurring as a result of technological and infrastructural development. Some of the basic characteristics of the peasant economy remain intact, however. First, unpaid family work continues to make a significant contribution to production activities, thereby reducing production costs. A policy implication of this is that the training activities carried out under the Special Development Projects should cover all family members and not just household heads. Second, in many cases the diversification of crops is for self-consumption needs rather than for the market. This is not taken into account by the various state settlement bodies, particularly the banks and credit institutions that usually grant loans to farmers who have diversified their crops for commercial purposes. It would be pertinent therefore to recommend that credit should be extended to cover self-consumption crops, particularly to settlers in the pioneering stage, without the need for immediate repayment.

Surveys carried out in the Puno forest, Alto Huallaga, Huallaga Central, and Alto Marañón show that the level of occupational diversification is low among settlers. Most of them work on their own plots of land and specialize in agriculture. It would therefore be advisable for the settlers, particularly in the pioneer accumulation phase, to diversify their activities and sources of income.

Another aspect that is typical of peasant economies is the role of intermediaries, who are in a virtually monopsonistic position and take advantage of the unorganized peasant population scattered throughout the forest highlands. The most immediate and visible consequences of this situation are the low prices that farmers receive for their produce. Moreover, the further the settlements are from the urban centers, the more merchants will try to compensate for transport costs by reducing the prices paid to settlers.

Thus, even if the land is used more satisfactorily and the subdivision of landholdings is controlled, it will not be possible to guarantee the profitability and consolidation of family farms unless prices and marketing methods are improved. In this connection, the state should step up its participation by fixing minimum prices, establishing a basic market infrastructure, and regulating the activities of intermediaries.

The practice of shifting cultivation has resulted in an "extensive" use of the land. A significant proportion of the agricultural land is now uncultivated. Although this has been done largely to maintain soil fertility, measures should be taken to use land more intensively and to adopt more appropriate technologies.

There is also some evidence that land disputes between migrants and indigenous communities have led to social tensions and inter-ethnic conflicts. It is important, therefore, to take effective measures to reduce such conflicts. If possible, social services such as education and health should be made available to both groups, and a suitable social climate generated for their integration.

Overall, the analysis in this study suggests that the achievements of the land settlement programs have fallen far short of expectations. This is largely because land development in the forest highlands had been characterized by a piecemeal approach, and no serious consideration has been given to improving agricultural technology or solving the problems of large-scale deforestation. Moreover, there has been a neglect of complementary investments in forestry, industries, and services in colonization areas that would have generated alternative employment and improved the living standards of the settlers. The lack of credit and marketing facilities has also been a major constraint on crop production, crop diversification, and new land development. There is thus an urgent need to provide effective marketing infrastructure and credit as well as educational and training programs for settlers. Finally, the problem of reckless deforestation requires an imaginative and innovative approach in the interest of maintaining the ecological balance.

## NOTES

1. The total population of the country increased by 2.2 percent 191 between 1940 and 1961; by 2.9 percent between 1961 and 1972; and by 2.6 percent between 1972 and 1981 (Aramburú 1982: Table 1).

2. Although in recent decades a distinction has been made.

3. This figure is obtained by dividing the total rural population of the forest highlands in the 1972 census (507,066 inhabitants) by five (Aramburú 1981).

4. Migrations to the city are usually individual rather than family migrations.

5. These are bodies that have recently been set up with full autonomous powers and management. At the present time, there are seven Special Development Projects in the forest area: Jaén-San Ignacio y Bagua, Alto Mayo, Bajo Mayo-Huallaga Central, Alto Huallaga, Madre de Dios, and Satipo-Chanchamayo. There is, in addition, Pichis-Palcazú, which includes both high- and lowlands.

6. In 1967, a survey of 136 families in Alto Huallaga showed that the average monthly family income was U.S. $130, that is, only U.S. $20 less than 13 years later. Although there may have been some underestimation of income in 1980 because of the clandestine nature of coca production, account must also be taken

of the impact of the economic crisis that has been affecting the country since 1976.

7. This privileged situation may since have changed because of massive migration from other areas.

8. Although only 30 to 40 percent of the land is used.

9. Periaherrera includes the sub-basins of the El Alto and Bajo Mayo as regions of Huallaga Central.

10. Despite structural changes, however, production for self-consumption and nonmonetary incomes is still characteristic of the indigenous communities, as compared with the settlement farmers.

## BIBLIOGRAPHY

Aramburú, C. 1981. *Estudio social de la colonización Tingo-María-Tocache-Campanilla*. Washington, D.C.: USAID.

———. 1982. "Expansión de la frontera agraria y demográfica de la Selva Alta Peruana." *Colonización en la Amazonía*. Lima: CIPA (February).

Aramburú C., and A. Ponce. 1980. *Organización socio-económica de la familia campesina y migración en tres regiones del Perú*. Lima: INANDEP (September).

Bedoya, E. 1981. *La destrucción del equilibrio ecológico en las cooperativas del Alto Huallaga*. Document Series no. 1. Lima: CIPA.

———. 1982a. "Colonizaciones en la Ceja de Selva a través del Enganche: El caso Saipai en Tingo María." *Colonización en la Amazonía*. Lima: CIPA.

———. 1982b. *Historia económica de una gran propriedad de la Ceja de Selva: El caso Saipai 1950–1970*. University of Syracuse, USAID.

———. 1983. *Tendencias en el proceso colonizador de la Selva Alta: Estudio de siete regiones*. Lima: Labor Migration Project ILO-DGE.

Cencira. 1974. *Diagnóstico socio-económico de la colonización Tingo María-Campanilla y Tocache*. Cencira, Lima.

Chirif, A. 1972. "Ocupación territorial de la Amazonía y marginación de la población nativa." *América Indígena*. (Mexico) 35, no. 2.

Durand, E. 1983. *Recomendaciones para formular políticas de colonización*. Cencira, Lima. Mimeo.

Gonzáles, A. 1983. *Colonizaciones y patrones de asentamiento en el Alto Mayo*. Lima: Migration Project, ILO/DGE.

Helmsing, B. 1983. *Colonos, colonización y produccion agrícola en los países andinos*. Mimeo.

International Labor Organisation/Dirección General del Empleo. 1984. *Condiciones sobre el poblamiento en Alto Mayo*. Workshop course: Employment, Labour Migration and Regional Development, Labour Migration Project, Moyobareba, Lima.

Lesevic, B. 1983. "Dinámica demográfica y colonización en la Selva Alta Peruana entre 1940 y 1981." Paper presented to Seminar on Population and Settlements in the Peruvian Forest Highlands of the Amazon, Lima, National Population Council, November.

Martínez, H. 1976. *Las colonizaciones selváticos dirigidas en el Peru: Antecedentes, actualidad y perspectivas* (version preliminar). Estudios de población y desarollo, Centro de Estudios de Poblacion y Desarollo, Lima, Peru, July.

Martínez, I. 1983. "Mercados laborales en la Selva Alta." Paper presented at Seminar on Population and Settlements in the Peruvian Forest Highlands, Lima, CNP, November.

Mora, C. 1982. "Las comunidades nativas y la colonización en la Selva Alta." Paper presented at Seminar on Population and Settlements in the Peruvian Forest Highlands, Lima, CNP, November.

Nelson, M. 1973. *Development of Tropical Lands*. Baltimore, MD: Johns Hopkins University Press.

Peri, P. 1983. *Migraciones, tecnología y empleo agrícola*. Lima: Labor Migration Project, ILO/DGE.

Periaherrera, T. 1983. "Uso de recursos naturales en la Selva Alta." Paper presented at Seminar on Population and Settlements in the Peruvian Forest Highlands, Lima, CNP, November.

Shoemaker, R. 1981. "Colonization and Urbanization in Peru: Empirical and Theoretical Perspective." *Rice University Studies*, Lima. Mimeo.

Teddy, P. 1983. "Uso de recursos naturales en la Selva Alta". Paper presented at Seminar on Population and Settlements in the Peruvian Forest Highlands, Lima, CNP, November.

Varese, S. 1974. *La sal de los cerros. Una aproximación al mundo Campa*. Retablo del papel, ed. Lima.

Werlich, D. 1975. *The Conquest and Settlement of the Peruvian Montana*. Ann Arbor, MI: University Microfilms.

Table 11.1
Size and growth of population by natural regions, 1940-81

| Natural regions | 1940 No. | % | 1960 No. | % | 1972 No. | % | 1981 No. | % | Annual growth rate (%) 1940-61 | 1961-72 | 1972-81 |
|---|---|---|---|---|---|---|---|---|---|---|---|
| Coast | 1,759,573 | 28.3 | 3,859,443 | 39.0 | 6,242,993 | 46.1 | 8,512,944 | 50.0 | 3.8 | 4.5 | 3.5 |
| Metropolitan Lima | (645,172) | (10.4) | (1,845,910) | (18.7) | (3,302,523) | (24.4) | (4,600,891) | (27.0) | (5.1) | (5.5) | (3.7) |
| Sierra | 4,033,952 | 65.0 | 5,182,093 | 52.3 | 5,953,293 | 44.0 | 6,704,390 | 39.4 | 1.2 | 1.2 | 1.3 |
| Forest highlands | 414,452 | 6.7 | 865,210 | 8.7 | 1,341,922 | 9.9 | 1,813,887 | 10.6 | 3.6 | 4.1 | 3.4 |
| Peru, total | 6,207,977 | 100.0 | 9,906,746 | 100.0 | 13,538,208 | 100.0 | 17,031,221 | 100.0 | 2.2 | 2.9 | 2.6 |

Source: Aramburú (1982: p. 12, Table 1).

381

Table 11.2
Land tenure in the forest region

| Area (hectares) | No. of plots | Percentage | Total hectares | Percentage |
|---|---|---|---|---|
| Less than 1 | 12,956 | 9.40 | 4,653.22 | 0.19 |
| 1 to less than 5 | 50,959 | 36.97 | 120,228.66 | 4.94 |
| 5 to less than 500 | 73,579 | 53.38 | 1,596,669.50 | 65.65 |
| 500 and above | 291 | 0.21 | 612,864.20 | 25.20 |
| Unspecified | 39 | 0.03 | 97,770.12 | 4.02 |
| Total | 137,824 | 100.00 | 2,432,185.7 | 100.00 |

Source: Agricultural census, 1972, National Bureau of Statistics and Census, Lima, 1975.


Table 11.3
Clearing of forest areas for shifting cultivation, 1925-99

| Period | Area (hectares) |
|---|---|
| 1925-74 | 4,500,000 |
| 1975-79 | 925,918 |
| 1980-84 | 1,641,231 |
| 1985-89 | 2,868,192 |
| 1990-94 | 5,006,383 |
| 1995-99 | 8,822,834 |
| Total | 23,764,558 |

Source: Martínez (1976: 20).

Table 11.4
Rank classification of the basins of the forest highlands according
to some indicators of development

| Forest highland basin | Mortality[a] | Development and socioeconomic diversification[b] | Basic housing and other services[c] | Total |
|---|---|---|---|---|
| Alto Mayo | 1 | 2 | 2 | 5 |
| Chanchamayo | 5 | 3 | 1 | 9 |
| Pichis-Palcazú and Oxapampa | 3 | 4 | 4 | 11 |
| Alto Huallaga | 4 | 1 | 6 | 11 |
| Huallaga Central, Bajo Mayo | 2 | 7 | 7 | 16 |
| Perené, Ene, and Tambo (Satipo) | 7 | 5 | 5 | 17 |
| Alto Urubamba | 9 | 6 | 3 | 18 |
| Alto Marañón | 5 | 8 | 9 | 22 |
| Pachitea | 8 | 11 | 8 | 27 |
| Apurimac | 10 | 12 | 10 | 32 |
| Tambopata | 11 | 10 | 11 | 32 |
| Inambari | 12 | 9 | 12 | 33 |
| Alto Madre de Dios-Manú | 13 | 13 | 13 | 39 |

Source: Lesevic (1983).

[a] Life expectancy at birth, together with infant mortality rate and the likelihood of death before the age of 2 years.

[b] Percentage of population aged 5 years and above that is literate; percentage of the economically active population with incomplete secondary education; percentage wage earners; percentage nonagricultural labor force, percentage nonagricultural wage earners; percentage of labor force in professional, technical and administrative occupations; economic activity rate; percentage of economically active population employed.

[c] Percentage of dwellings with access to drinking water; percentage of dwellings with electricity; percentage of dwellings with bath or shower; percentage of dwellings with latrine or lavatory; percentage of dwellings with electric, gas, or kerosene cooking facilities.

Table 11.5
Family labor input and incomes in agricultural households

| Region | No. of families surveyed (1) | Average no. of workers per family (2) | Average no. of workers per family excluding unpaid workers (3) | Average monthly family income (in current soles) (4) | Average monthly family income (in constant soles; 1974 = 100) (5) | Standard deviation of family income in column 5 (6) | Coefficient of variation = (6) ÷ (5) (7) |
|---|---|---|---|---|---|---|---|
| Cañete | 115 | 3.1 | 1.8 | 14,807.35 (June 1977) | 5,541.26 | 5,833.40 | 1.053 |
| Bajo piura | 103 | 2.8 | 1.9 | 11,500.00 (Aug. 1977) | 4,071.00 | 2,626.33 | 0.645 |
| Puno forest | 145 | 2.4 | 1.2 | 14,213.79 (Oct. 1978) | 2,875.77 | 2,933.40 | 1.020 |
| Puno sierra | 206 | 2.0 | 1.4 | 8,924.76 (Dec. 1978) | 1,728.87 | 1,287.77 | 0.745 |

Source: Aramburú and Ponce (1980: Table 43).

384

Table 11.6
Direct production costs and gross profits of rice cultivation
in Alto Mayo (in soles)

| Type of cultivation | Gross income per ha. | Direct production costs per ha. (Total costs per ha.) | Profit per ha. |
|---|---|---|---|
| 1978/79 Campaign | | | |
| Rice (irrigation) | 212,000 | 110,000 | 102,000 |
| Rice (dry culture) | 95,000 | 56,000 | 39,000 |
| 1982 Campaign | | | |
| Rice (mechanical irrigation) | 990,000 | 1,013,958 (1,172,637) | -23,958 -182,637 |
| Rice (irrigation by yoke) | 990,000 | 1,108,008 (1,266,687) | -118,008 -276,687 |
| Rice (dry culture) | 440,000 | 450,395 (529,734) | -10,395 -89,734 |

Source:  Peri (1983).

Table 11.7
Distribution of cultivated land by crop, 1979 (in thousands
of hectares)

| Crops (1) | Forest highlands (2) | Peru (3) | (2) as percentage of (3) |
|---|---|---|---|
| Seasonal crops | 189.0 | 1,711.8 | 11.0 |
| Permanent crops | 202.4 | 299.3 | 67.6 |
| Fodder crops | 135.9 | 381.6 | 35.6 |
| Total | 527.3 | 2,392.7 | 22.0 |

Source:  Periaherrera (1983: Table 13).

Table 11.8
Land owned by indigenous communities, 1974

| Community | No. of families | Total land owned (hectares) |
|---|---|---|
| Alto Sondobeni | 16 | 60 |
| Campamento Portillo | 18 | 100 |
| Cushibiani | 22 | 50 |
| Paureli | 27 | 100 |
| San Pascual | 18 | 30 |
| Sta. Rose de Panakiari | 26 | 100 |
| Yavironi | 23 | 70 |
| Total | 150 | 510 |

Source:   Shoemaker (1981: 168).

# Index

accessibility, 101–2
Acuna, Teodoro, 298
*adat* (customary) law, 62
administration, effect of on settlement programs, 35
African socialism, 241
age limit, 98
Agrarian Land Reform Code, 136
agrarian problems, alleviation of, 144
Agrarian Reform, Department of, 137
Agrarian Reform Act, 358
agrarian reform program, 89
agrarian revolution, 262–64
agregados, 334, 337
agricultural cooperatives, 358, 359
Agricultural Cooperatives Program, 222
agricultural development, 15–17
Agricultural Development International of Israel (Agridev), 240
Agricultural Machinery and Equipment Corporation, 135
agricultural output, 143

agricultural production, decline in, 250
*Agricultural Sector Review*, 223
agricultural settlements, 211
agricultural settlers, vs. indigenous communities, 373–76
Agriculture, Department of, 101
alang-alang grass (imperata cylindrica), 71, 76
All-Ethiopian Peasants' Association, 171, 172
American frontier zones, recent trends in, 271–307
anti-villagization, 260
archipelago, Indonesian, 64
Arusha Declaration (1967), 21
Associacao de Crédito e Assistencia Rural (ACAR), 323
Awash Valley Authority, 168, 169

balance-of-payments, 361; deterioration in, 206
barbasco trade, 297

Belaúnde, Fernando, 358
benefit-cost analysis, 4, 41
Bilut Valley scheme, 96, 103
block method, cultural practices, 105, 106
Board of Investments (BOI), 136
Brazil: colonization experience in, 317–39; colonization policy, 318–24
Brazilian Institute of Land Reform (IBRA), 318
British-American Tobacco Company (BAT), 240
budget allocation, transmigration and, 72–73
Bureau of Resettlement of the Ministry of Agrarian Reform, 136, 137, 146

Campas, 374
cash crops, 89, 262, 292
cattle ranchers, 276
CDP/SDA resettlement program, implementation of, 222
Central Industrial Region (CIR), 136
chain migration, 62, 75
Chief Inspector of Mines, 101
children, retention of, 279
child-spacing, 259
choice land, 176
Christianity, 374
Chuping Sugar Cane Project, 106
civilization, concept of, 374
classification system, used by RRC, 170
Coastal Development Project (CDP), 202, 204, 208, 212, 219, 224, 226
coffee frontier movement, 320
coffee plantation owners, 276
coffee trade, 297
colonial government, U.S., 131
colonial period (Philippines), 130–33
colonial settlement schemes, 238–39
colonists: characteristics of, 280–82; inequality among, 294; lack of capital and, 284; strategies, 279–96
colonization, 272; consolidation phase of, 291–96; direct, 318, 326; experience, in Brazil, 317–39; government

attitudes toward, 274; large-scale, 8; pioneer phase of, 283–91; vs. production intensification, 41; role of state in, 318; schemes, record of, 1; selection phase of, 280–83
colonization policies: current, 363–64; ecology and, 363; of Peru, 357–61
colonization programs, 39; primary objective of, 272
colonization zones: population mobility in, 275–79; retention in, 275–79
Commonwealth Act(s): 441, 133; 461(1939), 135; 604(1940), 135
Commonwealth period (Philippines), 133–34
communal farms, 34, 239, 249, 250, 261, 263; modernization of, 264
communal production, 245
Communist party, Indonesian, 53
Companhia Brasileira de Alimentos (COBAL), 323
Companhia Brasileira de Armazenamento (CIBRAZEM), 323
compensation, 116
compulsion, formation of Ujamaa village and, 246–47
consolidation phase program recommendations, 295–96
contract work, introduction of, 103
cooperative farming, 34, 173
cooperative settlements, 241
Court of Agrarian Relations, 136
cover crop (stylosanthus), 71
credit, unavailability of, 284
cultural practices, of settlers, 105–6

decentralization system, flaws in, 92
deforestation, 26, 43, 364, 376, 378
Dega zone, 162
demographic profile, of Philippines, 143
dependency, relationship of, 35
depletion, 302
de Samaniego, Jacinta, 298
detribalization, 373
Directorate for Land Planning (PTPT), 57

Directorate-General of Transmigration, 60, 61
Directorate of Regional and City Planning (DITADA), 56
Director of Geological Surveys, 101
drought, 203, 219
dry zone, 8
Durand, Eduardo, 363

ecological deterioration, 26; reduction of, 205
economic analysis, scheme performance and, 4
economic policies, and land settlement, 130–37
economic rehabilitation, 226
economic resources, development of, 206–7
education, 215; goals, 215
educational programs, 226
educational qualifications, settler selection, 98
*Education for Self-Reliance*, 257
elementary school program, 216
employment: nonagricultural, 23; nonfarm, 252; off-farm, 18, 288, 295, 302
employment opportunities: non-farm, 23–24; off-farm, 273; utilization of, 250–53
employment search, 114
encomienda system, 131
equipment disuse, rate of, 180
Ethiopia, land settlements in, 161–83
exchange labor, 141
export crops, 262

fair income, 116
fallback option, 278
family labor, reliance on, 338
family planning, 74, 259
famine, 167
farm(s): as commercial venture, 33; communal, 239, 250, 261, 263, 264
farmers, exploitation of, 371
farming: communal, 34, 249; cooperative, 34, 173; subsistence, 373

farm size, principles used in determining, 30
federal grants, 94
Federal Land Consolidation and Rehabilitation Authority (FELCRA), 12, 95
Federal Land Development Authority (FELDA), 3, 9, 15, 16, 17, 18, 23, 27, 28, 30, 32, 35, 89–118; achievements and assessments, 108–15; implementation strategy, 95–108; policy issues, 90–95
federal loans, 94
FELDA Latex Handling Corporation, 106
FELDA Marketing Corporation, 106
FELDA Mills Corporation, 106
financial targets, 220
First Five-Year Development Plan (1957–1961), 166
First National Development Plan, 319
fiscal incentives, 319
fishing settlements, 211
Five-Year Development Plan (FYDP), 220
fluoride, 260
Food and Agriculture Organization of the United Nations (FAO), 367
food production, 247
food security, 222
foreign trade balance, 218
forest clearance, 101
Forest Department, 101
forest highlands, use of land in, 371–72
forestry agencies, 70
Franciscan missionaries, 374
freehold tenure, 34
Fringe Alienation Schemes, 93, 94–95; failure of, 95; financing of, 94
frontier: closing of, 135; opening of, 130–33
frontier area, development of, 142–43
frontier migration, impact of, 143
frontier population, stabilization of, 306

Gezira Scheme (Sudan), 30
Gini coefficient, 21, 254

government resettlement programs, direct, 132–33
"green revolution," 41
Group Settlement Schemes, deficiencies of, 93–94
growth centers, 43

haciendas, 356, 359
Hardjono, Joan, 75
Harvard Advisory Group, 164
harvest (bawon) laborers, 49
health, 215–16; expenditures, 215; facilities, 20, 258–59; standards, 20
homestead concept, 131
household incomes, differences in, 368
housing, 226; lack of, 23; programs, 214
human capital, development of, 291
human resources, development of, 107

illiteracy rates, 256
ILO mission report, 10, 27, 145, 168, 205
implementation, FELDA's strategy of, 95–108
import substitution, 134, 136
incentives: formation of Ujamaa village and, 245–46; lack of, 35
income: distribution of, 33, 333; incentives, 212; maldistribution of, 147; settler, 110–11
income levels, settlers and, 17–19
indigenous communities: vs. agricultural settlers, 373–76; effects of resettlement programs on, 372–76
indigenous population, 59–60
Indonesia: program problems, 69–70; transmigration in, 48–76; transmigration policies in, 51–61
industrialization, 134
industries: agro-based, 117; import substitution, 134; small-scale, 246, 252
influenza, 334, 335
infrastructure assessment, 216–17
inheritance laws, 146

initiative, as selective criteria, 96
in-migration, 374
institutional credit, access to, 39
Instituto Nacional de Colonizacao e Reforma Agraria (INCRA), 318, 323, 326, 327, 337
intake, settler, 109–10
Inter-Governmental Group for Indonesia (IGGI), 73
Interisland Migration Division of the Bureau of Labor, 132
interstate resettlement, incidence of, 113
inter-zonal turnover, 279
Investment Incentives Act (1967), 136
irrigation, lack of, 23
Italian occupation, of Ethiopia, 165

Japanese settlers, 299

kampong (village), 15
Kolla zone, 161

labor force, recruitment of, 104
labor-land ratios, 165, 169
labor opportunities, utilization of, 250–53
labor-shortage zones, 285
labor utilization, 250–53
land: communal ownership, 165; demand vs. capacity, 90; fast-depleting resources, 116; fragmentation, 162; irrigated, 221; ownership of, 101; preparation, 56–57; private ownership of, 372; quality of, 16; rain-fed, 221; rent, 112; in resettlement projects, 16; shortage, 70–71; unalienated, 99; unusable, 70; unutilized, 95
land administration, 163–64
land alienation, 90–93; initiation of, 91; method of, 90
land concentration, 24–25; process of, 294–95
land development, 90–93
Land Development Ordinance (1956), 111
land grant orders, 163

landholdings, inequalities in, 116
landless, provision of land for, 12–14
landlord-tenant relationships, 130
land reform, 318; colonization as substitute for, 274
Land Registration Act (1902), 131
land settlement(s), 1; agricultural production in, 249–50; case studies, 137–41; costs and benefits of, 260–62; definition of, 3; economic policies and, 130–37; in Ethiopia, 161–83; in Malaysia, 89–118; in Philippines, 129–48; policies of, 2; programs, 38–41; in United Republic of Tanzania, 237–64
Land Settlement Development Corporation (LASEDECO), 135, 140
land tenure system, 24, 320, 332; effect of on settlement programs, 33–35
land titles, 335–37
land-titling system, 295
land use planning, 239
large-scale colonization, concept of, 8
Leguia, Augusto, 358
life expectancy, 338; rise in, 259
literacy campaigns, 175
literacy rate, 175
loan eligibility requirements, 305
loan recovery, system of, 112
loan repayment, settler, 111–12
loans: government agency, 285; repayment of, 290–91

Magsaysay, Ramon, 144
Mahaweli Development Board, 27
malaria, 334, 335; incidence of, 216, 226
malaria control programs, 171
Malaysia, land settlement in, 89–118
management structure, 107
marga groups, 71
maternal and child health (MCH) program, 259
migrant population, age structure of, 330
migrants: Andean, 356, 365; assistance to, 57–59; characteristics of, 138–39; improved welfare of, 17–21; long-distance, 166; origins of, 138–39; rural-urban, 114; short-distance, 166
migrant selection, 69
migrant workers, 281
migration: inter-regional, 248; interstate, 113; intrastate, 113; rural-rural, 9; rural-urban, 9, 117; second-generation, 114–15; self-financed, 138; spontaneous, 26, 61–63, 65, 74, 137; urban, 117; voluntary, 52
migration flows, 13
migration process, 139
mineral clearance, 101
minifundia-latifundia pattern, 25, 294
minifundistas, 39, 274
minifundization, process of, 281
Ministry of Agrarian Reform (MAR), 146
Ministry of Land Reform and Administration, 164
minority groups: assimilation of, 144–45; pacification of, 144–45
money shortage, 71
mortality rates, 287, 331, 338
Muslims, 131, 145; uprisings, 147
Muslim separatists, 10

national economy, diversification of, 206–7
National Institute of Colonization and Land Reform (INCRA), 285
National Integration Program (PIN), 319, 321, 322
National Irrigation Board (NIB), 21
National Land Settlement Administration (NLSA), 133
National Office for Agrarian Reform (ONRA), 367
National Resettlement and Rehabilitation Administration (NARRA), 135, 140
national security, 10
Netherlands colonization policy, 49, 50, 53, 62, 65
Netherlands colonization program, 56–57

new areas, development of, 10
new community, establishment of, 274
New People's Army (NPA), 144
nomadic-hunters-cultivators , 169
nomadic population, 162
nomads, 43, 169 ; mass exodus of, 203; resettlement schemes, 208–16
nomad settlers, retention of, 217–18
nonagricultural employment, scarcity of, 23
nonfarm employment, 252
nucleated settlements, 241

occupational diversification, 367, 370
O'Connor, James, 327
off-farm employment, 18, 295, 302, 304; negative consequences of, 288
oil palm, 89, 100; expansion of industry, 109; payback period for, 109
OPEC oil prices, 50
operation maduka, 251
ordinary least squares (OLS) method, 177
out-migration, 23, 115, 321

Pahang Tenggara regional development studies, 100
parasitic infections, incidence of, 287
Paredes, Juan, 297
patta (land ownership), 34
Paulista plantation movement, 319
PAYP (plan as you proceed), 56
peasant economy, in forest highlands, 365–71
perpetual pioneer, 304
person-land ratios, 130
persuasion, formation of Ujamaa village and, 244–45
Peru: colonization policies of, 357–61; settlement policies in, 355–78
Philippines: land settlements in, 129–48; and relationship with U.S., 131
physical targets, 220
pioneer phase program recommendations, 289–91
planned settlement programs, objectives of, 168

planned settlements, 166–76; impact of, 248–56; negative aspects of, 363; objectives of, 361–63
planning, effect of on settlement programs, 28–29
Planning Commission Office, 164
plot size, effect of on settlement programs, 30–31
podzolic soils, 55
poles of attraction, 43
policy implications, 224–27, 303–7, 376–78
policymakers, U.S., 131
population: center of concentration, 177; imbalance, 50, 74; need for control, 74; redistribution, 7, 8–10, 113–14, 247–48; redistribution programs, 130; relocation, 273
population census, 250
population distribution, 244–48; goals, 223–24
population growth, 259
population mobility, in colonization zones, 275–79
population movements: government-sponsored, 129; spontaneous, 129
postcolonial settlement schemes, 239–40
post-independence period (Philippines), 134–35
poverty, 7; reduction of, 253
primary education, 257–58
private contractors (mandor), 62
production intensification, vs. colonization, 41
production management units (PMUs), 58
profit maximization, 263, 365
program achievements, assessment of, 141–45, 176–81
projects, employment-generating, 252
property rights, 146
public land, disposition of, 131
Public Lands and Homestead Acts, 137
Public Works, Department of, 56, 57, 61

Quaker colonists, 300
quality of life, improvement of, 329
quota system, 113

rations, 217
recontracting, 141
refugee camps, 208
regional awareness period (Philippines), 136–37
regional development, 67–69; promotion of, 14
rehabilitation centers, 170
Relief and Rehabilitation Commission (RRC), 167, 168, 169, 170, 176, 180; administrative organization of, 171
relief camps, 36, 204, 226
rent-wage ratio, 140
*Report of the Working Party Set Up to Consider the Development of New Areas for Land Settlement*, 91
resettled households, average size of, 8
resettlement objectives, 218–19
resettlement program (Somalia), 204
resettlement projects, implementation of, 7
resettlements, 129, 262–64
respiratory infections, 287
retention: in colonization zones, 275–29; settler, 22, 260
Rice and Corn Production Administration (RCPA), 135
rice production, 54, 68
Rice Share Tenancy Act (1933), 135
roads, lack of, 23
Rondonia: demographic changes in, 328; demographic characteristics of, 329; economic characteristics of, 331–33; family characteristics of, 328–29; population growth in, 330–31; socio-economic changes in, 328
Rondonia settlers: achievements of, 333; frustrations of, 333; health of, 333–35; living conditions of, 333–35; migration patterns of, 335; socio-economic characteristics of, 337–38

rubber, 89, 100; payback period for, 109
rubber boom, 356
rural development: alternative strategies for, 272–75; primary objective of programs, 272
rural income distribution, 253
rural integrated development programs (RIDEPS), 252
rural population, expected increase in, 224
rural surplus population, solution for absorption of, 40
rural urbanism, 322
Ruvuma Development Association (RDA), 240, 241

satellite settlements, 29
scheme development, pattern of, 102–5
Scheme Development Committee (SDC), 108
SDA/CDP program implementation, 220–23
SDA/CDP schemes, 225
secondary level school program, 216
Second Five-Year Development Plan, 166, 253, 257
Second Malaysia Plan, 103
seed communities, 62
Selassie, Haile, 163
selection criteria, ethnic-biased, 114
selection phase program recommendations, 282–83
selection system, 97
self-sufficiency: attainment of, 173; in food production, 218
services, provision of, 256–57
Settlement Authority, 168
settlement costs, 26–28, 178–80; sharing of, 183
Settlement Development Agency (SDA), 11, 12, 202, 204, 208, 212, 219, 224, 226
settlement infrastructure, 178–80
settlement model, low-cost, 171
settlement organization, 208–9

settlement policies: overview of, 20–45; in Peru, 355–78
settlement population, male-female ratios in, 175
settlement productivity, 176–78
settlement programs: causes of failure of, 2; types of, 2
settlements: cooperative, 241; low-cost, 182; management of, 173–74; nucleated, 237, 241; organization of, 173–74; size, 99–102; spontaneous, 36–38, 164–66, 240, 278, 282; typology of, 169–71
settlement schemes: abandonment of, 22–23; capital-intensive, 237; colonial, 238–39; evaluation of, 3; inadequate management of, 225; postcolonial, 239–40
settler dependency, effect of on settlement programs, 35–36
settler population: age distribution for, 174; socioeconomic characteristics of, 174–76
settler retention, 181
settlers: achievement-oriented, 107; background of, 210–12; employment characteristics of, 211–12; occupational profile of, 176; origins of, 210; retention of, 260; social characteristics of, 210–11; successes and failures of, 296–303; work attitudes of, 212
settler selection, 95–99; effect of on settlement programs, 31–33; requirements for, 97
sex ratio, 329
sindicatos (cooperatives), 290
single-issue projects, avoidance of, 147
site identification, 53–56
site selection, 101–2; effect of on settlement programs, 29
slash-and-burn agriculture, 281, 284
slash-and-mulch system, 284
Small Industries Development Organization (SIDO), 252
small-scale industries, 246, 252
social differentiation, 367

social dislocation, 255
Socialism and Rural Development, 242, 243
social objectives, 21–22
social security system, 250
social services: access to, 214–16; provision of, 207
social services assessment, 216–17
social stability, 175
social tensions, 25–26
Social Welfare Department, 53
social welfare families, 67
sociopolitical structure, 208, 209–10
soil conservation, 238
soil depletion, 307
soil erosion, 302
soil suitability, 101
spontaneous migration, 26, 61–63, 65, 74, 137
spontaneous settlements, 36–38, 164–66, 240, 278, 282; effect of on settlement programs, 36–38; retention capability of, 278
squatting, 332
Suez Canal, 206
sugar imports, 17
Supreme Revolutionary Council, 207
survey data, 177
swamp reclamation, 54, 76

Tanganyika Agricultural Corporation (TAC), 240
TANU Youth League (TYL), 240, 241
tariffs, 134
tax incentives, 134
teacher shortage, 215
technical knowledge, need for, 76
tenancy ratios, 144
tenant evictions, 165
tenant-farmer ratios, 144
tenant-land ratios, 140
terracing, 239
Third Five-Year Development Plan, 166, 253, 257, 260
Third Malaysia Plan (1976–1980), 115
Third World countries, 253
Three Year Development Plan (TYDP), 218, 222, 223

tidal irrigation, 54
trade policy, changes in, 130–33
Trans-Amazon colonization program, 276
Trans-Amazon Highway, 277, 321
transmigrants: government-sponsored, 64, 65; number of, 63–65; selection of, 51–53; semi-assisted (spontan), 57; three principles of selection, 51
transmigrant welfare, 65–67
transmigration: budget allocation and, 72–73; financial constraints and, 71; goal of, 62; in Indonesia, 48–76; land shortage and, 70–71; policies in Indonesia, 51–61
transmigration sites, land limit for, 70
transport costs, 293
Transport Service Company, 106
tribal society, restructuring of, 207–8
tropics, transition to life in, 274
trypanosomiasis control programs, 171
tsetse fly infestation, 238

ujamaa: definition of, 241–42; objectives of, 241–44; strategies for implementing, 242–43
ujamaa villages: formation of, 244–48; institutional structure of, 243–44
unemployment, 7
United Republic of Tanzania, land settlement and population redistribution in, 237–64
United States: colonial policy, 131; and relationship with Philippines, 131
universal primary education (UPE), 257
unutilized land, availability of, 95

urban centers, 224
urban growth, 206
urbanization, increase in, 321
urban-rural income gap, 248
USAID program, 165

Vega, Guillermo, 298
veterinary campaigns, 205
Victoria Federation Co-operative Union, 240
Villages and Ujamaa Villages Act, 242, 244, 251
Village Settlement Agency (VSA), 239
villagization, 249, 253, 262; benefit of, 262; forced, 246; position of women and, 255; social consequences of, 255; strategy, 19
villagization program, 256–60
voluntary migration, 52

wages: minimum, 253; non-taxable, 253
war refugees, settlement of, 11
water, lack of, 23
water supply, rural, 259–60
Welamo Agricultural Development Unit (WADU), 167
wet zone, 8
Weynadega zone, 162
work discipline, lack of, 35
work incentives, 212, 226
working party, 96; recommendations of, 91–92
World Bank, 16, 18, 56, 58, 66, 70, 73, 76, 146, 223, 239, 254, 327; assisted projects, 57
World Bank mission, 209
world economic depression, 360
World Food Program, 58
World War II, 135, 137, 138, 147, 163